Here is what readers say about this book:
(Continued from back cover)

"It is a well-written, concise, easy understandable book on complex topic. It is a treasure of wisdom and knowledge."
Dr. A Rolfes, Newrybar, Australia

"It is one of the most comprehensive and easy to understand books."
Terrence Mohammed, Jamaica, NY

"This book presents information in a well-organized, simplistic manner, which was understandable to me as a novice."
Rose Mary Shaw, Yellow Springs, Ohio

"This book is packed with excellent material, explaining in simple terms the central concepts, beliefs and terms encountered in religion...veritably a treasure-house to anyone."
Dr. Alagappa Alagappan, Honorary President, The Hindu Temple Society of North America, New York

"...provides a well-crafted and complete overview of the fundamental concepts of Hinduism...an invaluable resource."
Hinduism Today, U.S.A.

"I find it an invaluable resource."
W. Jay Wood, Associate Professor, Wheaton College, Illinois

"I have read many books about Hinduism and Indian culture, but this is the best one I have ever encountered."
Deepa Patel, Burlington, New Jersey

"It combines erudition with simplicity of style that is rare among authors of books on Hinduism."
Bandana Purkayastha, Weatogue, Connecticut

"I enjoyed the book very much. I learned a lot of things...."
Nisha Patel, 13-years old, Voorhees, New Jersey

"It is extremely well-written and easy to understand."
Tejal Shah, T Royal Oak, Michigan

"...lucidly explains Hinduism in a nutshell."
News India-Times, New York.

The Hindu Mind

Fundamentals of Hindu Religion
And Philosophy for All Ages

Bansi Pandit

Third Edition

Dharma Publications
2005

Published by
Dharma Publications

First Edition	1992
Second Edition	1993
Reprinted	1996
Third Edition	1998
Reprinted	2005

To obtain a copy of this book or to send your
comments and suggestions, please contact the publisher at:

Dharma Publications
925 Maryknoll Circle
Glen Ellyn, IL 60137
E-mail: dharma@hindunet.org

Softcover $24.95 (U.S.A.) $28.95 (Canada)
Hardcover $32.00 (U.S A) $36.00 (Canada)

To order by mail in U.S.A,
add $ 4 for postage and handling.

Library of Congress Catalog Card No. 97-094062
Softcover: ISBN 0-9634798-4-9
Hardcover: ISBN 0-9634798-2-2

Printed in the United States of America.

Dedicated to:

Paramahamsa Sri Ramakrishna (1836-1886),
Swami Vivekananda (1863-1902),
Sri Aurobindo Ghose (1872-1950),
Swami Ram Tirth (1873-1906),
Ramana Maharshi (1879-1950),
Swami Ramdas (1884-1963),
Swami Sivananda Saraswati (1887-1963),
Paramahansa Yogananda (1893-1952),
Swami Chinmayananda (1916-1993),
sages and saints of the past and present
of all religions--who have taught the same truth
in different languages, at different times,
and to different peoples--and to my parents,
who brought me into this world.

Other Books by Bansi Pandit

Hindu Dharma

Softcover, ISBN 0-9634798-3-0, 136 pages.
Includes nine color plates of popular Hindu deities.
$9.00   (U.S.A.)
$13.00   (Canada)
To order by mail, add $3 or postage and handling.

Explore Hinduism

Softcover, ISBN 1-8728838-1-8

Author's Note:

The author conducts presentations on various aspects of the Hindu heritage for those who desire to obtain a better understanding of the Hindu religious and spiritual principles and practices. In the past, such talks have been given successfully at various institutions to numerous audiences, especially the youth and young adults. The presentations use overhead color transparencies or slides and are given over one or two days, depending upon the specific needs of the audience. The cost of these presentations is minimal to defray traveling expenses. For information, please contact the author at:

Dharma Publications
925 Maryknoll Circle
Glen Ellyn, IL 60137
E-mail: dharma@hindunet.org

ACKNOWLEDGMENT

To my wife, Vijay, who inspired me to embark on this work. To my sons, Rajiv and Rahul, who independently reviewed the entire manuscript several times and provided valuable suggestions. Their comments helped to improve both the detail and the presentation of the material for the benefit of the readers.

Seven Social Sins:

Politics without principles
Wealth without work
Pleasure without conscience
Knowledge without character
Commerce without morality
Science without humanity
Worship without sacrifice

(Quoted by Mahatma Gandhi
in *Young India*, 1925)

Foreword

In this remarkable and highly rewarding book, *The Hindu Mind*, the author Bansi Pandit has met head-on two pressing challenges of our times: (1) how to cull and distill the essential features of the enormously vast and deep Hindu heritage so varied in scope, in the short span of a handy volume, in an easily understandable, highly engaging and readable style, and (2) how to make it highly rational, objective, interesting, relevant, and meaningful to our new generation and future generations of Hindu youth. They are growing up fast, with the full impact and influences of westernization, in all its best and worst forms, at the same time deprived of the opportunities to know, understand, and appreciate their own rich time-tested spiritual heritage and thus their own true selves. Also, Hindu adult men and women, many of them professionals in their own fields, yet unaware and uninformed, desirous of acquiring an intellectual sensibility for the rich religious and cultural "Great Tradition of Hindu religion"--profound with its illuminating wisdom, life-sustaining moral values, and splendid aesthetic expressions--will also find this volume highly rewarding.

Bansi Pandit fully yet succinctly explores, with great clarity, all the visible and tangible aspects of Hindu religion: the scriptures, epics, symbols and symbolisms, teachings, deities, the important Hindu paradigms such as the "four-goals" and "four-stages" models, rituals, and festivals--that is, all the Hindu institutional machinery, all which constitutes the "hardware" of Hindu religion. But more important are his significant contributions illuminating Hindu religion's "software", that has been running the great machinery of Hindu religion in its world's longest history. In his philosophical discussions, enhanced by a rational, scientific, and truly moral sensibility that is distinctly unique to Hindu religion, Pandit also discusses the why of things. He unravels the genius and vision of Hindu religion flowing down from the wisdom and wizardry found inside the Vedas and unfolding through the course of Hindu history, showing the secret of its universal and cosmic outlook and cosmic consciousness. This drive and impulse, that has always throbbed, has enabled Hindu religion to keep itself reinvigorating and re-inventing, again and again. The author emphasizes the purity of reason and true knowledge that are essential for recognizing the brotherhood and oneness of all mankind, found in Hindu religion. The Hindus have always felt and believed that the essential Self, the vital essence in man, is the same as that found in all forms of life--a tiny gnat, an ant, an elephant, a tiger, and a butterfly--indeed the same as that found in the whole universe. *Bhagavad Gita* declares: "The ones full of wisdom, the true *pundits*, behold and relate to a learned Brahmin, a cow or an elephant, or a dog, or a dog-eater, with the same equanimity of vision and evenness of love." (BG 5.18)

The author also recognizes, clarifies, and removes the various stereotypes, harmful misconceptions and partial understandings, which many non-Hindus have long nurtured and written about. The cross-references, faithful drawings of the sacred deities, and well-arranged and organized charts and tables, all make the book highly informative and modern.

I wish and hope this valuable volume finds, in many different ways, the wide use, appreciation, and circulation it truly deserves--as a text in Hindu heritage classes in our Hindu temples, as a meaningful gift for our graduating Hindu youth, and as a basis for study and discussion in the Hindu homes. The author deserves our congratulations and gratitude.

T. K. Venkateswaran
Emeritus Professor of Hinduism and Comparative Religion,
University of Detroit; *Former Research Scholar,*
Harvard University

Preface

Hinduism, the religion of Hindus (originally known as *Sanatana Dharma*), is the oldest surviving religion in the world. Unlike other religions of the world, Hinduism did not originate from a single person, a single book, or at a single point in time. The religious and philosophical literature of Hindu religion is vast, diverse, and covers thousands of years of accumulated spiritual experiences of a large number of Hindu sages and saints. Therefore, it is difficult, almost impossible, for a beginner to know where to start to learn about Hindu religion without screening volumes of literature.

Though there are numerous books available on Hindu religion, most of them are not suitable for study by the beginners. The language and writing styles of most of the books on Hinduism are too complex for beginners to comprehend. To that extent, this book has been specially prepared to include simple language, modern writing and communication skills, and clarity of thought for easy comprehension by the readers of all ages.

A two-fold need for this book has been recognized. First, there are those who are curious and wish to learn the basic concepts of Hindu religion without indulging in extensive time-consuming research or becoming mired in the complexities of Hindu religious thought. Second, there are children born in Hindu families, especially outside India, who may lack the environment or the opportunity to receive some basic education in their own religion during their formative years. As a result, such children may feel somewhat empty in their adult lives, or have great difficulty generating a deep conviction of their own being.

The purpose of this book, therefore, is to assist the students of all ages in assimilating the fundamental concepts of Hinduism, and to provide them with a road map for further travels in the land of Hindu religion, if they so desire.

The Contents of the book

Since the express purpose of this book is to present the fundamentals of Hindu religious and philosophical thought in an easily understandable format, a serious effort has been made to provide the material in a logical manner and to keep the language simple and straightforward. Basic concepts are stressed with the hope that once the student has acquired an understanding of the fundamentals of Hindu religion, he (or she) can proceed on his own accord to gain a better understanding of the higher teachings contained in other books. Accordingly, this book includes the following special features:

- The book is divided into five parts. Parts I through IV discuss all essential aspects of the Hindu religious tradition. To broaden the reader's understanding of the material presented, Part V of the book includes tables, appendices, works cited, suggested readings for higher studies, a glossary and an index. Figures are included with their respective chapters.

- Commonly asked questions with answers pertaining to various aspects of Hindu religion have been included at the ends of Parts I through IV.

- Each chapter is complete in itself and can be read independently of the others. The reader may, therefore, find some material repeated.

- Cross-references to other sections of the book have been frequently provided in each chapter, as necessary, for a more comprehensive understanding of the contents.

- Whenever a Sanskrit word initially appears in a chapter, the English translation is provided in parenthesis. However, the meanings of many Sanskrit words cannot possibly be conveyed through simple, one-word translations. To this extent, a glossary with a pronunciation guide is provided in Part V of the book.

With Part I as a background, each chapter in Parts I through IV is essentially self-contained. This arrangement provides flexibility in arranging a course for teaching Hindu religion. Various chapters in Parts II, III, and IV can be read in a different sequence without difficulty.

In conclusion, the author wishes to express his sincere thanks and appreciation to Swami Brahmarupananda, who reviewed the original manuscript with patience and provided many suggestions on the technical content of the book. His encouragement and assistance are deeply appreciated. The author is also grateful to Prof. Subhash Kak for his review of the original manuscript and recommendations for its improvement. The author is indebted to Prof. Rajeshwari Vijay Pandharipande for her review of the manuscript, advice and support, and to Dr. C. L. Shastri for his encouragement and technical support.

Finally the author wishes to express his deep appreciation to Prof. T. K. Venkateswaran for his kindness in writing the foreword and for providing wise counsel and an outstanding stimulus.

Bansi Pandit

Even if you be the worst sinner among all the sinners, you will cross (the ocean of) all sin by the boat of knowledge alone.

(Bhagavad Gita 4.36)

Contents

Part III
Hindu Epics

Part IV
Other Topics

Part V
References

Appendices:

Miscellaneous:

Part I
Religion and Philosophy

Every morning in Africa, a gazelle wakes up and knows that it must run faster than the fastest lion or get killed. Every morning in Africa, a lion wakes up and knows that it must run faster than the slowest gazelle or starve to death. So whether you are a gazelle or a lion, when you wake up in the morning run as fast as you can.

(anonymous)

Chapter 1
Origin of Hindu Religion

Hindu religion is the oldest surviving religion in the world. Inspired by divine revelations ("by the breath of God"), the ancient rishis (sages and seers) sang divine songs in the forests and on the river banks of India, many thousands of years before Moses, Buddha or Christ. Over many centuries these divine songs continued to be recited by the sages, whose combined wisdom eventually gave birth to the Hindu religion popularly known as Hinduism today. The original name of the Hindu religion is *Sanatana Dharma* (Eternal or Universal Righteousness). In this book, the terms *Hindu religion, Hinduism, Hindu dharma*, and *Sanatana Dharma* are used synonymously.

Though the genesis of the term *Hindu* is somewhat controversial, the consensus among scholars is that as early as 500 BCE, the ancient Persians called the Indian people living on the banks of the river Indus (known as *Sindhu* in Sanskrit) as *Sindhus*. In the Persian language, the word *Sindhu* became *Hindu* and the people living in India came to be known as Hindus.[1,25]

Unlike other religions of the world, Hindu religion neither originated from a single founder or a single scripture, nor did it begin at a particular point in time. It is impossible to define the exact place and time of its origin. The date of approximately 1500 BCE, usually stated to be the origin of Hindu religion in the standard text books, is based upon the old Aryan Invasion Theory (see Chapter 39) that has now lost its credibility. According to this theory, the Vedic Aryans came from Central Asia, invaded India around 1500 BCE, destroyed the more advanced indigenous Harappan civilization, and established the Vedic culture in India. Based upon the current archaeological and literary evidence, modern scholars have concluded that there never

was an Aryan invasion and that the Rig Vedic people, who
called themselves Aryans (the word *Arya* in Sanskrit means
wise), were indigenous to India and were present as one of
the original ethnic groups since 6500 BCE or earlier.[10]

Sanatana Dharma thus flourished from the pre-historic
times in India in the form of a monotheistic Hindu
pantheon (i.e. the worship of one Supreme Lord in various
ways and forms). Meanwhile a number of social vices
appeared in Hindu society in the form of excessive religious
rituals, animal sacrifices, rigid operation of the caste system,
and self-declared Brahmin superiority over other castes.

In a period marked by rebellion, Buddhism and Jainism
emerged in India. Buddhism dominated for a period of
approximately 1000 years (200 BCE-800 AD). However, its
influence in India gradually eroded due to internal strife in
its organization and the resistance put up by Sanatanists (the
followers of Sanatana Dharma). The rise of Buddhism,
however, opened the eyes of Sanatanists. They accepted
much of Buddha's message and included him as an
incarnation of Lord Vishnu. Buddha's message of deep
friendship (*mahamaitri*) and unlimited compassion (*mahakar-
una*) toward fellow beings was incorporated into Sanatana
Dharma as Bhakti (devotion) Yoga. The worship of Lord
Shiva, Divine Mother, Sri Rama and Sri Krishna through
Bhakti Yoga became very popular among Hindus. In about
700 AD, Adi Shankaracharya (a famous saint, philosopher,
and scholar) played a leading role in opposing Buddhism
and upholding the cause of Sanatana Dharma in India. He
also brought the teachings of the Bhagavad Gita to the
forefront.

Chronology

Following are the major milestones in the development
of the Hindu religious tradition. It should be recognized
that authorities differ on the dates prior to approximately
500 BCE to which some of the events are assigned (see also
Table T-1). The following dates are, however, considered
conservative (lower estimates) by many modern scholars:[26]

Rig Vedic Period (6500 or earlier-2000 BCE)

This is the period in which the hymns of the Rig Veda, the oldest Hindu scripture, were developed.

Brahmana and Aranyaka Period (2000-1500 BCE)[28e]

The *Brahmanas* (explanatory treatises for using the Vedic hymns in rituals), *Aranyakas* (philosophical interpretations of the hymns), and the early *Upanishads* (Vedic philosophy) were added to the collection of the Vedic hymns. During this period the Hindu mind evolved from the worship of the natural forces to the conception of a single, all-encompassing Universal Spirit, called *Brahman* by the seers of the Upanishads.

Sutra Period (1500-500 BCE)

In this period, the Upanishads were composed and *Mimamsa, Nyaya, Sankhya,* and *Brahma Sutra* (aphorisms on Upanishads) were recorded. These writings later led to the development of the six popular schools of Hindu philosophy (see chapter 6). The development of Buddhism and Jainism also took place in this period.

Epic Period (700 BCE-300 AD)

The *Mahabharata*, originally composed around 2000 BCE (though the actual Mahabharata war occurred much earlier) was expanded during this period. The *Ramayana*, which was written as a poem by sage Valmiki during this period, was further enhanced sometime later. The *Bhagavad Gita* (a part of the Mahabharata), the *Laws of Manu* (Hindu code of conduct), some of the earlier *Puranas* (mythological literature), Philosophical Sutras, and the higher teachings of the Upanishads were made available to the common people through simplified translations.

Puranic Period (300-1500 AD)

During this time Puranic and Tantric literature (see chapter 3) was developed. The Philosophical Sutras for the

six popular schools (see chapter 6) of Hindu philosophy
were also interpreted.

Darshana Period (750-1000 AD)

The establishment of Shankara's Advaita Vedanta
philosophy (see chapter 7) and the decline of Buddhism in
India are the two main landmarks of this period. This was
also the beginning of the devotional movement spearheaded
by the twelve mystic poets of South India, known as Alvars.

Bhakti Movement (1000-1800 AD)

This period experienced the rise of devotional worship
expounded by Alvars, Nayanars, Tulsidas, Kabir, Surdas,
Tukaram, Ramprasad, Ramanuja, Ramananda, Guru
Nanak, Mira Bai, Vallabha, Chaitanya, and many other
religious teachers and saints.

Modern Hindu Renaissance

History has not been kind to Hindus and their religion
in India. A long and brutal spell of foreign domination and
religious fervor of the foreign missionaries brought
numerous challenges to the survival of Hindu religion in
India. At the same time, India has had the good fortune of
producing a number of illustrious religious and spiritual
leaders who revolutionized Hindu religion by opposing
certain inhumane social practices--including the vices of the
caste system--and excessive ritualism. There were many
leaders of the modern Hindu renaissance, including Ram
Mohan Roy, Swami Dayananda Sarasvati, Paramahamsa
Ramakrishna, Swami Vivekananda, Sri Aurobindo Ghose,
Ramana Maharshi, and Mahatma Gandhi.

Hindu Religion and the West

The insights of Sanatana Dharma spread to other parts
of the world through emissaries who visited India and from
Indians who visited foreign lands. The forerunner of this
movement to the Western world was Swami Vivekananda.
He was a popular speaker at the World Parliament of

Religions in Chicago, held in September of 1893. Building upon the popularity he had gained at the World Parliament, he later toured America and Europe to expound the teachings of the Vedas and the Upanishads. He also founded the Ramakrishna Mission in India, a well-known worldwide organization, dedicated to religious universalism and social work. Later, Paramahansa Yogananda, author of *Autobiography of a Yogi*, came to the United States in 1920 and helped spread the universal ideals of Sanatana Dharma. He established the Self-Realization Fellowship in Los Angeles, California, to disseminate the Vedic teachings.

One of the most impressive twentieth century figures who greatly influenced the educated Westerners through his eloquent speeches and numerous writings is Dr. Sarvepalli Radhakrishnan (1888-1975), a former President of India and a well-known scholar of both Eastern and Western philosophies. Dr. Sarvepalli Radhakrishnan was, in the words of Professor Klaus Klostermaier, "a prolific writer, and an excellent speaker--he seems to embody what all are looking for: purified, spiritualized, non-secular Hindu religion, the 'religion of spirit' and 'the world religion of the future,' a valid and final answer to the great questions of our time."[25]

Ramana Maharshi (1879-1950), another modern spiritual genius and a well-known teacher of *Advaita Vedanta*, has had a profound spiritual impact on the West. Maharshi was first introduced to the Western world through the writings of Paul Brunton, a British journalist and scholar, who authored many works, such as *Maharshi and His Message* and *Passage to India*.

There are many more prominent figures who have generated significant Hindu spiritual influence in the Western world. Included are Swami Ram Tirtha, Swami Ramdas, Sri Aurobindo Ghose, Swami Shivananda of Rishikesh, J. Krishnamurti, Sri Satya Sai Baba, Ma Anandamai, Swami A. C. Bhaktivedanta, Mahatma Gandhi, Maharshi Mahesh Yogi, Swami Chinmayananda, Satguru Subramuniyaswami, and Amritanandmayi Ma.

Chapter 2
What Hindu Religion Is

Hindu religion is said to be like a huge tree with its numerous branches representing various schools of religious thought. The tree itself is rooted in the rich soil of the Vedas and the Upanishads. The Vedas represent the religious tradition, whereas the Upanishads represent the philosophy upon which that tradition is based. Some say that Hindu religion is an ocean that absorbs all streams and rivers of diverse religious thought, however straight or crooked they may appear to be. Hindu religion is essentially a fellowship of all those who believe in the sacredness of the individual, personal experiential realization of the Divine through spiritual practice and moral discipline (unmediated by any authority, dogma, or belief), preservation and propagation of *dharma* (righteousness), complete freedom of thought in religious matters, harmony of religions (*sarva dharma samabhava*), non-violence (*ahimsa*) in word, deed, and thought, reverence for all forms of life, and the law of karma: *As you sow, so shall you reap.* The following paragraphs describe the essential features of Hindu religious thought and practice:

Existence of the Reality

Hindus believe that there is only one Reality or Truth, which cannot be limited to any one name, form, or personality. This Reality is the substratum of all things and beings of the world and yet transcends them all. It is the ultimate source and cause of all existence. It has two aspects, the transcendental (impersonal) and the immanent (personal).

In its transcendental aspect, the Reality is called by various names, such as Supreme or Cosmic Self, Supreme Being, Ultimate Reality, Universal Spirit and *Nirguna Brahman.* In this impersonal aspect, the Reality is formless, attributeless, immutable, indeterminate, and unapproachable by the human mind.\ As such, the Reality cannot even be called Creator, since It exists prior to all forms including that of the Creator. All that can be said about the transcendental aspect of the Reality is that It is of the nature of absolute existence, absolute knowledge, and absolute bliss (*sat-chit-ananda*).

In its immanent aspect, the Reality is the Supreme Lord or the personal God of all religions. Viewed from the personal aspect, Hindus call the Reality by various names, such as *Saguna Brahman, Ishvara, Paramatma,* and the Divine Mother. In this aspect, the Reality is just and merciful creator, preserver and controller of the universe.| "In the Vedic view, there is no one God or Goddess for all humanity, but there is one Reality, or Truth, for all beings.|[28] Hindus worship the personal aspect of the Reality in various names and forms, both male and female, according to the choice of the devotees (see also discussion of *Brahman* in chapter 4).

The Sacredness of the Individual

The Sanskrit word *atman*, meaning "God within," is usually translated as the soul, self, or spirit (see also page 55). |An individual, according to Hindu view, is the atman living in a human body. Hindus declare that the atman is immortal and divine.| Whereas the physical body perishes following death, the atman cannot.[24] From the perfect human being to the lowest worm resides the same omnipresent and omniscient atman. |The differences between living beings exist not in the atman, but in the degree of its manifestation in a particular physical body.| Just as electricity accomplishes various functions in different electrical appliances, depending upon the design of the appliance, the atman manifests differently in various organisms, depending upon the type and construction of the physical body. The degree of manifestation of the atman is highest in the human body.]

In its liberated state of bliss and original purity, the atman is omnipresent, omnipotent, and omniscient. However, when it is associated with a particular human body, it gives rise to mind, intellect, and ego. Owing to the existence of *maya,* the original ignorance (see chapter 4), the atman mistakenly identifies itself with the body, mind, and intellect. This false identity is the cause of the atman's bondage to material existence and the consequent pain and suffering in the world. According to Hindu view, freedom (*moksha* or salvation) from this earthly bondage is the true goal of human life (see also chapters 4, 13, and 40 for further discussions of the atman).

Moksha (Union with God))

The ultimate goal of Hindu religious life is to attain moksha, that is union with the Divine or freedom from all physical limitations. This union can be achieved through true knowledge (*jnana*), devotion (*bhakti*), and righteous work (*karma*). Purity, self-control, truthfulness, non-violence, and compassion toward all forms of life are the necessary prerequisites for any spiritual path in Hindu religion. The Hindu religion emphasizes the importance of a true guru (spiritual master) for the attainment of Self-knowledge (*atman-jnana*). Self-knowledge is essential for spiritual perfection. "For, if we know God but do not know ourselves, the God we know is but a conceptual construct, a product of our imagination. / If we truly know ourselves, we know the Divine (not merely the Creator God) as our innermost reality."[28b] Refer to chapter 32 for additional discussion of moksha.

Guru-Disciple Relationship

A true guru is a God-realized master who guides his (her) disciple on the spiritual path. The function of a true guru is two-fold: first, he explains the scriptures and guides the disciple on the spiritual path; second, the guru teaches by setting an example with the daily acts of his own life. Sometimes by words and sometimes in silence, a true guru purifies the spirit of the disciple. According to Hindu view, a disciple who obeys his guru in humility and in reverence attains Self-knowledge.

In Hindu religion, a guru-disciple relationship is the highest and most sacred relationship in life. The *Katha Upanishad* declares: "To many it is not given to hear of the Self [God within]. Many, though they hear of it, do not understand it. Wonderful is he who speaks of it. Intelligent is he who learns of it. Blessed is he who, taught by a good teacher (guru), is able to understand it...." It must be recognized that a guru is akin to a traveler's guide, who provides the road map and helps the traveler on his journey. The disciple, however, must travel on his own accord, since the guru cannot carry him along the way and simply drop him at the destination.

Unity of Existence

Hindu religion proclaims that the universe is a manifestation of *Brahman* (Universal Spirit). Brahman is in all things and is the self (*atman*) of all living beings. Thus there is perfect unity behind the diversity of the world phenomena. The differences appear only when the universe is observed through the mind and senses alone. However, when the mind is transcended by the wise through spiritual experience, the Universal Spirit is seen as the sole essence of all things and beings. The doctrine of the unity of existence has given birth to the famous tenet of Hindu philosophy described as "O ne in all and all in O ne."

Harmony of Religions (*Sarva Dharma Samabhava*)

Hindu religion offers a number of ways to seek union with the Divine. Hindus declare that all true religions are but different paths to the Divine. This doctrine is included in the following verse of the Rig Veda (R.V. 1.164.46):

"Ekam sat vipraha, bahudha vadanti."
"Truth is one, the wise call it by various names."

Because of its belief in the omnipresence of the Supreme Reality in every individual, Hindu religion teaches tolerance and universal harmony. Hindu religion does not look with contempt even upon an atheist. In the words of Sir Monier-Williams (Eng. Sanskrit scholar, 1819-1899):

Chapter 2

"A characteristic of Hindu religion is its receptivity and all-comprehensiveness. It claims to be the one religion of humanity, of human nature, of the entire world. It cares not to oppose the progress of any other system. For it has no difficulty in including all other religions within its all-embracing arms and ever-widening fold."

Friedrich von Schlegel, the German philosopher and poet, was so impressed with the universal outlook of Hindu religion that he wrote:

"When one considers the sublime disposition underlying the truly universal education [of Vedic India]...then what is or has been called religion in Europe seems to us to be scarcely deserving of that name. And one feels compelled to advise those who wish to witness religion to travel to India for that purpose...."[28c]

The Doctrine of Incarnation

Hindus believe that God incarnates on earth to uphold righteousness, whenever there is a decline of virtue. Thus declares the Bhagavad Gita (BG 4.6, 4.7):

"Whenever there is a decline of righteousness and predominance of unrighteousness, I [God] embody Myself. For the protection of the good and for the destruction of evil-doers and for the re-establishment of dharma (righteousness), I am born from age to age."

Hindus believe that incarnations are not limited to Hindu religion alone. They appear in the form of sages, saints, holy men and women in all religious traditions to help re-establish dharma in accordance with the Divine will.

The Law of Karma and Rebirth

Hindus hold that God, who is all-loving and merciful, does not punish or reward anyone. We create our own destinies by our own thoughts and deeds. Every action of a person, in thought or deed, brings results, either good or bad, depending upon the moral quality of the action, in accordance with the adage, "As you sow, so shall you reap."¹ Human actions do not occur without consequences. Moral consequences of all actions are conserved by Nature.

If a person lives a good life on earth, he (she) will be born into a better life in the next incarnation. For example, a sinner who leads an immoral life will be born as a poor human in an agonizing environment in the next incarnation. [A person is born again and again to reap the fruits of his own actions.] This cycle of birth and death continues until the person attains moksha, or freedom from the cycle of birth and death. Refer to chapter 13 for further discussion on karma.

The Doctrine of Ahimsa

Ahimsa means non-violence, non-injury or non-killing. Hindu religion teaches that all forms of life are manifestations of the Supreme Self. [We must not be indifferent to the sufferings of others.] We must extend love and compassion to all living beings. [Violence out of passion to satisfy one's own interests and lack of compassion for others are the major causes of evil in the world.] Mahatma Gandhi, one of the most revered leaders of our time, was the greatest exponent of the doctrine of non-violence. Prior to his teachings, the practical application of this doctrine had been restricted only to individual actions, but he extended the concept of ahimsa to the actions of communities and nations. Refer to chapter 15 for further discussion of ahimsa.

Sacred Writings

Hindu religion is not derived from a single book. It has many sacred writings which serve as the source of its doctrines. As stated earlier, it is a religion of the accumulated experiences of ancient, medieval, as well as modern sages and seers. The most important sacred writings of Hindu religion include the the Vedas, Upanishads, Agamas, Puranas, Ramayana, Mahabharata, and Bhagavad Gita (see chapter 3 for a detailed discussion of Hindu scriptures).

The Creation

The Sanskrit word for creation is *srishti*, which means projecting a gross phenomenon from a subtle ̃substance. *Srishti* does not mean bringing out existence from non-existence or creating something from nothing. [Creation implies something arising from nothing, or non-existence becoming existence.] Hindus declare that non-existence can never be the source of creation. [Thus, the universe is more accurately said to be the *projection* of the Supreme Being rather than a creation.]

Hindus believe that the universe is beginning-less (*anadi*) and end-less (*ananta*). It is the inherent nature of the universe to evolve, devolve, and re-evolve eternally in cycles of creation, dissolution, and recreation. Thus, in Hindu religion there is no such thing as the initial creation. The creation is eternal and proceeds in cycles. Whenever the words beginning and end are used in Hindu scriptures, they simply mean the beginning and end of a particular cycle.

According to Manusmrti (a Hindu scripture), each cycle of creation is divided into four *yugas* (ages of the world): *satyayuga* (golden age), *tretayuga* (silver age), *dvaparayuga* (copper age), and *kaliyuga* (iron age). Each cycle of creation begins with satyayuga, evolves through tretayuga and dvaparayuga, and ends with kaliyuga. Satyayuga is the age of bliss and virtue, as the human intellect is very powerful and able to grasp and obey the spiritual laws underlying the operation of the universe. Spiritual knowledge diminishes and universal chaos increases as the creation evolves from satyayuga to kaliyuga.

Satyayuga lasts for a period of 4,800 divine years, tretayuga 3,600 divine years, dvaparayuga 2,400 divine years, and kaliyuga 1,200.[26] One human year is one divine day and 360 human years is one divine year. The total duration of one cycle of the four yugas is 12,000 divine years (or 4,320,000 human years) and is called *maha yuga*. One thousand *maha yugas* comprise one kalpa, which equals one day for Lord Brahma, while equally long is his night. Each such daytime of Brahma is the period of existence of the universe and each

such nighttime is the period of its dissolution. At the end of
Brahma's day the universe is dissolved by *pralaya* (cosmic
deluge or natural disaster) and at the end of Brahma's night
the process begins anew.

It must be noted that the cosmic deluge (apparent death
and destruction) at the end of *kalpa* is not a permanent
destruction. Cosmic deluge is a link between the end of one
kalpa and the beginning of the next one, in an endless process
of cyclic creation. At the beginning of a given cycle, the past
karma of the atman is the catalyst for the new creation of both
good and evil in the subsequent cycle. In Hindu scriptures,
the present age is described as kaliyuga, which began around
3100 BCE when Sri Krishna entered *mahasamadhi* (yogi's
conscious exit from the physical body).

The Hindu notion of time is cyclic and is different from
the Western notion of time, which is unidirectional. In the
Western religious systems, creation implies a first beginning.
This view is not accepted in Hindu religion, since such a view
would have to attribute the responsibility of all evil and
suffering in the world to God. Refer also to the discussion of
prakriti and sin in chapter 4.

Freedom of Thought

Many religions of the world discourage the intrusion of
logical reasoning into the realm of their religious faith. Hindu
religion, on the other hand, uses reason for the defense of its
faith. The Hindu scriptures teach us, says Dr. Sarvepalli
Radhakrishnan (a renowned philosopher, scholar, and former
President of India), ["that we should attain an insight into
reality by hearing (*shravana*), reflection (*manana*), and meditation (*nididhyasana*). The first gives us scriptural teaching, the
second a rational approach, and the third the way to assimilate
the truth heard and reflected on into our being."[2]

Hindus believe that wisdom is not an exclusive possession
of any particular race or religion. Therefore, Hindu religion
provides everyone with absolute freedom of thought. One is
free to question any belief and practice until one is convinced
of the truth behind it. One can argue on any aspect of Hindu

religion without fear of sin or hell. An open mind is all that is necessary to study Hindu religion.

Divine Grace

According to Hindu view, an individual is potentially divine and is not born a sinner. An individual sins because of ignorance (*maya*), which is the root cause of all evils. In Hindu religion, there is no such thing as Original Sin. Hindus declare that Divine grace cures all the sins that are committed by an individual due to one's ignorance of one's own true nature. The promise of God's grace for one's salvation is included in the Bhagavad Gita as Sri Krishna speaks to Arjuna:

"Abandoning all duties, take refuge in Me alone. I will liberate thee from all sins; grieve not." (BG 18.66)

"All duties" in the above verse means all actions, righteous or unrighteous. Since one cannot live in this world without performing actions (BG 3.5), abandoning all duties really means that one should surrender all actions to God, that is perform all work without craving for the fruits of one's actions. The same idea is expressed in the Mahabharata, as follows:

"The Lord provides what one lacks and protects what one has, in the case of all those self-disciplined seekers who are wise, who tread the path of spiritual freedom, and who perform selfless work without sensual cravings...." (Mahabharata Shanti Parva 348.72)

The doctrine of grace is also referred to in the Katha Upanishad 2.20, which states that an individual attains salvation through Divine grace:

"In this physical world the atman flutters about thinking that it is different from the Divine; when favored by the Divine, atman attains salvation (freedom from the cycle of birth and death in the physical world)."

Chapter 2

Summary of the Essential Features of Hindu Religion
The essential features of Hindu religion as described above can be summarized by the letters of the words **HINDU DHARMA** as shown below (see page 166 for a discussion of the commandments of Hindu religion):

Harmony of Religions *(sarva dharma samabhava)*: Hindus hold that all true religions lead to the same goal. They revere all great teachers and prophets of all religions, and respect their teachings as the same eternal truth adapted to the needs of different peoples at different times. A true Hindu would neither exploit nor forcibly convert anyone from another religion to Hindu religion. If another religion would say, "Your religion is false; convert to mine and the Kingdom of Heaven will be yours," Hindu religion would say, "Come to me as a Hindu, Christian, or Sikh and I will make you a better Hindu, better Christian, and better Sikh." Religious tolerance is the chief message of Hindu religious tradition.

Incarnation: Hindus believe that whenever righteousness declines and unrighteousness rises, God incarnates Himself on earth to restore righteousness.

Non-violence: Hindus believe in the doctrine of non-violence, non-injury, and non-killing (ahimsa).

Doctrine of Karma: Hindus believe in the Law of Karma and the doctrine of rebirth. Ignorance is viewed as the cause of bondage. Just as a blazing fire burns firewood to ashes, true knowledge (attained by the grace of God through a guru) burns all karma to ashes (BG 4.37).

Unity of Existence: Hindus believe in the unity of all existence. All things and beings are the manifestations of one Supreme Being. When the mind is transcended through spiritual experience, the Universal Spirit is seen as the sole essence of the universe.

Chapter 2

Dharma: Hindus believe that dharma is essential for accomplishing material and spiritual goals and for the growth of the individual and society. Dharma denotes righteousness and good moral and ethical practices in accordance with the scriptures. Dharma includes all duties--individual, social, and religious--and adherence to the just laws of the land. The enemies of dharma are cowardice, lust, greed, and anger.

Humanism: Hindus believe in the equality of all human beings, regardless of caste, color, or creed.

Atman: the basic teaching of Hindu religion is that the essence of all things and beings is the atman, infinite and eternal, unchanging and indivisible. The true nature of an individual is the atman, which is one with the underlying reality of the universe. There is but one being, one reality, and in the words of the Upanishads (Chandogya Upanishad 6.10.3), "Thou art that."

Reality: the Supreme Reality of the universe (Brahman of the Upanishads) is both formless and with form, impersonal and personal, transcendent and immanent. The Supreme Reality becomes manifest in various aspects and forms, and is known by various names. Hindu religion declares that there are various ways by which an individual, in accordance with his temperament, can realize God.

Moksha: the purpose of Hindu religious life is to make an individual a better person so that he (she) can live harmoniously in this world and seek union with God.

Authority: Hindu religion does not rely upon a single book. It has many sacred writings that provide authority for its doctrines, including the Vedas, Upanishads, Brahma Sutra, Agamas, and Bhagavad Gita.

Chapter 2

Chapter 3
Hindu Scriptures

Hindu scriptures are the most ancient and extensive religious writings in the world. It is difficult to correctly classify and date them because of the large number of authors involved over a period of thousands of years. In addition, an old tradition by early authors to remove their own names from their works further complicates the matter. In general, Hindu scriptures may be classified (see Figure F-1) into two divisions: (1) Sruti Scriptures, and (2) Smriti Scriptures.

Sruti Scriptures

Sruti scriptures include the primary scriptures of Hindu religion known as the Vedas. The Vedas teach the highest truths ever known to man, and form the supreme authority of Hindu religion. The word *Veda* is derived from the root word *"Vid,"* meaning "to know."

Sruti in Sanskrit means "that which is heard." Thus the Vedas are the eternal truths that the Vedic seers, called rishis, are said to have heard during their deep meditations. The Vedas are not considered the works of the human mind, but an expression of what has been realized through intuitive perception by Vedic rishis, who had powers to see beyond the physical phenomena. As such, Vedas are considered of divine origin. The Vedic truths were orally transmitted by the rishis to their disciples over thousands of years. At a later date, these were compiled by Sage Vyasa for the benefit of future generations. There are four Vedas: *Rig Veda, Yajur Veda, Sama Veda,* and *Atharva Veda.*

Four Vedas

The Vedas are the primary texts of the spiritual and religious records of the ancient culture and teachings of India.

Their teachings are based upon recognition of the sacred nature of all life and self-realization as the true goal of human life. Hindus call the Vedas by several names, such as *apau-rusheya* (meaning "not authored by *purusha*, or human being"), *anadi* ("without beginning in terms of time"), and *nishvasitam* ("the breath of *Ishvara*, God").

As a culture and way of life, the Vedas represent a tradition that accepts all valid approaches to truth and embodies the principles of universality and diversity. In Vedic culture, self-realization is not limited to the teachings of any one savior or holy book. There is no attempt to limit truth to a particular form, approach, or belief. Every individual is encouraged to discover truth for himself (herself) and no attempt is made to dictate what truth is supposed to be.

The Vedas prescribe rituals and meditations for attaining harmony in life. The rituals are intended to keep our daily actions in harmony with Divine Will, and meditations are prescribed for realizing our true identity. The ritualistic parts of the Vedas are called the *Karma Kanda* and the meditation portion of the Vedas is called the *Jnana Kanda*.

Rig Veda

Rig Veda, derived from the root word "*rik*," meaning "to praise," is a collection of *mantras* (i.e., chants or hymns). A mantra is a sacred "utterance" charged with mystic potency and richness. The Rig Veda is divided into ten books (each book called *mandala,* meaning "circle"), and further subdivided into chapters and sections. It includes 1,028 hymns, comprising 10,589 Sanskrit verses, and over 150,000 words. The Rig Vedic hymns of prayer and worship are addressed to Vedic deities, such as *Indra* (250 hymns), *Agni* (200 hymns), *Soma* (100 hymns), and numerous hymns addressed to *Surya*. Fewer but very important hymns are dedicated to other Vedic deities such as *Varuna, Ashvins,* and Goddesses *Ushas, Aditi,* and *Saraswati.* Most doctrines of Hindu religion have been, in one way or another, derived from the Rig Veda. O ne of the most profound and significant doctrines of the Rig Veda is "Truth is one, the wise call It by various names."[3] The Rig

Figure F-1: Classification of Major Scriptures

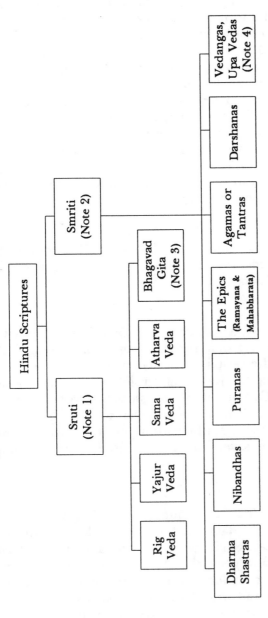

Notes

1. These are the Vedas, the primary scriptures of Hinduism, and the Bhagavad Gita. Each of the four Vedas (Rig, Yajur, Sama, and Atharva) consists of four parts: Samhitas, Brahmanas, Aranyakas, and Upanishads. Some *sampradayas* (religious traditions) also treat their Agamas as Sruti scriptures.
2. These are the secondary scriptures of Hinduism.
3. The Bhagavad Gita is a part of the epic (Mahabharata), but is considered as authoritative as the Sruti scriptures.
4. See Figure F-2 (pages 51 and 52) for further classification of these scriptures.

Vedic hymns reflect a devotee's relationship to the deities as a friend, as a child to his parents, as a servant to his master, or as a lover to his beloved.

In the Rig Veda we find the Vedic people worshipping the deities who were believed to control the destiny of mankind by controlling the forces of nature. These deities were conceived to be responsive to prayer, gifts, and sacrifices. Some hymns in the Rig Veda suggest that the Rig Vedic people were happy with the pleasures of earthly life and did not think too much about salvation. The thought that the Ultimate Reality (Brahman) is within, and can be realized by turning the mind inward rather than by appealing to the external deities, was later developed in the Upanishads.

Yajur Veda

The Yajur Veda, containing 3,988 verses, is a compilation of mantras and methods for use by priests in performing Vedic rituals and sacrifices.

Sama Veda

The Sama Veda, a collection of 1,540 verses, was set to music by the Vedic people for chanting during rituals. The use of music in the recital of the hymns eventually gave rise to Indian Carnatic (or Karnatic) music, the original classical music of India. Carnatic music is associated with devotional songs to deities and is based upon seven sounds: Sa, Re, Ga, Ma, Pa, Dha, and Ni. Mathematical permutations and combinations of these seven sounds are used to create tunes, known as *ragas*.

Atharva Veda

The Atharva Veda, a unique collection of 5,977 verses, was used to satisfy the daily needs of the people. This includes verses deemed necessary for success in agriculture, trade, progeny, health, and general welfare. Other verses relate to fostering love and understanding in relationships, such as between husband and wife, father and son, and teacher and student. Still other verses are designed to assist in procuring medicine and fighting one's enemies. The Sanskrit word *Ayurveda* means science of life. The Ayurvedic system of medicine, based upon the use of herbs for the treatment of diseases, has its roots in the Atharva Veda.

Format of the Vedas

Each Veda is divided into four main sections: Samhitas or mantras, Brahmanas, Aranyakas, and Upanishads.

Samhitas or Mantras

The word *Samhita* literally means "to put together." Samhitas (or mantras) are the basic texts containing hymns of prayer and worship, put together to address the earlier Vedic deities who represented natural forces and phenomena. These hymns were sung at times of worship and sacrifice, giving rise to the ritualism of the early Vedic period.

Brahmanas

Brahmanas emphasize and discuss the sacrificial rituals and the correct techniques for their performance. They include explanatory treatises for using mantras in rituals and reveal the mystical power of the sacrifices. They are called Brahmanas because they discuss the duties of the Brahmins (priests) pertaining to the sacrificial rituals.

Aranyakas

Aranyakas ("the forest books"; that is, the books meditated upon in the seclusion of the forests) mark a transition from the Brahmanical sacrificial rituals to philosophical and metaphysical speculation, which eventually culminated into Upanishadic thought. Aranyakas provide mystical interpretations of the mantras and rituals, put together in the seclusion of the forests, which ultimately gave rise to asceticism. The knowledge attained by ascetics was viewed as revelations.

Upanishads

Upanishads are the divine revelations received by ancient saints and seers. They represent the essence of the Vedas, the greatest truths ever known to mankind. The Upanishads are arguably humanity's most profound philosophical inquiry. They are the first perceptions of the unity of all, the oneness of individual and Reality. The basic teaching of the Upanishads is that the essence of all things and beings--from a blade of grass to the perfect human being--is the Divine Spirit, called Brahman. The true nature of an individual is this Divine Spirit. There is only one being, one Reality, and in the words of the Upanishads, *"Tat tvam asi,"* meaning "That thou art."

The word Upanishad consists of three parts: *Upa* (near), *Ni* (down), and *Shad* (sit). Thus Upanishad means "sitting near a teacher and receiving the secret teachings." Free from theology and dogma, the Upanishads remain the primary source of inspiration and guidance for millions of Hindus and non-Hindus alike. They have influenced many Western thinkers, including von Goethe, Arthur Schopenhauer, and Ralph Waldo Emerson.

The Upanishads, the concluding portions of the Vedas, focus on philosophical questions such as the purpose of life, origin of the universe, concepts of time, space, and matter, as well as concepts of atman, Brahman, maya, immortality, rebirth, karma, and the world. According to Max Muller, "The conception of the world as deduced from the Vedas, and chiefly from the Upanishads, is indeed astounding."[28d]

No one knows with certainty how many Upanishads originally existed, who wrote them, and when they were written. A total of 108 Upanishads have been preserved. Some of these are in prose, some in verse, and range from a few hundred to several thousand words. They are not an organized system of philosophy, since the sages and seers who revealed them were not preachers of the philosophical systems. Of the 108 Upanishads preserved, the following twelve are considered to be the principal Upanishads:

- **Katha Upanishad**

This Upanishad is a dialogue between Nachiketa, a wise and sincere disciple who wants to know the Truth, and the King of Death. In poetic language, this Upanishad reveals the secret knowledge of the Self: "Wonderful is he who speaks of it (the Self); intelligent is he who learns of it; blessed is he who, taught by a good guru, is able to understand it." It also explains the process of yoga for Self-realization.

• **Isha Upanishad**
With only 18 verses, the Isha Upanishad is one of the shortest. It provides additional discussion on the Self, teaches the path of moderation, and cautions the seeker against the path of extremes. Thus the Upanishad declares: "To darkness are they doomed who devote themselves only to meditation or only to work. Those who devote themselves both to life in the world and to meditation, by life in the world they overcome death, and by meditation they achieve immortality."

• **Kena Upanishad**
"That which is not heard by the ear, but by which the ear hears, know that to be Brahman. That which is not seen by the eye, but by which the eye sees, know that to be Brahman." According to this Upanishad, Brahman is the essence of all things and beings in the world. Brahman is beyond the comprehension of the mind and intellect: "One who thinks he knows Brahman, knows not," declares this Upanishad.

• **Prasna Upanishad**
This Upanishad is a dialogue between Sage Pippalada and many disciples, such as Sukesha, Satyakama, Gargya, Kousalya, Bhargava, and Kabandhi. In the dialogue the sage answers many questions asked by the disciples, including the following: How do creatures come into existence? What powers hold the body together? How does the life force enter and exit the body? When an individual sleeps or dreams, who is it within that individual's body who sleeps or dreams?

• **Mundaka Upanishad**
According to this Upanishad, knowledge is of two kinds, higher and lower. Higher knowledge is that by which one realizes the Ultimate Reality (Brahman). Lower knowledge

pertains to rituals, sacrifices, ceremonies, etymology, and astronomy, among other things. This Upanishad declares, "Brahman sees all, knows all; He is knowledge itself. From Him are born breath, mind, sense organs, and ether, air, fire, water, and the earth [the Panchamahabhutas--see chapter 37]. He is not known through the study of scriptures, nor through the subtlety of intellect, nor through much learning; but by him who longs for Him is He known."

- **Mandukya Upanishad**
  This is the shortest of the twelve Upanishads, but is considered the most important one. According to this Upanishad, the embodied self (atman living in a body) normally passes through three states of consciousness: waking, dream, and deep sleep. In the waking state, the self is conscious only of external objects. In the dream state, the self enjoys subtle impressions in the mind left by its past actions. In deep sleep the subtle impressions of the mind disappear and the self experiences bliss. Beyond the three states that are experienced by common people lies the fourth state; it exists beyond all senses, understanding, and expression. It is in this fourth state, known as the *Turiya* state, where the world of duality disappears and atman is realized.

- **Taittiriya Upanishad**
  This Upanishad declares that the universe emanates from Brahman in the following manner: "From Brahman arises *akasha* (gravitational energy); from akasha arises *vayu* (kinetic energy); from vayu arises *tejas* (radiation); from tejas arises *ap* (electricity) and from ap arises *prithvi* (magnetism)." See chapter 37 for a discussion of how this Upanishadic statement is in full agreement with the stellar evolution of the universe as proposed by science.
  To the youth, this Upanishad provides the following inspiration: "If the youth is morally pure, intelligent and knowledgeable, hopeful and possessing the skills of leading others, single-minded and unshakable in his thoughts, healthy and strong, for him the whole world is filled with treasures."

Chapter 3

To the men and women, this Upanishad delivers the following message: "Speak the truth; follow the path of righteousness; never postpone your duty. In married life nourish nobler generations; never neglect both worldly and spiritual realities; be skilled and dynamic. Be studious and share your wisdom with others and be ever grateful to the deities, your forefathers, and parents."

• **Aitareya Upanishad**
This upanishad declares that Brahman is the source, sustenance, and end of the universe. Without Him the eye cannot see, the ear cannot hear, the skin cannot feel, the tongue cannot speak, and the mind cannot think. He is the waking man in the wakeful state, dreamer in dreams, and deep sleeper in the dreamless sleep; but He transcends all these states. His true nature is pure consciousness.

• **Chandogya Upanishad**
This is one of the most popular and longest Upanishads. Through stories, parables, and dialogues, this Upanishad illustrates that everything visible and invisible has emanated from Brahman. It declares that the universe is born of Existence (Brahman) and not of non-existence (nothingness or void), as some may argue. "How could existence be born of non-existence?" asks this Upanishad.
The Chandogya Upanishad depicts an interesting story in which truthfulness is emphasized as the highest virtue: a boy goes to a sage for spiritual instruction. In order to check the boy's qualifications before accepting him, the sage asks the boy what the name of his father is. The boy replies that he does not know the name of his father, since his mother led an immoral life and does not know who his father is. The sage immediately accepts the boy because he speaks the truth, the only essential qualification for attaining the highest knowledge.

Chapter 3

- **Brihadaranyaka Upanishad**
This Upanishad is one of the oldest and longest. Through interesting conversations between Yajnavalkya, one of the great Upanishadic sages, and many students, this Upanishad teaches that Brahman is within all. "Brahman is the seer of the sight, the hearer of the sound, thinker of the thought, and knower of the known," declares this Upanishad. Both manifest and the unmanifest are different aspects of Brahman. This Upanishad includes the following prayer, the most popular among Hindus (Shukla Yajur Veda Brihadaranyaka Upanishad 1.3.28):

> "Lead me from unreal to real;
> Lead me from darkness to light;
> Lead me from death to immortality."

- **Kaivalya Upanishad**
This Upanishad begins with a disciple's request to his guru, "Master, teach me the knowledge of Brahman." The teacher advises the student to seek Brahman by acquiring faith in the word of the scriptures and in the guru. The teacher explains that Brahman is O ne without beginning, middle, or end. He is all-pervading, infinite wisdom, and bliss. As atman, Brahman dwells in the hearts of all beings.

- **Svetasvatara Upanishad**
According to this Upanishad, the Self supports both the perishable and the imperishable, as well as the manifest and the unmanifest. Due to cosmic ignorance (*maya*), the embodied atman becomes forgetful of its own divine nature and attaches itself to worldly pleasure and is thus bound to material existence. This Upanishad teaches that creation has existed eternally and that the mind, matter, and cosmic ignorance are the three aspects of Brahman. The Self is the destroyer of ignorance, or maya. The Upanishad prescribes meditation for realization of the Self.

Smriti Scriptures

Smriti means "that which is remembered." Smriti scriptures are derived from the Vedas and are considered to be of human origin and not of divine origin. They were written to explain and elaborate the Vedas, making them understandable and more meaningful to the general population. All authoritative writings outside the Vedas and Bhagavad Gita are collectively referred to as Smriti. These scriptures may be classified as follows (see Figure F-1 on page 39):

Dharma Shastras

These writings describe the codes of human conduct, righteousness, personal hygiene, social administration, and ethical and moral duties. The best known Dharma Shastra is the *Manu Smriti* or the Code of Manu, containing 2,694 stanzas in twelve chapters. Manu, the 65th ancestor of *Bhagavan* (incarnation of God in human form) Rama, prescribed Hindu conduct on the basis of self-control, non-injury, compassion, and non-attachment, all of which were emphasized as necessary prerequisites for a just and virtuous society (see also chapter 16). *Manu Smriti* is a code of laws for righteous living, which continue to dominate Hindu ethics. The other important works of this category are *Yajnavalkya Smriti* and *Gautama Smriti*, written by sages Yajnavalkya and Gautama, respectively.

Nibandhas

Nibandhas are the digests, manuals, and encyclopedias of the Vedic laws pertaining to human conduct, worship, and rituals. They also include topics such as gift-giving, pilgrimages, and the maintenance of the human body.

Puranas

The Puranas form the largest body of Smriti literature. They exist in question-and-answer form and explain the subtle teachings of the Vedas through stories and legends of the ancient kings, heroes, sages, and divine personalities. The Puranas are second only to the epics as popular instruments of religious teachings. There are eighteen major Puranas: six of these are devoted to Lord Vishnu, six to Lord Brahma, and the remaining six to Lord Shiva. Their author is Sage Vyasa, who also wrote the Mahabharata. Of all the Puranas, the most popular Purana is the *Bhagavata Purana*, which is devoted to Lord Vishnu.

The *Bhagavata Purana* includes 15,000 stanzas arranged in twelve chapters. A major portion of this popular scripture is a dialogue between Sage Suka (son of Sage Vyasa) and King Parikshit. The *Bhagavata Purana* includes stories of all the incarnations of Lord Vishnu, with the story of Sri Krishna described in great detail. This scripture teaches the different ways of offering devotion to God, such as listening to stories of God described in scriptures, meditating, singing devotional songs, adoring pictures and images of God, and performing all work in the spirit of service for the Lord.

The Epics

The two great epics (*itihasas*) of Hindu religion are the Ramayana and the Mahabharata. These are the most popular scriptural books among Hindus. The Ramayana was originally written by Sage Valmiki. The story describes how Lord Vishnu appeared on earth as Bhagavan Rama and killed King Ravana, who had oppressed his kingdom through his lust for power. The epic illustrates the ideals of personal, social, and public life. It also illustrates the ideals of brotherhood, friendship, and chastity for both men and women. See chapter 30 for a detailed discussion of the Ramayana.

Sage Vyasa is the author of the Mahabharata, which is sometimes called the fifth Veda because of its deep influence on Hindus of all walks of life. It is a story of the great war that took place between the Kauravas and the Pandavas for the ownership of the ancient kingdom of Kurukshetra. On one side were the five Pandava brothers and on the other were their cousins, one-hundred Kaurava brothers. In the battle-field Sri Krishna was the charioteer of Arjuna, one of the Pandava brothers. Upon seeing his friends and relatives gathered on the other side of the battlefield, Arjuna told Krishna that he was not prepared to kill his own friends and relatives for the sake of a kingdom. This led to an immortal dialogue between Krishna and Arjuna, known as the *Bhagavad Gita*, often called the Bible of Hindus. The message of the Bhagavad Gita is universal and includes the basic beliefs of Hindu religion. Refer to chapter 31 for a detailed discussion of the epic Mahabharata.

Agamas or Tantras

The Agamas, also known as Tantras, are the sectarian scriptures of the three major theological traditions of Hindu religion, namely Vaishnavism, Shaivism, and Shaktism. The Vaishnava-Agamas adore the Ultimate Reality as Lord Vishnu; the Shiva-Agamas revere the Ultimate Reality as Lord Shiva; and the Shakti-Agamas venerate the Ultimate Reality as Divine Mother of the universe.

The Shiva Agama has led to the school of philosophy known as *Shiva Siddhanta* in South India, and to the *Pratyabhijna* system of Shaivism in Kashmir. Similarly, there are two main schools in the Vaishnava Agama, the *Pancharatra* and the *Vaikhanasa*, the former being more popular among the devotees of Lord Vishnu. Each Agama consists of four parts. The first part includes philosophical and spiritual knowledge. The second part covers yoga and mental discipline. The third part specifies rules for the construction of temples and for sculpting and carving the figures of deities for worship in the temples. The fourth part of the Agamas includes rules pertaining to the observances of religious rites, rituals, and festivals.

Vedangas and Upa Vedas

Vedangas means "the limbs of the Vedas." The Vedangas consist of six treatises and are regarded as auxiliary to, and in some sense a part of, the Vedas. The following six Vedangas discuss the following subjects: Siksha (correct pronunciation), Chandas (metre), Nirukta (etymology), Vyakarana (grammar), Jyotisha (astronomy), and Kalpa (rules governing rites and rituals). The Upa Vedas or the subsidiary Vedas include Ayurvedic medicine, military science, music, dance and politics. Refer to Figure F-2 for additional discussion of these scriptures.

Darshanas

The religious literature in this category can be classified into two divisions, heterodox and orthodox (see Figure F-2). The heterodox schools reject the authority of the Vedas and include Buddhists, Jains, and the Carvakas (materialists). The orthodox schools accept the Vedas and the Vedic literature as authoritative. There are six orthodox schools (see Figure F-4) divided into two groups. The two Mimamsa schools are directly based on the Vedic literature. The Nyaya, Vaiseshika, Sankhya, and Yoga schools are based on slightly different religious ideology, but are consistent with the Vedas. Each Darshana or school has its writings attributed to its founder, including a number of commentaries written later by the followers of these schools.

Other Smriti Scriptures

This category includes many other religious writings, such as *Yoga Vasishtha* and *Panchatantra*. *Yoga Vasishtha*, the dialogue between Bhagavan Rama and Sage Vasishtha, comprises 29,000 Sanskrit verses and is said to have been written by Valmiki, a prominent sage and author of the epic Ramayana. In poetic language and through curious stories and philosophical discourses, *Yoga Vasishtha* expounds Vedanta philosophy with seemingly more emphasis on the Advaitic doctrine of the Vedanta philosophy.

Panchatantra is a celebrated collection of popular stories comprising five books. The characters of the Panchatantra are animals, serpents, birds, and fish, who are generally endowed with human or superhuman qualities. The stories are narrated by a priest who imparts worldly knowledge to the sons of an ancient king. A variety of translations and adaptations of Panchatantra are now available in the West, including a version of the life of Buddha that resulted in the creation of the legend of Saint Josaphat.[25b]

Figure F-2: Classification of Other Scriptures

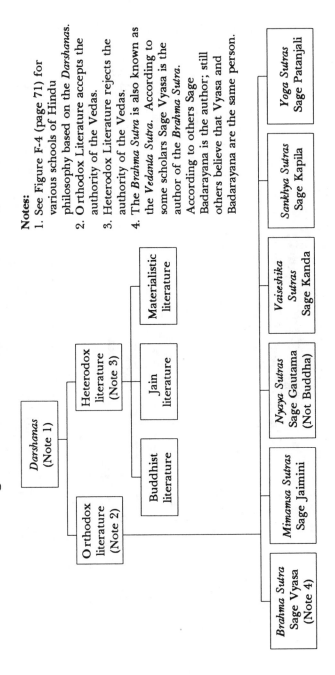

Notes:

1. See Figure F-4 (page 71) for various schools of Hindu philosophy based on the *Darshanas*.

2. Orthodox Literature accepts the authority of the Vedas.

3. Heterodox Literature rejects the authority of the Vedas.

4. The *Brahma Sutra* is also known as the *Vedanta Sutra*. According to some scholars Sage Vyasa is the author of the *Brahma Sutra*. According to others Sage Badarayana is the author; still others believe that Vyasa and Badarayana are the same person.

Darshanas
(Note 1)

Orthodox literature
(Note 2)

Heterodox literature
(Note 3)

Buddhist literature

Jain literature

Materialistic literature

Brahma Sutra
Sage Vyasa
(Note 4)

Mimamsa Sutras
Sage Jaimini

Nyaya Sutras
Sage Gautama
(Not Buddha)

Vaiseshika Sutras
Sage Kanda

Samkhya Sutras
Sage Kapila

Yoga Sutras
Sage Patanjali

Figure F-2 (Continued)
Classification of Other Scriptures

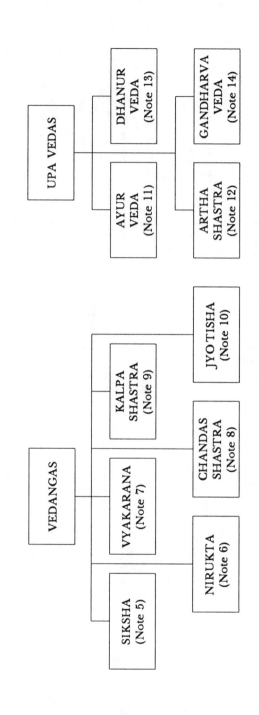

Figure F-2
Classification of Other Scriptures
Notes (Contd.):

5. Siksha, written by Sage Panini, includes the science of phonetics, pronunciation, and accent.

6. Nirukta teaches the science of linguistics and provides etymology of the words used in the Vedic mantras.

7. Vyakarana describes the science of the Sanskrit grammar as developed by Sage Panini.

8. Chandas Shastra teaches the art of versification and the use of meters in prose and poetry.

9. Kalpa Shastra describes the science of the Vedic rites and rituals.

10. Jyotisha teaches the science of astronomy and astrology.

11. Ayur Veda teaches the science of the ancient system of Indian medicine that uses natural herbs and plants to cure diseases. Maharshi Charaka was the first physician of the human race, who formulated a code of ethics for physicians. Refer to chapter 38 for further discussion on this subject.

12. Artha Shastra is a manual of ethics for kings written by Kautilya. In addition to providing guidance for ruling the country, this manual includes instructions for conducting espionage and fighting the enemy.

13. Dhanur Veda teaches the science of archery and the use of weapons in war. It also specifies the rules of warfare and treatment and protection of the prisoners of war.

14. Gandharva Veda is the science of music and dance. Sage Bharata is the author of Natyashastra, an ancient manual of dramatic art. The science of sound and acoustics was fully developed by the ancient Hindus, which gave birth to a variety of musical instruments of ancient India, such as drums, flute, and veena (lute).

Chapter 4
Hindu View of God and Individual

Hindu sages tell us that the essence of all things and beings is *Brahman*. What is this Brahman? The Chandogya Upanishad 6-8 explains; "Bring a fruit from this banyan tree," says the father. The son, Svetaketu, brings it. "Break it." "It is broken, revered sir." "What do you see in this?" "Tiny little seeds." "Break one of these seeds, my child." "It is broken, revered sir." "What do you see in it?" "Nothing, sir." "My dear child, from the subtle essence which you do not perceive, stands this mighty banyan tree. That subtle essence is the ground and root of all there is. That subtle essence is Brahman. That which is tiny (*anima*) is the atman of all. That thou art (*Tat Tvam Asi*), my dear boy."

Brahman

According to Hindu view, the Reality (the *Brahman* of the Upanishads) can be viewed from two aspects: transcendental (impersonal) and immanent (personal). In its transcendental aspect, the Reality is called *Nirguna Brahman*, that is, Brahman without attributes. It is conceived of as one and undifferentiated, both static and dynamic, and as the ultimate principle underlying the universe. "Brahman is He whom speech cannot express, and from whom the mind, unable to reach Him, comes away baffled," states the Taittiriya Upanishad.

Nirguna Brahman is not an object of prayer, but of meditation and knowledge. It cannot be described, and the most one can say is that it is absolute existence, absolute knowledge, and absolute bliss (*sat-chit-ananda*). It is unborn, self-existent, all-pervading, and the ground and the essence of all things and beings in the universe. According to the Maitri Upanishad, "Brahman is immeasurable, unapproachable, beyond conception, beyond birth, beyond reasoning, and beyond thought."

God

In its immanent (personal) aspect, the Reality is called *Saguna Brahman*, that is, Brahman with attributes. Saguna Brahman is the personal God, the creator, the preserver, and the controller of the universe. In Hindu religion, the personal aspect of Brahman is worshipped in both male and female forms (see Figure F-3). From the male aspect, the Reality is called by various Sanskrit names, such as *Ishvara, Parameshvara, Paramatma, Maheshvara,* and *Purusha.* Although there are subtle differences in the meanings of these Sanskrit names, they generally denote the Reality as creator, preserver, and controller of the universe. From the female aspect, the Reality is called by names such as Divine Mother, Durga, and Kali.

It must be recognized that the personal concept of the Reality in Hindu religion, as denoted by the above Sanskrit names, is the same as the concept of God in Christianity except for one notable difference: God in Hindu religion is not the creator of the individual soul (atman). The atman is divine and eternal. In Christianity, God is the creator of the individual souls. Refer to Table T-3 for Hindu and Christian concepts of God and Table T-5 for a comparison of the major religious principles of Hinduism, Christianity and Judaism.

Atman

According to Hindu view, *atman* is the inner essence of an individual. It is pure, divine, immortal, perfect, omnipresent, omnipotent, and omniscient. In the words of Sage Yajnavalkya (Brihadaranyaka Upanishad IV.5.15):

"The Self (*atman*), described as not this, not this (*neti neti*), is imperceptible, for it cannot be perceived. It is indestructible, for it cannot be destroyed. Being unfettered, it never feels pain, nor can it be injured. Being unattached, it never attaches to anything."

When associated with a body and under the influence of cosmic ignorance (*avidya* or *maya*), the atman forgets its true nature and mistakenly identifies itself with the body-mind apparatus. This wrong identification is the cause of its bondage to material existence and the consequent pleasure, pain, and suffering in the perpetual cycle of birth and death in the phenomenal world. Thus the ultimate goal of Hindu religious life is to transcend individuality, to realize one's own true nature, which is potentially divine and pure. This realization is called *moksha*, or the liberation of the soul from the cycle of birth and death, resulting in union with God.

Although the Sanskrit word atman is generally translated as soul, atman and soul are not interchangeable, in light of the Western definition of the soul. What Westerners call soul, Hindus call *manas* (or sukshma sharira), the subtle faculty of the mind, intellect, and the ego (see chapter 13). In Hindu view, the mind, intellect, and ego appear and exist only because of the presence of the atman in the physical body. Atman is also sometimes translated as spirit or self.

Hindu Deities

Hindus believe in the existence of one and only one Supreme Being (the Brahman of the Upanishads), but they worship Him in various forms known as deities or gods (note small *g*). The Hindu worship of many deities (gods) is not polytheism, but *monotheistic polytheism*. The monotheistic Hindu pantheon is an affirmation that the Supreme Being can be known in many ways and worshipped in many forms. The tradition of worshipping many gods or deities is based upon the following logic:

• Hindu religion recognizes the diversity of the human mind and the potential for a different level of spiritual develop-ment in each individual. Hindu religion does not, there-fore, thrust everyone into the pigeonhole of a single creed. The Mahabharata declares:

"Akaasat patitam toyam yatha gacchati sagram, sarva deva namaskarah kesavam prati gacchati."

"Just as the rain water that falls from the sky eventually reaches the ocean, so also all the worship offered to Him, by whatever name you wish, or in whatever form you

Figure F-3: Understanding God in Hinduism

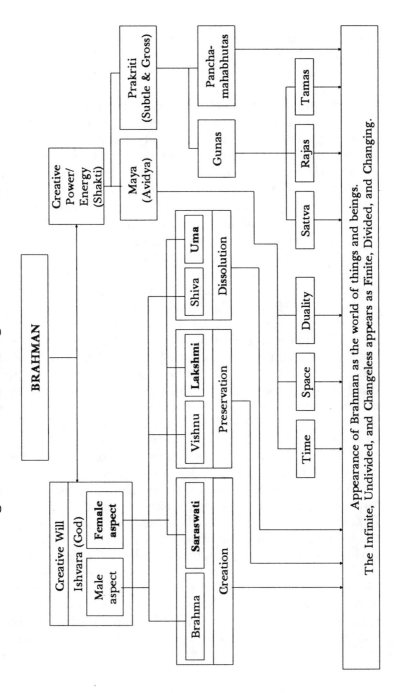

like, ultimately goes to the one (the only one) Ultimate,
Infinite, Supreme Reality."

• Being the creator of the innumerable forms in this
  universe, the Supreme Being must be able to assume any
  form to please His devotees. Furthermore, the Supreme
  Being cannot be said to have only one particular form or
  one particular name because that would imply putting
  limitations on His infinite power. This is why Hindus
  worship various names and forms of the Supreme Reality.
  No name or form is considered superior or inferior to the
  others because all are various manifestations of one Supreme Being. This idea is further brought forth clearly
  in the following doctrine of the *Atharva Veda*:

> "He is the One, the One alone,
>   in Him all deities become One alone."

Worshipping a particular form of the Supreme Being does
not limit or contradict the worship of other forms of the
Supreme Being. This logic is best understood by the use of
the following contemporary analogy: when we work in an
office, we wear a suit and tie or a dress. While working around
the house, we wear work pants and perhaps a T-shirt. When
we play tennis, we wear sportswear, and so on. The point
here is that in all these cases, one is the same person, merely
wearing different outfits to do various jobs.

When a devotee chooses to worship one form of the
Supreme Being, the chosen deity is called *Ishta-deva*, or
Ishta-devata. This Ishta-deva becomes the object of the devotee's love and adoration, satisfying his spiritual longing. In
early Vedic texts an attempt was made to fix the number of
deities (gods) at thirty-three. These thirty-three deities were
divided into three groups of eleven each. One group was
associated with heaven, the other with earth, and the third
with the waters and atmosphere. The leader of the first group
was known as the sun god (Surya), the leader of the second
group as the god of fire (Agni), and the leader of the third

group as the god of wind (Indra). In later days the number thirty-three was expanded to thirty-three crores (330 million). The concept of 330 million deities (or gods) may sound ludicrous, but it has deep symbolic significance.

According to Hindu view, atman is the manifestation of Brahman in each and every living being, from the perfect man to the lowest worm. Thus Hindus worship God in all beings, realizing that all beings are different manifestations of the Reality. In ancient times it was believed that 330 million living beings existed in nature. Since each living being was believed to be a particular manifestation of Brahman, the existence of the 330 million manifestations gave rise to the concept of an equal number of deities. Actually, all 330 million deities could not have been worshipped. Instead, the 330 million *number* was used to give symbolic expression to the fundamental Hindu doctrine that God lives in the hearts of all beings, and as such He has immense and uncountable manifestations.

The following are some of the major deities worshipped in contemporary Hindu religion. Their place in a typical monotheistic Hindu Pantheon is illustrated in Figure F-3.

Brahma

In Hindu religion, Lord Brahma (not to be confused with *Brahman* of the Upanishads) is the god of creation. He represents the creative aspect of the Supreme Being. By worshipping Brahma, a Hindu worships the Supreme Being as the creator of the universe. The symbolism of Lord Brahma is discussed in chapter 20.

Saraswati

Goddess Saraswati means "the essence of one's own self." Saraswati denotes that aspect of the Supreme Reality which represents knowledge, learning, and wisdom. In Hindu mythology, Saraswati is the divine spouse of Brahma, the god of creation. Since correct knowledge is necessary for anything to be created, Saraswati provides knowledge necessary for creation. She represents the status to which womanhood has been elevated and revered in Hindu religion. The symbolism of Goddess Saraswati is discussed in chapter 25.

Chapter 4

Vishnu

Lord Vishnu is the god of preservation. Thus the Supreme Reality is known as Vishnu when It is conceived to be engaged in the preservation of the universe. Vishnu is an important member of the Hindu Trinity, consisting of Brahma, Vishnu, and Shiva (see chapter 29). Vishnu is also known by the name of Vasudeva. Bhagavan Rama and Bhagavan Krishna are the two most popular incarnations of Lord Vishnu worshipped by Hindus. Refer to chapter 21 for a discussion of the symbolism associated with Lord Vishnu.

Lakshmi

Goddess Lakshmi, the divine spouse of Lord Vishnu, is the goddess of wealth and prosperity, which she provides to Vishnu for the sustenance of the universe. She is the symbol of all that Hindus consider sacred, chaste, and pure in womanhood. Refer to chapter 24 for a discussion of the symbolism of Lakshmi.

Shiva

Lord Shiva is the deity of dissolution and re-creation in the continuous cycle of creation, preservation, dissolution, and recreation. He is the third member of the Hindu Trinity, with the other two being Brahma and Vishnu. Lord Shiva represents the aspect of the Supreme Reality that is responsible for dissolution of the old and recreation of the new. Refer to chapter 22 for a discussion of the symbolism of Lord Shiva.

Durga

Goddess Durga, the Hindu deity of energy and power (*shakti*), is the divine spouse of Lord Shiva. She represents one of the popular manifestations of the Supreme Reality in the form of the Divine Mother of the universe. She is also known and worshipped by many other names, such as Parvati, Kali, Shakti, Uma, Mrudani, Chandika, and Devi. Durga puja (worship of Goddess Durga) is one of the most popular and colorful annual festivals of Hindus in India. Refer to chapter 23 for symbolism associated with Goddess Durga.

Chapter 4

The Concept of Maya

Maya, one of the key terms in Hindu religious tradition, is used in various connotations, implying a principle, power, or process. Since in Hindu view non-existence can never be the source of creation (just as a plant can never sprout without a seed), maya is the metaphysical principle that is used in Hindu religion to explain the projection of the phenomenal world by Brahman.

There are two predominant views among Hindu scholars relating to the concept of maya. In some philosophical systems, maya refers to the mysterious power (or the cosmic energy) of the Supreme Being with which He projects the universe from Himself. Because of maya things and beings are brought into existence, incarnations are born, humans play their roles on the stage of life, and the divine play of life (*leela*) continues age after age (*yuge yuge*).

In other philosophical systems including Advaita Vedanta, maya is thought of as cosmic illusion or ignorance (*avidya*) that deludes the atman into forgetting its own divine nature. This forgetfulness of its true nature further causes the atman to mistakenly identify itself with the body and mind, assume individuality, and thus subject itself to the physical limitations in the phenomenal world (*samsara*).

This mistaken identification of the atman with the body and mind (i.e., *veiling* the truth and *projecting* it as something else) is said to be, in Hindu scriptures, analogous to mistaking a rope for a snake in dull light. In this classical rope-snake analogy, the rope represents the atman, the snake represents the individual or individuality, and the dull light denotes maya. Refer to chapter 37 for discussion of the triple powers of maya (*sattva, rajas,* and *tamas*) that cause the phenomenon of *veiling* the truth and *projecting* it as something else.

Maya can be explained in yet another way. In Hindu view, atman provides sentience to a sentient being and gives rise to faculties of the mind and intellect in a human body. In the absence of a body, atman does not say "I." In the absence of atman, the inert body does not say "I" either. However, when the two meet, a mysterious power in the form of "I-thought" appears. This mysterious "I-thought," also called ego, is the

Chapter 4

result of maya. This aspect of maya is explained by Parama-hamsa Sri Ramakrishna: "Maya is nothing but the egotism of the embodied atman. This egotism has covered everything like a veil. All troubles come to an end when the ego dies. This maya, that is to say, the ego, is like a cloud. The sun cannot be seen on account of a thin patch of cloud; when that disappears one sees the sun. If by the grace of the guru one's ego vanishes, then one sees God."[4]

Prakriti and Gunas

The concept of prakriti is used in Sankhya philosophy (see chapter 6) to explain the evolution of the universe. Prakriti is defined as the ultimate unconscious primal matter or the ultimate cosmic energy, the material cause of the universe.

Prakriti is the source of the five great elements earth, water, fire, air, and ether, known as *Panchamahabhutas* (see chapter 37). These five great elements comprise all material objects and the bodies of plants, trees, insects, animals, and human beings. All beings in the world are the products of the union of the atman (or *Purusha* of Sankhya philosophy) and prakriti. Thus *Brahman*, through its *shakti,* is both the material and the efficient cause of the universe. Thus, the multiplicity of the created world has behind it the perfect unity of all existence, the Brahman of the Upanishads, as illustrated in Figure F-3.

Prakriti has three inherent properties or attributes, known as the three gunas: *sattva, rajas,* and *tamas.* In Sanskrit, *guna* means "quality." Sattva represents the qualities of goodness, balance, and harmony. Rajas represents passion, restlessness, and activity. Tamas represents dullness, inertia, and laziness.

Prakriti and maya are similar concepts. Prakriti is the primal matter with the qualities of sattva, rajas, and tamas, whereas maya is cosmic ignorance with the triple powers of sattva, rajas, and tamas (see chapter 37).

The *gunas* are the attributes of all matter, gross and subtle. When they are in a state of equilibrium, *prakriti* is by definition in equilibrium, and the creative activity of the Supreme Being, *Ishvara,* is at a stand-still. This state of existence is called *pralaya* (cosmic deluge--see creation in chapter 2). When the cyclic process of cosmic deluge is complete, the *gunas* begin to stir by Divine Will and *prakriti* begins on the course of evolution. The individual souls are embodied according to their karma. Thus a new cycle of creation begins in an endless process of creation, sustenance, dissolution, and re-creation. In Hindu view, the mind is believed to be a subtle form of matter. Thus the three gunas determine the character of an individual, depending upon the proportion in which they are present, as elaborated in the following table:

Individuals	Sattva	Rajas	Tamas
Intellectuals, educators and creative thinkers	high	low	low
Politicians and administrators	medium to high	high	low to medium
Businessmen, employers, and skilled labor	medium	high	medium
Non-skilled labor	low	medium	high

The above four-fold classification of individuals, based upon their inherent qualities, was known as the *Varna* system of the Vedas. In the *Varna* system, the creative thinkers and the educators were known as *Brahmins*, the politicians and administrators as *Kshatriyas*, the businessmen, employers and skilled laborers as *Vaisyas*, and the non-skilled laborers as *Shudras*. The *Varna* system classified an individual into one of the above four classes based upon his or her aptitude, ability, character, and achievements. All these qualities depend upon an individual's manifestation of prakriti (i.e. the *gunas*). Thus the three attributes of prakriti, the *gunas*, were used to determine an individual's natural classification into the *Varna* system, as explained in the following verse of the Bhagavad Gita:

"The four-fold classification of human beings was created by Me in accordance with their *gunas* and *karma* [qualities and actions]. Although I am the author of that, yet know Me to be the non-doer and changeless." (BG 4.13)

Chapter 4

It is interesting to note that the problems and conflicts among the four classes of the *Varna* system that existed in the Vedic period are synonymous to those that exist today in contemporary society. For example, the conflict between politicians and the independent thinkers of a modern society is typical of the conflict that existed between *Brahmins* and *Kshatriyas* of the *Varna* system. Similarly the conflict of interest between the businesses and the trade unions of a modern society is typical of the conflict that existed between the *Kshatriyas* and the *Shudras* of the *Varna* system.

In accordance with the three powers of nature (*sattva, rajas,* and *tamas*), the Bhagavad Gita expounds upon the three-fold natural classification of individuals, the quality of work performed by them, the knowledge acquired by them, and the quality of their wisdom, steadiness, and concepts of pleasure, as follows (BG 18.20 through 18.39):

Parameter	Sattvic (Pure)	Rajasic (Impure)	Tamsic (Ignorance)
Individual	Free from ego, attachments, and not affected by success or failure	Greedy, slave of passions, and affected by pleasure and pain	Without self-harmony, vulgar, arrogant, deceitful and despondent
Work	Performed without selfishness, lust, greed, hate, or desire	Performed with desire for reward	Performed with a confused mind without considering what may follow
Knowledge	Perceiving God in all beings	Failing to perceive God in all beings	Perceiving beings different from each other and independ. of God
Wisdom	Can discriminate between fear and courage, bondage and liberation, and knows which actions to take and not to take	No clear vision of what is right and what is wrong and which actions to take	Thinking that wrong actions are correct and taking actions which should not be taken

(Table continued from previous page)

Parameter	Sattvic (Pure)	Rajasic (Impure)	Tamsic (Ignorance)
Steadiness	Attaches to self-harmony and peace	Attaches to desire for wealth, power, name and fame	Attaches to laziness, fear, self-pity, depression and lust
Pleasure	Arises from clear vision of the Spirit	Arises from craving of the senses for the objects of their desire	Arises from dullness, sleep, laziness, or carelessness

Sin in Hindu Religion

An individual is not born a sinner in Hindu religion. "Each person is potentially divine. The goal is to manifest this divinity within, by controlling nature, [both] external and internal. Do this either by work or worship or psychic control, or philosophy [by one or more, or all of these] and be free," declares Swami Vivekananda.[5]

The doctrine of sin as expounded by Christianity (see Table T-3) is not accepted in Hindu religion. According to Hindu view, man commits sin only because of his ignorance of his own true nature. Due to *avidya* (ignorance) that leads to false knowledge, man perceives himself to be an independent entity, different from other beings and separate from God. The imagined separation between himself and the Divine makes the individual forget his real nature, and his intimate relationship with the Divine. Under this delusion, the individual behaves in petty ways and attaches himself to fear, craving, and anger. In Hindu view, *ignorance* of Self is the root cause of all evils in the world. Self-knowledge is thus essential for eliminating evil, since knowledge destroys ignorance just as a fire burns wood to ashes. Thus we hear the words of Sri Krishna in the Bhagavad Gita:

"Even if you are the greatest sinner among all sinners, by the raft of knowledge alone, you will easily cross the entire ocean of sin." (BG 4.36)

Chapter 4

Chapter 5
Worship of God in the
Form of Mother

"O Mother Divine, the refuge of the lowly and afflicted
and the savior supreme. O Thou, the remover of the
suffering of all. O *Narayani,* salutations to Thee."
(From *Devi-Mahatmyam,* a Sanskrit Scripture)

"If God is our father, why cannot God be our mother? If
we are the children of our heavenly Father, why cannot we be
the children of our heavenly Mother?" This rhetorical question is the basis of why Hindus recognize and accept both male
and female aspects of Nature and worship the Reality in the
form of Mother, Father, Friend, Master, Guru, and Savior.
Thus Lord Krishna declares in the Bhagavad Gita:

"I am the Father and the Mother of this universe, and
the Creator of all. I am the Highest to be known, the
Purifier, the holy O M, and the three Vedas." (BG 9.17)

The worship of God in the form of Mother is a unique feature of Hindu religious tradition. Through the ages, the doctrine of the Motherhood of God has established a firm root
among Hindus. Today they worship the Divine Mother in
many popular forms such as Durga, Lakshmi, and Saraswati.
Refer to chapters 23 through 25 for a discussion of the symbolism of these forms of the Divine Mother.

By worshipping God as the Divine Mother, a Hindu can
more easily attribute motherly traits to the Lord, such as tenderness and forgivingness. "Wife and children may desert a
man, but his mother, never!" The natural love between a
mother and her child is the best expression of the Lord's unconditional love for us as children of God. In the most repre-

sentative Hindu view, the universe is the manifestation of the creative power (*shakti*) of Brahman, whose essence is absolute existence, consciousness, and bliss (*sat-chit-ananda*). Since all created forms proceed from the womb of the mother, the creative power of God is recognized by Hindus as the female principle or the motherly aspect of nature. In this sense we are all children of the Divine Mother, who nourishes us throughout our existence.

To a Hindu, the motherly aspect of God in nature is full of beauty, gentleness, kindness, and tenderness. When we look upon all the glorious and beautiful things in nature and experience a feeling of tenderness within us, we feel the motherly instinct of God. The worship of God in the form of Mother is a unique contribution of the Hindu mind. When a devotee worships God as Divine Mother, he (she) appeals to Her tenderness and unconditional love. Such love unites the devotee with God, like a child with its mother. Just as a child feels safe and secure in the lap of its mother, a devotee feels safe and secure in the presence of the Divine Mother. Paramahamsa Sri Ramakrishna worshipped the Divine Mother Kali during his entire life, established a personal relationship with Her, and constantly enjoyed Her presence by his side.

In Hindu religion, Divine Mother is the first manifestation of the creative principle of the Ultimate Reality. Thus with the name of Divine Mother comes the idea of the divine power, omnipotence, omnipresence, love, intelligence, and wisdom. Just as a child believes its mother to be all-powerful, and capable of doing anything for the child, a devotee believes the Divine Mother to be all-merciful, all-powerful and eternally guiding and protecting him.

The worship of God as Mother has had a significant impact on Hindus. The position of women in the Hindu religion is dignified because each woman is considered a manifestation of the Divine Mother. Hindus view man and woman as the two wings of the same bird. Thus, a man is considered incomplete without a woman, since "*it is not possible for a bird to fly on only one wing,*" says Swami Vivekananda. Through the worship of Divine Mother, Hindus offer reverence to the womanhood that is unparalleled in human history.

Chapter 5

Chapter 6
Different Schools of Hindu Philosophy

Hindu religion was not founded by a particular person, prophet, or incarnation. As such, Hindu religious tradition is not a single and simple system of theories, principles, or practices. It consists of a diverse body of ideas and experiences accumulated over thousands of years by sages and saints. Since in many cases the ideas and spiritual experiences of sages and saints are diverse, Hindu religious thought has attempted to synthesize these various beliefs. The result is a unified body of concepts based upon diverse principles and practices. This *unity within diversity* is made possible by five basic features of Hindu religion: common ideals, common beliefs, common scriptures, common deities, and common practices. The essential characteristics of Hindu religious thought can be summarized as follows:

1. There is no vivid distinction between Hindu religion and philosophy. They go hand-in-hand. For example, the first three sections of the Vedas may be called religion, but the last section, called Upanishad, is only philosophy. In Hindu religion, there is a definite philosophical basis for every religious act. No religious act is based upon dogma or blind faith.

2. Hindu thought presents a unified view of the universe. The entire universe is believed to be a manifestation of Brahman, the ground and seed of all things and beings in the universe. As such, there is no absolute distinction between material and immaterial, or animate and inanimate. All distinctions are relative and appear only at the level of the mind and the senses. Once the mind and the senses are transcended through spiritual experience, only Brahman remains.

3. Since the Supreme Reality manifests itself in various ways, and therefore can be conceived in many ways, Hindus accept all diverse data and experiences as a valid basis for their philosophy. All possibilities and alternatives are evaluated and none are rejected beforehand. Thus, Hindu philosophy insists on the synthesis of all experiences and teaches the doctrine of harmony. Universal brotherhood is the chief message of Hindu religious tradition.

4. Hindu philosophy is not based upon curiosity or purely upon intellectual pastime or philosophical discourses. Having originated from a deeply recognized need to be free from the pain and suffering of this world, Hindu religious philosophy is both a way of life as well as a way of thought.

5. Rational thought and inference are considered important tools for attaining knowledge and cognition of the physical world. However, the Reality transcends both reason and logic. In the spiritual domain, therefore, Hindu sages consider intuition to be superior to reason. Thus, Hindu philosophy recognizes intuition as a superior means for knowing the Ultimate Truth and emphasizes introspection as an important tool for developing intuition.

6. All systems of Hindu philosophy believe that the individual self (atman) is immortal and passes from one body to another. This continuous cycle of birth and death is governed by the Law of Karma (see chapter 13).

Hindu Religious Thought

Hindu religious thought can be divided into two major systems: the heterodox and the orthodox (see Figure F-4). The heterodox system (called *nastika* in Sanskrit) rejects the authority of the Vedas. This system includes Carvaka (Materialism), Jainism, and Buddhism. The Carvaka system denies existence of the individual self (atman) apart from the body and rejects the notion of moksha (salvation) for the atman. This system of philosophy never gained popularity among

Hindus. Refer to chapters 10 and 11 for discussions of Buddhism and Jainism.

The orthodox system (called *astika* in Sanskrit) accepts the authority of the Vedas. It includes six schools of Hindu religious philosophy in the following order of popularity: Uttara Mimamsa or Vedanta, Purva Mimamsa, Yoga, Sankhya, Nyaya, and Vaiseshika. These schools of philosophy are based on complex ideas that are beyond the scope of this work. Therefore, only a brief introduction to these schools is provided below:

Uttara Mimamsa or Vedanta

Uttara Mimamsa, the "latter inquiry," also called Vedanta, is the philosophy of the Upanishads. *Vedanta*, the "end of the Vedas," refers to the teachings of the Upanishads, the concluding sections of the four Vedas. Vedanta is also a popular term used to denote collectively the teachings of the *Upanishads, Brahma Sutra, Bhagavad Gita,* and many other writings that elaborate upon the teachings of the Upanishads. The subject of Uttara Mimamsa is the knowledge of *Brahman* and its scriptural source is *jnana-kanda* (philosophical part) of the Vedas. There are several varieties of Vedantic Systems and all maintain that Brahman is the highest reality. Refer to chapter 7 for a discussion of the Vedanta philosophy and its three popular schools: Advaita, Visishtadvaita, and Dvaita.

Purva Mimamsa

Purva Mimamsa, the "earlier inquiry," founded by Sage Jaimini, is a religion of ritualism which is directly based on the Vedas. This system believes in the efficacy of the mantra and thus emphasizes the Vedic rites and rituals as a means for liberation of the atman from its bondage to material existence. The scriptural basis of Purva Mimamsa is the *karma-kanda* (ritualistic part) of the Vedas. According to the *Mimamsa Sutra,* "Dharma is that which is indicated by the Vedic rites and rituals as conducive to the highest good." The two foremost philosophers of this school are Prabhakara and Kumarila Bhatt.

Figure F-4: Classification of Hindu Philosophy

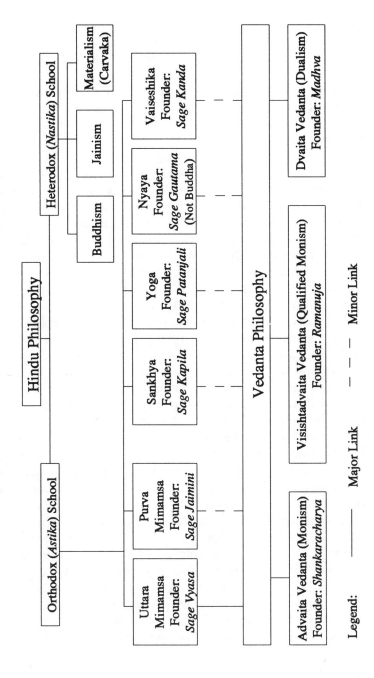

Yoga

This system accepts the metaphysical views of the Sankhya philosophy, but advocates a system of mental and physical exercises as spiritual discipline for liberation of the atman from worldly bondage. Refer to chapter 8 for a discussion of the yoga philosophy.

Sankhya

This system, founded by Sage Kapila, advocates an evolutionary view of the universe based upon continuity of life from the lowest to the highest level of existence. According to Sankhya, there are two ultimate realities which exist independently in the universe. O ne is the plurality of selves, called *Purusha*, and the second is the unlimited primal matter, called *prakriti* (see page 62). Purusha is pure consciousness, but inactive, and prakriti is unlimited cosmic energy devoid of consciousness. The contact between Purusha and prakriti gives rise to the world of things and beings.

Prakriti is said to be made up of three subtle elements known as the three gunas (see page 62). These are *sattva* (virtue), *rajas* (passion), and *tamas* (dullness). These three elements enter, in different proportions, into the material composition of all things and beings in the world, thus making each different in nature and character. For example, an individual is truthful and wise if sattva predominates in him. He is active and energetic if rajas predominates, and dull and lazy if tamas predominates.

The cause of the soul's misery and suffering in the world, according to the Sankhya philosophy, is its mistaken identification with the body, mind, intellect, and ego. The dissolution of this identification is necessary for liberation of the self from bondage to material existence. Since the false identification of the self with the body and mind is due to its ignorance of its own true nature, the Sankhya system emphasizes true knowledge of the self as a means for salvation. The true knowledge can be attained by proper discrimination between the self and the non-self. The non-self is comprised of the material world, including the body, mind, and intellect.

Chapter 6

Nyaya and Vaiseshika

Nyaya means "theory of inference." This school, founded by Sage Gautama (not Buddha), is more a system of logic than a system of religious practices. However, logic here is practiced for the purpose of attaining salvation. This school is primarily interested in logical analysis of the world and the use of inference and reason as a means to acquire true knowledge. Nyaya philosophy enjoys considerable respect among Western scholars, since it illustrates the subtleties and intricacies of the Indian logic.

Vaiseshika means "study of ultimate particulars." This school, also known as the Atomic School of Hindu religion, was founded by Sage Kanada. According to this philosophy, salvation results from the knowledge gained by cognition of six categories: substance, quality, action, class concept, species, and inherence.

Both of these systems acknowledge the existence of God as the Supreme Soul, Who is omnipotent, omniscient, guiding, and controlling the universe. Individual souls (*jivas*) are believed to be infinite in number and separate from the Supreme Soul, experiencing the limitations of the worldly life, and governed by the Law of Karma. The aim of both of these systems is the liberation of the individual soul (*jiva*) from worldly bondage by means of true knowledge of the Ultimate Reality.

Other Systems of Hindu Religious Thought

The following are other chief types of religious and philosophical thought in Hindu religion:

1. The Natural Dualistic Monism of Nimbarka
   (*Dvait-advaita*)
2. The Suprarational Dualistic Monism of Chaitanya
   (*Achintya Bhedabheda, "inconceivable duality and non-duality"*)
3. The Pure Monism of Vallabha (*Suddh-advaita*)
4. The Superpersonalism of the Bhagavad Gita
   (*Ishvara-Vada*)
5. The Spiritual Dynamism of Tantra *(Shakti-Vada)*

Chapter 6

Vedanta Philosophy

Vedanta, literally "the end of the Vedas," is the name given to the teachings of the Upanishads and various other religious writings that interpret, expand, or elaborate upon the teachings of the Upanishads. The Upanishads alone are not an organized and systematized philosophy for easy comprehension. The Upanishadic teachings were first systematized in approximately 500-200 BCE by Sage Badarayana and are known as the *Brahma Sutra* ("aphorisms concerning Brahman") or the Vedanta Sutra.

The Brahma Sutra contains 550 aphorisms and summarizes the basic philosophy of the Upanishads in four treatises (*adhyayas*). The predominant view among scholars is that the Brahma Sutra reflects the philosophical positions of the Chandogya Upanishad more than that of any other Upanishad. The aphorisms of the Brahma Sutra are very short and some consist of only one or two words. These aphorisms cannot be comprehended without a commentary. The traditional commentaries written on the Brahma Sutra constitute the basis of various philosophical systems, some of which provide diametrically opposed interpretations of the same short sutra.

The three major commentaries on the Brahma Sutra were provided by the medieval scholars Shankaracharya, Ramanujacharya, and Madhvacharya. Their differing interpretations gave rise to the three popular systems of Vedanta philosophy: *Advaita Vedanta* (non-dualism) of Shankara, *Visishtadvaita* (qualified non-dualism) of Ramanuja, and *Dvaita* (dualism) of Madhva. These systems differ more in detail than in substance. The basic difference in these systems is in their beliefs pertaining to the interrelationships between Brahman, the world, and the atman. There are several other Vedantic systems such as those of Bhaskara, Nimbarka, Srikantha,

Sripati, Baladeva, Vallabha, and Suka.   All these systems
maintain that Brahman is the highest reality.

Advaita Vedanta

The Advaita school of Vedanta is based upon the interpretations of Vedanta provided by Adi Shankaracharya, a
medieval sage and scholar, often called the genius of Hindu
metaphysical tradition.   Shankaracharya (788-820 AD) was
born into a Brahmin family in the city of Cochin, in South
India.   He received his education in Benares and became an
ascetic when he was a boy.   By the age of eight he was well
versed with the four Vedas, and by the age of twelve he had
mastered all Hindu scriptures.   He became a religious and
spiritual teacher as well as a reformer, establishing four
monasteries in India: one at Badrinath in the Himalayas, a
second at Dwarika on the West Coast, a third at Puri on the
East Coast, and the fourth at Sringeri in the state of Mysore.
These monasteries are to this day popular centers of learning
and pilgrimage in India.

Shankaracharya travelled throughout India and filled his
short life of thirty-two years with unprecedented religious and
spiritual activity.   His chief works are his commentaries on the
Brahma Sutra, the ten principal Upanishads, and the Bhagavad Gita.   He also wrote various other books on the Advaita
philosophy, such as *Upadesasahasri* (A Thousand Teachings),
Viveka Chudamani (Crest Jewel of Discrimination), *Atmabodhah*,
Bhaja Govindam, and his most popular devotional poem,
Saundarya Lahiri.

Shankaracharya's Advaita Vedanta is a philosophy of
oneness of all creation (matter as well as consciousness).
Advaita means monism or non-dualism.   Advaita Vedanta is
a very popular system of philosophy and has many followers
among Hindus.   This school of philosophy is especially popular among scientific and intellectual communities of Hindus
and non-Hindus alike.   Advaita Vedanta provides a complete
unified theory of everything in the universe, a goal that
modern physics is striving to achieve (see chapter 10 of *The
Tao of Physics* by Fritjof Capra, Bantam Books).

Chapter 7

According to Advaita Vedanta, everything inanimate and animate is nothing but Brahman. Brahman is the Absolute Reality and there is no other Reality but Brahman. In the words of Shankaracharya:

'Brahman satyam jagan mithya, jeevo Brahmaiva naparh." [6]

"Brahman alone is truth, the world is unreal. Atman (the individual soul) is Brahman only and none other."

When Shankara says that the world is unreal, it should not be construed to mean that the world is totally unreal. "To understand Shankara's statements one must always see them in the frame of reference in which they are made: all his assertions are explicit or implicit comparisons with absolute reality, which alone is of interest to him."[25c] To the "common" person, the world is real as long as he (or she) is in the grip of maya (nescience) and perceives the world through the mind and the senses alone. However, when the mind and senses are transcended through spiritual experience, the world of things and beings disappears altogether and what remains is Brahman, which is the only reality.

In the realm of matter, Einstein's equation $E=mc^2$ confirms that the cosmic matter is actually cosmic energy. Since modern science has not yet accounted for human consciousness in its scientific investigations, it cannot yet prove that the cosmic energy has actually arisen from the cosmic consciousness. Therefore, modern science cannot currently explain the unity of all things and beings in the world as Shankara did. For this reason, it is said that Shankara had already started where Einstein ended several centuries later.

Visishtadvaita

Ramanujacharya (1055-1137 AD) was the chief exponent of this school of Vedanta philosophy. He was born into a Brahmin family in Bhutapuri in South India. He was a saint and a scholar and taught Vedanta at the sacred shrine of Srirangam near modern day Tiruchirappalli.

Deeply influenced by the devotional poetry of the South Indian mystics known as Alvars, Ramanuja believed that devotion (bhakti) was the central teaching of Vedanta. He neither favored strict monism taught by Shankara two centuries earlier, nor the pure dualism taught by Madhva (discussed below) approximately two centuries later. Unlike Shankara, Ramanuja favored devotion over knowledge as a means of self-realization. He proclaimed self-surrender as an expeditious path for salvation. He attempted to synthesize theism with monism and formulated a school of religious thought known as *Visishtadvaita*, meaning qualified monism or qualified non-dualism.

Both Visishtadvaita and Advaita Vedanta hold that Brahman is the only independent and Absolute Reality that pervades the entire universe. In Advaita Vedanta, however, Brahman is attributeless, but in Visishtadvaita the individual selves and the material objects are internal distinctions of Brahman. There are many followers of this school of Vedanta among Hindus. Among the chief works of Ramanuja are *Vedarthsamgraha* ("Compendium of the Sense of the Veda"), *Vedantasara* ("Essence of Vedanta") and his commentary on the Bhagavad Gita and the Brahma Sutra. The two most suitable works of Visishtadvaita for beginners are *Yatindra-mata-dipika* by Srinivasadasa and *Vedanta Karikavali* by Bucci Venkatacharya.

Dvaita

This school of philosophy was developed by Madhvacharya (1199-1278 AD), who was born in Udipi, near Mangalore on the West Coast of India. He was a *Vaishnava* (worshipper of Lord Vishnu) saint and a religious reformer. He developed a system of philosophy that combines dualism with theism and is known as Dvaita, "the philosophy of the two."

According to Dvaita Vedanta, there are two categories of the Ultimate Reality. Brahman or God is the *Absolute Reality* and is called by various names, such as Narayana, Vishnu, and Hari, among others. Individual selves (*jivas*) and material objects (*prakriti*) are *relative realities*, that is eternally existing, distinct from each other but dependent on God. There are many followers of this school of religious tradition among

Hindus. The chief works of Madhva include his commentaries on the Brahma Sutra, Bhagavad Gita, and other religious and metaphysical treatises. The most systematic introduction to the philosophy of Dvaita Vedanta may be found in *Vada-Vali*, a philosophical manual written by Jayatirtha, a fourteenth century Vedantic scholar.

Similarities and Differences

The following is a summary of the major similarities and differences between Advaita, Visishtadvaita, and Dvaita schools of Vedanta philosophy:

1. Advaita declares that Brahman is the only Absolute Reality. Brahman is free from internal and external distinctions. Individual selves and material objects are not real, but are illusory appearances made possible by the operation of a magical power, called maya (see chapter 4 for a discussion of maya). Maya is not separate from Brahman, but is indistinguishable from Him, just as the burning power of fire is inseparable from the fire itself.

Like Advaita, Visishtadvaita also declares that Brahman is the only Absolute and independent Reality and accepts the Advaita view that Brahman is free from external distinctions. However, Visishtadvaita declares that Brahman possesses internal distinctions, since the conscious selves and the unconscious matter (prakriti) are His internal parts. Thus, according to Visishtadvaita, Brahman is the unity qualified by many internal parts or attributes.

Dvaita declares that there are two categories of the Ultimate Reality. Brahman as a personal God is the Absolute Reality, and the individual jivas (souls) and the material objects are the relative realities, distinct from each other and dependent upon God.

2. According to Advaita, the world is not a creation, but an illusory appearance of Brahman. The world appearance is taken for real by those who have not realized Brahman. The wise are not deluded by the illusory power of maya, since

they can see right through it and find nothing else but Brahman. Both the Visishtadvaita and Dvaita schools believe that creation is a real act of Brahman and He creates the world out of unconscious matter (prakriti) in accordance with the past deeds (karma) of the selves.

3. All three schools agree that individual souls are not created by Brahman or God. Advaita declares that in its liberated state, atman (individual soul) is identical with Brahman. Visishtadvaita and Dvaita declare that in its liberated state atman is not identical, but distinct from Brahman or God. In that state, however, the atman is untainted by imperfections, is free from ignorance (avidya) and bondage, and as such enjoys the eternal bliss of complete union with Brahman.

4. All three schools agree that ignorance (avidya) causes the atman to forget its divine nature and to mistakenly identify itself with the body-mind apparatus. This false identification of the atman with the body, mind, and intellect is the cause of its bondage to material existence and consequent suffering.

5. In order to liberate the atman from bondage, all three schools recommend the study of the scriptures, performing work without the desire for reward, and complete self-surrender to Brahman with intense devotion, meditation, and prayer. However, Advaita emphasizes true knowledge of the self and Brahman as an essential prerequisite for attaining liberation (moksha). The other two schools favor devotion and self-surrender over knowledge as a means of self-realization.

6. All three schools have produced an unbroken tradition of acharyas, saints and scholars from the past down to our time. Their institutions are still the major centers of spirituality and mysticism in India.

Chapter 7

Chapter 8
Yoga Philosophy

Yogic tradition among Hindus began thousands of years ago in India. While the Upanishads are the original source of yoga philosophy, yoga is expounded in many sections of the Hindu epic Mahabharata. The Bhagavad Gita gives a universal expression to the yogic teachings.

Etymologically, the Sanskrit word *yoga* is derived from the root word *yuj*, meaning union. A person who seeks after this union is called a yogin or yogi. Vedanta defines yoga as a means of uniting the individual being (*jivatman*) with the Cosmic Self (*Paramatman*). When the word *yoga* is used by Westerners, it generally means *Hatha Yoga*, which is an ancient Hindu system of physical exercises and breathing techniques designed to maintain a healthy body. Hindu Scriptures use the word *yoga* as a synonym for *sadhana*, meaning a spiritual discipline.

There are four main disciplines of yoga: *Karma Yoga, Bhakti Yoga, Jnana Yoga*, and *Raja Yoga*. A worker who seeks union between himself and the Universal Self through selfless service to humankind is called a *karma-yogi*. A person who seeks union between himself (or herself) and God through selfless love and devotion is called a *bhakta* or *bhakti-yogi*. An intellectual who seeks union in all of existence through divine knowledge is called a *jnana-yogi*. A mystic who seeks union between his individual self (atman) and the Universal Self (Brahman) by controlling his mind and senses is called a *raja-yogi*.

Although yoga is classified into the above four different disciplines, none of these is exclusive, superior, or inferior to others. All are equally important and are treated likewise in Hindu scriptures. The suitability of a particular discipline, however, depends upon the mental, intellectual, and emotional dimensions and karmic association of one's personality.

Karma Yoga

The word *karma* (derived from the Sanskrit root *kri*, meaning "to do"), denotes an action that brings back results in this life or in future lives. Karma Yoga (or the yoga of action) teaches that work performed in the spirit of service to God and for the welfare of mankind leads to salvation (moksha) of the individual self. Good actions bring one closer to his spiritual goal and bad actions take him farther away from this goal. Good actions are those that are performed for the welfare of others, without desire for the fruits (rewards) thereof. Bad actions are those that are performed with selfish motives, without consideration for others.

According to Hindu view, actions that lead to spiritual emancipation must satisfy the following conditions:

- One must respect all forms of life, from the lowest to the highest, with the understanding that the same self resides in all beings, from the perfect human to the lowest worm.

- There must be sincere feelings of love and compassion toward all creatures. Work, with love, is freedom for the worker, and work without love is his bondage.

- Work must be performed purely for its own sake. This means that all actions must be performed without expectation of reward (*nishkama-karma*). Thus we hear the words of Sri Krishna in the Bhagavad Gita 2.47:

Karmany evaa 'dhikaaras-te, maa phaleshu kadaacana.
Maa karmaphalahetur bhur, maa te sango 'stv akarmani.

"Thy choice is in action alone, but never in the results thereof. Never consider thyself the cause of the results of thy actions, but never cease to do thy work."

The above verse provides the basis for the Hindu philosophy of work. Unfortunately this verse has been misinterpreted by some scholars to mean that one should perform actions without expecting results. Could Krishna have told

Arjuna not to expect victory in the battle that Krishna was
encouraging Arjuna to fight? What then does the above verse
truly mean? We know from our experiences that there are choices in
our actions, but there are no choices in the results we receive.
Giordano Bruno (Ital. philos., 1548-1600) says, "I have fought
much. Victory is in the hands of fate." Krishna's advice in
the above verse is very clear: we should plan our actions
certainly expecting the results we wish to achieve. However,
we should not despair if the results do not arrive as expected.
As Swami Dayananda advises, "perform action expecting
results; act so that you can achieve what you desire; plan and
execute your work; but if the result is totally contrary to your
expectations, in spite of all wishing and willing, do not react
and call yourself a failure."[30] "Arise! Awake! and stop not till
the goal is reached," said Swami Vivekananda. Thus "be not
attached to the fruits of action" simply means to "plan and
perform actions to achieve what one desires, but to not react
negatively to the results of actions (i.e., call oneself a failure)
if such results are contrary to one's expectations."

According to Hindu religion, a karma-yogi may or may
not believe in a particular religion or religious doctrine or even
in God, but good karma (selfless actions) will naturally lead
him to salvation. In the following words, the Bhagavad Gita
teaches that work is both beautiful and holy and declares that
individuals attain perfection when they offer their work as
worship to God:

> "Whosoever performs actions, surrendering them to
> Brahman [God] and abandoning all attachments, is
> not polluted by sin, just as a lotus leaf is not polluted
> by water." (BG 5.10)

Bhakti Yoga

Bhakti Yoga is a path of selfless devotion, worship,
reverence, self-surrender, and adoration of God. The devotee
on this path worships God in whatever form he or she holds
Him dear. This path of spiritual realization is more suited to

those who are naturally endowed with an emotional bent of mind. The devotee on this path initially chooses a deity (*Ishta-deva*), in accordance with his or her temperament, to accomplish the spiritual goals. He offers his love and devotion to his Ishta-deva. Since it is the ego (*ahankara*) that keeps an individual separated from God, the aim of this spiritual path is to dissolve the individual ego through devotion and self-surrender to the will of the Lord.

A devotee on the path of bhakti actively engages himself or herself in various devotional activities, such as constant remembrance and repetition of God's names, singing *bhajans* (devotional songs) in praise of the Lord, and offering flowers and incense for puja (worship). These and other devotional activities expand the heart of the devotee, who sees the light of his chosen deity pervading the whole universe in and around him. His love gradually expands to embrace the entire creation of God. This is the highest consciousness to which the devotee is raised by his selfless devotion to God.

The path of bhakti is said to be the easiest to follow, but this is not so. Performing certain rituals to please God, using beads, or offering a fruit or flower to Him are not enough to achieve significant progress on this path. The devotee must completely surrender his or her self to the will of the Lord. This self-surrender is very difficult to accomplish because self-surrender for a worldly person is a battle against the so-called seven enemies of the soul: lust (*kama*), attachment (*moha*), egoism (*ahankara*), anger (*krodha*), jealousy (*matsarya*), pride (*mada*), and greed (*lobha*).

The path of bhakti is generally characterized by the following four features:

- The spiritual guidance of a competent teacher (guru) is generally needed so that the devotee is not distracted by the seven enemies of the soul identified above.

- The study of scriptures, constant remembrance of the names of the Lord, and unconditional self-surrender to the Lord are the essential elements of this yogic discipline.

Chapter 8

- The performance of one's duties in the spirit of non-attachment (*vairagya*) and dedicating all work performed as worship to God is essential for achieving spiritual success on this path.

- The devotee's adherence to *ahimsa* (non-injury, non-violence) in thought, action, and speech is required, since ahimsa is the true expression of love.

According to Hindu religion, bhakti is the bond of union between an individual and God, and therefore, between one individual and another, as God lives in the hearts of all beings. The praise of bhakti as a means of salvation is expressed throughout the Bhagavad Gita, especially in the following words of Sri Krishna:

"Even if the most wicked worships Me [God] with undivided devotion, he should be considered as good, for he is rightly resolved. He shall soon become pure and attain lasting peace. This is My word of promise, that he who loves Me shall never perish." (BG 9.30, 31)

Bhakti yoga teaches mankind to love God as the atman in all creatures, and thus experience the joy hidden otherwise. Thus Sri Krishna declares in the Bhagavad Gita:

"He who hates none and is friendly and compassionate to all creatures, who is free from thoughts of 'I' or 'mine', who is equal-minded in pleasure and pain and who is forgiving; who is ever content and meditative, self-subjugated and whose determination is strong, with the mind and intellect dedicated to Me; he who is thus devoted to Me is dear to Me." (BG 12.13 and 12.14)

Hindu sages tell us that bhakti develops progressively to bring about union between an individual and God. Accordingly, Hindu scriptures describe various degrees and forms of bhakti as shown in Figure F-5.

Figure F-5: Degrees and Forms of Bhakti

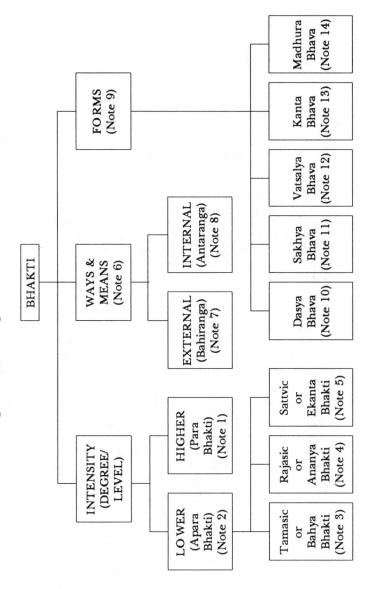

Notes for Figure F-5:

1. *Para bhakti* is the highest kind of bhakti in the form of meditation
    on the formless (*nirguna*) aspect of Brahman. This path is difficult
    and thus suitable for only a few, as declared in the Bhagavad Gita
    (BG 12.5), "Greater is the trouble of those whose minds are set on
    the Unmanifested; for the goal of the Unmanifested is very hard
    for the mortals to attain."

2. *Apara bhakti* (or *gauni bhakti*) is based upon the belief that the
    Supreme Lord is the creative source of man and the world, Who
    transcends and yet is immanent in the world. This type of bhakti
    is classified into three categories: *bahya (tamasic), ananya (rajasic),
    and ekanta (sattvic).*

3. *Bahya bhakti* (also known as the tamasic bhakti) is the devotee's love
    and adoration towards God, based upon an unenlightened view
    (or feeling) that God dwells (external to the devotee) in shrines,
    temples, and holy places. Most devotees on this path usually desire
    and pray for material and/or spiritual gifts. A majority of the
    religious rites and rituals of the ordinary people are examples of
    bahya bhakti, and the popular religion does not generally rise above
    this level.

4. *Ananya bhakti* (also known as the rajasic bhakti) is passionate
    devotion towards one's *Ishta-Devata* (chosen deity), and based upon
    strict monotheism. Here the intense devotion purifies the heart
    of the devotee, dissolves his sins, and thereby accelerates his
    spiritual progress. There is, however, one danger associated with
    this kind of devotion. In the absence of jnana (right knowledge)
    this devotion may give rise to sentimentalism, bigotry, and intoler-
    ance towards those who cherish different concepts of God and use
    different methods to realize Him. Historically, this type of bhakti
    has created some sectarian animosity among Hindus, but it has
    never degraded into any kind of noticeable violence between
    Hindus themselves. The history shows, however, that in many
    other religions of the world this kind of monotheistic devotion has
    resulted in iconoclastic zeal and subsequent violence.

5. *Ekanta bhakti* (also known as the sattvic bhakti) is the purest and
    the highest level of devotion to God. Here the devotee consecrates
    all his actions to God and loves Him for His sake and not for the
    sake of any gifts whatsoever. Not only does the devotee feel God
    in his own heart, he also feels Him in the hearts of all beings. The
    devotee does not care about caste or culture, power or wealth, rites
    or rituals, or rank or profession. He is absorbed in the true love

Chapter 8

of God and sees all things and beings in Him, and Him in all things and beings.

6. Hindu scriptures teach various ways and means of bhakti for one's spiritual growth.

7. External means include various religious practices such as offerings to God, readings of the scriptures, chanting of sacred hymns, repeating the name of the Lord (Satnam or Ramnam), and seeking the grace of the Guru.

8. The internal means include renunciation (of the fruits of one's actions; that is, performing all actions without desire for reward), right knowledge, meditation, and practice of yoga.

9. Hindu scriptures describe nineteen different forms of devotion between the devotee and God, expressed in human relationships. Of these, the following five are considered most important:

10. *Dasya bhava* is a type of bhakti in which the devotee's feeling towards God is that of a servant to the master. An example of this kind of devotion is that of Hanuman towards Rama in Ramayana.

11. *Sakhya bhava* is the devotee's bhakti towards God that is similar to that of a friend to friend. An example of this type of devotion is that of Sudama towards Krishna in the Bhagavata Purana.

12. *Vatsalya bhava* is the feeling of the devotee towards God similar to that of the parents towards their child. An example of this type of devotion is that of Yashoda to child Krishna.

13. *Kanta bhava* is the type of bhakti between the devotee and God in which the devotion is similar to that of a person to his or her spouse. An example of this type of devotion is that of Sita towards Rama in Ramayana.

14. *Madhura bhava* is the bhakti of the devotee towards God similar to the love of a lover to the beloved. An example of this kind of bhakti is that of the gopis, like Radha, towards Krishna.

Note that Hindu religion upholds progressive bhakti, and maintains that a devotee should proceed from the *bahya bhakti* to *ananya bhakti*, from *ananya* to *ekanta*, and finally from *ekanta* to *para bhakti*. Since there are no provisions for *mudha bhakti* (blind faith) in Hindu religion, the devotee should develop an open mind and be very careful lest his devotion turns into emotion and his love into a mere sentiment.

Chapter 8

Jnana Yoga

The path of Jnana Yoga is generally suited to those who are gifted with strong mental and intellectual faculties. This path emphasizes true knowledge regarding the nature of the self, and requires sharp intellect coupled with intense spiritual longing. Since ignorance (*avidya*) obscures the self from achieving salvation, the aim of this path is to destroy ignorance by discrimination and contemplation on Truth. This path is generally characterized by the following three features:

- Listening to the scriptures and the discourses from spiritual teachers (gurus) who are themselves well-established in Truth. The company of truly awakened souls strengthens the power of right discrimination and accelerates the unfolding of the true Self.

- Discriminating truth from falsity and intense contemplation on the guru's words. Thoughtful contemplation gradually weakens the ego and frees the atman from its wrong identification with the body and mind.

- Practice of shifting the focus of attention from the mortal aspect of one's being to the immortal aspect of being, and intense contemplation therein.

Jnana is the highest teaching of the Upanishads and the central theme of the Bhagavad Gita. As stated in the following verses of the Bhagavad Gita, Jnana is considered a supreme purifier:

"Nothing indeed purifies in this world like wisdom. He who lives in self-harmony finds it [wisdom] in time within himself, by himself." (BG 4.38)

"Noble are all those (who worship Me), but I regard the wise as My very Self; for with soul ever steadfast, a man of vision is established in Me alone and I am his goal supreme." (BG 7.18)

Chapter 8

Raja Yoga

Raja Yoga is a psychophysical method or a technique of training the mind and developing its subtle powers of perception to discover spiritual truths that provide the basis for religious principles and practices. Raja means "king" and Raja Yoga is said to be the royal road to spirituality. Raja Yoga is a scientific and systematic path (comprising of body postures, breath control, and concentration) generally suited to persons with a scientific mind and outlook. The purpose of this path is to lead one to the super-conscious state (*samadhi*) in which one is united with the Cosmic Consciousness.

The science of Raja Yoga was systematized and codified by Patanjali Maharishi around 200 BCE. His work, known as "Yoga Sutras of Patanjali" or "The Aphorisms on Yoga by Patanjali," consists of 196 Sanskrit slokas (verses). *Sutra* literally means "thread" and Yoga Sutras are combinations of words threaded together to delineate the science of yoga. The Sutra itself is divided into four *pads* (sections): *samadhi* (contemplation) *sadhana* (practice), *vibhuti* (accomplishment), and *kaivalya* (absoluteness). According to Yoga Sutras, *chitta vritti nirodhah* (restraint of the modifications of the mind-stuff) is the practice of yoga and *svarupe avasthanam* (abiding in one's own nature) is the result.[31]

Sage Patanjali is not the creator of the doctrine of Raja Yoga, since Raja Yoga practices were known among Hindu ascetics and mystics long before him. However, it is due to him that the science of Raja Yoga, previously hidden in the mystic tradition, became an organized system of philosophy. The several commentaries on Patanjali's work were later written by sages and scholars, among whom Sage Vyasa's work is very popular, owing to its style, organization, and depth.

The purpose of Raja Yoga is to purify the body and mind for developing perfect concentration. Perfect concentration leads to perfect meditation, which eventually leads one to the super-conscious state (*samadhi*) in which one is united with the Ultimate Reality. Raja Yoga is also called *Ashtanga Yoga*, "The Yoga of eight limbs or steps." *Ashta* means eight and *anga* means limb or part. The eight steps or limbs of this yogic discipline are: *yama, niyama, asana, pranayama, pratyahara, dharna, dhyana, and samadhi.*

Yama (restraints)

Yama constitutes moral and ethical discipline and includes five restraints: *ahimsa* (restraint from violence), *satya* (restraint from falsehood), *asteya* (restraint from stealing), *brahmacharya* (restraint from sex), and *aparigraha* (restraint from avarice).

Niyama (observances)

Niyama constitutes spiritual discipline and includes five observances: *shaucha* (cleanliness of body and purity of mind), *santosha* (contentment), *tapasya* (austerity), *svadhyaya* (scriptural study), and *Ishvara-prani-dhana* (surrender to God).

Asana (posture or seat)

Asana (a suitable body posture; see page 405) assists in focusing the mind inward. Regular practice of asana increases body endurance, willpower, and resistance to bodily diseases, as well as the tone of muscles and nerves.

Pranayama (breath control)

Pranayama involves a series of breathing exercises designed to ensure smooth (long and deep) breathing. In addition to its physiological benefits, smooth breathing helps to eliminate unwanted thoughts, thus producing a calm effect on the mind. Sages tell us that short and irregular breathing increases mental activity, resulting in more unwanted thoughts that further distract the mind. Thus pranayama prepares the mind for subsequent concentration and meditation.

Pratyahara

Pratyahara means withdrawing the mind from sense perception so that it can focus on one thought. Pratyahara includes several methods designed to divert the mind from sense objects.

Dharna (concentration)

Focusing of the mind on one thought is called dharna. Once pratyahara has been established, the mind is then directed to an object of concentration. The object of concentration may be a picture of a deity, a mantra, one's own breath, or a part of the body, among other things.

Dhyana (meditation)

Meditation is a state of mind in which the mind is in an absolute state of non-doing. Meditation is not a religion, but a scientific technique by which the meditator can tune in and tap the vast resource of wisdom that is hidden in his own self. Like a hidden gold mine, the wisdom within one's own self is untapped in most people. According to Hindu religion, the atman is the source of unlimited power and wisdom in a human being, and meditation is the means of contacting this great wisdom.

According to Hindu scriptures, an individual is the atman clothed in a physical body. When associated with the physical body, the atman gives rise to mind (*manas*), intellect (*buddhi*), and ego (*ahankara*). The mind of an ordinary individual routinely passes through the three states of consciousness: waking state (*jagrat*), dream state (*svapna*), and deep-sleep (*sushupati*) state. Hindu sages tell us that when the mind is in a state of perfect non-doing, it can enter the fourth state of consciousness (known as samadhi, the *turiya* state, or the super-conscious state) and realize union with God. Upon attaining the *turiya* state, an individual attains moksha, or freedom from the perpetual cycle of birth and death. A person who attains the *turiya* state while still in the human body is known as a *jivanmukta* (liberated soul).

Although thousands of books have been written on meditation and thousands of gurus have, or are, teaching it, confusion concerning what meditation is and how to achieve it is still considerable. Contrary to popular perception, meditation is not an action that one can perform, but a phenomenon that occurs spontaneously and effortlessly when the mind is in a thoughtless state or a state of non-doing. When an individual says that he or she meditates, this only means that he or she is using a certain meditation technique to create a situation in which meditation can occur spontaneously.

Meditation is distinguished from concentration only by its uninterrupted nature. In Hindu scriptures, concentration is analogous to pouring a thin stream of water, whereas meditation is analogous to pouring a thin stream of oil. Both streams will fall towards one place, but the stream of water may not fall as smoothly as that of oil. Water has a tendency of splitting into drops, thus creating an irregular stream.

There are many techniques of meditation described in Hindu religious literature. These techniques may be broadly classified into three categories: direct meditation, indirect meditation, and inquiry meditation. *Direct meditation* is uninterrupted concentration, or a current of unified thought, directed towards an object of meditation, such as a divine thought, a picture of a deity, a mantra, or any object the meditator may use to symbolize God. *Indirect meditation* consists of watching one's own thoughts without becoming involved in them. Another method of indirect meditation involves observing one's own breathing. These processes eventually lead to the thoughtless state whereby meditation occurs spontaneously. In the *inquiry method* of meditation, the meditator stills the body and mind and whenever a thought appears he inquires, "Who am I?" This inquiry eventually leads to the thoughtless state whereby meditation occurs effortlessly. Refer to Appendix A-1 for step-by-step instructions on meditation for a beginner.

Samadhi

Samadhi, "union with God," the eighth and final step of Patanjali's Ashtanga Yoga, is attained when the devotee realizes the super-conscious state (in deep meditation) and becomes one with God. There are two forms of samadhi: conscious and superconscious. In conscious samadhi a yogi attains supernatural powers (called *siddhis*) by the strength of his yogic practices. These *siddhis* are in the forms of clairvoyance, mind reading, thought transmission, and other miracles.

If these *siddhis* are practiced, they are said to become obstacles for attaining the final stage of superconscious samadhi, communion with God.

Superconscious samadhi is generally said to be of two types: *savikalpa samadhi* and *nirvikalpa samadhi*. *Savikalpa* means being separated and *nirvikalpa* means no separation. In *savikalpa samadhi* the devotee maintains a separate identity (subject-object relationship) from God. In *nirvikalpa samadhi* the subject-object relationship ends and the devotee becomes one with God.

The difference between these samadhis is explained by Paramahansa Yogananda: "In the initial states of God-communion (*savikalpa samadhi*) the devotee's consciousness merges with the cosmic spirit and his life force is withdrawn from the body, which appears dead, motionless, or rigid. The yogi is fully aware of his bodily condition of suspended animation. As he progresses to higher spiritual states (*nirvikalpa samadhi*), however, he communes with God, without bodily fixation."[7]

Other Forms of Yoga

There are several other forms of yoga, such as Hatha Yoga, Mantra Yoga, Laya Yoga, and Tantra Yoga. All these, however, are either branches or subdivisions of the four main divisions of yoga stated above. Hatha Yoga is a branch of Raja Yoga and includes the first four steps (yama, niyama, asana and pranayama) of Raja Yoga. Yogis discovered very early that suitable body postures and regulated breathing were of great help in focusing one's mind inward. This led to the discovery of Hatha Yoga. Today Hatha Yoga is an integral part of popular health maintenance and body-building activities in many countries. The simple principles and practices of Hatha Yoga (such as *surya namaskara*[8]) are excellent for preserving the health and vitality of the body and mind. They improve one's posture and retard the aging and decay of the body. Hatha Yoga teaches the science of physical health and hygiene for men and women.

Mantra Yoga is a subdivision of Bhakti Yoga. Sacred words or syllables are repeated while meditating upon their

meanings. Such repetitions are usually silent in order to focus
the aspirant's mind inward rather than on sense objects.

Laya Yoga is a variation of Raja Yoga. *Laya* means
merging the mind in the Self through concentration on a
sound or a sacred thought. This path is generally followed
by those who have mastered the knowledge of subtle body
centers (*chakras*) and the energy that flows through the subtle
channels in the body, from *kundalini* (energy stored at the base
of the spine) to the higher centers in the body.

According to the Tantric literature, there are three major
channels (*nadis*) in a human body, known as *sushumna, ida,* and
pingala. These channels originate at the base of the spinal
column (*muladhara*) and extend to the top of the head.
Sushumna runs through the center of the spinal column and
is connected to the topmost point in the head, known as
sahasrara. Ida and *pingala* run parallel to *sushumna* on the left
and the right side of the spinal column, respectively, and meet
each other at a point between the eyebrows, known as *ajna
chakra.* There are seven energy centers (see Table T-4),
known as *chakras* (psychic centers), located in a human body.
These chakras are vital centers of the body's energy system.

The chakras are not visible to the naked eye, but can be
perceived by yogis in deep meditation. These chakras are said
to appear like lotus flowers of various colors, located at
different spots in a human body. In each person one chakra
is innately more active than others.

Individual karma and nature determine which chakra is
more active. The awakening of chakras leads to spiritual
enlightenment. The following are the seven chakras of the
human body:

- *Muladhara chakra* is located at the base of the spine, possesses
  four petals, and controls smell.

- *Swadhisthana chakra* is located at the base of the genitals,
  possesses six petals, and controls taste.

- *Manipura chakra* is located opposite to the navel, possesses
  ten petals, and controls sight.

• *Anahata chakra* is located near the heart, possesses twelve petals, and controls the sense of touch.

• *Vishuddha chakra* is located at the medulla oblongata, possesses sixteen petals, and controls hearing.

• *Ajna chakra* is located between the eyebrows, possesses two petals, and controls the mind.

• *Sahasrara chakra* is located at the top of the head, possesses 1000 petals, and is the center of the cosmic consciousness in the body.

According to Tantra Yoga (a variation of Raja Yoga), *kundalini shakti* (coiled energy) is the mysterious power (also called serpent power) that resides at the base of the spinal column (*muladhara chakra*) of every individual. In ordinary persons this energy is usually inactive and analogous to a coiled serpent. When awakened by meditation or pranayama, this power begins to move upward within *sushumna nadi*. In its ascent, *kundalini shakti* activates the chakras and brings about total purification and rejuvenation of the entire being. When *kundalini shakti* reaches *sahasrara chakra*, the spiritual center at the top of the head, the mind enters the super-conscious state (*samadhi*) and the individual attains moksha (liberation from the cycle of birth and death), or union with God.

Kundalini Shakti is also called *Chiti Shakti* or Divine Mother. In the words of Swami Muktananda, "She is both worldly life and spiritual life. The glory of this supreme Shakti is marvelous. She is the knowledge of the enlightened and the fruit of action of the active. She is the ecstatic state of the *bhaktas* and the dynamic Kundalini of yogis. In fact, she is the beauty of the whole world." [32]

Chapter 9
Philosophy of the Bhagavad Gita

"He who studies this sacred dialogue of ours, by him I consider myself worshipped through the sacrifice of wisdom. He who listens to it with faith and without scoffing, even he, being liberated from evil, shall attain to the sacred regions of of righteous." (BG 18.70-71)

The Bhagavad Gita, the age-old Sanskrit religious classic of Hindus, is one of the three pillars of Hindu religion (with the *Upanishads* and the *Brahma Sutra* as the other two). The Bhagavad Gita (also referred to as Gita) is a spiritual dialogue between Lord Krishna, a Hindu incarnation of God, and Arjuna, one of the heroes of the Mahabharata, an ancient Hindu epic. An unknown Hindu saint has described the Gita in the following words: "If the Upanishads (sacred Hindu Scriptures) are the cows, the Lord Himself is the milker, Arjuna the calf, and those of purified understanding are the drinkers of the milk, the supreme nectar of the Gita." Since the Bhagavad Gita represents a summary of the Upanishadic teachings, it is sometimes called an *Upanishad of the Upanishads.*

The two words *Bhagavad* and *Gita* mean "the song of the Lord." The Bhagavad Gita, however, is not a lyric, but a philosophical poem, which was authored by Sage Vyasa, the legendary compiler of the Mahabharata. In its present form, the Gita constitutes Chapters 23 to 40 of the *Bhishmaparva* part of the epic Mahabharata.

The Bhagavad Gita has inspired countless Hindus since its composition. It has also inspired many Western thinkers, such as Henry David Thoreau (1817-1862), Ralph Waldo Emerson (1803-1882), and Maxine Elliott (1871-1940). Although the original date of composition of the Gita is not clear, its teachings are timeless, and as such, the exact time of the revelation of this scripture is of little spiritual significance.

The original text of the Bhagavad Gita is in Sanskrit, but translations are available in all major languages of the world. The first English translation was by Charles Wilkins in 1785. The setting of the Gita is the battlefield of Kurukshetra, where armies of the Pandavas and their cousins, the Kauravas, are ready for the historic battle of the Mahabharata. The battle resulted from a family dispute between the Pandavas and the Kauravas over the succession of the ancient kingdom of Kurukshetra, about one hundred miles from modern day Delhi. Before the battle ensued, Arjuna told Krishna (who was Arjuna's friend, counselor, and charioteer) to drive his chariot between the two armies so that Arjuna could see who he had to fight.

At the sight of his own relatives, friends, and teachers arrayed on the opposite side of the battlefield, Arjuna was overwhelmed with grief and he refused to fight, saying, "Shall I kill my own masters who, though greedy of my kingdom, are yet my sacred teachers? I would rather eat in this life the food of a beggar than eat royal food tasting of their blood." In order to dispel Arjuna's fear and delusion, Sri Krishna speaks to Arjuna the eternal words of wisdom that are recorded in the Bhagavad Gita as an immortal dialogue between Sri Krishna and Arjuna.

The Bhagavad Gita consists of 700 Sanskrit slokas (verses) arranged in eighteen chapters. It is a book of light, love, and life (i.e. jnana, bhakti, and karma). If a person were to be given an instruction manual telling him how to live life on earth, the Gita would indeed be such a manual: "Who are we? Why are we born? What is the goal of life? What are the means? What are good and bad actions? What should we do when one duty conflicts with another?" These and many other questions are raised and answered in the Bhagavad Gita. It is only after hearing the immortal words of wisdom from Krishna that Arjuna's doubts and delusions are dispelled, as he addresses Krishna, "By thy grace I remember my light, and now gone is my delusion. My doubts are no more, my faith is firm, and now I can say 'Thy will be done.'" (BG 18.73)

Chapter 9

If we wish to understand the spiritual meaning of the Bhagavad Gita, we must forget everything about the actual Mahabharata war, the stories of Arjuna and Krishna, and the Pandavas and Kauravas. The great Mahabharata war in the Gita is symbolic of the great spiritual struggle of the human soul. In the following verses the war imagery is used by Krishna to expound the wisdom of the Vedas and the Upanishads:

> "Kill, therefore, with the sword of wisdom the doubt lying in thy heart, born of ignorance. Armed with the weapon of yoga, arise, O great warrior, arise. Know the Self to be superior to the intellect and let Him give you the spiritual strength. Be a warrior and kill desire, the powerful enemy of the soul." (BG 3.43 and 4.42)

Scholars say that there are three great secrets included in the Gita. First, one must perform all duties in the world, abandoning all attachment for the fruits of action. Second, one must discriminate between the self and the non-self. Third, one must realize that everything that exists, movable or immovable, visible or invisible, is nothing but Brahman.

To those who might see repetitions or apparent contradictions in the teachings of this great scripture, the following words of Shankaracharya's commentary on the Bhagavad Gita come to light: "If a hundred scriptures should declare that fire is cold or that it is dark, we would suppose that they intend quite a different meaning from the apparent one."[9]

Philosophy of the Bhagavad Gita

The philosophy of the Gita is an outstanding synthesis of the philosophy of the Upanishads and various other streams of Hindu religious thought that existed during the epic period (see Table T-1). The apparently diverse views of the dualistic and non-dualistic systems of Hindu philosophy, and the exclusive views of various other schools of Hindu religious tradition, find a happy marriage in the universal spirit of the

Gita. Although the interpretations may vary, the philosophy of the Bhagavad Gita can be summarized as follows:

1. The Ultimate Reality has two aspects, transcendent (impersonal) and the immanent (personal).

2. In its transcendent aspect, the Ultimate Reality is the Brahman of Advaita Vedanta, which is indeterminate, unapproachable, formless, and attributeless.

3. In its immanent aspect, the Ultimate Reality is the Supreme God, the creator, sustainer, controller, and the moral governor of the universe. He is the father, mother, friend, guide, and the savior of the world.

4. The Supreme Lord has created the universe out of Himself. Everything in the universe is a manifestation of the Supreme Lord. There are two aspects of His nature, the higher aspect and the lower aspect (see chapter 13 of the Bhagavad Gita). His higher nature is manifested as individual selves and His lower nature is manifested as the material world, which consists of eight elements: earth, water, fire, air, space, mind, intellect, and ego. These eight elements constitute the whole world of matter (*prakriti*), or nature, with its three intrinsic qualities of sattva, rajas, and tamas. The whole world of things and beings is evolved by the manifestation of the above two aspects of God's nature in the form of individual selves and matter (*prakriti*).

5. The Supreme Lord pervades the entire universe and is the inner ruler of all beings. All things and beings in the world are centered in Him, like beads on a string. He is the origin and the end of everything in the universe. There is nothing higher than Him. He pervades everything and everything is in Him, yet He transcends them all and He is not in them (see Bhagavad Gita, chapter 9, verses 4, 5 and 6).

6. Individual selves are pure, eternal, conscious, beyond space and time, beyond birth and death, changeless, immuta-

ble, and are the expressions of the higher nature of the Supreme Lord. By mistakenly identifying itself with the ego, an individual self becomes deluded, feeling limited and subjected to the pleasure and pain of this world. This false identification of the self with material existence is the cause of its bondage to the world. Liberation from such bondage is the highest goal of human life. This liberation is attained when the self gives up its identification with the limited ego and realizes its true nature of purity and divinity.

7. The Bhagavad Gita recommends the four paths, as previously explained, for the liberation (moksha) of the self: action (Karma Yoga), meditation (Raja Yoga), devotion (Bhakti Yoga), and knowledge (Jnana Yoga). These paths are not exclusive, but are interrelated and lead to the same goal. All these paths presuppose a fully moral and self-disciplined life. An individual can discover the existence of the Supreme Reality (as the very essence of his or her own self) by following one or more of these paths under the guidance of a qualified teacher (guru). A devotee may follow one or the other path depending on his or her taste and temperament.

8. The Bhagavad Gita teaches that the Supreme Lord speaks and understands all our languages, accepts our worship and prayers in whatever form we offer Him, and makes Himself visible to us in whatever direction we seek Him. This comprehensive universal outlook of Hindu religion is reflected fully in the spirit of the Gita.

In conclusion, as to the essence of the Bhagavad Gita, an unknown scholar has expressed it in the following words: "The essence of the Gita is the vision of all things in God and the vision of God in all things." Thus unity of life is the chief message of the Bhagavad Gita. To use the words of Dr. Sarvepalli Radhakrishnan, "We do not proceed on the same lines but that which we seek is the same. We may climb the mountain by different paths but the view from the summit is identical for all." [29]

Chapter 9

Chapter 10
Buddhism

Buddhism, an offshoot of Hindu dharma and one of the major religions of the world, is practiced by about one-fifth to one-fourth of the world population today. It is prevalent in Bhutan, Burma, China, Cambodia, Japan, Korea, Nepal, Tibet, Thailand, Sikhim, Sri Lanka, and Vietnam. Buddhism was founded in 528 BCE by Gautama Buddha, who was born in 563 BCE near Kapilavastu, one hundred miles north of modern day Benares, a city in India. Buddha's father, Suddhodana, a king of the Sakya tribe in northeast India, named his son Siddhartha Gautama. *Siddhartha* means "wish-fulfilling," as Gautama fulfilled his father's wish for a son and an heir-apparent to the throne. *Gautama* represents the family name. Gautama is sometimes referred to as *Sakyamuni*, or the king of the Sakyas. *Buddha* means an "enlightened one."

Warned by a sage that his son would either be a ruler or a wandering monk, Buddha's father raised the child in royal luxury and shielded him from witnessing any kind of pain or suffering. Although surrounded by princely entertainments, Buddha appeared to be feeling lonely and restless; something was constantly annoying the young prince's mind. Concerned about his loneliness, Buddha's father, after consulting his chief advisers, arranged a wedding for his prince.

Siddhartha was subsequently married to a beautiful girl named Yasodhara. In due course a son was born to the couple and was named Rahula. Great happiness filled the palace on the birth of the child, but nothing seemed to satisfy Buddha's inner restlessness.

One day while journeying through the city, Buddha witnessed what is known in Buddhist lore as the *Four Sights*. He saw a person crippled with old age, another suffering from disease, and yet another being carried to the cremation grounds. Lastly, he saw a wandering monk who appeared calm and peaceful. The first three sights convinced Siddhartha of life's sufferings and filled his heart with sadness. The fourth sight, that of a wandering monk, convinced him that the luxurious life that he was born into was not a solution to human suffering. O ne night, leaving his princely life behind, including his wife and the young child, Siddhartha abandoned the palace to live in a forest, determined to seek the remedy for human suffering. This event, known in Buddhist lore as the *Great Departure*, took place when Siddhartha was in his twenties.

In the seclusion of the forest, Gautama practiced extreme asceticism, thereby torturing his body and reducing it to bare bones. Although he attained some yogic powers by practicing such austerities, he soon recognized the futility of such practices as they did not provide a solution to the problem of human suffering. Subsequently, he began an indefinite period of meditation. It was during the full moon of May in 544 BCE, while seated under a Peepul tree in Gaya (near Patna in India), that Gautama attained Enlightenment. He discovered a higher state of consciousness as well as the method of attaining it. For many days he remained in the same spot, absorbed in Supreme Bliss. Later he decided to communicate to the world the knowledge he had attained. Thus, Gautama (now the All-Enlightened Buddha) delivered his initial great sermon, some time in his early thirties, at Sarnath (near Banaras) to the first five seekers who approached him. For the next forty years Buddha taught his philosophy to all. In the year 483 BCE he passed away at the age of eighty in Kusinara, the present day Kashi (Varanasi), in the Gorakhpur district of India.

Major Doctrines of the Philosophy of Buddhism

Buddha was primarily interested in alleviating human suffering (*duhkha*). He had no particular interest in metaphysical speculation, theological and philosophical discussions, or the abstract mysteries of the cosmos. He believed that such arguments had no direct bearing on the fundamental aspects of human suffering. The following are the four major doctrines advocated by Buddha:

1. *Impermanence of all Existence*: everything in nature is in a state of flux and there is nothing that exists permanently. There is no permanent being (atman or Self) but a continuous state of being and becoming in a perpetual chain of existences, in which one existence leads to another.

2. *Chain of Dependent Origination*: since all beings are subject to aging, decay, and death, suffering is a universal characteristic of all existence. The origin of suffering is the chain of causation, consisting of twelve links (i.e. states), in which each link or state is the effect of the preceding one and the cause of the following one. The first link in the chain of causation is birth, caused by the ignorance of the previous birth (i.e. death without attaining nirvana). *Nirvana* is the attainment of final enlightenment or freedom from rebirth. The new birth exhibits individual traits (individuality) that are a carry-over from the previous birth. The individual becomes conscious of his or her self and expresses individuality through the faculty of the mind and senses. The mind and senses interact with things and beings of the world and generate sensations which in turn give rise to attachment with names and forms of the world. Following old age, decay, and death of the individual, this attachment or craving causes a new state of existence (rebirth) to come into being, which has its own old age, decay, and death. This chain of causation in which one existence leads to another, in a perpetual cycle of birth and death, is called the Chain of Dependent Origination in Buddhism.

3. *Karma and Samsara*: Buddhism denies the existence of any permanent being (atman or Self). In Buddhist view, the karma of an individual 'A' causes the birth of another individual 'B,' just like the flame of candle 'A' lights candle 'B.' Nothing permanent transmigrates from 'A' (upon its death) to 'B' (upon its birth) and the only connection between 'A' and 'B' is that of causation. Although there is no identity

retained between one birth and another, the karma of one
being (i.e. actions performed in ignorance) bring a new being
into existence, thus perpetuating the suffering in samsara (the
life experiences in the phenomenal world). The suffering can
be annihilated by performing right actions, leading to nirvana.

4. *Nirvana: nirvana* (similar to moksha in Hindu dharma)
is the highest goal of human life in Buddhism. Nirvana refers
to a state (attained by Buddha) in which there is no craving
for life and all karmic effects are annihilated. After attaining
nirvana, one does not, upon death, bring another individual
into existence. Since nirvana annihilates the root cause of the
suffering in samsara, rebirth is not possible after attaining
nirvana.

Buddha's Teachings

Buddhism, unlike many other faiths, places greater emphasis on man as the creator of his own destiny. There are
no saviors who will provide salvation. Only individual human
effort can lead to nirvana. Buddhism does not recognize
sacred books or divine personalities and rejects authoritarian-
ism. Buddha did not call himself a savior or a messiah. He
believed that ignorance, not sin, is the cause of human
suffering. Ignorance can be overcome by right knowledge
and right effort. The following are the major elements of
Buddha's teachings, known in Buddhist lore as the *Four Noble
Truths*:

1. Suffering is a universal characteristic of all existence.

2. Suffering is caused by man's ignorance, desires,
   greed, and craving.

3. Suffering has a definite cause and can be overcome
   by eliminating its cause.

4. Suffering can be overcome by following Buddha's
   Eight-Fold Path:

(1) Right understanding	(6) Right effort
(2) Right purpose	(7) Right kind of awareness
(3) Right speech	(8) Right meditation
(4) Right conduct	
(5) Right livelihood	

Hindu Dharma and Buddhism

Buddhism is an offshoot of Hindu dharma and is considered as one of the heterodox schools of Hindu philosophy. The teachings of Buddhism are not significantly different from those of Hindu dharma, but are essentially the same as the teachings of the Jnana Yoga (path of knowledge) school of Hindu dharma. The following summarizes their major views:

- Buddhism and Hindu dharma both aim at transcending the phenomenal existence. Buddha rejected the ritualistic aspect of the Vedas, but did not deny the higher teachings of the Upanishads. The Vedic rituals in Hindu dharma are recommended for a beginner for attaining concentration and meditation on the spiritual path. This position is very clearly conveyed in the *Bhagavad Gita* in the following words:

    "To the knower of Truth, all the Vedas
    are of as little use as a small water-tank
    is during the time of a flood, when water
    is everywhere." (BG 2.46)

- Both Hindu dharma and Buddhism believe in the theory of karma and rebirth, with one major difference. Whereas Hindu dharma believes that the atman (individual self or spirit) transmigrates from one birth to another, Buddhism holds that nothing transmigrates from one birth to another. In Buddhist view, karmas of one individual give birth to another, but no identity is retained between the two individuals.

- In Hindu dharma, moksha annihilates all karmic effects and the atman is freed from the cycle of birth and death. In Buddhism, nirvana annihilates the karmic effects, and upon the death of an individual, no other individual is brought into existence, thus annihilating the suffering in samsara.

- Buddha opposed the caste system among Hindus. Hindus had originally accepted the caste system as a social tool for the smooth and efficient functioning of their society. Refer to chapter 17 for a discussion of the caste system that existed among Hindus in ancient times.

- Buddha declared that the Self and the world are both unreal. To a Hindu, the Self is immortal and the world is an illusive appearance. However, behind the illusive appearance of the universe lies the Ultimate Reality, which is the seed of all things and beings in the world.

- Buddha advocated a monastic life for attaining nirvana. Hindu dharma teaches that truth can be realized by all people from all walks of life, including householders.

- The goal of life according to Buddha is to attain nirvana. The goal of life according to Hindu dharma is to realize the Self. Both these concepts are essentially the same, in that both emphasize transcending the world of names and forms in order to attain liberation.

It must be noted that Buddha is recognized as the ninth incarnation of Lord Vishnu in Hinduism.

Chapter 11
Jainism

Jainism, an offshoot of Hindu dharma, is believed to be as ancient as the Vedic religion, since references to two of its twenty-four saints (*Tirthankaras*), Rishaba and Arishtanemi, are found in the Rigvedic mantras. Rishaba, the first of the twenty-four Tirthankaras, is the founder of the original Jain Dharma. Vardhamana Mahavira, a contemporary of Buddha, was the last Jain Tirthankara as well as the founder and organizer of modern day Jainism, practiced by several million people, most of whom live in India.

Vardhamana Mahavira was born in 599 BCE in a village near Patna in Bihar, India. He was called *Jina*, "the spiritual conqueror," or *Mahavira*, "the great hero." He received princely education in his young age. His family followed the teachings of Parsva, the twenty-third Tirthankara, whose teachings Mahavira later organized and consolidated. Mahavira renounced worldly life at the age of thirty-two, soon after the death of his parents. He led the life of a wandering ascetic, travelling from place to place in the eastern region of the Ganges valley in India. After attaining Kevala (the state of blessedness or liberation) he preached Jain Dharma to large audiences and organized the Jain community of monks and nuns. At the age of seventy-two in the year 527 BCE, while sitting alone and reciting the Jainist canon in a town called Pawapuri (near Patna in India), Mahavira passed into nirvana.

Jainism was founded as a protest movement against excessive Vedic rituals and practices. It spread slowly in the beginning. In the fourth century BCE a famous king, Chandragupta, who had defeated the Greek invader Alexander, became a Jain and vigorously spread Jainism throughout India. In the first century BCE a split occurred in the followers of Jainism, giving rise to two sects: *Svetambara* (the white-clad) and the *Digambara* (the sky-clad). Monks of the

Svetambara sect wore clothes of white color (symbolizing renunciation), whereas the monks of the Digambara sect insisted on following the Mahavira's example of total nudity. The discarding of clothes by Digambaras symbolized the severing of attachment with the world. The two sects also disagreed over some of the Jain teachings. Both sects eventually evolved their own writings.

Jain Religious Thought

According to Jainism, the universe is neither created nor sustained by a supernatural being. It is beginning-less (*anadi*), endless (*ananta*) and operates in accordance with natural law. The reality has two independent and distinct categories, *Jiva* (soul) and *Ajiva*. Jiva characterizes consciousness whereas Ajiva is inanimate, without consciousness or life. Jiva is either in a liberated state or in an unliberated (bound) state. In its liberated state, the Jiva is perfect knowledge, purity, peace and power. In the unliberated or bound state, Jiva possesses a body and is associated with karmic forces, that is, subtle particles of matter that permeate the soul. Because of its association with the karmic forces, the original glory of the soul becomes tainted, just as the brightness of gold is diminished by a coating of rust, or the brightness of a lamp is blurred by a layer of soot. The aim of the Jain teachings is, therefore, to eliminate the association of Jiva with karma and restore the soul to its original glory.

Ajiva, the second component of reality, consists of five entities: matter (*pudgala*), space (*akasha*), time (*kala*), dharma, and adharma. These five entities govern the material phenomena in the universe. Matter forms human bodies and the material objects. Time and space are needed for the existence of material objects. Dharma and adharma are the principles of motion and rest; they govern the state in which material objects exist in space and time.

Jain Teachings

The major teachings of Jainism can be summarized as follows:

Chapter 11

- Ahimsa is the doctrine of non-killing, non-violence, and non-injury. It is the central doctrine of Jainism and the first of the five great vows taught by Mahavira, the last Tirthankara. In Jainism the doctrine of ahimsa is extended to all forms of human, animal, and plant life.

- Jainism believes in the Law of Karma, in the sense of cause and effect. According to this law, each person is responsible for the moral consequences of his or her actions and must reap their fruits in this or the future life. There is no escape from the effects of one's actions. Good actions liberate the person from the clutches of karma and bad actions drag one back into the claws of karma.

- Jainism teaches that *himsa* (violence), *nirdaya* (lack of compassion), *krodha* (anger), *mada* (pride), *moha* (delusion), *lobha* (greed), *dvesha* (hatred), and *trishna* (craving) are the primary causes of suffering and injustice in the world. These desires and passions are also the enemies of the soul and cause its bondage in the world. Jainism teaches that right knowledge, right faith, and right conduct must be practiced simultaneously to conquer these enemies.

- Attachment to material objects is the primary cause of bondage and leads to greed and jealousy, which further leads to suffering and injustice in the world. Renouncing attachment to material objects is a necessary condition for attaining joy and peace in the world and thereafter.

- Jainism strongly emphasizes the practice of asceticism throughout one's life. It is a means for physical and mental purification leading to inner peace. Asceticism eliminates the tendency of possessiveness, destroys the effects of karmic forces, and leads the soul to its original glory and splendor.

- Jainism teaches the practice of the *Five Vows* and the *Three Jewels* for curing worldly ills and for attaining Kevala (liberation). The Five Vows are: *ahimsa* (non-violence), *satya* (truthfulness), *asteya* (non-stealing), *brahmacharya* (chastity), and *aparigraha* (non-attachment or renunciation of material things). The Three Jewels are: right faith, right knowledge, and right conduct.

Hindu Dharma and Jainism

Jainism is one of the theological traditions (*sampradayas*) of Hindu dharma and is classified as one of the heterodox schools of Hindu philosophy. The similarities and differences in their major religious views are summarized below:

- Jainism rejects the ritualistic content of the Vedas, but does not necessarily deny their higher teachings. The Vedic rituals are recommended in Hindu dharma to beginners for concentration and meditation on the spiritual path. This position is clearly brought forth in the Bhagavad Gita: "To the knower of Truth, all the Vedas are of as little use as a small water-tank is during the time of flood, when water is everywhere." (BG 2.46)

- Jainism opposes the caste system. The caste system, based upon division of labor, was accepted by ancient Hindus as a social tool for the smooth functioning of their society. Practice of the caste system, however, violates the basic tenets of Hindu scriptures, such as Upanishads and Bhagavad Gita. Refer to chapter 17 for a detailed discussion of the caste system.

- Jainism does not believe in the existence of God as creator, sustainer, and moral governor of the world. Jains believe that the universe has existed eternally in accordance with natural law. Hindu dharma believes that the Ultimate Reality has two aspects: personal and impersonal. In the personal aspect, the Ultimate Reality is God, the creator, sustainer, and the moral governor of the universe. In the impersonal aspect, the Ultimate Reality is devoid of qualities and attributes and is beyond the reach of thought. Although there are several different views, the most representative Hindu view is that the universe is the projection of Brahman, projected by Him out of Himself.

• Both believe in the immortality of the atman and in the Law of Karma. The doctrine of ahimsa is common as both apply this to all human, animal, and plant forms of life.

• The goal of life according to Jainism is to attain Kevala. In Hindu dharma the goal is liberation or Moksha. Both of these concepts are essentially the same, in that both emphasize transcending the world of names and forms to realize the Truth.

• Jainism emphasizes that everyone reaches *Kevala* through his or her own efforts. There is no savior or redeemer who will do this for him or her. The path advocated is that of selfless work without fear of punishment or desire for rewards. Jainism emphasizes more strongly the doctrine of ahimsa and the practice of asceticism. These teachings are essentially the same as those of Karma Yoga and Jnana Yoga in Hindu dharma.

• The ethical code of Jainism is the most severe of all Hindu religious schools. Complete indifference to the objects of the world is defined as the highest character in Jainism. According to the Jain teachings, the atman regains its original pure state (i.e., attains kevala) only after it sheds off all karmic particles that it becomes associated with during its earthly sojourn. This can be achieved through faith in Jain teachings, true knowledge, righteous work, and high character. Of all the Hindu religious traditions, Jainism attaches highest importance to ahimsa and vegetarianism.

Chapter 12
Sikhism

Sikhism, another offshoot of Hinduism, is the religion of Sikhs, the majority of whom live in Punjab, India. However, Sikhs are also found in significant numbers in other parts of India, as well as in Britain, Canada, and the United States. A Sikh is one who believes in the Ten Gurus of the Sikh religion as well as the *Guru Granth Sahib*, the holy scripture of Sikhism. A guru is a spiritual guide who dispels ignorance or darkness. The word "Sikh" is derived from the Sanskrit word *Sisya*, meaning disciple. Sikhism was founded in the fifteenth century by Guru Nanak, the first guru of the Sikh tradition. Present day Sikhism, however, is based upon the teachings of the Ten Gurus, which includes Guru Nanak and nine other Gurus who succeeded him.

Guru Nanak was born on April 15, 1469 in the village of Talwandi (now known as Nanak Sahib) about fifty-five miles west of modern day Lahore in Pakistan. Nanak was born in a Kshatriya (warrior class) family of Hindus. His father was a revenue official in the village of Talwandi. Nanak received early education in Sanskrit from a village pandit, and in Persian and Arabic in the Talwandi Muslim school. At the age of sixteen he was employed in a local revenue court. He was married at the age of nineteen and later became the father of two sons. Even at this young age Nanak was leading a spiritual life. He would rise very early in the morning, bathe in a nearby river, meditate, and sing *kirtan*a (devotional prayers) before beginning his daily work. Regular meditations and *kirtana* continued in late evenings as well.

At the age of thirty, Nanak had a mystical experience that changed his life. One day while bathing in a river, he disappeared from sight and was believed to have drowned. According to the *Janamsakhis* (traditional biographies of Sikhism) Nanak was called by God and directed to lead a spiritual mission that was explained to him in the following words: "Nanak, I am with thee. Through thee will my name be magnified. Go in the world and let your life be one of praise for the name of God, charity, service and prayer."

It is said that Nanak was missing for three days and nights. Appearing on the fourth day, he declared: "There is no Hindu, there is no Muslim." Following this event, Nanak was honored as a Guru and he preached his spiritual message wherever he went.

Accompanied by a musician and a disciple named Mardana, Guru Nanak travelled extensively, undertaking four long journeys. On his first journey he travelled eastward, visited both Hindu and Muslim places of pilgrimage, and held discussions on religious and spiritual matters with ascetics and holy men. On one of his journeys he travelled to Haridwar, where a well-known incident took place. There he saw Hindu pilgrims throwing handfuls of water eastward in the direction of the rising sun. This was an offering to their dead ancestors believed to be in the heavens. Nanak also began throwing handfuls of water, but in the opposite direction. When questioned, Nanak answered: "If you can send water to your dead ancestors in heaven, I should be able to send it to my fields in Punjab." Nanak rejected religious rituals and preached against them.

Guru Nanak's second journey led him southward, visiting places as far as Sri Lanka. His third journey was to the northern regions of the Himalayas. On his last journey, in the year 1518, Nanak travelled westward and visited Mecca and Medina in the Middle East. On this journey another famous incident occurred. Guru Nanak fell asleep with his feet inadvertently pointing toward Kabah, the Muslim holy place. Angered by this act, a Muslim priest rudely woke Nanak and pointed out the apparent sin Nanak had committed by placing his feet toward the house of God. "Then turn my feet in some other direction where God does not exist," answered Nanak.

By the time Nanak returned home, he was too old to travel and decided to settle with his family. He built a new township named Kartarpur, translated as the "abode of the creator."

Chapter 12

The Kartarpur community established itself around Nanak and was united in loyalty to him and the message he taught. This was the beginning of Sikhism. Twenty days before his death, Nanak initiated one of his disciples, by the name of Lehna, as a Guru and renamed him Angad. Later, other gurus followed and the religious leadership was handed down from Guru Nanak through a succession of gurus, listed here with their terms of guruship: Angad (1538-1552), Amar Das (1552-1574), Ram Das (1574-1581), Arjun (1581-1606), Hargobind (1606-1645), Hari Rai (1645-1661), Hari Krishan (1661-1664), Tegh Bahadur (1664-1675), and Guru Gobind Singh (1675-1708).

Two major religious acts of Guru Gobind Singh, the tenth and the last guru, are of great importance to the Sikh religion. The last guru organized a new brotherhood of Sikhs, called *Khalsa* (pure one). The male members of the Khalsa tradition were instructed to observe the "five k's": leave their hair and beard uncut (*kesh*), to wear a comb (*kanga*), shorts (*kacha*), steel wrist ring (*kadda*), and to carry a sword (*kirpan*). The members of the Khalsa tradition were also instructed not to drink or smoke. The initiated men took the name "Singh" (lion) and the women admitted to the Khalsa tradition took the name "Kaur" (princess). The first five persons initiated into the Khalsa tradition were called *panj pyares* (the beloved five). Guru Gobind Singh also declared himself to be the last human guru and declared the Guru Granth Sahib (the Sikh holy scripture) to be the eternal guru of the Sikh religion.

Major Teachings of Sikhism

The following are essential characteristics of Sikh religious thought and a summary of its major teachings:

- Sikh religious philosophy is monistic, or non-dualistic. The Ultimate Reality is conceived of as the unity of all existence. God is both *saguna* (with attributes) and *nirguna* (without attributes).   God is called by various names, such as *Sat* (truth), *Sat Guru* (true guru), *Akal Purkh* (timeless being), *Kartar* (creator), and *Wahi-guru* (praise to the lord).

Chapter 12

- God is the creator of the universe, and its existence and continued survival depends on His *hukam* (will).

- Man is unique in the world because he has the ability to discriminate and establish a divine relationship with God. Due to maya (illusion) man sees the world distinct from God. This duality results in his attachment to the things of the world and leads him to forget God. Attachment to material objects is the primary cause of rebirth, on the basis of past karma (action).

- The only way to achieve liberation (*mukti*) from the cycle of birth and death is by being God-conscious (*gurmukh*).

- Because God is within, rituals are unnecessary, but *right conduct* is essential. Physical renunciation of the world is unnecessary and futile. Sikhism emphasizes living as a householder and devoting life to the service (*seva*) of others.

- The institution of guruship is an essential characteristic of Sikh religion. No one can achieve moksha (liberation) without the help of a true guru. The guru is not to be worshipped, but must be respected, consulted and obeyed.

- Sikhism does not believe in the incarnation of God in a human form. The company of holy men is prescribed as an essential prerequisite for spiritual progress.

- Sikhism strongly disapproves of asceticism and self-mortification as a path to enlightenment.

- Sikhism prescribes the singing of the names of God, such as *Nam Simran*, and singing of devotional prayers (*kirtana*) as the best way to conquer lust, anger, greed, attachment, and pride---the five sins comprising maya. The influence of maya is believed to lead man away from God. The soul (*Jiva*) is an integral part of Brahman (God). Jiva is immortal

and pure. The physical body decays, but Jiva continues
forever.

Hindu Dharma and Sikhism

➤ Sikhism arose from the Indian Sant (holy person) Tradition, essentially within a Hindu cultural environment. Guru
Nanak accepted the teachings of the Upanishads but rejected
the ritualism of the Vedas. Thus the religious views of Sikhism
are essentially the same as those of Hindu dharma with the
following major exceptions and clarifications:

- Hindu dharma teaches Karma Yoga, Raja Yoga, Jnana
  Yoga, and Bhakti Yoga as the four main paths for the
  realization of God. Although these paths are not exclusive,
  the seeker on the spiritual path chooses one or the other
  path that suits his or her temperament. Sikhism does not
  necessarily reject Jnana and Raja Yogas, but emphasizes
  Bhakti Yoga, in conjunction with Karma Yoga, as an
  effective spiritual discipline for worldly life as well as for
  the realization of God.

- Unlike Hindu dharma, Sikhism does not believe in the
  incarnation of God in a human form.

- Sikhism rejects ritualism. Hindu dharma accepts ritualism
  as a tool for beginners for attaining concentration and
  meditation. As stated earlier, ritualism is not compulsory in
  Hindu dharma

- Sikhism rejects the caste system. The caste system was a
  social structure, based upon division of labor, accepted by
  ancient Hindus for efficient functioning of their society.
  Practice of the caste system, however, violates the fundamental tenets of Hindu dharma as expounded by scriptures
  such as the Bhagavad Gita and Upanishads. Refer to
  chapter 17 for a discussion of the caste system.

Chapter 13
Karma and Reincarnation

The Hindu theory of reincarnation or rebirth explains the evolution of the individual atman, through many lives on earth, until it attains liberation (moksha) from the cycle of birth and death. The belief in rebirth is common to several ancient religions. In Hindu religion, however, reincarnation or rebirth is not merely a belief, but a doctrine that is based upon definite metaphysical and ethical grounds. The Hindu theory of reincarnation is based upon four basic principles: permanence of the atman, existence of maya (the original ignorance), liberation (moksha) of the atman from samsara, and the Law of Karma.

Permanence of the Atman (soul)

Three views are possible regarding the life of the atman. One is that the life of the atman is the same as that of the body and that the atman perishes at the death of the body. A second view is that the atman is born with the body, but does not perish at the death of the body. Still a third view is that the atman has neither a beginning nor an end.

All systems of Hindu philosophy (except Carvaka, the materialistic philosophy) view the atman as a permanent entity. According to Hindu thought, the atman is immortal, pure, omnipresent, and omniscient. In every human being and in every animal, however weak or wicked, great or small, resides the omnipresent and omniscient atman. The difference among creatures is not in the atman, but in its manifestation in the physical body that the atman occupies.

The level of manifestation of the atman in a particular body depends upon the physical construct of that body. In a human body the atman has the highest manifestation. According to the most representative Hindu view, the human body with which the atman is associated consists of three bodies: physical (*sthula-sharira*), subtle (*sukshma-sharira*), and causal (*karana-sharira*).

The atman experiences the external world through these three bodies.   The *physical* body, which is produced and sustained by food, is the abode of all experiences of the atman relating to the external world.   It is also the abode of consciousness in the waking state.   At the death of an individual only the physical body dies and is eventually dissolved back into matter.

The second body, called the *subtle* body, is comprised of subtler matter than that of the physical body. The subtle body is the abode of dream consciousness and the mental and the intellectual functions of the individual. It is this subtle body that serves as the medium by which the atman transmigrates from one physical body to another in the process of reincarnation.   The subtle body does not perish at death and, therefore, individuality does not end at death. This doctrine is expressed in the following words of the Bhagavad Gita:

> "When the Lord [atman] obtains a body and when He leaves it, He carries the mind and its impressions along, just as the wind carries along scents from the flowers." (BG 15.8)

The third body that the atman assumes is known as the *causal* body.   This body is the last sheath of the atman and consists of an idea-matrix for the subtle and the physical bodies.   According to Hindu scriptures, the causal body is comprised of 35 idea-elements corresponding to 16 basic elements of the physical body and 19 elements of the subtle body.   The presence of the causal body is indicated in the deep-sleep state when the physical and the subtle bodies temporarily cease to function.

Theory of Pancha Kosha

According to the theory of pancha kosha (*pancha* means five and *kosha* means sheath) taught by the Taittiriya Upanishad, the three bodies--physical, subtle, and causal--discussed above consist of five sheaths (or body cells): *annamaya kosha* (physical sheath composed of food), *pranamaya kosha* (prana or vital sheath), *manomaya kosha* (mental sheath), *vijnanamaya kosha* (intellectual sheath), and *anandamaya kosha* (bliss sheath). The physical sheath represents the physical body of the individual, which is the essence of the food consumed. The vital sheath is linked with the function of breathing. This sheath causes the senses to function and sustains life in the human and animal species. The mental sheath is the basis for human perception, cognition, memory, and understanding. The intellectual sheath is the basis for the human functions associated with intellect, egoism, and imagination. The fifth sheath is the sheath of bliss, the pure spirit or atman.

The two sheaths *vijnanamaya kosha* and *anandamaya kosha* are the bodies that go from birth to birth; the other three sheaths are grown again in each life. Sri Aurobindo explains the process: "When the atman returns to birth, it takes up with its mental, vital, and physical sheaths so much of its karma as is useful to it in the new life for further experience." Just as a snake sheds its skin, the atman drops all the sheaths or body coverings when it attains eternal perfection or *moksha* from samsara.

Existence of Maya (the original ignorance)

According to the most representative Hindu view, the atman, when associated with a physical body, identifies itself with the body under the influence of maya. Maya is the cosmic illusion or the original ignorance. Sri Krishna speaks of its power in the Bhagavad Gita:

> "I am not manifest to all, being veiled by yoga-maya.
> And in its delusion the world knows Me not, the
> unborn and immutable." (BG 7.25)

Under the influence of maya, the atman forgets its divine nature, identifies itself with the body and mind, assumes individuality, and thus enjoys pleasures and suffers pain in the world. Maya has two powers: the power of veiling the

Ultimate Reality, and the power of falsely projecting the
Ultimate Reality as something else (see discussion of maya in
chapter 4). These dual powers of maya create a mirage-like
effect, similar to falsely identifying a rope as a snake in dull
light or mistaking sand for water in a desert. Under the
influence of maya, the atman does not change, but forgets its
divine nature and becomes a part of the phenomenal world,
which is also projected by maya.

In Hindu view, the cause of human birth is not O riginal
Sin (from Christian doctrine), but the original ignorance,
called maya. The difference between these two concepts is
that the O riginal Sin (see page 65) is a moral error whereas
the original ignorance (maya) is the lack of the right knowledge
of the Ultimate Reality, a metaphysical error.

Liberation (Moksha) of the Atman From Samsara

In Hindu view, the birth and death of an individual is in
reality the birth and death of the physical body that the atman
occupies during its appearance in the phenomenal world. The
atman is potentially divine and immortal, and it assumes
innumerable physical bodies in order to reap the fruits of its
past actions. In this process the atman goes through the
perpetual cycle of birth and death, called *samsara*, until it
attains liberation (*moksha*). During each birth the atman
undergoes sufferings and enjoyments as regulated by its past
karma, creates new good or bad karma (based upon the quality
of its actions) and also has the opportunity to attain *moksha*
through a spiritual discipline, in accordance with the scriptures. In Hindu view, the human birth is of supreme
importance because it provides a rare opportunity for the
atman to gain spiritual perfection, and thereby free itself from
physical limitations of samsara.

In Hinduism, the evolutionary process is forward-acting.
This means that once the atman has attained a human body
in the process of its normal evolution from the lower to higher
forms of life, it will always assume a human body in its
subsequent incarnations regardless of the quality of its past
karma. However, as stated above, the quality of human life in

a particular incarnation will, in part, depend upon the quality of one's accumulated past karma.

For a Hindu, the goal of life is to attain liberation from the experiences of the phenomenal life (i.e. freedom from the cycle of birth and death). Moksha, or liberation, is the realization by the atman of its true nature, which is immortal, pure, omnipresent, and omnipotent. The concept of moksha is the answer provided by Hindus to the age-old question of the purpose of life. According to Hindu view, the ignorance caused by maya is the cause of the atman's bondage to the phenomenal world, and the cure is right knowledge.

Liberation is the birth-right of every individual. It is the individual himself who is responsible for his own salvation. No savior or redeemer can achieve this task for him.

According to Hindu scriptures, moksha is not the result of some change or modification of the atman. Moksha does not imply that the atman acquires something that it does not already have. Moksha simply means freedom of the individual from ignorance, realization of one's own true nature, and liberation from the cycle of birth and death. In a liberated state, an individual develops universality of outlook and freedom from all worldly attachments. The concept of moksha in Hindu thought is of great moral and ethical significance, as it provides an incentive for righteous living in the world.

The Law of Karma

The word *karma* denotes an action that brings back results in this life or in future lives. The doctrine of karma is based upon the theory of cause and effect. This theory of cause and effect differs from the Christian notion that God punishes the wicked and rewards the virtuous. The underlying basis for this difference is that Hindu dharma is a god-loving religion rather than god-fearing.

The Law of Karma is the answer provided by Hindu dharma to the question of why suffering and inequalities exist in the world: "Why should one person be different from another in his looks, abilities, and character? Why is one born a king and another a beggar? A just and merciful God cannot create such inequalities." The doctrine of karma, a law of actions and their retribution, can be viewed as the law of causation (cause and effect) applied to the moral realm. The law that every action has a reaction works in the scientific world as well as in the moral world.

Every human action inevitably leads to results, good or bad, depending upon the moral quality of the deed. There is no such thing as action without results. "As we sow, so shall we reap," is the law that governs all deeds. Actions that are morally good produce good results and those that are morally bad produce bad results. The Law of Karma conserves the moral consequences of all actions, and conditions our present and/or future lives accordingly. In part, the present life is determined by the results of past deeds: we are the effects of our own infinite past. Every child that is born in this world is born to work out its own past deeds.

According to the Law of Karma, we are the effects and we are the causes. What we did in the past has determined in part what we are today, and what we do today will determine our tomorrow (*agami karma*). There is no supernatural power that creates our destinies and nothing happens by mere chance or fate. We are the creators of our own destinies. If we are unhappy, it has been of our own thinking and doing. We can be happy, if we want to be so. Does this mean that we are the helpless creatures of our past (at least for the present) and that there is nothing we can do about it? The answer lies in a clear understanding of how the doctrine of karma works.

The past karma of an individual consists of two parts, *prarabdha karma* and *sanchita karma*. The prarabdha karma is the part of one's past karma which is to bear fruit in the present life of the individual. The sanchita karma is the accumulated karma of the previous births which is to bear fruit in the future. The prarabdha karma of an individual consists of two components: fixed and variable. The fixed component of karma is beyond our control and consists of that component of the past karma which determines one's parents, the family in which a child must be born, the general features of the physical body that the child will eventually develop, and the social and religious environment in which the child must grow.

The variable component of the past karma remains latent in the child in the form of *samskaras* (natural habits and tendencies). It is this variable part of the past karma that one can overcome by initiative and free will. The level of success one can achieve in diluting the effects of the variable component, however, depends upon the power of the samskaras and the strength of the individual will.

The past karma of an ordinary human being is either good, bad, or mixed. An individual's particular incarnation is determined by the overall balance of past karma. If the overall balance is positive (i.e. overall good karma), the individual will be born in an environment that would be naturally conducive toward the onward progress of his atman. In a particular incarnation, only those innate tendencies (samskaras) are manifested for which conditions are favorable in that incarnation and the remaining samskaras will remain inactive until a future incarnation in which conditions for the manifestation of the remaining tendencies will become available. The right environment is essential for manifestation of the samskaras. For example, if an individual is born as a professor (because of his overall good karma) and if he had been a gambler in his past incarnations, his innate gambling tendency will not find the right environment to manifest itself in the academic environment of his vocation. However, if he happens to be in the company of gamblers, he will exhibit a natural love for gambling because of the residual impressions of his past karma. This is why Hindu dharma stresses the importance of a right environment and an association with those who are pure-minded.

Every human action, be it physical or mental, produces two effects. First, depending upon the moral quality of an action, the appropriate fruits of the action will be rewarded later, either in the same life or in a future life. Second, the action leaves residual impressions (samskaras) on the mind of the individual. These samskaras determine the character of the individual. Thus, actions determine the personal conduct and this conduct molds the character, in a revolving chain of cause and effect. The *Brihadaranyaka Upanishad* declares thus: "A man becomes good by performing good deeds and evil by performing evil deeds."

The Law of Karma determines the results of all of one's deeds in accordance with their moral quality. To reap the fruits of one's actions, good or bad, an individual must be born again and again in the physical world. Thus, the Law of Karma binds an individual to the cycle of birth and death. Freedom from this cycle can be achieved by adherence to the doctrine of *nishkama karma*. According to this doctrine, an individual who performs actions without attachment to their fruits (see also the discussion of Karma Yoga in chapter 8) is freed from the bondage of birth and death, thereby attaining that state which is beyond all suffering (BG 2.51).

Destiny and Free Will

According to the Bhagavad Gita (BG 3.27), all human actions are caused by prakriti (nature), and the following are the five causes of whatever action an individual performs with his body, speech, and mind (BG 18.14):

1. The body
2. The agent (ego)
3. Various senses (means of perception)
4. Different functions of various sorts (means of action)
5. The divine will (*daivam*)

The combined effect of the above first four factors is called the individual effort, which includes one's willpower, initiative and drive, enthusiasm, education and training, material resources, interface with other parties involved in the venture, and other factors that may depend upon a given situation. All these factors are usually known and can thus be maximized by an individual to ensure success in a particular endeavor. The divine will is an unknown and unknowable factor in human lives. It presents an element of uncertainty in all human actions.

Chapter 13

Another factor that determines the outcome of one's action is one's destiny, the fruits of one's past actions in accordance with the Law of Karma. Destiny is also an unknown factor and thus cannot be predicted.

⤙ Since success in any human endeavor depends upon the above five variables plus destiny, individual success may thus be mathematically represented as the product of the following variables:

$$S = E \, x \, W \, x \, D$$

In the above equation, S represents individual success, E the individual effort, W the divine will, and D the destiny (effect of karma).

As stated above, the divine will is an unknown factor. We may, however, assume that if the work is righteous, is performed without longing for results, and with an understanding that is free from egoism (see BG 3.27), the Divine Power will help to bring the work to a successful conclusion. With this assumption, W may be set equal to one and the above equation reduces to:

$$S = E \, x \, D$$

This is the simplified form of the Equation of Success. In this equation S can range from zero to one. When S equals zero, there is zero success, or complete failure. When S equals one, there is one-hundred percent success.

E also ranges from zero to one. When E equals zero, there is zero or no effort. When E equals one, there is one-hundred percent effort.

Likewise D ranges from zero to one. If D equals zero, there is zero destiny or bad karma. If D equals one, there is good fortune or good karma.

From the above equation, it follows that even if D is equal to one (good karma), S will be equal to zero if E equals zero. Thus, even with the best karma, success is directly proportional to one's effort.

Chapter 13

Even when **D** equals one, the only way **S** can equal one is by having **E** equal one. Therefore, we can logically conclude that **destiny (or karma) alone cannot lead to success unless effort is maximized.** This is why, in the following words of the Bhagavad Gita, Krishna guarantees Arjuna success in the war with the Kauravas, informing Arjuna that his (Arjuna's) destiny favors his winning of the battle. However, as explained above, Krishna must still (and does) advise Arjuna to fight:

> "Arise [O h Arjuna!], conquer thy enemies [make **E**=1]; enjoy thy kingdom and win thy glory [**S**=1]. Through the fate of their karma, I have already doomed them to die [**D**=1]; be thou merely an instrumental cause. (BG 11.33)

Again, from the Equation of Success, it follows that if **D** is equal to zero, **S** will be equal to zero, even if **E** equals one. This is the power of one's predetermined destiny. Since a person's destiny in the present life is based upon his karma from previous incarnations, he has no control on the impact of his pre-determined destiny on his present life. All he can do is maximize his effort in the present life.

Although the impact of an individual's *destiny* cannot be underestimated, it is the *effort* that he must control by utilizing his free will. O n a broader level, this means that *one must do the best one can and not worry about the results.* In other words, one must not become attached to the fruits of one's actions. This leads to the fundamental doctrine of Hinduism, *work without attachment,* declared in the Bhagavad Gita:

> "The wise, possessed with knowledge, renouncing the fruits of their actions, become freed from the bondage of birth and reach that state which is beyond all evil." (BG 2.51)

Refer to Q5 on page 158 to understand what renunciation of the fruit of action really means.

Chapter 13

Chapter 14
Deity Worship and Ritualism

A human being cannot conceptualize anything without some sort of a mental image. A Hindu associates his mental image of the infinite attributes of the Supreme Lord with sacred images, called deities, and uses such images, as symbols to concentrate his mind on the worship of the Lord. Just as we associate the idea of infinity with the image of the blue sky, or the idea of holiness with a cross or a place of worship, a Hindu associates the ideas of the attributes of the Supreme Lord, such as omnipresence and omnipotence, with various sacred images and forms. Therefore, when a Hindu worships an image, he does not worship the inanimateness of the image, but rather the holiness, sacredness, purity, omnipresence, and omnipotence that are symbolized by such a sacred image. Deity worship in Hindu religion is characterized by the following features:

- Hindu religion is monotheistic polytheism: There is no henotheism in Hindu religion. There is only one omnipresent and omnipotent God, Who Hindus worship by different names and in different forms. "A rose called by any other name would still smell as sweet." Thus we hear the eternal words of Sri Krishna in the Bhagavad Gita:

  "In whatever way men love Me, in the same way they find My love; various are the ways for men, but in the end they all come to Me." (BG 4.11)

- Hindus believe that the Absolute can be realized through meditation and contemplation. The images and forms are simply symbols.

• Sacred images are used as tools of worship and meditation. Images have been found very helpful for success in meditation. They help the mind to focus on the Supreme Being during worship and meditation.

• The use of sacred images as symbols in the worship of the Supreme Lord is neither compulsory in Hindu religion nor is it needed by all. The use of images in worship is only an aid for those who prefer it.

• The use of sacred images in worship in meditation has produced a countless number of Hindu sages and saints. One of the greatest sages of modern times, Paramahamsa Sri Ramakrishna (1836-1886 AD), worshipped images of the Divine Mother Kali throughout his life. If image worship can produce spiritual giants like Sri Ramakrishna, then its value in worship and meditation cannot be discounted.

Ritualism

Ritualism in Hindu religion often has been criticized by non-Hindus and sometimes by Hindus themselves. The reasons for such criticism are three-fold. Firstly, not everyone understands the *purpose* of rituals. Secondly, not all understand the *meaning* of the rituals. Finally, ritualism defeats its own purpose, when practiced excessively.

Regarding the purpose or the scope of ritualism, its practice is meant as a tool for a beginner in his (or her) religious life. In the predominant Hindu view, ritualism creates a sacred environment, generates devotion for worship and thereby helps a beginner to concentrate his mind on worship, prayer, and meditation. However, everyone may not need this tool. If a person can concentrate his mind on the spiritual path without distraction, ritualism is not needed and thus is not compulsory in Hindu religion.

In the advanced stages of one's religious life, there is absolutely no need for religious rites or ceremonies. This position is very clearly stated in the following words of the Bhagavad Gita:

Chapter 14

"To the knower of Truth, all Vedas are of as little use as a small water-tank is during the time of a flood, when water is everywhere." (BG 2.46)

The above position is also reiterated by Swami Vivekananda in the following words: "It is good to be born in a church but not to die there."

A ritual is completely useless if performed mechanically without understanding its meaning. For a ritual to be an effective tool in worship and meditation, one must concentrate one's mind on the meaning of the ritual while performing it.

In Hindu religion, each religious act or ceremony has a definite philosophical basis, and no ritual is based upon dogma or blind faith. For example, a common practice for a Hindu is to offer a coconut in a temple. The priest breaks the coconut and pours its milk at the feet of the Lord. There is deep meaning behind this religious act. A coconut has three parts: an outer skin, a hard shell, and milk within the hard shell. The outer skin is fluffy and beautiful and symbolizes the human body, with its external beauty. The hard shell denotes the ego, and milk symbolizes the soul. This ritual signifies that when the ego is killed (symbolized by the breaking of the hard shell by the priest), the soul is united with God (symbolized by pouring of the milk at the feet of the Lord).

Lastly, there is a problem with excessive ritualism. Blind faith, unaided by knowledge, can lead to excessive ritualism. One of the examples of excessive ritualism is the use of large quantities of food items, such as milk and honey, by some priests for bathing (*snana* or *abhisheka*) the deities during *pujas*. Sometimes large quantities of food are thrown around the deities as an offering. This practice may have started in old days by rich kings and queens whenever they conducted worships in palaces or temples. This practice of wasting large quantities of food in the name of an offering to deities is, however, against the true spirit of Hindu worship. In today's world there is so much poverty and hunger that wastage of food is neither warranted nor desirable. What brings a devotee closer to the Lord is the quality of devotion (*bhavana*) towards Him and not the quantity of food offered during worship. Thus Lord Krishna declares in the Bhagavad Gita:

> "O ne who offers to Me with devotion only a leaf, a flower, a fruit, or even a little water, this I accept, because it was offered with love by [one who is] pure-hearted." (BG 9.26)

Just as meditation without physical work has no value, nor work without meditation, ritualism without knowledge is useless. The hands and heart must work together to perform true service; so must ritualism be combined with knowledge, meditation, and self-less work for attaining success in religious and spiritual life.

Purpose of Religious Rites and Ceremonies

The purpose of Hindu religious rites and ceremonies is to help promote growth of moral qualities. A symbolic material offering to deities during worship, with sincerity and devotion, is a rite that leads to the spirit of self-sacrifice, a virtue in itself. Similarly, other rites such as alms-giving promote generosity, and fasting leads to self-control. The five daily sacrifices (see *pancha maha yagnas* in chapter 32) that a householder is enjoined to offer to gods, sages, forefathers, humans, and other living beings are intended to develop devotion to the family, society, and kindness to animals.

In Hindu view, the rites and rituals enjoined by scriptures are the means for the purification of the ego, which is the end of all rites and rituals. However, when the rites and rituals are made ends in themselves, they become impediments for the progress of the individual. Inward righteousness is more important than outward righteousness, and moral and ethical excellence is far superior than ceremonial purity.

In conclusion, deity worship and ritualism are effective means for religious and spiritual pursuit in Hindu religion. They embody the religious wisdom and experiences of Hindu sages and saints through the ages. However, in our enthusiasm for the means, we should not overlook the ends.

Chapter 14

Chapter 15
Ahimsa and Vegetarianism

O ne of the essential doctrines of Hindu religion is *ahimsa paramo dharmah,* or ahimsa is the highest virtue. Ahimsa literally means non-violence or non-injury. Although ahimsa is generally spoken more as a cardinal virtue of Buddhism and Jainism, its roots are embedded in the rich soil of the Vedas and Upanishads, the primary Hindu scriptures.

"You must not use your God-given body for killing God's creatures, whether they are human, animal or whatever." (Yajur Veda Samhita 12.32)

The doctrine of ahimsa is based upon the fundamental doctrine of Hindu religion: *Vasudhaiva Kutumbakam,* or all life-forms are one family. This means that Brahman, the eternal all-pervading Supreme Being, dwells in all living beings, whether human, animal, or insect. Thus an injury in *thought, word, or deed* against a living being is a sin against all of creation, including the sinner himself. Hindu scriptures (such as Rig Veda 10.37.11, Atharva Veda 19.48.5 and 10.191.4, Devikalottara Agama and Sandilya Upanishad) declare that injury should not be caused to any living creature.

Ahimsa teaches that one must consider all living beings in the image of one's own self and thus not commit acts of violence in thought, word, or deed against other living creatures. The doctrine of ahimsa includes the following essential elements:

• From the standpoint of non-injury, ahimsa means universal love for all beings. Since the Supreme Self is present in all beings, the love between living beings is the love of God.

- It is impossible to sustain one's existence in the physical world without injury or destruction of some creatures. In all situations and circumstances restraint must be intelligently applied in order to travel on the path of ahimsa.

- Anger and hatred cannot coexist with ahimsa. Anger blinds reason and leads one to violence. A follower of the path of ahimsa must be humble and perform his duties in the spirit of total detachment. An individual who is worried about name and fame and attached to material pleasures is apt to commit violence to protect his or her selfish interests.

- Greed and possessiveness are the two main causes of social injustice and the suffering of mankind. A follower of ahimsa must not hoard wealth above and beyond his or her legitimate needs.

- Fearless action is an essential element of ahimsa. Evil must be resisted, but with ill-will against none. Cowardice has no place on the path of ahimsa. This idea is clearly expressed by Mahatma Gandhi, the epitome of non-violence, in the following words: "I would rather have India resort to arms in order to defend her honor than that she should in a cowardly manner become or remain a helpless witness of her own dishonor."

- Compassion is an essential element of ahimsa. One must not be satisfied solely with one's own well-being, but must strive to alleviate the suffering of all mankind.

- A follower of ahimsa must practice austerities (*tapasya*), but extreme austerities are against the true spirit of ahimsa.

- Ahimsa implies equal rights and opportunities for all, regardless of differences in caste, color, creed, race, sex, and religion. The boundaries of faith, nation, or state are alien to the spirit of ahimsa.

- Ahimsa teaches reverence for plants and trees. The care of plants and trees was taught by Hindu sages, who asked people to protect the *Vana Devata*, the heavenly being which resides inside trees. By applying the doctrine of ahimsa to plant life, Hindus were the first to recognize the importance of protecting the environment.

In summary, one can say that true ahimsa is a life of non-violence but not inaction, tolerance but not fearfulness, love but not attachment, strength but not ill-will, peace but not cowardice, and complete freedom from greed, hatred, anger, and enmity.

Vegetarianism

Vegetarianism is a necessary corollary of the doctrine of ahimsa. Hindu religion, therefore, ordains vegetarianism as an essential virtue. Vegetarianism is not merely a code of eating habits, but is based upon a deeply recognized need to create a balanced state of body and mind. Meat-eating is not only detrimental to one's spiritual life, but also to the environment we live in and the physical body we possess. The Hindu philosophy of vegetarianism is, therefore, based upon spiritual, ecological, economic and health considerations as discussed below:

Spiritual Considerations

The highest purpose of life in Hindu religion is to transcend ordinary consciousness and seek the unity of all existence. The entire universe is the manifestation of one Supreme Brahman. "All is One and One is in all." For those who wish to follow a path of self-knowledge and God-realization, it is essential to extend love, kindness, and compassion to all forms of life and recognize them as integral parts of nature.

To live in this world, however, we must destroy some life. The simple process of ordinary breathing involves the killing of bacteria that have life. Even the plants we eat have life. At the same time, killing a bird or an animal for food and cutting an eggplant in a garden do not involve the same level of pain and agony. In order to extend our love, kindness, and compassion to all forms of life and at the same time be able to live in the world, Hindu sages tell us that we must consume only those foods that cause the least possible pain. Accordingly, they have divided all forms of life into five different categories based upon the number of senses each species possesses and the number of elements (*tattwas*) the physical body of the particular life form is comprised of.

According to Hindu thought, the entire universe consists of five elements (*tattwas*): ether, air, fire, water, and earth (see chapter 37). The same elements also enter into the constitution of the physical bodies of all life forms, as follows:

Life Form	Sense Organs	Tattwas of the Physical Body
Human Beings	touch, taste, sight, sound, smell, mind	space, air, fire, water, earth
Quadrupeds (4-legged animals)	touch, sound, sight, taste, smell	air, fire, water, earth
Birds	touch, sound, sight, taste	air, fire, water
Reptiles, worms, and insects	touch, sound, sight	fire, earth
Roots, vegetables, and fruits	touch, sound	water, earth

The sages further tell us that life forms which involve the least amount of pain are those that possess the least number of senses and whose bodies are made of the least number of elements. Interestingly, the legal punishment for destroying life forms is based upon the concept of least pain. In all countries of the world, the killing of six-sensed life forms (human beings) is considered a heinous crime and carries the maximum punishment. The four- and five-sensed life forms carry less punishment. There is no punishment for destroying the two- and three-sensed life forms. Thus Hindu thinkers concluded that as long as living involves the destruction of life, the killing of roots, vegetables, and fruits involves the least pain and agony (see also Question 3 on page 156). Therefore, this type of food is recommended for the healthy growth of the body, mind, and intellect.

According to the *Chandogya Upanishad*, "The mind is made of food. The gross component of the food eaten passes through the body as excrement. The finer component of the food forms the body, and the finest or the subtlest component of the food forms our minds." A more direct translation of this ancient truth is, "You are what you eat."

Through their own spiritual experiences, Hindu sages discovered that the food we eat determines the temperament we possess. Accordingly, they divided food into three categories: *sattvic* (pure), *rajasic* (energizing), and *tamasic* (dull). The sattvic foods produce calmness and serenity of mind and include plants, vegetables, nuts, fruits, grains, pulses and moderate quantities of milk products. The rajasic foods contribute to the restlessness of mind and include onions, garlic, peppers, spices, and sour and bitter foods. Tamasic foods lead to the degeneration of the human nature and include meat, alcoholic beverages, and stale foods. For additional discussion of these three different categories of foods, refer to verses 7 through 10 of chapter 17 of the Bhagavad Gita.

Ecological and Economic Considerations

Tropical rain forests are being continuously destroyed to make room for cattle production for meat. It has been estimated that 260 million acres of U.S. forest land has been cleared to make pasture land to produce livestock. Due to the destruction of the rain forests and related habitats, the current rate of extinction of life-forms is estimated to be 1,000 species per year. Meat-based diets also contribute to water pollution due to contaminated runoff and swage from the slaughter-houses and feedlots. Studies show that the production of livestock creates ten times more pollution than the residential areas and three times more than the industry. The fresh water resources of the planet are also becoming depleted. Only sixty pounds of water are required to grow a pound of wheat, whereas 2,500 to 6,000 pounds of water are required to produce one pound of meat. The fossil fuel resources also are being depleted at an alarming rate. It takes two calories of fossil fuel energy to produce a calorie of soybean protein, whereas it takes 78 calories of fossil fuel energy to produce one calorie of beef protein.

Vegetarianism is the most economic alternative for the human race. To illustrate, it takes ten acres of pasture land to produce a given amount of animal protein. It takes only one acre of land to produce the same amount of vegetable protein. Thus nine acres of land are wasted when meat is produced. In addition, an average animal eats approximately sixteen pounds of grain to produce only one pound of meat. Thus fifteen pounds of grain are wasted in the process. According to Harvard nutritionist Jean Mayer, reducing meat production by only ten percent would release enough grain to feed sixty million people.

Health Considerations

Although there are many types of vegetarians, the two main types are vegan and lacto-ovo. Vegans avoid meat, fish, fowl, eggs, and dairy products. Lacto-ovos avoid meat, fish, and fowl, but eat dairy products and eggs.

Meat-based diets and dairy products are known to be the highest in cholesterol and saturated fats. The nutritional and medical research has repeatedly shown that people whose diets are high in cholesterol and saturated fats have a high risk of death by coronary heart disease and stroke. Since vegetarians tend to eat fewer calories than omnivores, they are slimmer, with lower blood pressure and cholesterol, and a lesser incidence of diabetes. Since vegetarian diets are lower in saturated fats and higher in fiber, their intake provides substances (such as beta carotene) that protect against cancer.

(For additional information on this subject, refer to sources included in Suggested Readings chapter of this book.)

Chapter 15

Chapter 16
Hindu Ethics

Hindu ethics does not owe its origin to dogmatic notions of good and evil or heaven and hell. Hindu ethics is dictated by the need to harmonize an individual's desires, emotions, and ambitions in order to lead a harmonious life on earth, with the ultimate aim of Hindu religious life being the realization of the self. Self-realization, according to Hindu view, is the awareness and the consciousness of the Self, the source and the essence of human existence and freedom.

Hindu scriptures declare that an individual consists of the physical body (*sharira*), mind (*manas*), intellect (*buddhi*), and the self (*atman*). Based upon this four-fold division of the human personality, an individual needs worldly property (*artha*) to maintain his own physical body and to satisfy the needs of his family and dependents. To satisfy the mind and intellect, he needs to fulfill his desires and intellectual pursuits (*kama*). To satisfy his soul, he must attain liberation (*moksha*) or union with God, the ultimate aim of human life.

While satisfying the individual needs of artha and kama, as stated above, one must reconcile those actions designed to achieve individual good with those actions motivated by social good. Every individual must play his or her part for the good of society, the nation, and the world. One must act within the limits of *dharma*. Dharma stands for righteousness, duty, moral and social laws (see chapter 32 for further discussion of dharma). Thus, we see that there are four principal goals of human life: dharma, artha, kama, and moksha.

Dharma comes first, indicating that the other three cannot be fulfilled without fulfilling the obligations of dharma. Moksha is the final goal, since its attainment is only possible when the other three (dharma, artha, and kama) are fulfilled.

Although dharma has different meanings in different contexts, from the ethical standpoint, dharma is a system of moral and ethical values. Hindu dharma recognizes seven vices which divert an individual from the path of dharma and lead a person to commit sin. These are craving (*trishna*), anger (*krodha*), greed (*lobha*), attachment (*moha*), pride (*mada*), jealousy (*matsarya*), and egoism (*ahankara*).

Dharma helps an individual to evolve his intellect so that he can achieve artha and kama while fulfilling his duties and obligations to the society, state, nation, and the world. A balanced and stable mind is necessary for selfless action and for enjoying worldly pleasures without being attached to them. This has been beautifully expressed in the Bhagavad Gita 2.51:

> "The wise, possessed with knowledge, abandoning the fruits of their actions, become freed from the fetters of birth and reach that state which is beyond all evil."

Hindu ethics does not advocate suppressing genuine desires and emotions. It seeks to satisfy them in a controlled manner so that all the energy is not wasted for pure worldly pursuits. Sufficient energy must remain for intellectual and spiritual evolution. Some of the virtues that bring about an intellectual evolution in an individual are truthfulness, non-violence, love, justice, compassion, courage, wisdom, tolerance, contentment, forgiveness, purity of thought, word, and deed, and self-control. Other virtues that form the core of Hindu ethics are listed in verses one through four of chapter 16 in the Bhagavad Gita.

Although the commandments of Hindu ethics are basically the same as those of other major religions of the world, Hindu ethics places more emphasis on the following virtues:

Self-control, Charity, and Compassion

These three virtues form the foundation for a life of virtue and goodness. Their importance is conveyed in the following parable found in the *Brihadaranyaka Upanishad 5.2.1-3*:

Once upon a time, the gods, men, and demons asked their teacher (Sage Prajapati) for his final advice. To the gods, Prajapati said: "da," which they understood to mean *damayata*, or the practice of self-control. To the men, Prajapati said, "da," which they understood to mean *datta*, or the practice of charity. To the demons, Prajapati said, "da," which they understood to mean *dayadhvam*, the practice of compassion. The Upanishad further tells us that Prajapati reminds all human beings, through the natural sound "da-da-da" produced by thundering of the clouds, to always practice these three cardinal virtues.

Renunciation

The concept of renunciation in Hindu dharma has been largely misunderstood by non-Hindus and Hindus alike. Renunciation does not mean renunciation *of action*. It means renunciation *in action*. What must be renounced is not the action, but attachment to the fruits of the action. O ne cannot run away from worldly responsibilities, but must cultivate virtue and goodness in the spirit of non-attachment.

"Therefore, without attachment, perform always the work that has to be done, for man attains highest by doing work without attachment." (BG. 3.19)

Truthfulness

Hindu sages tell us that truth must be practiced in thought, speech and actions. Truthfulness is more the practice of sincerity than of speaking factually. The intent of speaking truth should not be merely to hurt others. There is a popular saying in Sanskrit: "*Satyam vada priyam, vada na vada satyam apriyam,*" meaning "speak the truth, but not to hurt other's feelings. The truth that you speak should be pleasing to others."

An example of speaking truth, but not to hurt others may be found in the following story: with a knife in his hand, a butcher was chasing a cow, which suddenly disappeared from his sight. The butcher stops and asks a priest--walking on the road--as to which way the cow went. The priest directs the butcher in the wrong direction, thus saving the cow from the butcher's knife.

The importance of truthfulness in one's character is obvious and is illustrated in the following parable found in the *Chandogya Upanishad*:

A boy asks a teacher for spiritual instruction. In order to determine whether the boy is worthy of receiving spiritual instruction, the teacher asks the boy, among other questions, what the name of his father is. The boy replies, "I do not know my father's name because my mother has led an immoral life and she does not know who my father is." The teacher immediately accepts the boy for spiritual instruction because truthfulness is the only criterion of an individual's character.

Hindu sages tell us that truthfulness leads to true knowledge and bliss. As Mahatma Gandhi explains, "Where there is no Truth (*Sat*), there can be no true knowledge. That is why the word *chit* or knowledge is associated with the name of God. And where there is true knowledge, there is always bliss *(ananda)*. Sorrow has no place there. And even as Truth is eternal, so is bliss derived from It. Hence we can know God as *sat-chit-ananda*, one Who combines in Himself Truth, Knowledge, and Bliss." [13]

Non-violence

Non-violence (ahimsa) is one of the essential tenets of Hindu ethics. All of creation is the manifestation of one Supreme Self and, as such, one must look at all beings in the image of the Self, treating them with kindness and compassion. One must not be satisfied solely with one's own well-being, but must strive for the well-being of mankind. Refer to chapter 15 for a detailed discussion of the doctrine of ahimsa.

Yajna

Yajna, literally meaning "sacrifice," is used in various connotations, implying ritual worship as well as the principle of sacrifice and surrender. As ritual worship, yajna involves offering materials such as clarified butter, grains, seeds, spices, and leaves and branches of certain sacred trees to the sacred fire, while chanting special *mantras* by trained priests in order to lead a moral and ethical life, one must be truthful. The concepts of morality may change from time to time, but truth is unchangeable. No one is able to conceal the truth permanently.

Shaucha (purity of body and mind): Purity is of two kinds: physical and mental. Physical purity means keeping one's body clean inwardly and outwardly. Inward cleaning can be promoted by following the laws of good health and consuming the *sattvic* foods (foods that promote health, mental power, strength, long life, and are soothing and nourishing-- see verses 7 through 10 of chapter 17 of the Bhagavad Gita). Outward cleaning implies wearing clean clothes and keeping the body clean. Mental purity means being free from negative thoughts of lust, greed, anger, hate, pride, jealousy, etc. According to the Hindu sages, mental cleaning can be accomplished through good association (*satsanga*) with wise, calm, and harmonious people. Study of scriptures and reflection upon the teachings of the sages and saints promotes the purity of the mind and keeps it free from fear, greed, hate, anger, and other disturbing sentiments.

Vidya (knowledge): Hindu scriptures declare that knowledge is of two kinds: the lower knowledge (*apara-vidya*) and the higher knowledge (*para-vidya*). The lower knowledge implies the worldly knowledge (in arts and sciences) which is necessary to live in the world. The higher knowledge is the spiritual knowledge which teaches one how to overcome an unexpected adversity, accomplish goals in spite of obstacles, and attain mental and spiritual strength to face the struggles of life. This spiritual knowledge can be acquired through study of scriptures, associations with holy people, and by performance of selfless work (*nishakama karma*). The spiritual knowledge helps an individual to lead a life that is individually rewarding, socially beneficial, and spiritually uplifting. The goal of the spiritual knowledge is the ultimate communion of the individual with God.

accordance with scriptural injunctions. Hindu sages tell us that sacred fire is the medium through which the material gifts offered as oblations are actually transformed into spiritual substance, which is received by the deity that is being worshipped.

As a principle of sacrifice and surrender, yajna involves the act of offering the best and the most useful one has for the welfare of others. The Rig Vedic hymn to the Supreme Being (*Purusha Sukta*, Rig Veda X.90) describes the creation of the universe by the Supreme Being, out of Himself, as an act of yajna (initial sacrifice). The entire creation functions on the principle of yajna, declares the Bhagavad Gita (BG 3.14 - 3.16). The waters sacrifice to form clouds, clouds to form rains, rains to grow food, and food sacrifices to feed the humans. The humans in turn must sacrifice to serve creation.

Yajna has both ethical and spiritual dimensions. Giving a worker his fair wages, sharing one's wealth with all those who are responsible for its growth, helping the poor and needy, resisting wickedness, and sharing knowledge and experience with others are all different forms of yajna. The food that we consume, the clothes we wear, and the means of transport available to us are all the result of the sacrifices made by others (i.e., other people's yajna).

Competition, cooperation, and yajna are the three components of human action. Competition alone is the basis of the animal behavior. Competition and cooperation are the characteristics of human life. When yajna is added to the human endeavors, divinity comes into play. Man is born to give and not to grab. One who takes more than he gives is called a thief (BG 3.12). A righteous man strikes a reasonable balance between giving and taking. An enlightened man is one who gives a lot more than he takes. "Whatever you offer to the Lord is returned to you, magnified many fold. Take care, therefore, that you do not offer anything bad to Him," advises Sri Ramakrishna. Just as fuel that gives away itself to the fire in turn becomes fire itself, a person who performs all his duties in the spirit of yajna becomes pure and divine himself. This is the spiritual dimension of yajna.

Sages tell us that when work is performed as yajna, the effect of that work is transformed into an invisible power, which in the Vedic terminology is called *apurva*. The sun burns itself for the welfare of creation. Thus, the work performed by the sun is yajna. Due to the sun's yajna, water converts into invisible water vapor, which forms clouds and eventually rain. The rain has the power to grow food and thereby sustain creation. In this example, heating of the water by the sun is yajna, and the invisible water vapor is *apurva*. In the case of a human being, the apurva is the spiritual power which is naturally developed as result of yajna. Thus yajna intensifies one's spiritual power, which in turn helps one to attain supreme good in life on earth and thereafter.

Ten Major Virtues

The philosophy of Hindu ethics may be summarized by the following ten major virtues, known as *Dharma Lakshanas*, in Manu Smriti, a Hindu scripture:

Akrodha (absence of anger): Anger clouds reason, resulting in a loss of discrimination between right and wrong and virtue and vice. When the discriminative faculty is ruined, the person loses self-identity and perishes, says the Bhagavad Gita (BG 2.63). An angry person hurts himself or herself and others in three different ways: physically (through violent actions), verbally (through harsh words), and mentally (through ill will). The control of anger must be practiced as an ideal in itself.

Asteya (non-stealing): Stealing is generally defined to be the taking away, by force or unjust means, of the property of another person(s). In the Hindu ethical system, stealing also includes hoarding over and above one's legitimate needs, obstructing other people's progress, taking away their opportunities, or acquiring something through illegal or immoral means. The lack of control over one's senses and one's greed usually generates an urge to steal. A person established in *asteya* is free from greed and thus has no urge to steal. Nature keeps him surrounded by an abundance of things he needs.

Atma vinigraha (control of the mind): A disturbed mind cannot distinguish right from wrong or virtue from vice. The art of concentration brings wisdom and in in-depth comprehension, improves memory, harmonizes thoughts and action and strengthens the mind. A strong mind protects an propagates moral and ethical values.

Dama (self-control or control of the senses): The sens must be controlled so that they can operate under the directi of reason. Self-control does not mean self-denial; it mea moderation in satisfying one's desires and avoidance indulgence. A man of self-control frees himself from lo talk, harmful gossip, over-eating, excessive drinking, keeps his body and mind under control. A slave of the ser cannot distinguish right from wrong. According to Bhagavad Gita (BG 2.62 and 2.63), attachment to senses ca longing for sense objects, which in turn ruins the discrim tive faculty. The lack of discrimination between what sh or what should not to be done leads to delusion. A delu man becomes unfit to realize the goal of life.

Dhee (purity of intellect): The purity of intellect is important than intellectualism. A man of pure intellect is from fear, bad temper, bad moods, and unpredictable b ior. Hindu sages tell us that pure intellect is espe promoted by the study of scriptures, contemplation on and noble thoughts, and regular meditation.

Dhriti (firmness or persistence): One must be fi one's convictions in order to discover truth. A wavering cannot reach truth. A virtuous life is possible only beca one's commitment to lead such a life.

Kshama (forgiveness or forbearance): Forgiven forbearance is the cardinal virtue of moral and ethic Forgiveness maintains the serenity of the mind e provocative situations in one's life.

Satya (truthfulness): *Satya* does not mean merely sp the truth. It means to be truthful in thoughts, wor deeds, and in our relationships with other human bei

What Hindu Religion is Not

Hindu religion, the oldest surviving religion in the world, has influenced non-Hindus of many cultures and backgrounds. Unfortunately, some of the books written in English by non-Hindus, many influential people of other religions who speak about Hinduism, and sometimes the media present a picture of Hinduism that is neither true nor objective. In general, there are three reasons for the misrepresentation of Hindu religion.

First, the religious and the metaphysical concepts of Hinduism, as expressed by Sanskrit words in Hindu religious writings, do not have an adequate translation in English or any other language. Moreover, many of the concepts themselves do not exist in Christianity or Western theology. For example, the Sanskrit words *dharma, maya, moksha, samsara, karma, sadhana,* and *Brahman* do not have technically adequate translations in English.

Second, the lack of an adequate understanding with regard to the essence of Hinduism has contributed to some of the misrepresentation of Hindu religion. In the absence of any dogmatic affirmations concerning the nature of God in Hindu religion, some non-Hindus are confused as to what Hindu religion is all about. For example, it may be difficult for some non-Hindus to understand how four different individuals can be called Hindus if one of them believes in Advaita (non-dualism), the second in Dvaita (dualism), the third in polytheism, and the fourth in atheism.

The third reason for the misrepresentation of Hinduism is that some authors obtain all their information about Hinduism from just one source. In doing so, they fail to do justice to a religion that does not draw its authority from a particular book or from a particular founder.

The intent of this chapter is not to address each and every misrepresentation of Hindu religion. The following, however, are some of the major aspects of Hinduism that have been commonly mistaken or confused:

The World, an Illusion

Persons unfamiliar with Hindu religion often believe that Hinduism regards the world as an illusion, and therefore does not encourage its followers to work diligently in this world. This misunderstanding arises when the Sanskrit term *maya* is inadequately translated as "illusion." Maya is the original ignorance (*avidya*) that causes the mind and senses to perceive the superficial diversity rather than the underlying unity of existence. All things and beings in the world are different manifestations of one Supreme Reality, known as *Brahman* in the Upanishads. The goal of Hindu religious life is to transcend maya and attain moksha, or union with God. Hindu religion's formula for transcending maya is dharma, artha, kama, and moksha (see chapter 32). This formula requires a person to perform all duties and live a life of righteousness (dharma) in the world, earn wealth (artha), and fulfill genuine desires (kama) before the fourth (and last) goal of moksha can be realized. The Bhagavad Gita expounds Karma Yoga, the discipline of action, in more verses (approximately 113 out of 700) than any other Yoga.

The life of Rama in the story of Ramayana (see chapter 30) is the Hindu ideal view of the perfect life in this world. The Mahabharata (see chapter 31) teaches that one must discharge one's duties and obligations. The Ramayana and the Mahabharata are not epics of inaction, but of responsibility and action.

Caste System

The caste system is often perceived to be an integral part of Hindu religion. This erroneous perception arises when people mix the ancient social tradition (caste system) with Hindu religious philosophy. When the Vedas refer to the four-fold division of society, they use the Sanskrit word *varna* meaning "class," and not the word *jati* meaning "caste." The word *varna* was mistakenly translated as "caste" by the Portuguese during their period of colonial establishment in India. This mix-up is quite significant because the Varna System of the Vedas (see chapter 4) was designed to achieve division of labor and help society operate efficiently. Varna was not conferred on an individual on the basis of his parentage. As stated in the Bhagavad Gita (BG 4.1), Varna was conferred on the basis of the intrinsic nature of an individual, which is a combination of the three gunas: *sattva, rajas, and tamas* (see chapter 4). Thus it is the combination of the gunas which established the identity of an individual in the Varna System. The following examples illustrate that the Varna System of the Vedas was based upon one's aptitude and natural capabilities (see *prakriti* and *gunas* in chapter 4) and not on the hereditary caste structure:

- Sage Vyasa, a Brahmin sage and the most revered author of the major Hindu scriptures, was the son of Satyavati, a low caste woman. Vyasa's father, Sage Parasara, had fallen in love with Satyavati, a fisherwoman, and had married her. Vyasa's deep knowledge of the Vedas later determined the caste of Vyasa as a Brahmin sage, and not his birth to a low caste fisherwoman.

- Sage Valmiki, the celebrated author of the epic Ramayana, was a low caste hunter. He came to be known as a Brahmin sage on the basis of his profound knowledge of the scriptures and his authorship of Ramayana.

- Sage Vidura, a Brahmin sage who gave religious instruction to king Dhritarashtra, was born to a low caste woman servant of the palace. His caste as a Brahmin sage was determined on the basis of his wisdom and knowledge of *Dharma Shastras* (scriptures).

Chapter 17

• The Kauravas and Pandavas were the descendants of
Satyavati, a low caste fisher-woman, and the sons of Sage
Vyasa. Vyasa's father was the Brahmin Sage Parasara,
the grandson of Sage Vasishtha. In spite of this mixed
heredity, the Kauravas and Pandavas were known as
Kshatriyas on the basis of their occupation.

In the Mahabharata, Yudhishthira defines a *Brahmin* as
one who is truthful, forgiving, and kind. He clearly points
out that a Brahmin is not a Brahmin just because he is born
in a Brahmin family, nor is a Shudra a Shudra because his
parents are Shudras.

In one of the most interesting stories in the *Chandogya
Upanishad*, Satyakama asks his mother, "I wish to receive
religious instruction, tell me of what family am I?"

The mother replies, "I do not know, my son. I was a
servant in my young age, moving from house to house, when
I conceived you. I do not know of what family you are. I am
Jabala and you are Satyakama. Say that you are Satyakama
Jabala." Satyakama went to the sage Gautama (not Buddha)
and said to him, "Sir, I wish to receive religious instruction
from you. Would you accept me as your student?"

"Of what family are you," asks the sage.

"I do not know, sir. In her young age my mother went
from house to house as a servant and conceived me. She does
not know of what family I am. My mother is Jabala and I am
Satyakama. Therefore, I am Satyakama Jabala."

"No one other than a true Brahmin would speak the truth
like this. I will initiate you," replies the sage.

Although Brahmins were generally initiated into higher
religious education, an honest character and not birth determined Satyakama's eligibility for religious instruction. This
shows that the practice of the Varna System was based on
conduct and character, not birth.

The Varna System must have started as analogous to
professional guilds, but as a result of exploitation by some
priests and socio-economic elements of society, this system
became hereditary and degenerated over the centuries. As
the Varna System became increasingly rigid and based on

inheritance, it was enveloped by another social system known as the caste system. Thus, this caste system determined the *social* structure of ancient Hindu society. The caste system could not have been a part of Hindu religious philosophy, since it violates fundamental Hindu doctrine, according to which there is no absolute distinction between individuals, since the same atman dwells in the hearts of all beings. Thus there is no religious sanction whatsoever to the concept of the caste system in Hindu religion.

330 Million Gods

Hindu religion is labelled as a religion of 330 million gods. This misunderstanding arises when people fail to grasp the symbolism of the Hindu pantheon. Hindus worship the nameless and formless Supreme Reality by various names and forms. Each god or deity is a particular manifestation of the one Supreme Reality (see chapter 4). Hindu religion can therefore be considered *monotheistic polytheism.*

According to Hindu religion, the Lord lives in each and every being as the atman. Thus each living being is an individualized and particularized manifestation of God. In ancient times it was believed that there were 330 million living beings. This gave rise to the concept of 330 million deities or gods. Actually, 330 million gods could not have possibly been worshipped, since 330 million names could not have been designed for them. The number "330 million" was simply used to convey a symbolic expression of the fundamental Hindu doctrine that God lives in the hearts of all living beings.

Women in Hindu Religion

Hindu religion has been occasionally criticized as encouraging inequality between men and women, towards the detriment of Hindu women. This inaccurate presumption again arises when people combine social and religious issues. In religious matters, Hindus have elevated women to the level of divinity. For example, only Hindus worship God in the form of Divine Mother. In Hindu religion the deities for knowledge, learning, and material wealth are female and not male.

The past social inconsistencies and injustices of women in
India have been a result of the social structure that did not
arise from Hindu scriptures, but from humans who failed to
correctly incorporate the teachings of the scriptures, such as
the Upanishads and Bhagavad Gita, into their social philosophy. (See also answer to Question 9 on page 367 for additional
discussion on this subject.)

Deity Worship is Not Idol Worship

Hindus are often labelled as idol worshippers by some
non-Hindus, especially the followers of the semitic religions.
Hindu deities are routinely called idols by the news media.
An intelligent examination of the Hindu view of God (see
chapter 4) shows that Hindu deity worship cannot be equated
with idol worship.

Webster's Dictionary defines idol as a "false god" or "a
form or appearance visible but without substance." Since a
Hindu deity represents a particular manifestation of the
Ultimate Reality (Brahman of the Upanishads), a Hindu deity
is as real as the Reality itself. The "substance" that the deity
represents is the Ultimate Relity and none other. Thus a
Hindu deity is neither a false god nor is it without "substance."
How can Hindu deity worship be called idol worship?

A sacred image used in Hindu worship symbolizes the deity
to be worshipped by the devotees. The image itself is not
God, but a symbol of God. Just as one associates the idea of
infinity with the image of the blue sky or the idea of holiness
with the image of a church, a mosque or a cross, a Hindu
associates his ideas of purity, truth, omnipresence, and omnipotence with the sacred images and forms.

It is interesting to note that when sacred images are used
in other religious traditions, they are called icons and regarded
as holy works of art; but when sacred images are used by
Hindus, they are called idols. In the words of Dr. David
Frawley, a Vedic scholar from the U.S., "An image of Christ
as the good shepherd is called an icon and viewed with respect.
An image of Krishna as the good cow herder--which is a
similar image of the Divine as watching over the souls of

men--is called an idol, which encourages one to look inferiorly upon it. This is the prejudice and negative stereotyping in language of the worst order."

There are two implications associated with falsely labeling Hindu deity worship as idol worship. Firstly, Hindus are looked down upon as idolaters and Hindu religion is denigrated as an idolatrous tradition. Secondly, such labeling "inflames the sentiments of anti-idolatry religions like Christianity and Islam, as both the Bible and Koran, at least in places, instruct their followers to oppose idolaters and smash their temples and images. The use of the term idol in the press, particularly in the Indian press, is thus careless, insensitive, inflammatory and communal," acknowledges Dr. Frawley.

Holy Cow

Hindu religion is often said to be the religion of the holy cow. But Hindu religion is also a religion of the holy bull (the bull is the vehicle of Shiva), the holy elephant (Ganesha has an elephant head), the holy monkey (Hanuman), and other animals. Actually, all animals are holy to Hindus. Seeing God everywhere, Hindus have a reverence for everything, plants and trees, rivers and oceans, cows and ants. The same atman that lives in a worm also lives in the heart of a human being. The only difference is in the level of manifestation of the atman in a particular body, depending upon the type of physical body. In a human body, the atman has the highest manifestation. This is why all living creatures are holy to a Hindu and ahimsa is an essential doctrine of Hindu religion.

One reason why Hindus treat cows with special reverence is that a cow has been traditionally perceived as a second mother of a child when her milk is fed to the child. As Mary is the mother of God to Christians, the cow to Hindus is the mother of life. Cows were also associated with the childhood of Lord Krishna, who was a cowherd boy himself.

Sometimes criticism is brought against Hindu religion stating that Hindu religion's taboo on cow slaughter and beef eating is responsible for India's poverty and starvation in some parts of the country. In his article on *Mother Cow*, Marvin

Harris challenges this criticism and shows that the religious rules to protect cattle in India are ecologically rational.[35] He shows that far from being parasites on Indian society, Indian cattle plow and produce fuel, milk, and hides, and without them agricultural life in India would be impossible.

Mythology is Not the Answer

Some of the confusion regarding Hindu religion is created by Hindus themselves, when Hindu mythology is relied upon in order to explain Hindu beliefs and practices. Mythology was developed to inspire the common people, allowing the masses to grasp the spiritual truths easily and without confusion. Mythology was not created to convince an inquisitive mind about the validity of one's religion. The following conversation between a mother and her 12-year old son illustrates the futility of relying on mythology to defend one's religious beliefs and practices:

Son: "Why do Hindus worship a god who does not have a human head (referring to a picture of Ganesha)?"

Mother: "Do not talk like that. Ganesha is the god of success and the remover of obstacles. He is the son of Lord Shiva."

Son: "How did Lord Shiva get stuck with an elephant-headed son? Since Shiva is God himself, could he not create a son with the proper head?"

Mother: "One day Parvati (Shiva's wife) was in her home alone. She wanted to take a bath, but there was nobody home to guard her privacy. She created Ganesha from a mold that she formed from the dust of her body. She instructed Ganesha to guard the main gate of the house. In the meantime Lord Shiva, who had been away from home, returned. Not knowing who Shiva was, Ganesha prevented Shiva from entering the house. Shiva was enraged for not being allowed to enter his own home. Angered, Shiva cut off the head of Ganesha and walked into his own home.

When Parvati came to know what had occurred, she begged Shiva to bring Ganesha back to life. Shiva ordered his servants to go into the forest and bring the head of the first creature they set their eyes upon. The servants saw an elephant in the forest, cut its head, and brought the elephant-head to Shiva. Shiva put the elephant-head on the body of Ganesha and brought him back to life. To restore respect and dignity to Ganesha, Shiva appointed him the god of success and the remover of obstacles. Shiva also ordained Ganesha to be worshipped first in all religious functions, before any other deity is worshipped."

Son: "This story of the creation of Lord Ganesha is unbelievable, in that God would become so angry so as to behead a child (see also Question 3 on page 237). How could the Lord, Who is supposed to be able to see all that is going on in the world without even moving from His abode, not know that His own wife had created a child? With all the power He is supposed to possess, why could He not put the same head back on the body instead of transplanting an elephant's head?"

Mother: No answer. (She was unable to come up with intelligent answers from mythology to the questions posed by her 12-year old son.)

Mythology may explain how a certain belief has arisen, but it cannot explain why the belief exists. Only philosophy can provide meaningful justification for religious beliefs and practices. Lord Ganesha is the son of Lord Shiva in mythology, but allegorically, he is only a symbolic representation of some of the highest ideals of Hindu scriptures. Refer to chapter 19 for a detailed discussion of the symbolism of Lord Ganesha.

Chapter 17

Questions and Answers
Part I

From 1990 to 1993 the author had an opportunity to address questions from students at several university campuses, as well as youth and adults at temples and community gatherings, on various aspects of the Hindu religious tradition. Many of these questions and their answers are included below, and in the similar sections at the ends of the other parts of this book. Some of these questions were also asked by the readers of the earlier editions of this work.

Q1. What does it mean to be a Hindu? What is the daily routine of a devout Hindu?

A. A Hindu is one who performs all duties and responsibilities associated with his (her) stage in life in accordance with Hindu scriptures. In addition to the duties and responsibilities pertaining to one's normal profession, a Hindu is enjoined by Hindu dharma to perform the following seven duties:

1. Worship the family deity (*Ishta-devata*--see chapter 4) through daily prayers and meditations, visit temples, and undertake pilgrimages. These practices are significant in assisting the devotee with his goal of becoming God-conscious in all daily activities.

2. Study scriptures and regulate one's personal and social life in accordance with their teachings. Recognize Four Goals, Three Debts, and Four Stages of Hindu religious life. Utilize the moral and ethical principles of the scriptures to accomplish *dharma, artha, kama, and moksha* (see chapter 32).

3. Believe in the basic doctrines of the Hindu religious tradition represented by the letters of the words *HINDU DHARMA* (refer to chapter 2)

4. Believe that all deities (gods and goddesses) are various forms of one Supreme Lord and that different religions and different paths are like different radii of a circle, each leading to the same center, representing the Supreme Lord.

5. Treat sages, saints, holy men and women, teachers, parents, and all elders with respect and reverence.

6. Help the needy, handicapped, sick, poor, and the less fortunate.

7. Serve guests with love, respect, and reverence.

The daily routine of a devout Hindu is to perform the five dharmas (*pancha maha yagnas*), as discussed under *Grhastha ashrama* in chapter 32.

Q2. *Is Hinduism a religion or a way of life?*

A. Hinduism is both a religion as well as a way of life. In a sense, every religion is a way of life. As a religion, Hinduism is called *Sanatana Dharma*, meaning eternal religion or righteousness. Unlike other religions, Hinduism did not originate from a single founder or prophet. Instead, Hindu religion is based upon the superconscious experiences of a galaxy of *rishis*, each of whom could have claimed prophethood. The Hindu religion is based upon the teachings of the Vedas and comprises eternal values of life--a botanical garden of human virtues that is free from religious dictatorship and dogma. Freedom of thought is the main feature of the Hindu religious tradition.

As a way of life, Hindus consider all of mankind as one big family of the Supreme Lord. Hindu religion teaches non-violence, recommends vegetarianism, and emphasizes respect and reverence for the elderly. Hindus are taught to

respect all elders in and outside the family. To a Hindu,
everything in the universe, animate or inanimate, is divine,
and non-violence is a direct consequence of this broad view
of divinity. A premium is placed on personal character,
personal and social responsibilities of an individual, chastity
in marriage, and family values. Simple living and high
thinking is the hallmark of the Hindu way of life. Refer to
Question 2 on page 359 for a discussion of the major
characteristics of Hindu culture.

*Q3. Non-vegetarianism is a highly debated topic in Hindu
religion. Some justify non-vegetarianism on the basis that
Hindu scriptures, as they claim, do not prohibit eating meat.
Others argue in favor of vegetarianism, but cannot find
adequate scriptural support for their position. In view of this
confusion, please explain what position Hindu scriptures have
taken on this issue? If I am not a vegetarian, can I still be
called a Hindu?*

A. Yes, if you are not a vegetarian you are very much a
Hindu. No one loses Hindu religion by being a non-vegetar-
ian.
    Hindus treat the cow as the second mother of humanity.
Just as a human mother feeds her child, milk products
derived from the cow can feed all of humanity from birth to
death. For this reason, Hindu scriptures (Manu Smriti 5.56)
prohibit eating cow-meat (beef). Apart from this prohibition,
there are no direct religious injunctions in Hindu scriptures
against eating other kinds of meat. Although meat-eating is
not directly prohibited, Hindu scriptures *strongly* recommend
vegetarianism for living a healthy, happy and holy life while
not causing injury to any living creature (Mahabharata
18.115.8, 18.116.37-41, 115.40 and 115.47, Mahabharata
Shantiparva 262.47, Bhagavad Gita 13.27-28, and Tirukural
260, 312, 321, and 324--see Chapter 15 for additional scriptures). For reasons stated in Chapter 15, vegetarianism is the
hallmark of the Hindu religious tradition.
    Hindu scriptures say, "*jeevo jeevasya jeevanam*," meaning
"one life form can only survive by consuming another life

form." No one can survive by eating sand. This being the case, there is a wide spectrum of life forms that one can eat. In deciding what one should eat and what one should not eat, a human being is expected to use compassion. Thus depending upon the level of compassion, one may select certain foods and reject others. There are two extremes in this process. With zero compassion, one could eat a fellow-being. With infinite compassion, one may end up drinking milk only. Leaving aside both of these extremes, Hindu religion expects each human being to exercise his or her own level of compassion in deciding what to eat and what not to eat.

The Vedic people were meat-eaters. When their level of compassion diminished, giving rise to excessive animal sacrifices, Jainism appeared in India as a movement of compassion toward all forms of life. Jainism raised the level of human compassion in India and the doctrines of ahimsa and vegetarianism became firmly rooted in Hindu religion. Some Jains, however, went even further. They would also not eat fresh fruits or vegetables. They would eat only those fruits or vegetables that were ripe and fell from the trees and plants themselves.

Although there is no direct scriptural injunction in Hindu religion against non-vegetarianism, other than the one against eating cow-meat, a majority of Hindus are vegetarians because of the many benefits of vegetarianism as discussed in chapter 15.

Q4. Most of the Hindu beliefs and practices take authority from the primary scriptures, the Vedas, the Upanishads (a part of the Vedas) and the Bhagavad Gita. What about the secondary scriptures (such as Puranas, the two epics, and Agamas)?

A. Not most, but all Hindu beliefs and practices take authority from the primary scriptures. In the event of a question or conflict between the primary and the secondary scriptures, the primary scriptures govern.

The secondary scriptures (see chapter 3) were written by various sages, saints, and holy persons at different times to

interpret, illustrate, and expound teachings of the primary
scriptures for the benefit of the general population, who
could not comprehend the higher teachings of the primary
scriptures. The primary scriptures are the soul of Hindu
religion.

The purpose of the secondary scriptures is to regulate
individual and social life, from time to time, in accordance
with the eternal principles of the primary scriptures. Like a
living organism, Hindu religion responds to the environment
and adapts itself to the needs of the hour. The necessary
adjustments are incorporated by sages and saints in the form
of new laws and new secondary scriptures. This flexibility
has allowed Hindu religion to survive thousands of years.
Unlike the ancient Greek and Roman societies that arose,
lived, and died, Hindu society has survived through onslaughts of time. The backbone of Hindu society has been
the Hindu religious tradition, which is humanity's oldest
religion.

*Q5. The Bhagavad Gita teaches that one must work without
attachment to the fruits of one's actions. In real life the fruits
of one's actions are the incentives that drive one to work. In
practical life, is it possible to work without attachment? If a
student did not care about the fruits of his or her school
activities, what would motivate him or her to attain excellence?*

A. The philosophy of work taught by the Bhagavad Gita is
the philosophy of duties and responsibilities. In this system,
everyone in society is supposed to perform duties for the sake
of duties. The fruit that comes must be used as a *means* for
the discharge of the duties. The *means* include maintenance
of the individual's physical body, his household, and other
needs that he or she must satisfy in order to live a normal life.

If everyone in society performed his or her duties very
well, the rights and privileges of all individuals in that society
would be met spontaneously. For example, I have a right to
own a nice house, educate my children, and live a comfortable
life. If the builder of my house performed his work well, the
teachers performed their duties well to bring excellence to the

educational system, and everyone else in society performed his or her work well, my rights and privileges would be automatically satisfied. In this system of work, the performance of duties and responsibilities by individuals ensures the rights and privileges of others. There is no incentive for immoral and unethical conduct in performing work. One performs one's duties in the service of the Supreme Lord and without waiting for the fruits of action. A society based upon this philosophy will naturally be moral and ethical.

The philosophy of work taught by the Bhagavad Gita does not promote unfair competition. Every individual is supposed to do the best he or she can and establish excellence as a goal. Thus, excellence is itself the incentive in this system of work. This does not mean that an individual should not study, plan, and set goals for one's actions. In fact, without these steps there would be no excellence possible in work.

The philosophy of work that exists in much of Western culture is the philosophy of rights and privileges. In this system, the driving force for action is the fruit of action itself. That being the case, an individual can justify any means to reach the end. A society based upon this system is bound to enter into a *rat-race* without regard for other fellow-beings. The hunger for the fruits of action can force an individual to use immoral and unethical means to accomplish the end. Thus, a society based upon this philosophy runs the risk of being immoral and unethical.

Take the example of two students, number 1 and 2. Both are students in chemistry. Student 1 wants to acquire a good understanding of chemistry. He is not particularly concerned about the grades he may receive, but he wants to understand the fundamentals of chemistry so that he can eventually attain a deep understanding of the subject. He spends time studying in the library, discusses the subject with his peers, regularly consults his teachers, and always completes his homework on time.

Student 2 wants to be number 1 in class by obtaining the highest grades, regardless of what it takes. He also visits the library and reads the books and journals, but whenever he finds a useful book in the library, he hides it so that no one else can find it, lest someone else should get higher grades than he. He also thinks of many other mischiefs to beat his competitors in class.

In the above example, student 1 is unaware of his competition. He achieves the highest grades in class because of his excellent knowledge of the subject. He is also loved and respected by all. Student 2 becomes frustrated because he fails to be number 1 in class. Even if Student 1 did not achieve the highest grades, he does not become frustrated, since his only goal is to perform with excellence, regardless of whether or not he received the fruits of his work (i.e. the highest grades.

The philosophy of work taught by the Bhagavad Gita is based upon common sense and human nature, as studied by the ancient sages. The sages say that one who is attached to the fruits of his or her actions is more likely to become frustrated when the fruits do not arrive as expected. On the other hand, one who is not attached to the fruits of actions, but strives for excellence in work is more likely to receive better results. Thus, one must study, plan, and set goals, but not be attached to the fruits of one's actions. One's best performance should be the goal for work and excellence should be the incentive that drives one to work.

Q6. I am an engineer by profession. I draw a salary and support my family. The incentive for my work is the raise in the salary that I receive at regular intervals. My boss is very happy with my work and I have been receiving decent raises. Am I attached to the fruits of my actions? If so, what am I supposed to do to comply with the teachings of the Bhagavad Gita?

A. Yes, you are attached to the fruits of your actions. The following example will explain this:

Attachment or detachment to the fruits of action are two different modes of one's own mental attitude (*bhavana*). Take the example of two engineers, number 1 and 2. Both are equally qualified, work in the same office, perform more or less the same work, and draw pretty much the same salary each. Both are married, have children, and maintain independent households. Engineer 1 thinks that he needs more and more money to support his family. In his view the family is the goal and the job is the means. He is generally preoccupied with thoughts of how much money he is earning now, how much he will be making in the future, and how much more other people in the office are earning. He does not mind occasionally asking his friends how much they are earning.

Engineer 2 takes a different attitude. He wants to do an excellent job in his office and is always thinking about the ways and means to improve the quality of his work, control wastage in the company, and bring more efficiency to the working environment of his company. He thinks that if he can help the company, by his efficient performance, to keep their production costs low, the company can make their products available to more people at a reduced cost. This would be his contribution to serve the people, and through his service to the people he would be serving God. He thinks that for him to work efficiently in his office he must have a happy family behind him. To him, the family is the means and his job is the goal.

In this example both engineers are doing the same thing. Both are earning just about the same money and both are using their salaries to support their families and discharge other responsibilities. The only difference is in their mental attitude. For engineer 1, the family is the goal and the job is the means, whereas for engineer 2, the job is the goal and the family the means. It may be said here that engineer 1 is attached to the fruits of his actions, whereas engineer 2 is not, and the latter is in compliance with the teachings of the Bhagavad Gita. Thus, one's mental attitude determines one's attachment or detachment to one's actions.

Now let us look at the practical side of this example. Engineer 2, who is actually detached from the fruits of his actions, more likely will make a higher salary than the other engineer. Since engineer 2 is dedicated to his job, and is working hard to improve his performance, his efforts are more likely to be recognized and compensated by his company than those of engineer 1. This shows that the philosophy of work taught by the Bhagavad Gita, based upon excellence as an incentive as well as the goal, is far superior than the philosophy of work that is based upon material incentive.

Q7. With numerous scriptures, religious philosophies, codes of laws, and innumerable forms of worship, what does Hindu religion actually represent?

A. Hindu religion is like a fruit tree, with its roots representing the Vedas and the Upanishads, the thick trunk symbolizing the spiritual experiences of numerous sages and saints, its branches representing various theological traditions, and the fruit itself, in different shapes and sizes, symbolizing various sects and sub-sects. The major features of Hindu religion are its unity behind the apparent diversity of views, freedom of thought, doctrine of ahimsa, respect and reverence for all religions, and belief in the divinity of the human race. Unlike other religions, Hindu religion does not claim a monopoly on wisdom, engage itself in false propaganda to degrade other religions, and does not approve of forcible conversions.

Hindus look upon the whole world as one family. With open arms, they welcome all people of all religions as their brethren. They respect the scriptures of other religions and revere their prophets. Hindu scriptures say that the cows may be of different colors, but the milk of all the cows is of one color.

Q8. Christians tend to view their religion as the only one which boasts a kind, loving, and most importantly, a personal God. They claim that the God of the Hindus is cold and impersonal, and the person who follows Hindu religion is alone in the world. How does one respond to such criticism?

A. First, we must understand that there is only one God and He is God of all religions. If He is kind and loving to Christians, He cannot be cold and impersonal to non-Christians. We may call Him by different names and worship Him in various forms, but "*He is the One, the One alone. In Him all deities become One*," declares the Atharva Veda.

Unlike many other religions, Hindu religion is a God-loving and not a God-fearing religion. Hindus worship God both as Father and Mother. To a Hindu, God is very personal, as declared by Lord Krishna in the Bhagavad Gita:

"I am the Father of this universe. I am the Mother of this universe, and the Creator of all. I am the Highest to be known, the Purifier, the holy O M, and the three Vedas. I am the Way, and the Master who watches in silence; thy friend and thy shelter and thy abode of peace. I am the beginning and the middle and the end of all things...." (BG 9.17 and 9.18)

Q9. If each human birth is the result of the actions of past karma, what determined the first human birth in the series of births?

A. According to Hindu religion, the universe has existed eternally in cycles. There never was a time when the universe did not exist. Whenever the words *beginning* and *end* appear in Hindu scriptures, they refer to the beginning and end of a particular cycle.

At the beginning of a given cycle of creation, the past karma of the soul is the catalyst for the human birth in that cycle. Upon attaining a human body, karma accumulates due to the operation of maya and binds the soul to material existence.

Q10. If whatever we do is the result of our past actions, is not karma just another name for fate?

A. If fate means something inevitable that is determined and controlled by supernatural power, then karma and fate are not the same. Karma is the effect of one's past deeds. In Hindu view, God does not create an individual's fate or destiny. The individual himself, by virtue of his own actions, determines his fate or destiny. Past deeds determine the present and the present deeds will determine the future, in accordance with the Law of Karma.

Q11. If the present life is determined by our past karma, how can there be any free will?

A. The answer to this question can be found in the following words of Dr. S. Radhakrishnan: "The cards in the game of life are given to us, we do not select them. They are traced to our past karma, but we can call as we please, lead what suit we will, and as we play, we gain or lose. And there is freedom." Refer also to the discussion of destiny and free will in chapter 13.

Q12. If one must reap the fruits of all of one's good and bad deeds, how can there be moksha, since even good deeds will bring fruits and keep the individual bound to the physical world?

A. According to the doctrine of *nishkama karma*, actions performed without desire for fruits and in the spirit of complete surrender to God do not subject an individual to the effects of karma. In other words, good deeds that are performed with the desire to reap the fruits of such deeds would still subject one to the effects of karma. As stated in the Bhagavad Gita:

> "He who performs actions, surrendering them to Brahman and abandoning all attachment, is not polluted by sin, as a lotus leaf is not polluted by water." (BG 5.10)

Q13. By what mechanism does karma operate on future births?

A. The subtle (also called astral) body is the medium by which the soul transmigrates from one body to another. Refer to the discussion under the Immortality of the Soul in chapter 13.

Q14. Could you describe the process of reincarnation?

A. As explained in chapter 13, the soul possesses three bodies, physical, astral, and causal. Upon death the soul leaves the physical body and enters the astral world in its astral body. The astral world is a spiritual world of light and joy where each soul finds its own place such that the surroundings and the conditions reflect the kind of life it has pursued on earth. The soul lives in the astral world until its next incarnation on earth. An individual's allotted span in the physical and astral worlds is predetermined by Nature in accordance with the Law of Karma. In the astral world the soul undergoes experiences to fulfill some of its earthly desires which it did not have an opportunity to satisfy on earth.

When the soul's allotted span in the astral world is over, the soul returns to the physical world to be reincarnated again. It chooses a home and the family which can best fulfill its evolution in accordance with its karmic history. For a detailed discussion of the astral world and how the soul lives in that world refer to chapter 43 of *Autobiography of a Yogi*, both listed in Suggested Readings.

Q15. Why do Hindus reject the idea of the atonement of sins and adhere to their theory of karma?

A. Hindus do not reject the idea of seeking God's grace for alleviating human misery. Sri Krishna says:

"Abandoning all duties, take refuge in Me alone. I will liberate thee from all sins; grieve not." (BG 18.66)

Hindus believe that mere atonement alone is not enough. O ne must perform righteous work as well. In Hindu view, the universe is governed by God's laws, both physical and spiritual. A violation of these laws brings human misery. We experience this fact in our daily lives. If we violate the laws of good health, we become sick and suffer. The law of gravity has no mercy for anyone (even a saint!) who decides

to jump from the top of a cliff. A man who has committed a
murder may tell the judge in court, "Sir, I am sorry. I will
not do it again." Will the judge, even if he is exceedingly
merciful, let the man go because he expressed remorse for his
sins?

Hindus believe that violation of God's laws is handled by
Nature in accordance with the universal law of justice, known
as the Law of Karma in Hindu religion. In Hindu view, God
does not punish anyone, since He is too merciful for this. We
punish ourselves through our ignorance (BG 5.15) and we
cannot blame God. He has established His laws and we have
no choice, but to follow them.

Karma is basically a form of energy. We project this
energy to our surroundings through our thoughts, words,
and deeds. Because of the law of conservation of energy, the
energy we project returns to us, in time, as fruits of our
actions. The Law of Karma is the divine law of justice, and
like gravity, it treats everyone the same.

Q16. Are Hindus saying that Jesus Christ suffered on the Cross because of his past bad karma?

A. No. All prophets and incarnations are the messengers of
God. They are liberated souls (*jivanmuktas*) and they come on
earth not because of their karma, but because of their
compassion to aid the suffering of humanity. The actions of
the liberated souls are pure, free of attachment and are not
subject to the Law of Karma (BG. 5.7).

Q17. Does Hinduism have commandments?

A. The term "commandments" implies religious directives
dictated by a person (generally the founder of the religion) or
a single book (usually the scripture of the religion). Since
Hinduism does not have a single founder or a single scripture, the term "commandments" is generally not used in
Hindu religious literature. Instead, the term "doctrines" is
normally used to illustrate Hindu religious beliefs and practices. Although there are numerous doctrines in Hindu

scriptures, the following are considered the major doctrines of Hinduism:

Ten Major Doctrines of Hindu Religious Thought

- "Truth is one, wise call It by various names." (Rig Veda 1.164.46)

- Just as the rain water that falls from the sky eventually reaches the ocean, so also the worship by any name and form finds way to the Supreme. (Mahabharata)

- Each human being is potentially divine. The goal is to manifest one's divinity by controlling nature, external and internal. This is the whole of religion. (Swami Vivekananda)

- "All of mankind is one family." (Hitopadesh; Subhashita Ratna Bhandagare)

- Law of Karma (*As you sow, so shall you reap*). (Mahabharata Shantiparva 299.42; BG 18.60)

- "That mode of living which is founded upon total harmlessness towards all creatures or [in case of actual necessity] upon a minimum of such harm, is the highest morality." (Mahabharata Shantiparva 262.5-6)

- Whenever there is a decline of virtue, God incarnates Himself on earth to uphold righteousness. (BG 4.7, 4.8)

- The one who destroys dharma is annihilated. The one who protects dharma is protected by dharma. (Mahabharata Vanaparva 313.128)

- There is nothing like wisdom which can make us pure on this earth (BG 4.38) "Let the noble thoughts come from all sides." Acquire knowledge, put it into practice, gain wisdom, and then distribute it freely.

- Knowledge, sacrifice, service and renunciation-in-action are the guiding principles of Hindu life. (Hindu Scriptures)

Ten Major Doctrines of Conduct

- Surrender your mind and heart to the Lord. Be *atman*-conscious rather than body, mind, and intellect-conscious. See God in whatever you see. (BG 6.31, 8.7, and 18.65)

- Perform all your duties in the spirit of service to the Lord. Renounce selfishness and never abandon your duties for fear of pain. (BG 4.20, 5.10, 9.27, 18.4 to 18.8 and 18.12)

- Perform all thy work without expectation of reward. (BG 18.9)

- "You must not use your God-given body for killing God's creatures, whether they are human, animal or whatever." (Yajur Veda Samhita 12.32)

- "Speak the truth; do not fail to pay attention to truth...." (Taittiriya Upanishad 1.11) "There is nothing higher than truth...." (Mahabharata Shantiparva 109.4-5)

- "It is sinful to covet the property of others, taking what has not been given, abusing others by speaking untruth, and talking idly...." (The Laws of Manu)

- "Let your mother be treated like a god; let your father be treated like a god; let your teacher be treated like a god." (Taittiriya Upanishad 1.11)

- One must not neglect one's duties and responsibilities or commit adultery. (The Laws of Manu X.24)

- "That act or exertion by which others are not benefited, or that act in consequence of which one has to feel shame, should never be done...." (Mahabharata Shantiparva 124.65-6)

- "Righteousness is what prevents injury to creatures; righteousness is what leads to advancement and growth...." (Mahabharata Shantiparva 109.9-11)

Q18. *Hindu religion teaches four main spiritual paths-- Bhakti Yoga, Karma Yoga, Raja Yoga, and Jnana Yoga--for self-realization. Are any of these paths better than the others?*

A. No. None of these paths is better than the others and none is exclusive either. No one can live without performing work (BG 3.8) and one cannot perform any significant work in life without proper knowledge of, devotion to, and concentration on that work. Take the case of an engineer who designs and manufacturers radios. Before he can do his job he must have the right knowledge (*jnana Yoga*) of how a radio operates. During the design process he must concentrate (*Raja Yoga*) on his work and every step of his way he must be dedicated, and love (*Bhakti Yoga*) and enjoy what he is doing. Thus we see that although from an overall standpoint this engineer may be called a *Karma Yogi*, he needs to combine all the above four yogas to perform his work successfully.

All the above four spiritual disciplines have a common destination. O ne may choose any one of these paths as an overall discipline to suit his or her bent of mind. But the individual must use the other three to support the major discipline chosen, since none of these paths is complete to the exclusion of the other three.

Q19. The Bhagavad Gita teaches that one should perform one's duty, but should not expect the fruits of one's efforts. The Satyanarayana Puja story guarantees instant desired reward. Please reconcile these two apparent contradictions.

A. The doctrine of *adhikara* (see Q4 on page 275) requires that the religious instruction for an individual should be graded to match the spiritual competence of the individual. The work without attachment taught by the Bhagavad Gita is the highest spiritual discipline for attaining *moksha*, the goal of Hindu religious life. This spiritual discipline may not (and it does not) correspond to the spiritual competence of every individual in society. There are many people who are not much interested in *moksha*, but wish to perform righteous work. They want to offer sincere prayers to the Lord for attaining success in their work. The *Satyanarayana Puja* offers a method of offering such prayers to the Lord for attaining success in a given venture.

Q20. What are sins and what are their prescribed penances?

A. The Hindu definition of sin is very comprehensive. It includes several views that range from the ancient belief that sin is a disease to the most exalted one which holds that sin is a denial of the soul or betrayal of the self. Other views describe sin as a self-centered desire, breach of dharma, or lack of spiritual harmony. Hindus divide sins into three groups: sins of thought, sins of the word, and sins of deed. To a Hindu an evil thought or harsh word is as much of a sin as a wicked deed. According to the Bhagavad Gita, lust (*kama*), anger (*krodha*), and greed (*lobha*), known as the "the triple gate of hell," are the root causes of all sins:

> "Triple is the gate of hell, destructive of the soul--lust, anger, and greed. Therefore one should forsake these three. The man who escapes these three gates of darkness and works for the good of his soul, reaches the supreme goal." (BG 16.21-16.22)

➤ The recommended penances for sins are giving alms, fasting, performing religious rites prescribed in the scriptures, and performing selfless service for the poor and needy. Penances do not turn the sinner away from sins. They are confirmatory rites that show the sinner's repentance and public confession after he or she has turned away from sins. What turns away a sinner from sins is the change of heart that must come from within. Such a transformation is possible with a proper spiritual environment, right knowledge, and constant association with the pure and holy. As said above, the penances purify the sinner only after he has turned away from sin.

Q21. What are the cardinal virtues of Hindu religion?

A. The Hindu theory of ethics is much the same as that of any other civilized nation. But if Hindus have anywhere distinguished themselves, it is in their special emphasis on purity (of body and mind), truthfulness, non-violence, sacrifice (obligatory duties enjoined by scriptures), self-control, and renunciation (*in* action and not *of* action). These six virtues are the distinctive marks of the religious spirit of Hindus. Refer to chapter 16 for a detailed discussion of the Hindu theory of ethics.

The concept of sacrifice has dominated the entire Hindu view of life. The Sanskrit word for sacrifice is *yajna*, but *yajna* does not mean killing, as may be construed by the word sacrifice. Yajna (see also page 140) means "playing one's role in life to help sustain the functioning of the universe." The form and extent of sacrifice have varied from time to time, but its underlying principle has endured for ages.

Q22. Is there a Hindu diet code?

A. As explained in chapter 15, the Bhagavad Gita (BG 17.7-10) divides all foods on the basis of their inherent characteristics and spiritual compatibility. Foods such as cereal, rice, barley, wheat, beans, mustard seeds, coconut, milk, curd, clarified butter, and the numerous fruits, grains, pulses, nuts, and vegetables have all along been recommended foods for Hindus. Foods such as fish, flesh, and eggs are considered detrimental to the mental tranquillity necessary for meditation and worship.

Q23. All religions have some strengths and weaknesses. What are the strengths and weakness of Hindu religion ?

A. The major strengths of Hindu religion are its adaptability, recognition of the potential divinity of the human race, freedom of thought, universal outlook, non-violence, freedom from religious dictatorship and dogma, and reliance on reason to support its beliefs and practices.

There are no weaknesses in Hindu religion as far as religious philosophy is concerned. Sometimes criticism is brought against Hindu religion stating that it has not provided political and economic stability to India. Critics attribute India's poverty and political chaos to Hindu religion. To this effect, Dr. Radhakrishnan replies, "Let us frankly recognize that the efficiency of a religion is to be judged by the development of religious qualities such as self-confidence, inner calm, gentleness of the spirit, love of neighbor, mercy to all creation, destruction of tyrannous desires, and the aspiration of spiritual freedom, and there are no trustworthy statistics to tell us that these qualities are found more in efficient nations [other religions]."[16]

According to Dr. Radhakrishnan, "It is not right to complain that India has failed because she has followed after things spiritual. She has failed because she has not followed after them sufficiently. She has not learned to make spirit entirely the master of life, but has created in recent times a gulf between spirit and life and has rested in a compromise. Some of our holy men are inclined to become creatures set apart, beings who take flight from the temporal in order to cling to the heart of the eternal. If, in our eagerness to seek after God, we ignore the interest of humanity, we may produce a few giants but will not elevate the race. We have shown how high individuals can rise by spiritual culture and how low a race can fall by its one-sidedness."[17]

One mistake of Hindus in India in the past has been that they did not take to the cult of the nation. As Dr. Radhakrishnan said, "We did not make our country a national goddess, with an historic destiny, a sacred mission, and a right of expansion. We did not worship Mother India (*Bharat Mata*) as others do: e.g. 'Britannia,' 'La France,' 'The Fatherland.' We did not tell the people that the enemy of India is the enemy of God, and if the enemy said he, too, had a god, he could only be a false god. All the same, Indian culture has failed to give political expression to its spiritual ideals. The importance of wealth and power to give expression to spirit, though theoretically recognized, was not practically realized. India has suffered for this negligence."[18]

Q24. Is it difficult to learn and practice Hindu religion? If so, what should be done to resolve such difficulties?

A. Hindu religion, a religion essentially free from dogmatism, is easy to learn and follow, provided one approaches it with an open mind. There are five problem areas one should be aware of in studying Hindu religion. These are discussed below:

Diversity: One often fails to see the underlying unity amidst the bewildering variety of Hindu sects and sub-sects, with their own customs, symbols and forms of worship, and amidst many schools of philosophy and systems of theology, with their different texts and scriptures and their commentaries, and commentaries on commentaries. It is sometimes difficult for a beginner to understand how four persons can all be Hindus when one of them is a monist (advaitist), another a dualist, third an atheist, and fourth a ritualist, busy in his rituals. One should understand that Hindus are not Hindus because they believe in one scripture or they worship together in one church. They are Hindus because there is underlying unity in their religious life. The following five elements contribute to such unity: common scriptures, common deities, common ideals, common beliefs, and common practices.

Unique Concepts: One of the major difficulties in understanding Hindu religion correctly is that the original religious concepts were developed in Sanskrit and this language has lost its stature as the primary language among the general population. These religious concepts are unique to Hindu religion and cannot be adequately translated word for word into English or any other language. Concepts such as *Brahman, maya, gunas*, and *prakriti* do not exist in Western theology or other religions. One-word translations into English that most authors provide do not convey the true meanings, thus causing confusion and misunderstanding. The student of Hindu religion should be aware of this problem and should try to understand these concepts correctly and not depend entirely on their one-word translations.

One of the best examples of this problem is the word *yajna*, which has been often translated as *sacrifice*. The word *sacrifice* in rituals has the connotation of animal-killing, and thus *yajna* is construed to mean animal sacrifice. *Yajna* actually means giving alms, giving gifts to the needy, or surrendering something for the sake of something else. In Hindu view, proper functioning of the universe needs a balance between the opposing forces operating in the universe, and everyone should perform yajna (i.e. play his or her appointed role in life in accordance with one's dharma) to help maintain the necessary balance. See also discussion of unique concepts in answer to Question 21 above.

Symbolism: Hindu religion uses symbolism extensively to illustrate and explain the profound teachings of the scriptures, which otherwise cannot be grasped by the general population. Sometimes criticism is brought against Hindu symbolism in that it does not use real symbols. For example, Goddess Lakshmi is shown sitting on a lotus flower (see chapter 24) and a question is raised as to how someone can sit on a flower. The student of Hindu religion should remember that in Hindu symbolism, the reality of the symbol itself is not considered. What is important is the message the symbol conveys.

Scriptures: This can be a major problem area for the beginner. There are many scriptures, in at least eight different categories, with numerous texts in each category. A beginner is lost as to what he or she should study and how much to study in the limited time available these days. A detailed indexing of the major scriptures including the Vedas, the Bhagavad Gita, the Upanishads, the epics, and the Laws of Manu is needed to solve this problem. Without such indexing, it is almost impossible for a beginner to know what Hindu scriptures contain. For example, many of us are unaware that a gold mine of Hindu wisdom is buried in one section of the Mahabharata, called *Shantiparva*.

The indexing should be detailed enough to allow the student of Hindu religion to easily identify those sections of all major scriptures that apply to his or her area of interest. For example, if a student wants to know what Hindu scriptures say regarding women's rights and the role of women in Hindu society, he or she should be able to consult an index and identify all applicable scriptures with their chapters, sections or paragraphs pertaining to the rights and privileges of women in Hindu society. This work is needed to make accessible the wisdom of the Hindu sages to all future students of Hindu religion .

Mythology: Hindu *philosophy* and not *mythology* is the basis of Hindu religious beliefs and practices. Mythology was developed to inspire the common people, allowing the masses to grasp the spiritual truths easily. There are some stories in the Puranas that appear to establish superiority of one sect over another or that of one deity over another.

During the periods of conflict between various cults and sects of Hindus in India, unfortunately many interpolations were introduced into the original Puranas to establish the superiority of one god over another or that of one sect over another. It is now difficult to correctly identify the old text from the new additions that were incorporated when the fever of sectarianism rose high in India. Therefore, such stories that attempt to establish superiority of one god over another or that of one sect over another should be ignored altogether.

Q25. Why do Hindu scriptures insist on having a guru? Isn't it possible to attain spiritual perfection without a guru?

A. To achieve spiritual progress without a guru is theoretically possible, but practically very difficult. In this age of *kaliyuga* (see chapter 2) where material thoughts have established a strong hold on the individual, the guidance of a spiritual master is highly recommended by scriptures in order for an individual to attain self-realization. In Sanskrit, the syllable *gu* means "darkness or ignorance," and *ru* means "dispeller or remover." A guru gives initiation (*diksha*) to a pupil and guides the pupil on his or her spiritual path.

If the disciple is compared to a traveler, where self-realization is analogous to one's final destination, the guru can be called the traveler's guide, who provides a detailed road map leading to the destination, as well as other helpful instructions. The guru may walk side-by-side with the traveler to guide the journey, but a guru cannot lift the traveler on his own shoulders and simply deliver him or her to the final destination. Thus the guru's role is limited to providing a correct road map and the necessary instructions.

Q26. What should be done to get Hindu youth interested in their heritage?

A. We must act individually as well as at the community level. Individually, never stop youth from asking questions. The basis of Hindu religious principles and practices is not mythology, but philosophy. Therefore, answer questions based upon philosophy, while quoting mythology, as appropriate, to cite examples to illustrate the philosophy. Explain the purpose of religious sacraments before you ask youth to participate in religious rites and ceremonies. Blind faith and dogma are alien to Hindu religion, which is essentially a tradition of study, learning and experimentation.

Religious education must be imparted to a child when he (or she) is young so that the child can grow up with good character and convictions. All members of the family should worship the family deity (*Ishta Devata*) together daily through *puja, bhajans,* prayers, and meditation. A family that prays together stays together. It is important to implant good tendencies (*samskars*) in children when they are young.

At the community level, Hindus must address the following important issues:

• Establish community facilities to educate ourselves and our youngsters regarding Hindu heritage. Innovative ways must be developed to make learning Hindu religion fun for the youth and young adults.

• Develop new traditions for the Hindu community to work and learn together. These new traditions could be regular talks and seminars on Hindu dharma nationwide, pilgrimages, festivals, and performance of common *samskars*, such as birth, marriage, and death. Using religious practices from Bharat (India), Hindus should learn to develop and share some common traditions, leaving aside linguistic differences, customs and personal preferences. In the long run, the future generations will benefit from such common traditions.

- Create awareness about our heritage in local communities through programs such as inviting neighbors, friends and colleagues to religious functions and festivals.

- Be volunteers at local schools to teach Hindu Dharma, culture and history. Be volunteers at local libraries and hospitals and serve the needy through community projects.

- Last, but not the least, learn to deal with distorted information about Hindu heritage in text books and in the media.

Q27. What is the difference between r̥tam and satyam, as in the common prayer: r̥tam vadiṣyāmi, satyam vadiṣyāmi?

A. *R̥tam* means "the lower truth" and *r̥tam vadiṣyāmi* means "I will speak the lower truth." *Satyam* means "higher truth" and *satyam vadiṣyāmi* means "I will speak the higher truth." What is lower truth? The truths that we normally speak during our daily lives in this phenomenal world (samsara) are called lower truths or worldly truths, since they are associated with the transient nature of this world. The lower truths are perceived by the mind and senses and are a part of our dharma. Our adherence to these truths helps us to eventually transcend the mind and senses and attain the higher truth, that is satyam. The higher truth is that the only reality is Brahman and this world has only a relative existence. In the Upanishads, the higher truth is indicated by statements such as *aham Brahmasmi* (I am Brahman), *tat tvam asmi* (that thou are) and *sarvam khalvidam Brahma* (everything is Brahman).

Q28. What is important, one's country or one's religion?

A. Religion and country cannot be separated. If religion is worship, country is the deity, the Mother Goddess to be worshipped. If there is no deity, there is no worship. The defense of the homeland and protection of her honor is the essential part of the Vedic tradition, as is clearly stated in the following verse of the Rig Veda:

"When in my dwelling-place I see the wicked enemies of gods, O King (the god Soma), chase their hatred away. O Bounteous One, dispel our foes."
(Rig. VIII, LXVIII: 9)

The above verse affirms that one's homeland is the dwelling place of gods and must be protected from the enemies, (internal and external) at all costs. First try to "chase their hatred away," that is bring reason and logic into their heads. If they persist in their wicked ways, banish them from the land.

Q29. What is the significance of performing homam/havan?

A. A *homam* or *havan* creates a sacred environment for divine contemplation and removes mental contaminants, such as lust, craving, restlessness, fear, worry, anger, and jealousy. These are the practical benefits which can be derived from religious rites and sacraments, when they are observed with sincerity and devotion. From the standpoint of Hindu scriptures, a *homam* or *havan* accrues the highest religious merit (*punya*).[25e]

Q30. How does one focus his/her mind and keep it from wandering?

A. The mind wanders due to uncontrolled indulgence in the sense objects, or by harboring the thoughts of insecurity and fear of both known and unknown. A major cause of mental restlessness is the lust and craving for sense objects (BG 2.60, 2.67, and 2.70). The sages tell us that the mind is always looking for permanent peace and permanent peace does not arise by satisfying one's desires, but from the desirelessness itself. Only temporary peace results when a desire is fulfilled. Some of our desires are a biological necessity. There is nothing wrong with having genuine desires and working towards their fulfillment in one's life. Thus, the first step for focusing the mind is to intelligently screen one's desires, let go the unnecessary ones, and entertain only the genuine desires.

The second step is to practice some sort of dispassion in one's daily life. We must learn to act and offer all the fruits of our actions to our Ishta Devata (family deity), and to accept the results as prasad (Divine Grace). Thus our actions (karma) coupled with devotion (bhakti) facilitates detachment in life. All our actions are propelled by desires rooted in our emotions. As we learn to surrender the fruits of our actions to the Lord, our hearts are filed with bhakti and emotions transformed to devotion, thus eliminating unnecessary worries. In modern society, worry kills more people than work itself.

The mind attains peace, intelligence, and wisdom through regular practice of yoga, meditation, religious rites and ceremonies, worship of the Ishta Devata, presence of God (japam or kirtan), study of the lives and teachings of the great souls, study of scriptures and holy books, satsangh (holy company), working for the good (not pleasure) of others, social service, and prayers with deep yearning in the heart for God (BG 6.35).

Food plays an important role in our mental development and constitution. O ne must consume sattvic foods (vegetarian diet including milk products) and perform physical exercises regularly. If the body is not healthy, the mind cannot be peaceful. Food is an important factor for the peace of the mind. The Chandogya Upanishad says that the food we eat affects us in three different ways. The gross component of the food becomes the excrement. The subtle component is transformed into flesh, blood and the bones, and the subtlest component of the food makes up our minds. When the food is pure, the mind becomes pure. High-protein and high-calorie (tamasic and rajasic) foods contribute to mental restlessness, whereas the sattvic foods (BG 17.7 through 17.10) contribute to mental peace, and wisdom.

Last, but not the least, one must live a life of moderation.
The mind cannot be peaceful if one's lifestyle is based upon
the extremes. Too much food or too little food, too much
sleep or too little sleep, too much work or too little work, too
much meditation or too little meditation, too much rest or too
little rest are not conducive to a peaceful mind (BG 6.16 and
6.17).

*Q31   Hindus say that the Vedas are revelations. If they are
revelations, how do you explain the shift from many gods in the
early Vedic texts to the monism of the Upanishads?*

A. Vedas are *apaurusheya*, meaning that they "have no human
origin." Vedas are not revelations in the Biblical sense, but
insights into the Cosmic Law (*Dharma*), which transcends
personalities and temporal events. Hindu religion retains
many gods (note small g) as different names and forms of the
One Ultimate Reality (*Brahman* of the Upanishads). There is
both monism and pluralism in the Vedic and Hindu view,
unlike Biblical traditions that have an exclusive monotheism
that is intolerant of pluralism (many gods) and of monism
(the idea of the Supreme Self or *Parabrahma* beyond God or
Ishvara).

*Q32.   Hindus say that the Reality is the oneness of Brahman
and that Moksha (liberation from the cycle of birth and death)
is attained by realizing that the concept of an individual self is
an illusion.   How do you respond to Descarte's assertion: "I
think, therefore I am"? If our problem is metaphysical (what
we are) and not moral (what we do), what is the basis for
morality in Hindu/Vedic tradition?*

A. Thought implies consciousness and is dependent upon it.
Therefore, in the Vedantic view the correct principle is "I am,
therefore, I think." What is consciousness? Exploring consciousness is what the Vedic quest is all about. This is both a
metaphysical and a moral or ethical concern, because consciousness implies unity, which presumes an ethical and moral
code in life.

Part II
Symbolism of Hindu Deities

You are all gods, if you only knew it. Self-realization is the knowing—in body, mind, and soul—that we are one with the omnipresence of God; that we do not have to pray that it come to us, that we are not merely near it at all times, but that God's omnipresence is our omnipresence; that we are just as much a part of Him now as we ever will be. All we have to do is to improve our knowing.

(Paramahansa Yogananda}

Chapter 18
Significance of Symbolism

Just as a work of art reflects the imagination of an artist, symbolism in religion expresses the attributes and the qualities of Reality as conceived by the seekers of Truth. Viewed from the impersonal aspect, Reality is devoid of qualities and attributes and is beyond the reach of thought. From the personal aspect, Reality has infinite attributes, such as omnipresence, omnipotence, love, and compassion. The infinite attributes and qualities of Reality are symbolized in Hindu religion in various ways, such as pictures, images and icons of deities. The religious and spiritual teachings are symbolized as well in religious rituals and as sacred articles used in worship.

The teachings of the Upanishads are subtle and sometimes beyond the comprehension of an average person. Symbolism helps such a seeker to concentrate his (her) mind on the worship and meditation of God. Just as a map is used by a traveler as an aid for reaching his destination, symbolism is used by a devotee as an aid in comprehending the Infinite Reality, and for traveling on the spiritual path to his final destination of union with God.

Symbolism in Hindu dharma is sublime and profound. Each act of Hindu worship reflects some deep spiritual significance as illustrated in chapter 14. If correctly understood, symbolism greatly aids a devotee in realizing the spiritual goal. The beauty and efficacy of religious rituals cannot be appreciated without proper knowledge of the significance of such acts. Symbolism in Hindu religion is a subject that can occupy a volume of its own. The purpose here is to illustrate the significance of some of the common symbols, icons, and sacred articles used in Hindu religion. The subsequent ten chapters explain the symbolism of some of the popular Hindu deities.

- **Anjali:** A gesture of reverence and greeting, in which two palms are softly held together and slightly cupped. Anjali held near the chest is used to greet equals, at the eye level to greet the elders and guru, and above the head to offer salutations to God.

- **Bilva** (weed-apple or bael tree): Bilva leaves are considered very auspicious for the worship of Lord Shiva.

- **Bindi** or **bindu** (*tilak*): Hindus wear a tilak (a red dot by women and an elongated dot by men) on their foreheads, between the two eyes. This point, known by various names such as *Ajna Chakra*, Spiritual Eye, and Third Eye, is said to be the major nerve center in the human body. In ancient times, Hindus used red lead powder (*sindhoor*) or sandal-wood paste to place dots on their foreheads. According to Hindu sages, red lead and sandalwood paste have cooling properties. Therefore, placing a red lead or sandalwood paste dot on the forehead between the eyes cools the nerve center associated with that location. The sages tell us that, consequently, the mind becomes calm and quiet. The tilak is also a reminder of the wedding vows. The most popular is the red tilak worn by Hindu married women to symbolize their marriage and the wedding vows. The religious significance of tilak has been largely forgotten these days and it is now used more for fashion than for religious reasons.

- **Camphor:** When camphor is lit, it burns and leaves little or no residue behind. This illustrates that spiritual knowledge (symbolized by the light of the camphor) completely purifies the mind of a devotee, leaving no impurities behind. The fragrance of the camphor also disinfects and purifies the air at the place of worship.

- **Coconut**--see page 129.

- **Cow** is the symbol of Mother Earth, which nourishes and sustains life. This symbolism arises from the fact that cow's milk is like that of a mother's milk to a child. In Hindu dharma, Mother Earth is revered as a deity and is called by

various names such as Goddess *Bhumi* or *Prithvi.* The
sanctity of the cow has been maintained by Hindus since the
Rig Vedic times. In Hindu dharma, all animals are held in
special regard, as many of them serve as vehicles (*vahanas*)
of the Hindu deities.

- *Dhupa* (incense): The fragrance of dhupa symbolizes the
  force with which sense objects attract the mind. The
  burning of dhupa symbolizes the destruction of the craving
  for sense objects. The fragrance of dhupa also spiritualizes
  the environment, symbolizes the love of God, frees the mind
  from worldly distractions, and helps it to concentrate during
  meditation and worship.

- *Dhvaja*, a red or orange flag or banner flown above the
  temples, is a symbol of victory over unrighteousness and a
  reminder that "righteousness will ultimately prevail."

- *Ghanta* (bell): The ringing of a bell during prayer or
  worship eliminates distracting sounds and helps the mind
  to concentrate on the object of worship.

- *Kalasha* is a pot of water (pitcher, jar, etc.), topped with
  mango leaves and a husked coconut, and used in a puja to
  represent the deity to be worshipped. Kalasha is also the
  name given to the pot-like spires installed at the top of a
  temple roof.

- *Kamandalu* (water pot), an earthen or wooden water pot
  carried by a *Sadhus* (holy persons), symbolizes freedom from
  worldly attachments and intense desire to seek the Divine
  through a spiritual discipline.

- *Kuttuvilaku*, the standing lamp used in temples and shrines
  for puja, symbolizes the divine light that dispels *avidya*, the
  main cause of human bondage in the world.

- **Lotus flower** symbolizes spiritual knowledge and power.
  The lotus grows out of mud, unfolds into a beautiful flower,
  lives in water all the time, but is not wetted by it. This
  conveys the idea that a spiritual aspirant, while living in the

world, should remain unaffected by the worldly attractions, and should work towards spiritual unfoldment.

- **Mango** leaves and mango fruit symbolize auspiciousness and the happy fulfillment of the genuine human desires.

- *Namaskara* or *pranama*: To greet another person, a Hindu joins his (her) hands with palms together, bows down in front of the other person, and says, *"namaskara," "namaste"* or *"pranama."* In Hindu view, the Supreme Being dwells in the heart of each being as the *atman.* The joining of hands symbolizes the idea that in the meeting of two persons, the Self actually meets Itself. Joining hands also symbolizes humility. Thus when a Hindu joins his (her) hands and says *namaskara*, he actually says in humility, "I bow to God in you; I love you and respect you, as there is no one like you."

- *Paduka*, the sacred sandals worn by sages, saints, and *Sadhus*, is the traditional icon of the guru. Holy sandals represent the holy feet of the guru and are worshipped as the source of guru's grace, since in the presence of a guru, one traditionally bows down and touches his or her feet as a form of reverence.

- *Rudraksha*, meaning "eye of Rudra or Shiva," are the marble-sized, multi-faced reddish brown seeds of the Rudraksha tree (*Eleocar-pus ganitrus*), which grows in the Himalayas. A garland of Rudraksha beads (*Rudrakshamala*) is considered very auspicious for japa (recitation of mantra) and meditation. Holy persons, especially the devotees of Lord Shiva, wear the *Rudrakshamalas* on the ear-lobes, around the wrists, on the crown of the head, or around the neck to give special potency to the mantra chanted.

- **Saffron** color symbolizes purity, simplicity, and renunciation of worldly desires. Thus the flags on temples as well as the clothes worn by spiritually advanced people are usually of the saffron color.

- *Salagramas* or *Saligramas*, natural formations of stones in the Gandaki river in Nepal, are used to represent different incarnations of Lord Vishnu during worship and puja. The origin of the word "*Salagrama*" is traced to a remote village, called Salagrami, near the source of the river Gandaki in Nepal, where Lord Vishnu is lovingly called "*Salagrama*."

- **Shankha** is the conch shell (found in sea water) in the form of a multiple spiral, evolving from a single point into ever increasing spheres. Shankha thus symbolizes the origin of the universe from a singular source (*Brahman*). The sound of a conch is the same as the sound of the sacred syllable O M (see chapter 29). This sound spiritualizes the environment for worship or religious ceremony. A conch is blown during religious rites, ceremonies, worship and prayer in temples and shrines.

- **Shatkona** is a "six-pointed star" formed by two interlocking triangles. The three sides of the top triangle denote *sat* (absolute existence), *chit* (absolute consciousness), and *ananda* (absolute bliss). Thus, the top triangle symbolizes the unmanifested Reality. The three sides of the bottom triangle represent God, *atman*, and the world. Thus, the bottom triangle denotes the manifested Reality. The interlocking of the two triangle conveys the idea that the two aspects of the Reality are eternally connected.

- **Shivalinga**, meaning "Shiva symbol," is the main object of Shiva worship in temples and shrines. It consists of three parts. The bottom part which is four-sided remains under ground, the middle part which is eight-sided remains on a pedestal, and the top part which is actually worshipped is round. The three parts symbolize Brahma at the bottom, Vishnu in the middle, and Shiva on the top. The word *linga* is derived from the two Sanskrit words *laya* (dissolution) and *agaman* (re-creation). Thus, shivalinga symbolizes that entity in which the creation merges at the time of dissolution and out of which the universe reappears at the beginning of the new cycle of creation. The linga symbolizes both the creative and destructive power of the Lord and great sanctity is attached to it by the devotees.

Chapter 18

- **Swastika,** meaning "it is well," is the symbol of auspiciousness, prosperity, and good fortune. The four limbs of the Hindu swastika denote the four Vedas (symbolizing auspiciousness), four goals of life (denoting prosperity), four stages of life (signifying good fortune), four directions in space (symbolizing the Divine omnipresence), four seasons (symbolizing the cyclic nature of time), and four *yugas* of the world-cycle (symbolizing the natural evolution of the universe; see chapter 2). The Hindu swastika should not be confused with the Nazi swastika, which has a different design and a totally different meaning.

- **Tripundra,** literally meaning "three marks," is the sectarian mark of the devotees of Lord Shiva. Tripundra is comprised of three horizontal stripes of holy ashes (*vibhuti*) on the brow with a dot (*bindhu*) at the third-eye (center of forehead). The three stripes serve as a reminder of the three causes of human bondage: duality, *karma*, *maya*. Vibhuti (see below) symbolizes the transient nature of the physical body and the urgency to strive for spiritual perfection.

- **Trishula** is the three-pronged scepter Lord Shiva uses to destroy evil and the evil-doers. It symbolizes the three fundamental powers of the creative process: will (*iccha*), action (*kriya*), and knowledge (*jnana*).

- **Tulasi** plant is a very holy plant among Hindus. Its leaves are used for the ceremonial worship of Lord Vishnu. Tulasi plant is praised as destroying the evil of the present age and it is considered a bad omen to break its branches. Growing a tulasi plant in or outside one's home is considered very auspicious. The curative effect of the juice of tulasi leaves is well recognized in the Ayurvedic system of medicine.

- **Urdhvapundra,** a sectarian mark of the devotees of Lord Vishnu, is comprised of three vertical lines on one's forehead (two white lines with a red line in the middle). The white lines symbolize Lord Vishnu's footprints, resting upon a lotus base. The red line symbolizes Goddess Lakshmi, the divine consort of Lord Vishnu.

- **Vata**, the banyan tree, symbolizes the Hindu religious tradition. The roots of the banyan tree represent the Vedas, Upanishads and other scriptures. The trunk symbolizes the unity in diversity of the Hindu philosophy, and the numerous branches, in various sizes and shapes, symbolize the diverse sects and subsects of Hinduism.

- **Vahana:** The Sanskrit word *Vahana* denotes an animal, bird or a human being, used as a carrier (vehicle) for Hindu deities in Hindu mythology. Hindus offer worship to deities along with their vahanas. The pictures and images of the vahanas are generally placed next to their deities in temples, home shrines and all places of worship.

- **Vibhuti** is the holy ash prepared by burning cow dung along with sacred materials, such as milk, ghee and honey, during religious rites and ceremonies. Vibhuti symbolizes renunciation and purity. When burned, most things are reduced to ashes. The ashes, therefore, symbolically denote the transient nature of the phenomenal world. Placing vibhuti on one's forehead is a reminder that one must not be selfish and greedy, accumulating wealth merely for one's personal use. Instead, one must share wealth with his fellow beings, since we are all members of the universal family of the Lord. Vibhuti is considered very auspicious and is placed on the forehead for attaining purity of the heart and mind.

Significance of Puja

In Hindu dharma, *puja* is the most common form of ceremonial worship for honoring God (in the form of a picture or an image). Puja symbolizes a devotee's desire to offer love and devotion to the Lord, thereby surrendering his or her individuality to Him. Hindu dharma recognizes self-surrender as a supreme path to salvation. In a *puja*, a devotee decorates an image or a picture of one or more forms of God with clothes, flowers, garlands, and fragrant paste, and offers water, flowers, and foods of different kinds. A typical *puja* involves the following sixteen steps. With each step appropriate verses are read from a variety of scriptures:

1. Avahana (invocation): the worshipper invites the deity to the ceremony.
2. *Asana*: the deity is offered a seat.
3. *Svagata* (greeting): the devotee greets the deity.
4. *Padya*: the devotee symbolically washes the feet of the deity with sacred water.
5. *Arghya*: water is offered for symbolic cleaning of the deity's hands and face.
6. *Acamaniya*: the water is offered for sipping.
7. *Madhuparka*: the deity is offered the water/ honey drink.
8. *Snana or abhisheka*: the water is offered for symbolic bathing. If submersible, the image may be bathed.
9. *Vastra* (clothing): a cloth is wrapped around the deity and ornaments affixed to the form.
10. *Anulepana or gandha*: perfumes and/or ointments are applied to the image.
11. *Pushpa*: flowers are laid before the image, or garlands are draped around it.
12. *Dhupa*: incense is burned before the deity.
13. *Dipa or arati*: a burning lamp, lighted camphor and/or incense are waved in front of the deity.
14. *Naivedya or prasada*: sattvic foods (BG 17.8) such as fruits and foods cooked using rice, wheat flour, milk, clarified butter, and sugar, are offered to the deity. The remaining food is believed to be blessed by the deity and is later distributed to the devotees as *prasada*.
15. *Namaskara or pranama*: the devotees bow or prostrate before the image of the deity to offer homage.
16. *Visarjana or udvasana*: the ceremony ends, the deity returns to its heavenly abode, and the sacred food (*prasada*) is distributed to the devotees.

Chapter 18

Chapter 19
Lord Ganesha

Lord Ganesha, also called Ganapati or Vinayaka, is a Hindu deity (god) that in popular images and pictures is presented in the form of a human body with the head of an elephant. This blend of human and animal parts is a symbolic representation of a perfect human being, as conceived by Hindu sages.

In his images and pictures, Ganesha is depicted holding various objects in his hands, as illustrated in Figure F-6. Several other objects are also displayed in front of or around him. These objects, as well as the image of Ganesha himself, symbolize some of the highest ideals of the Hindu scriptures. The following are only the major symbols of Lord Ganesha, and a brief explanation of what they represent:

Elephant head, wide mouth, and large ears: the large head of the elephant symbolizes wisdom, understanding, and a discriminating intellect that one must possess to attain perfection in life. The wide mouth represents the normal human desire (as in the craving for savory foods) to enjoy life in the world. The large ears signify that a perfect human being is one who possesses a great capacity to listen to others and assimilate their ideas.

The trunk and two tusks with the left tusk broken: there is no known human instrument that has an operating range as wide as that of an elephant's trunk. It can uproot a tree and yet lift a needle off the ground. Similarly, the human mind must be strong enough to face the ups and downs of the external world and yet delicate enough to explore the subtle realms of the inner world. The two tusks denote the two sides of the human personality, wisdom and emotion. The right tusk represents wisdom and the left tusk represents emotion. The broken left tusk signifies that in order to attain perfection, emotion must be conquered with wisdom. In the mythology,

Ganesha is said to have written the epic Mahabharata with his broken left tusk, as was dictated to him by Sage Vyasa.

Elephant eyes: elephant eyes are often said to possess natural deceptiveness that allows them to perceive objects to be bigger than they really are. Thus the elephant eyes symbolize the idea that even if an individual gets bigger and bigger in wealth and wisdom, he should perceive others to be bigger than himself; that is, surrender his (her) pride to the Lord and attain humility and humbleness.

The four arms and various objects in the four hands: the four arms symbolize the four directions and indicate that the Lord is omnipresent and omnipotent. Ganesha carries a small axe in his upper right hand and a rope in his upper left hand. The Lord, when approached by a devotee, cuts his (devotee's) worldly attachments (symbolized by the axe), pulls him away (symbolized by the rope) from worldly temptations, and sets him on the path of Truth. The sweet ball (*laddu*, a popular food item) in the lower left hand indicates that he bestows peace and prosperity on his devotees. The lower right hand is shown in a blessing pose. This illustrates that Ganesha always blesses his devotees.

A human body with a big belly: the human body possesses a human heart, which is a symbol of kindness and compassion toward all. Ganesha's body is usually portrayed wearing red and yellow clothes. Yellow symbolizes purity, peace and truthfulness. Red symbolizes the activity in the world. These are the qualities of a perfect human being that is performing all the duties in the world, but with purity, peace, and truthfulness. The big belly conveys the idea that a perfect individual must have a large capacity to face all pleasant and unpleasant experiences of the world.

A mouse sitting near the feet of Ganesha and next to fresh food: a mouse symbolizes the human ego that can nibble everything good and noble in man. A mouse sitting near the feet of Ganesha indicates that a perfect man is one who has conquered his ego. A mouse sitting near fresh food, but not eating it, conveys the idea that a purified or controlled ego can live in the world without being affected by the temptations

LORD GANESHA

FIGURE F-6

of the world. The mouse is also the vehicle of Ganesha, signifying that one must control ego for wisdom to shine forth.

By worshipping Ganesha, a Hindu seeks God's blessings for achieving success in one's endeavors in the physical world and for attaining perfection thereafter. Since perfect success in all religious acts as well as in worldly affairs is the goal of all human beings, Hindus worship Ganesha to seek God's blessings before beginning such activities (see Popular Prayer below). For this reason, Ganesha is worshipped first in all religious functions and ceremonies.

In Hindu mythology, Lord Ganesha is the son of Lord Shiva and Goddess Parvati (a form of Goddess Durga). The other son of Shiva is Karttikeya, the Lord of Righteousness, who protects dharma by destroying evil. Karttikeya is also known as Kumara, Skanda, Subramanya, Shanmukha, or Muruga. Shanmukha (depicted as a six-headed deity, symbolizing five senses and the mind) signifies that five senses and the mind must be in harmony for mental, intellectual, and spiritual growth.

Subramanya has two consorts, Valli (symbolizing *jnana shakti*, the power of knowledge) and Devasena (symbolizing *kriya shakti*, the power of action). The vehicle of Subramanya is a peacock. The peacock is a bird whose behavior is unpredictable, as its moods are influenced by weather conditions. A peacock therefore symbolizes ego, which causes unpredictable behavior in human beings. The use of the peacock as a vehicle is intended to convey the idea that control of the ego is necessary for spiritual growth.

Popular Prayer to Lord Ganesha:

Om shuklam-bara-dharam vishnum, shashi-varnam chatur-bhujam. Prasanna-vadanam dhyaayet, sarva vighno-pashaan-taye.

Lord Ganesha, who is all-pervading, the embodiment of purity, who possesses an ever smiling face, a bright complexion (like a full moon) and four hands; to that deity, I pray for the removal of all obstacles.

Chapter 19

Chapter 20
Lord Brahma

Lord Brahma symbolizes the aspect of the Ultimate Reality (Brahman of the Upanishads) that is responsible for the creation of the universe. For this reason Brahma is called the Creator of the universe. He is the first member of the Hindu Trinity (see Figure F-17) that also includes Lord Vishnu and Lord Shiva. His divine consort is Saraswati, the goddess of learning and knowledge. She provides him with knowledge that is necessary for the purpose of creation.

Brahma is usually conceived of as a bearded, four-faced, four-armed deity. He carries a rosary in the upper right hand, a book in His upper left hand, a *kamandalu* (water pot) in His lower left hand, and holds His lower right hand in a grace-bestowing pose (see Figure F-7).

The *four faces* symbolize the sacred knowledge of the four Vedas (Rig, Yajur, Sama, and Atharva); this is the most prominent feature of any image of Brahma. Thus the four faces convey the idea that Brahma is the source of all knowledge necessary for the creation of the universe. The *four arms* represent the four directions and thus symbolize the omnipresence and omnipotence of Brahma.

The *four hands* symbolize the four parts of an individual's personality: mind (back right hand), intellect (back left hand), ego (front right hand), and the empirical self or conditioned consciousness (front left hand). The *rosary* symbolizes the time cycle through which the world moves from creation to sustenance, from sustenance to dissolution, and from dissolution to new creation. The rosary also symbolizes the materials used in the process of creation. Its position in the back right hand suggests the intelligent use of these materials in the process of creation.

A *book in the hand* symbolizing intellect (the back left hand) conveys the idea that right knowledge is important for any kind of creative work. A *water pot* (kamandalu) in the front left hand symbolizes the cosmic energy by which the Lord brings the universe into existence. The *hand symbolizing ego* (the front right hand) is shown in the pose of bestowing grace. This signifies that the Lord bestows grace and protects all those who surrender their ego to the Lord.

The color gold symbolizes activity and thus the *golden face* of Brahma indicates that the Lord is active when involved in the process of creation. The *white beard* denotes wisdom and the long beard conveys the idea that creation is an eternal process. The *crown* on the head of the Lord implies that the Lord has supreme power and authority over the process of creation.

The *lotus* symbolizes spiritual power, the creative power of the Ultimate Reality, the essence of all things and beings in the universe. Brahma sitting or standing on a lotus indicates that He represents the creative power of the Ultimate Reality. The color white symbolizes purity. Thus Brahma wearing *clothes that are off-white* represents the dual nature of creation, that is purity and impurity, happiness and unhappiness, vice and virtue, knowledge and ignorance, and so on.

In Hindu mythology, a *swan* is said to possess a unique discriminating faculty which enables it to distinguish pure milk from a mixture of milk and water. The swan is therefore used to symbolize the power of discrimination. Brahma uses the swan as a vehicle. This is intended to convey the idea that although creation is pluralistic in nature, there is only one Supreme Reality that the entire universe emanates from. This knowledge can be acquired by training one's mind and intellect to acquire the power of right discrimination.

As creation is the work of mind and intellect, Lord Brahma symbolizes the Universal Mind. From the standpoint of an individual, Brahma symbolizes one's own mind and intellect. Since an individual is naturally gifted with the mind and intellect, he or she may be said to have already realized Brahma. For this reason the worship of Brahma is not very popular among all Hindus (see also Question 1 on page 236). He is, however, worshipped by seekers of knowledge, such as students, teachers, scholars and scientists.

Chapter 20

LORD BRAHMA

FIGURE F-7

Chapter 21
Lord Vishnu

Lord Vishnu symbolizes the aspect of the Supreme Reality (Brahman of the Upanishads) that preserves and sustains all things and beings in the world. Although there are some variations in images and pictures of Lord Vishnu, He is generally symbolized by a human body with four arms. In His hands He is portrayed (see Figure F-8) carrying a conch (*shankha*), a mace (*gada*), and discus (*chakra*). He wears a crown, two earrings, a garland (*mala*) of flowers, and a gem around the neck. He has a blue body and wears yellow clothes. The Lord is shown standing on a thousand-headed snake (named Shesha Nag). The snake stands with its hoods open over the head of the Lord.

The *four arms* symbolize the four directions and indicate that the Lord is omnipresent and omnipotent. The two front arms signify the lord's activity in the visible (physical) world and the two back arms signify His activity in the spiritual (invisible) world. The right side of the body represents the activities of the mind and the intellect. The left side symbolizes the activities of the heart; that is, love, kindness, and compassion.

A *conch* in the upper left hand indicates that the Lord communicates with His devotees with love and understanding. When blowing His conch, He reminds his devotees to live in this world with kindness and compassion towards all living beings. A *chakra* in His upper right hand conveys the idea that the Lord uses this weapon to protect His devotees from evil. The *mace* denotes energy and a mace in the Lord's left lower hand signifies that He sustains the manifest world by the energy that He holds in Himself. His front right hand is depicted bestowing grace on His devotees.

The *snake* denotes the mind and the thousand heads of the snake signify the innumerable desires and passions of an

FIGURE F-8

individual. Just as a snake destroys its victim by its venom, an uncontrolled mind destroys the world by the venom of its possessiveness. The Lord has controlled all desires, and this is symbolized by showing Him seated or standing on the two coils of the snake. When a sincere devotee of the Lord controls his desires, the Lord fulfills the devotee's genuine desires and helps him on his path.

Some scholars use the snake to symbolize time. Just as a victim cannot escape when caught in the coil of a snake, mortal beings cannot escape the clutches of time. Since time and space are interconnected, the two coils of the snake can also represent time and space. Thus the Lord standing on the two coils of a snake denotes that He is beyond the reach of time and space.

The *blue sky* in the background of the Lord suggests that He pervades the entire universe. The blue color (e.g. of the sky) symbolizes infinity. The blue body of the Lord signifies that He has infinite attributes. He is nameless, formless, and immeasurable. The color yellow is associated with earthly existence and the *yellow clothes* of the Lord signify that He incarnates Himself on this earth to uphold righteousness and destroy evil and unrighteousness.

A *flower garland* around the Lord's neck is a symbol of the devotee's adoration for the Lord. A *gem* decorating His neck signifies that the Lord fulfills all genuine desires of His devotees and provides for their needs. The *crown* is a symbol of the Lord's supreme power and authority. The *two earrings* signify the dual nature of creation, such as knowledge and ignorance, happiness and unhappiness, and pleasure and pain.

The worship of Lord Vishnu is very popular among Hindus, especially among the followers of the Vaishnava tradition (Vaishnavism). He is the second member of the Hindu Trinity (see Figure F-17), which also includes Lord Brahma and Lord Shiva. Lord Vishnu is also known by other names, such as Vasudeva and Narayana. The following ten incarnations of Lord Vishnu are described in Hindu mythology and are popular among Hindus. These incarnations reveal the help rendered by God during various stages of human evolution. As shown below, the first two incarnations are in the animal form, the third one is half-human and half-animal, and the fourth and the subsequent ones are all in human form. These incarnations relate to human evolution, from aquatic life to human life, and are consistent with the modern theory of evolution suggested by science:

- Matsya (fish)--saves Sage Manu from floods and recovers the Vedas from demons.

- Kurma (tortoise)--sustains the earth on his back.

- Varaha (boar)--brings the earth back from the bottom of the ocean where it was dragged down by a demon, known as Hiranyaksha; Varaha kills the demon.

- Narasimha (man-lion)--kills the demon King Hiranyakashipu, who was planning to kill his own son, a devotee of Lord Vishnu.

- Vamana (dwarf)--the first human incarnation of the Lord; kills the demon King Mahabhali, who had deprived the gods of their possessions.

- Parasurama (the warrior with an axe)--saves Brahmins from the tyranny of the arrogant Kshatriyas.

- Rama--kills Ravana, the demon king of Lanka.

- Sri Krishna--the most popular incarnation; Krishna's contributions throughout his life include the teachings of the Bhagavad Gita to Arjuna.

- Buddha--Hindus consider Buddha as an incarnation of Lord Vishnu and accept his teachings, but do not directly worship him.

- Kalkin (a man on a white horse)--this incarnation is yet to come and will mark the end of all evil in the world.

Chapter 22
Lord Shiva

Lord Shiva is the third member of the Hindu Trinity (see Figure F-17), which also includes Lord Brahma and Lord Vishnu. Lord Shiva represents that aspect of the Supreme Reality (Brahman of the Upanishads) which continuously re-creates, in the cyclic process of creation, preservation, dissolution and re-creation. He annihilates evil, grants boons, bestows grace, destroys ignorance, and awakens wisdom in His devotees. Since the tasks of Lord Shiva are numerous, He cannot be symbolized in one form. For this reason the images of Shiva vary in symbolism. The symbolism discussed here includes only a few major symbols that are common to all pictures and images venerated by Hindus.

In His images, Lord Shiva is depicted in a human form (see Figure F-9). His body is naked and covered with ashes. The *naked body* indicates that He is free from attachments to the material things of the world. Since most things reduce to ashes when burned, ashes symbolize the essence of all things and beings in the world. The *ashes* on the body of the Lord signify that He is the source of the entire creation which emanates from Him.

Lord Shiva is depicted as having *three eyes*. The two eyes on the right and left side indicate His activity in the physical world. The third eye in the center of the forehead symbolizes knowledge (*jnana*), and is thus called the eye of wisdom or knowledge. The powerful gaze of Shiva's third eye annihilates evil, and is the reason that evil-doers fear His third eye.

The destructive power of Shiva is symbolized by the snakes around His neck. In some pictures Shiva is depicted holding a trident in His right back hand. In other pictures a trident is shown standing adjacent to Him. A *trident* has three edges, which denote the three qualities of nature: sattva (inactivity), rajas (activity), and tamas (non-activity). The trident signifies

LORD SHIVA

FIGURE F-9

that the Lord is beyond the three qualities of nature. The trident also symbolizes the weapon that the Lord uses to destroy evil and ignorance in the world.

A *damaru* (small drum) produces sound when vibrated. As per Hindu scriptures the sound of vibration (of the sacred syllable O M) is believed to be the source of creation. A damaru in one of Shiva's hands conveys the idea that He holds the entire creation in His hand, folding or unfolding it at His will. Since a tiger symbolizes power, the *tiger skin* on which the Lord sits indicates that He is the source of infinite power which He controls at will.

The crescent moon is shown on the side of the Lord's head as an ornament, and not as an integral part of His countenance. The waxing and waning phenomenon of the moon symbolizes the time cycle through which creation evolves from the beginning to the end and back to the beginning. Since the Lord is the Eternal Reality, the crescent moon is only one of His ornaments, and not an integral part of Him.

The moon also symbolizes the qualities of the heart such as love, kindness, and compassion. The crescent moon near the Lord's head conveys the idea that a devotee must develop these qualities in order to become closer to the Lord.

Shiva is depicted sitting on a *cremation ground*, symbolizing His ultimate control over birth and death. A *bull*, known as Nandi, is associated with Shiva and is said to be His vehicle. The bull symbolizes both power and ignorance. Shiva riding the bull suggests that the Lord removes ignorance and bestows power of wisdom on His devotees. The bull is called *Vrisha* in Sanskrit. In Sanskrit, Vrisha also means *Dharma* (righteousness). Thus a bull next to Shiva indicates that Shiva is the eternal companion of righteousness. Nandi also symbolizes a realized person (*sreshta purusha*) or a perfect person, who is absorbed permanently in the vision of the Reality.

When devotees visit a Shiva temple, they offer their salutations first to *Nandi*, the bull in front of the deity. The devotee places the index finger and thumb of his (her) right hand on the two horns of the bull, thus forming a full circle. This simple act has a deep philosophical significance. The index finger represents the ego-sense (*Jiva*) and the thumb denotes the Reality. Since the ego-sense of a worldly person is normally far removed from the Reality (symbolized by the opposite directions in which the thumb and the index finger are normally pointed), the individual does not experience the vision of the Reality (i.e. the vision of Lord Shiva), which is the Self within. By placing the thumb and index finger on the two horns of the bull, the devotee makes a contact between the ego-sense and the Reality, resulting in the dissolution of the ego. When the ego is dissolved, the Reality appears in its fullness, symbolized by the full circle formed by the index finger, the thumb and the two horns of the bull, which stand for wisdom (*viveka*) and renunciation (*vairagya*).

The worship of Shiva is very popular among Hindus, especially among Pashupata, Shaivist, Kaladamana, and Kapalika traditions. *Shivaratri* (see chapter 36) is an important annual festival of Hindus. On this day Shiva and His consort Parvati are worshipped in homes and temples.

Shiva is also called by other names such as Shankar, Mahadeva, Rudra, Ishvara, and Neela Kantha. There are numerous temples dedicated to Lord Shiva throughout India. The following temples are the most popular pilgrimage sites in India: Amarnath (Kashmir), Kedarnath (Himalayas), Eklingaji (near Udaipur), Bishveshvar (Benares), Tarakeshvar (West Bengal), Bhuvaneshwar (Orissa), Somnath (Kathiawar), as well as Conjeeveram, Jambukeshvara, Tiruvannamalai, Kalahasti, and Chidambaram in South India.

Two Most Auspicious Shiva Mantras:

Namah Shivaaya ca Shivataraaya ca.
Obeisance to Him, who is auspicious and exceedingly so.
Om Namah Shivaaya.
Salutations to Lord Shiva.

Popular Prayer to Shiva

Salutations to Thee, who is fond of forests, who is the nearest and the farthest! Salutations to Thee, who is the minutest and the biggest! Salutations to Thee, O three-eyed One, who is the oldest and the youngest! Salutations to Thee, who is everything and who transcends everything.

Chapter 22

Chapter 23
Goddess Durga

Goddess Durga is one of the most widely worshipped deities in the Hindu religion. The Sanskrit word *durga* means a fort or a place that is protected and thus difficult to reach. Durga, also called Divine Mother, protects mankind from evil and misery by destroying evil forces such as selfishness, jealousy, prejudice, hatred, anger, and ego.

In Her images, Goddess Durga is shown (see Figure F-10) in a female form, wearing red clothes. She has eighteen arms (for simplicity Figure F-10 shows only eight arms), carrying many weapons in Her hands. The red color symbolizes action and the *red clothes* convey the idea that She is always busy destroying evil and protecting mankind from pain and suffering caused by evil forces.

A tiger symbolizes unlimited power. *Durga riding a tiger* indicates that she possesses unlimited power and uses it to protect virtue and destroy evil. The *eighteen arms* of Durga indicate that she possesses the combined power of nine of the ten incarnations of Lord Vishnu (see chapter 21) that have appeared at different times. The tenth incarnation, the Kalkin (a man on a white horse), is still to come. This is intended to convey the idea that Goddess Durga represents the united front of all gods against the negative forces of evil and wickedness. The objects in the hands of the Goddess are intended to convey the following ideas:

• Red symbolizes action and a garland denotes victory. A *garland of red beads* (akashmala) indicates that Goddess Durga is actively involved in destroying and conquering the forces of evil (denoted by each individual bead) to protect Her devotees from pain and suffering.

GODDESS DURGA

FIGURE F-10

- A *lotus in half-bloom* signifies that a concerted effort (symbolized by the red color) is necessary to eradicate evil forces. The lotus will finally bloom, indicating that the Goddess helps the forces of righteousness to conquer the forces of wickedness.

- Other *weapons* in the hands of Durga such as an axe, mace, arrow, thunderbolt, spike, stick, sword, iron rod, and disc, convey the idea that one weapon cannot destroy all different kinds of enemies. Different weapons must be used to fight enemies depending upon the circumstances. For example, selfishness must be killed by detachment, jealousy by desirelessness, prejudice by self-knowledge, and ego by discrimination.

The worship of Goddess Durga is very popular among Hindus. She is also called by many other names, such as Shakti, Parvati, Ambika, and Kali. In the form of Uma, She is known as the divine spouse of Lord Shiva and is the mother of Her two sons, Ganesha and Karttikeya, and two daughters, Lakshmi and Saraswati. There are many temples dedicated to Durga's worship in India.

Durga is the object of a special worship during the annual festival of Durga Puja (see chapter 36), celebrated during the month of October. The special worship (*puja*) lasts for nine days. Goddess Durga is worshipped during the first three days, Goddess Lakshmi during the next three days, and Goddess Saraswati during the final three days of the festival. This order of worship has a special significance. Durga, as the destroyer of evil, is worshipped first so that the devotees can destroy their negative qualities, such as greed, anger, and ego. Next, Lakshmi (goddess of wealth) is worshipped to attain positive qualities, such as purity, self control, love, and kindness. Finally, Saraswati (goddess of learning) is worshipped to attain the highest knowledge. The highest knowledge can be attained only after all negative qualities are destroyed and the mind and intellect are purified.

Chapter 23

Chapter 24
Goddess Lakshmi

Lakshmi is the Goddess of wealth and prosperity, both material and spiritual. The word "Lakshmi" is derived from the Sanskrit word *laksme*, meaning "goal." Goddess Lakshmi, therefore, stands for the goal of life, which includes worldly prosperity as well as spiritual prosperity.

In Her images and pictures, Lakshmi is depicted in a female form with four arms and four hands (see Figure F-11). She wears red clothes with a golden lining and is seated on a lotus. She has gold coins, a half-open red lotus, and a golden, fully blossomed lotus in Her hands. An owl and four elephants are shown next to Her.

The *four arms* symbolizing the four directions denote omnipresence and omnipotence of the Goddess. The *red color* symbolizes activity. The *golden lining* (embroidery) on Her red dress denotes prosperity. The idea conveyed here is that the Goddess is always busy distributing wealth and prosperity to Her devotees. The seating of Lakshmi on *lotus* signifies that when one lives in this world, one can enjoy its wealth, yet not become obsessed with it. Such a living is analogous to a lotus that lives in water but does not become wet by it.

The four hands represent the four goals of human life: *dharma* (righteousness), *kama* (genuine desires), *artha* (wealth), and *moksha* (liberation) (see chapter 32). Since the front hands represent the activity in the physical world and the back hands indicate the activity in the spiritual world, these four goals are represented by front right, front left, back left, and the back right hands, respectively.

Since red symbolizes activity, a *half-blossomed* red lotus in the back left hand of Lakshmi conveys the idea that one must perform all duties in accordance with one's dharma. This leads to moksha (liberation), which is symbolized by a *full-blossomed lotus* in the back right hand of Lakshmi.

An owl is a night bird that dwells in darkness and cannot see in the daytime. An *owl sitting next to gold coins* signifies that one must not be blinded by material wealth and dwell in ignorance. The passion for possessiveness leads to suffering and injustice in the world.

The *four elephants* also symbolize the four goals of human life as described above. They are shown spraying water from golden vessels onto Goddess Lakshmi. The spraying of water denotes activity. The golden vessels denote wisdom and purity. The four elephants spraying water from the golden vessels on the Goddess convey the idea that continuous self-effort, in accordance with one's dharma and governed by wisdom and purity, leads to both material and spiritual prosperity.

In some pictures, only two (instead of four) white elephants are shown standing next to the Goddess. The two white elephants symbolize the name and fame associated with worldly wealth. The two white elephants standing next to the Goddess convey the idea that a devotee should not earn wealth merely for the sake of material desires, but should share it with others in order to bring happiness to others in addition to himself.

Goddess Lakshmi, also called *Shri*, is the divine spouse of Lord Vishnu (see chapter 21) and provides Him with wealth for the maintenance and preservation of creation. There are many temples dedicated to Her worship in India. Hindus also worship Lakshmi in their households. She is especially worshipped on the auspicious day of Diwali (see chapter 36), with religious rituals and ceremonies specifically devoted to Her.

A Popular Prayer to Goddess Lakshmi:
Namastestu mahaa maaye, shrrpiite surapuujit.
Shankha chakra gadaa haste, mahaa lakshmi namostu te.

Salutations to Thee, O Mahalakshmi, Who is the seat of all power and the source of all wealth, Who is worshipped by gods, and Who has a conch, a disc, and a mace in Her hands.

Chapter 24

GODDESS LAKSHMI

FIGURE F-11

Chapter 25
Goddess Saraswati

Saraswati is the Goddess of learning, knowledge, and wisdom. The Sanskrit word *sara* means "essence" and swa means "self." Thus Saraswati means "the essence of the self."

In Her popular images and pictures, Goddess Saraswati is generally depicted with four arms (some pictures may show only two arms), wearing white clothes and seated (or standing) on a lotus (see Figure F-12). She holds a book and a rosary in Her rear two hands, while the front two hands are engaged in the playing of a lute (*veena*). Her right leg is placed on Her left leg. She uses a swan as her vehicle. There is a peacock by Her side gazing at Her.

The *lotus* is a symbol of spiritual knowledge and power. A white lotus denotes supreme knowledge. By sitting or standing on a lotus, Saraswati signifies that She is Herself rooted in the Supreme Reality, and She symbolizes supreme knowledge. The white garments indicate that She is the embodiment of pure knowledge.

The *four arms* symbolizing the four directions denote Her omnipresence and omnipotence. The two front arms indicate Her activity in the physical world and the two back arms signify Her presence in the spiritual world. The *four hands* represent the four elements of the inner personality. The mind (*manas*) is represented by the front right hand, the intellect (*buddhi*) by the front left hand, the conditioned consciousness (*chitta*) by the rear left hand, and the ego (*ahankara*) by the rear right hand.

The *left side of the body* symbolizes the qualities of the heart and the *right side* symbolizes activities of the mind. A *book* in the rear left hand signifies that knowledge acquired must be used with love and kindness to promote prosperity of mankind.

GODDESS SARASWATI

FIGURE F-12

The *rosary* signifies concentration, meditation, and contemplation, leading to samadhi, or union with God. A rosary in the rear right hand representing ego conveys that true knowledge acquired with love and devotion melts the ego and results in liberation (moksha) of the seeker.

The Goddess is shown playing a *musical instrument* that is held in Her front hands, which denote mind and intellect. This symbol conveys that the seeker must tune his mind and intellect in order to live in perfect harmony with the world. Such harmonious living enables the individual to utilize acquired knowledge for the welfare of all mankind.

A *swan* is depicted sitting on the left side of the Goddess. A swan is said to have a sensitive beak that enables it to distinguish pure milk from a mixture of milk and water. A swan, therefore, symbolizes the power of discrimination, or the ability to discriminate between right and wrong or good and bad. Saraswati uses the swan as Her carrier. This indicates that one must acquire and apply knowledge with discrimination for the good of mankind. Knowledge that is dominated by ego can destroy the world. A perfect harmony between heart and intellect is essential for the proper application of knowledge.

A *peacock* is sitting next to the Goddess and is anxiously waiting to serve as Her vehicle. A peacock depicts unpredictable behavior since its moods can be influenced by the weather. Saraswati is using a swan as a vehicle and not the peacock. This signifies that one must use knowledge with discrimination for the good of mankind.

Saraswati is represented in Hindu mythology as the divine consort of Lord Brahma, the Creator of the universe. Since knowledge is necessary for creation, Saraswati symbolizes the creative power of Brahma. Goddess Saraswati is worshipped by all persons interested in knowledge, especially students, teachers, scholars, and scientists. She is the focus of a special worship during the annual festival of Vasant Panchami, celebrated during the month of Magha (January-February).

The name *Saraswati* first appeared in the Rig Veda as a sacred river. The Vedic Seers praised Her in the following words:

Chapter 25

O best Mother; O best river, O best Goddess
Saraswati...Unique among rivers, Saraswati flows pure
from the mountains to the ocean; revealing wealth and
the world's abundance....
   (Rig Veda II.41.16 and VII.95.1-2)

Since Rig Vedic times, Saraswati has been identified as
Goddess of Knowledge and Learning. Although Her mythical
associations are various and complex, Her primary role is as
the divine consort to Lord Brahma.

In some Puranas, Saraswati and Lakshmi are viewed as
daughters of Lord Shiva and Goddess Durga. Other Puranas
describe a quarrel among the three wives of Lord Vishnu--
Saraswati, Lakshmi, and Ganga--which became so fierce that
Vishnu sent Saraswati to Brahma and Ganga to Shiva. Still
other mythological stories ascribe the birth of Saraswati to the
body of Lord Brahma. Whatever the mythological associations
of Goddess Saraswati may be, She symbolizes the aspect of the
Supreme Reality (Brahman of the Upanishads) that bestows
upon us wisdom and intelligence so we may acquire worldly
as well as spiritual knowledge.

Prayers to Goddess Saraswati:

Saraswati namastu-bhyam, varade kaamaruupini.
Vidyaarambham karishyaami, siddhir bhavatu me sadaa.

Salutations to Thee, O Goddess Saraswati, Who is the
giver of boons and fullfiller of all desires. In the
knowledge I seek, O Goddess of Knowledge, may I
always accomplish my goals!

Jaya Saraswati namostu te, Jaya Saraswati namostu te
Hail Saraswati! Salutations to Thee!

May Goddess Saraswati protect me from all the worldly
evils and sorrows by entirely eliminating the dullness of
the intellect and kindling the light of knowledge!

Chapter 25

Chapter 26
Sri Rama and Sri Krishna

Bhagavan Sri Rama is the seventh incarnation of Lord Vishnu. The life story of Rama and the main purpose of his incarnation (to destroy the demon king Ravana) is described in the great epic Ramayana (see chapter 30). Rama's wife Sita is revered as an incarnation of Goddess Lakshmi, the divine consort of Lord Vishnu.

Rama is the symbol of an ideal man, as conceived by the Hindu mind. In the epic Ramayana, Rama's personality and actions depict him as the perfect son, devoted brother, true husband, trusted friend, ideal king, and noble adversary. Sita is the symbol of an ideal daughter, wife, mother, and queen. Whereas Rama symbolizes standards of perfection that can be conceived in all the facets of a man's life, Sita represents all that is great and noble in womanhood.

In images and pictures, Rama is shown carrying a bow and arrow (see Figure F-13). The bow and arrow convey that Rama is always ready to destroy evil and protect righteousness. He is himself an embodiment of dharma. Worship of Sri Rama is popular among all Hindus, as is evident by the numerous temples dedicated to him in India. In the temple images, Rama is usually shown with his faithful wife Sita, devoted brother Lakshmana, and his beloved devotee Hanuman. In the epic Ramayana, Hanuman, the monkey hero, aids Rama in rescuing his wife and battling Ravana, her abductor.

Bhagavan Sri Krishna is the eighth and the most popular incarnation of Lord Vishnu. Of all incarnations (see chapter 21), Sri Krishna is accepted as a full and complete incarnation (*purna avatara*) of Lord Vishnu. Krishna commands love, respect, and adoration from Hindus of all ages and walks of life. This universal appeal is unique and present only in the life and teachings of Sri Krishna.

LORD RAMA AND LORD KRISHNA

FIGURE F-13

The details of Krishna's childhood and youth are elaborated in devotional literature, such as the *Bhagavata Purana*, *Harivamsa*, and *Vishnu* and *Padma Puranas*. The epic Mahabharata depicts Krishna only as an adult. He is depicted as the teacher of the Bhagavad Gita to Arjuna, and as a friend, advisor, and charioteer of Arjuna in the Mahabharata war. The epic does not include the details of Krishna's childhood.

Krishna, the eighth incarnation of Lord Vishnu and the eighth child of his parents, was born at midnight in a prison on the eighth day of the dark fortnight of Bhadrapada (August-September). Krishna's father (Vasudeva) and his mother (Devaki, sister of King Kamsa) had been imprisoned by Kamsa, an evil king of Mathura. Kamsa was a cruel, oppressive, and arrogant king who terrorized his kingdom.

Kamsa had been told by astrologers that he would be killed by a son born to his own sister Devaki. Kamsa, therefore, imprisoned his sister and her husband in order to keep an eye on every child that would be born to them. He killed the first seven children of his sister soon after they were born. At the time Krishna was born, the prison guards fell asleep and Vasudeva managed to escape from prison and take infant Krishna to Gokula, where Krishna was exchanged for a baby girl born to *Yashoda* and *Nanda*. Vasudeva returned to prison with the baby girl. When Kamsa was informed by his prison guards that a girl, and not a boy, was born to Devaki, Kamsa decided to kill the girl anyway. He grabbed the girl in his hands and tried to kill her by striking her against the ground. The girl slipped away from his hands and flew into the sky, announcing, "Kamsa, the savior of the earth is already born and will kill you soon." Following this event, Kamsa ordered that all newly born babies be killed in his kingdom. He sent the most powerful demons and demonesses to accomplish this mission.

Krishna was raised in Gokula by the cowherd family of Yashoda and Nanda. His childhood was full of dangers, as Kamsa made every effort to have him killed. Even when he was only a little child, Krishna killed all the demons and demonesses that were ordered to kill him. Eventually, Krishna killed Kamsa, thus fulfilling the purpose of his incarnation.

Chapter 26

All other incarnations of God that descended on earth illustrate the Divine aspect of the human personality, but Krishna's incarnation represents the *human dimension of the Divine*. Thus in the stories of Krishna, he is depicted as a common person, wise and mischievous, happy and sad, laughing and crying, loving and hating, promising and deceiving, and enjoying and suffering. Whereas the Ramayana and Mahabharata illustrate the stories of Brahmins and Kshatriyas (the elite in ancient society), the stories of Krishna depict the common people of ancient India (cowherd men and women) and their ambitions, aspirations, conflicts, and religious and social problems.

Symbolically, Krishna is the manifestation of the nameless and formless Brahman in a human form. The popular images and pictures of Krishna show him with a blue complexion and wearing yellow clothes. The blue color symbolizes infinity and the yellow color denotes earth. Thus the two colors together convey that Krishna is the infinite consciousness that has descended on earth to take a human form.

Krishna is usually depicted as playing a flute (see Figure F-13). The flute symbolizes the human body and its holes represent the mind, senses, and the intellect. Krishna represents the consciousness. The music produced by the flute represents the functioning of the body, or its sentience. Krishna playing the flute and producing music illustrates that the body, mind, senses, and the intellect are inert in the absence of the consciousness. They become functional only when the consciousness resides in the body. Thus it is the pure Self in the body that expresses Itself through the mind, intellect, and senses, and produces the music of life.

Rama and Krishna are the two most venerable incarnations of Hinduism. However, their lives are in sharp contrast to each other, and some of the incidents of their lives are diametrically opposite. The following are just a few examples:

- Rama was born during broad daylight in the palace at Ayodhya, while Krishna was born at midnight in a prison at Mathura.

- Rama was the first child of his parents, who had performed religious rites and rituals in order to bear a child. Krishna was the eighth child of his parents, who, because of King Kamsa's vow to kill all their children, were not eager to have another child.

- Rama was of fair complexion whereas Krishna was of dark complexion.

- As a child, Rama was brought up in the royal luxury of the palace. Krishna, on the other hand, lived in a cowherd village under constant danger from his own uncle, King Kamsa.

- As a child Rama lived in nobility, and in his adult years, he lived as a commoner (when in exile). But Krishna lived as a commoner in his childhood, and in his adult years he lived in nobility.

- Rama had trouble living a peaceful life even with one woman, his own wife Sita. Krishna had no trouble living a peaceful life with many women around him.

- Rama's wife Sita was taken away from him by Ravana, whereas Krishna forcibly took Rukmini (who wanted to marry Krishna against her parent's wishes) from her parents and married her.

- Rama belonged to the solar dynasty whereas Krishna belonged to the lunar dynasty. Rama was a king whereas Krishna was a king-maker, but never a king. Rama lived in exile to fulfill the mission of his incarnation, whereas Krishna moved from palace to palace to fulfill his mission.

- Rama never claimed to be an incarnation, whereas Krishna declared himself to be an incarnation.

Chapter 26

- Rama was worried and confused in his battle with Ravana, whereas Krishna brought a worried and confused Arjuna back to his senses and encouraged him to fight the battle of the Mahabharata.

- Rama always carried arms when required and fought the battle with Ravana himself. Krishna never carried arms even when he was expected to do so. Although Krishna was always surrounded by wars, he never fought one himself.

- Rama always carried a bow and arrow in his hands and fought demons all his life. Krishna always carried a flute in his hands and played music all his life.

- Rama's name is chanted with the name of his legally wedded wife, Sita. Krishna's name is not chanted with the name of his legally wedded wife, Rukmini. Instead, Krishna's name is chanted with the name of his beloved devotee, Radha.

- Rama's sons lived independently, but were crowned by Rama himself. Krishna's sons and grandsons lived close to Krishna, but were annihilated during the life-time of Krishna. Rama left behind a prosperous Ayodhya, whereas Krishna left behind Dwarika in ruin.

- Rama symbolizes the living of a righteous life in the world, whereas Krishna symbolizes the goal of such a life. Whereas Rama is God in the form of a perfect man, Krishna is God himself. Whereas Rama symbolizes the perfect student, Krishna symbolizes the perfect teacher (guru) of such a student. For these reasons it is often said, "Live like Rama, and do what Krishna taught."

The above analysis of the lives of two great incarnations of Hindus illustrates the doctrine of unity within diversity, or harmony within differences, the major theme of the Hindu religious and spiritual tradition.

Chapter 26

Chapter 27
Radha and Krishna

Krishna was brought up in Vrindavan by the cowherd family of Yashoda and Nanda. His playmates were *gopas* (cowherd boys) and *gopis* (cowherd girls). As a cowherd boy, he led the cattle to the forest for grazing. He was the master of the flute and played his bamboo flute to the joy of all. He was loved dearly by cowherd men, women, and children.

Whenever Krishna played his flute, the cowherd boys and girls would run away from their homes and gather in the forest to dance with him. This dance is known as *Rasa Lila.* Each gopi thought of Krishna as her own. Krishna assumed multiple forms to allow each gopi to have her own Krishna. Of all the gopis, Radha (see Figure F-14) loved Krishna the most. She gave herself completely to Krishna without any expectations. Her love was of the purest kind.

When Krishna grew up, he married four women: Kalindi, Jambuvati, Rukmini, and Satyabhama. In order to rescue sixteen thousand women imprisoned by the demon king Bhaumasura, he also symbolically married all of these women in order to save them from the tyranny of the demon king. Although Krishna loved all his four wives, Radha was his favorite devotee.

The relationships of Krishna with his wives and gopis are symbolic. Although Krishna symbolically represents the human dimension of the Divine, he is not an ordinary person. He is the Divine in a concrete human form. Krishna's life, as depicted in Hindu mythology, raises two interesting questions: "Was Krishna a polygamist? Did he introduce the concept of dating?" Such questions are not valid, since these arise only when Krishna is viewed as an ordinary human being. However, since Krishna represents divinity in the human form, all of his actions symbolize spiritual ideas and concepts.

Krishna himself symbolizes Brahman, the sole basis of the universe. The four wives of Krishna denote the four direc-

RADHA AND KRISHNA

FIGURE F-14

tions, or the physical universe which emanates from Brahman by the operation of maya. The marriage relationship between Krishna and his four wives signifies the natural relationship between Brahman and the universe.

Gopis symbolize the individual souls trapped in physical bodies. Radha symbolizes the individual soul that is awakened to the love of Brahman and is absorbed in such love. The gopis' love for Krishna signifies the natural bond between the individual soul and Brahman. The Rasa Lila, the dance of the gopis and Krishna, indicates the union of the human and divine, the dance of the souls. The sound of Krishna's flute represents the call of the divine for the individual souls. The forest where Krishna plays his flute denotes the transition between the physical world and the spiritual world. In the forest, the gopis forget themselves and are absorbed in love for Krishna. This illustrates that when an individual soul responds to the call of the Divine, the soul enjoys union with the Divine and becomes absorbed in such union.

In the case of all the other deities, Hindus worship a particular deity with his (or her) spouse. In the case of Krishna, however, Hindus worship Krishna and his consort Radha, and not any of his spouses. This apparent contradiction is explained below: Krishna symbolizes the Supreme Lord, and his four wives symbolize all that the Supreme Lord has created and sustained in the universe. Krishna's marrying his wives of his own accord signifies that the Lord has created the universe of his own choice. Radha symbolizes an individual soul, the atman. When Krishna plays and dances with the gopis, his wives do not object to such a relationship and they unselfishly remain devoted to him. They neither complain nor are they affected by Krishna's spiritual relationship with Radha and the other gopis. This conveys the idea that the universe maintains its cosmic balance and is not impacted by the human aspiration to seek union with God.

It is important to note that when we try to understand Krishna's relationships with his wives and gopis, we do not fall into the trap of interpreting these relationships in the context of human weaknesses, such as lust and jealousy.

Chapter 27

The purpose of life is to seek union with God. Hindus show reverence to the divine relationship between the atman and Brahman by worshipping Radha and Krishna. To worship Krishna and one or all of His wives would mean worshipping the relationship between Brahman and the world seen through maya. This is a meaningless goal, since we already reside in the world of maya. As our actual goal is to transcend maya and seek union with Brahman, Hindus worship Radha and Krishna and not Krishna and Rukmini or any of his other wives.

The Ethics of Sri Krishna

Sri Krishna is the teacher of dharma in the Mahabharata and the Bhagavad Gita. In many instances his own actions in the Mahabharata war appear to be unorthodox and sometimes questionable. What then are the ethics of Krishna?

Generally speaking, ethical systems may be divided into two categories: heteronomous and autonomous. The former is fixed by authority of some sort. The Ten Commandments of Christianity are an example of this category of ethics. The latter is derived from sociological and existentialist considerations. Krishna's ethics take the middle path, in that there is no absolute right or absolute wrong. It is not enough that we follow the established norms of conduct. Instead, we must pay undivided attention to the intrinsic rightness or wrongness of our actions and decide what the best action would be in a given situation. All actions should be performed in the spirit of equability (*samatva*). If we renounce the fruit of our actions, our conduct will naturally become pure. "Therefore, unattached, perform the right deed," advises Krishna (BG 3.19).

The key element of Krishna's ethical teachings is *dharma*, the doctrine of human growth and harmony (see chapter 32). Dharma must be protected at all costs and by all means. Krishna does not advocate the disreputable maxim that the ends justify the means. He teaches that we should not be afraid to fight greater evil by lesser wrong, whenever preservation of dharma is at stake. This is the most important lesson one can learn from Krishna's seemingly unorthodox actions and behavior in the Mahabharata war.

Chapter 28
Hanuman

In the Hindu epic Ramayana (see chapter 30), Hanuman, also called Maruti, is the great monkey hero who assists Rama in his battle with Ravana. The battle is fought by Rama to rescue his wife Sita, who was kidnapped by Ravana. Hanuman is instrumental in locating Sita before the battle begins and arranging a huge army of monkeys to fight alongside Rama.

Whereas Lord Ganesha symbolizes the qualities of a perfect human being (see chapter 19), Hanuman (see Figure F-15) symbolizes the qualities of a perfect man as conceived by the Hindu mind. Why is a perfect man represented in the image of a monkey and not in the image of a man himself?

A perfect man is a man with a perfect mind. An ordinary mind is usually restless, unstable, and craves for sense objects all the time, in rapid succession. These are the qualities of a typical monkey, who is restless and jumps from one spot to another or from one tree to another. Thus a monkey symbolizes the mind, and a perfect monkey symbolizes a perfect mind, and therefore, a perfect man.

If we analyze the role of Hanuman in the story of Ramayana, we find that he exhibits perfect qualities as illustrated below:

- Humility: Hanuman is the symbol of humbleness. He is the embodiment of truthfulness and righteousness, the essential qualities of a perfect man. After his coronation, Rama distributed gifts to all those who had assisted him in his battle with Ravana. Turning towards Hanuman, he said, "There is nothing I can give you that would match the service you have rendered to me. All I can do is to give you my own self." Hearing these words of Rama, Hanuman, with his hands joined together in front of his mouth, head slightly bent in the

HANUMAN

FIGURE F-15

pose of service, stood by Rama, in all humility. To this day, this picture of Hanuman as a humble devotee of the Lord is the most popular among the admirers and worshipers of Hanuman.

- Admiration: a perfect man is one who is admired by his friends and respected by his foes. Hanuman is an example of such admiration and respect by his friends and enemies. In the story of Ramayana, even Inderjit (Ravana's son, a great warrior) and Ravana himself recognized Hanuman as an outstanding hero.

- Nobility: a perfect man is one who is noble, sincere, and provides sympathy for the sorrowful and hope for the hopeless. When Hanuman sees Sita for the first time in Ashoka Vana, where she was confined by Ravana, he gives her solace and imbibes her with hope for survival.

- Understanding: a perfect man must possess perfect knowledge and understanding. Hanuman is a scholar and has mastered the four Vedas. When he initially meets Rama, Hanuman's speech is so vibrant with Vedic knowledge that Rama himself acknowledges the depth and richness of Hanuman's dialogue.

- Mastery over ego: since the ego is the enemy of a person, Hanuman has killed his ego, thus becoming totally free from it. He never seeks credit for his great deeds of valor, which include the destruction of Lanka (the kingdom of Ravana) and the killing of Ravana's top generals.

- Achievements: a perfect man must be physically strong so that he can perform great deeds of valor. Hanuman is a monkey of unparalleled physical strength. He lifts hills and mountains on his shoulders, uproots trees, and moves large objects with his tail.

- Nishkama-Karma: a perfect person must perform all work in the spirit of service to the Lord and without any desire for the reward. Hanuman is the embodiment of selfless service. He performs all actions because of his love for the Lord. Hanuman's sincerity and selflessness are best expressed in the following words spoken to Rama: "Only give me this blessing that my affection for you may never diminish."

Hanuman is revered by Hindus as a perfect devotee of God. The worship of Hanuman, therefore, symbolizes the worship of the Supreme Lord for acquiring the following qualities, represented by the letters of the word HANUMAN:

H = Humility and hope
A = Admiration (truthfulness, devotion)
N = Nobility (sincerity, loyalty, modesty)
U = Understanding (knowledge)
M = Mastery over ego (kindness, compassion)
A = Achievements (strength)
N = Nishkama-karma (selfless work)

These are the qualities of perfection in the image of Hanuman as conceived of by the Hindu mind.

A Popular Prayer to Vera Hanuman (Maruti)

Manojavam maaruta tulya vegam jitendriyam buddhimataam varishtam, vaataatmajam vaanara yuuthamukhyam shrii raamaduutam shirasaa namaami.

Bowing down my head, I salute Hanuman, who travels faster than the mind and the wind, who has mastered the sense organs, who is the best among the intelligent, who is the son of the Wind God, who is the commander-in-chief of the army of *vaanaras* (monkeys), and who is the envoy of Bhagavan Sri Rama.

Chapter 29
The Sacred Syllable OM and the Hindu Trinity

The syllable O M (also called *pranava*), the most sacred symbol in Hinduism, is associated with symbolism as well as mysticism. Volumes have been written in Sanskrit illustrating the significance of this mystic symbol. Although this symbol is mentioned in all the Upanishads and in all Hindu scriptures, it is especially elaborated upon in the *Taittiriya, Chandogya,* and *Mundaka Upanishads*.

By its sound and form, O M (see Figure F-16) symbolizes the infinite Brahman and the entire universe. In Sanskrit the sounds of letters *A* and *U* produce, when combined together, the sound equivalent of letter *O*. Thus the sound produced by O M is obtained by superimposing the sounds produced by the three letters *A*, *U*, and *M*. O M is also called the "four-element syllable." The letters *A*, *U*, and *M* are the three elements and the fourth element is the *silence* from which the sound of O M arises, and back into which it subsides.

The sound produced by the letter *A* signifies all that is observed and perceived in the wakeful state of an individual, thus representing both the subject and the object, and all the experiences in the physical world. Therefore, the letter *A* symbolizes all that is known and knowable. The sound produced by the letter *U* represents the observer and the things observed in the dream state of an individual's consciousness, thus denoting the astral worlds and the worlds of heavens and hells. The sound produced by the letter *M* signifies all unknown in the state of deep sleep as well as all that is unknown in the wakeful state. Thus O M symbolizes the phenomenal world that contributes to our experiences in the universe.

Sacred Symbol OM

FIGURE F-16

The *silence*, the fourth element of OM as stated above, represents the underlying Reality that pervades the waking, dream, and the deep sleep states of one's consciousness. Thus OM symbolizes the infinite Brahman, the essence of all existence.

As shown in Figure F-16, the symbol of OM consists of three curves (curves 1, 2, and 3), one semicircle (curve 4), and a dot. The large lower curve 1 symbolizes the waking state (*jagrat*); the upper curve 2 denotes deep sleep (*sushupti*) or the unconscious state, and the lower curve 3 (which lies between deep sleep and the waking state) signifies the dream state (*svapna*). These three states of an individual's consciousness, and therefore the entire physical phenomenon, are represented by the three curves.

The dot signifies the Absolute (fourth or *turiya state* of consciousness), which illuminates the other three states. The semicircle symbolizes maya and separates the dot from the other three curves. The semicircle is open on the top, which means that the Absolute is infinite and is not affected by maya. Maya only effects the manifested phenomenon. In this way the form of OM represents the unmanifest and the manifest, the noumenon (attributeless Reality) and the phenomenon, and thus OM is an adequate symbol of God, personal and impersonal. This message is brought forth in the following passage of the Katha Upanishad:

> "The goal which all the Vedas declare, which all austerities aim at, and which humans desire when they lead the life of continence, I will tell you briefly: it is OM. This syllable OM is indeed Brahman. This syllable is the highest. Whosoever knows this syllable obtains all that he desires. This is the best support; this is the highest support. Whosoever knows this support is adored in the world of Brahman...."

> (Katha Upanishad I, ii, 15-17)

The sacred mantra *Om Tat Sat* (see chapter 35) is uttered by Hindus at the end of all prayers. Thus OM begins where

Chapter 29

all speech ends, the point where an individual's heart melts into divinity, and the unspeakable and inexpressible Reality is reached. In this way, the OM symbolizes the essence of all the scriptures.

Hindu scriptures declare that OM is the storehouse of mystic power. When correctly uttered, OM brings into play the entire vocal mechanism of a human being. When OM is uttered according to Vedic injections, the throat generates the sound A by beginning the sound from the bottom of the spine (Kundalini) and thus using the entire depth of the human system in producing this sound. The sound U begins at the throat and ends at the tip of the tongue. The sound M is concentrated at the terminal end of the vocal system, the lips.

According to Hindu scriptures, the sound of OM is the sound of creation, and this sound represents to our ears the sound of the cosmic energy of which all things are the manifestations. All vowel sounds are included in the correct pronunciation of OM. All consonants are the interruptions of the sounds of the vowels. All words are thus fragments of the syllable OM. To have the highest experience in life is to hear the sound of OM in deep silence.

Hindu scriptures tell us that the repetition of OM, in accordance with the Vedic methods, generates the mystic power that leads one's mind into deep concentration, meditation, and finally to *samadhi*, a state of higher consciousness. The mystic power of OM is confirmed by Lord Krishna Himself in the Bhagavad Gita:

"Uttering the monosyllable OM, the eternal word of Brahman, One who departs leaving the body [at death], he attains the supreme goal." (BG 8.13)

How to Chant OM

The following instructions should be used to chant OM correctly:

1. Take a deep breath.
2. Hold the breath as long as you can comfortably. Do not create any discomfort.

3. Speak O M during a slow and long exhaling phase, until the breath is totally out. This completes one chant.

4. Pause and repeat the above steps again and again.

The sound of O M is to be produced in a non-stop manner, by combining the sounds of *A, U* and *M*. The last sound (that of M), assumes a nasal tone when the lips have closed after speaking A and U.

The Hindu Trinity

The Hindu Trinity (see Figure F-17), also called *Trimurti* (meaning three forms), is the representation of the three manifestations of the Supreme Reality, as Brahma, Vishnu, and Shiva. Each of these manifestations is associated with a specific cosmic function. Brahma symbolizes creation, Vishnu preservation, and Shiva dissolution or destruction necessary for re-creation. It must be clearly understood that the members of the Hindu Trinity are not three different and independent gods, but three aspects of one Supreme Being, called Brahman (see chapter 4) by seers of the Upanishads.

Hindu Trinity

= Brahma + Vishnu + Shiva = Three Faces of the Divine
= Three Cosmic Functions of the Supreme Being
= Creation + Preservation + Dissolution
= **G**enerator + **O**perator + **D**estroyer
= **GOD**

In conclusion, O M (or AUM) symbolizes the Supreme Being and the universe. The sound of O M is the primal sound from which the universe has evolved. The sound of "AUM" also represents the Hindu Trinity as "A" denotes creation, "U" indicates sustenance, and "M" represents dissolution and re-creation. Correct chanting of O M quickly relaxes the mind and the body. When chanted in accordance with Vedic injections, O M generates mystic power that accelerates spiritual transformation.

Chapter 29

HINDU TRINITY

FIGURE F-17

Questions and Answers
Part II

Q1. Between Brahma, Vishnu, and Shiva, why is Brahma (the creator) worshipped the least? I am told that it is because Brahma was cursed by somebody. If that is true, this means that our God performed deeds bad enough to be cursed. It also means that there was somebody who possessed more power than our Creator. Please explain.

A. As explained in chapter 20, Brahma represents the creative power of Brahman, the Ultimate Reality. He symbolizes the Universal Mind, responsible for the creation of the universe. From the individual standpoint, Brahma is the god of the mind and intellect, the creative faculty of an individual. The worship of Brahma, therefore, indicates the worship of the Supreme Being for bestowing upon the individual greater mental and intellectual efficiency.

One could argue that the general population is not particularly interested in mental and intellectual pursuits, and instead is interested in wealth and power to procure the necessities of life. For this reason the worship of Brahma did not become popular among common people. The worship of Brahma is, however, popular among students, teachers, scholars, and intellectuals, who are particularly interested in mental and intellectual pursuits.

As explained under discussion of the Hindu Trinity (see page 234), Brahma, Vishnu, and Shiva are three different aspects of the same Reality, Brahman. No deity is superior or inferior to any other deity and any attempt to establish superiority among deities violates the spirit of Hindu religion.

Certain stories in the Puranas have tried to establish the superiority of one sect over another and that of one god over another. However, the *original* Puranas did not include any such stories. When the conflicts between various sects of Hindus climaxed, some of the original Puranas were altered and additions and interpolations were made to establish the superiority of some gods over others. Since these developments occurred a long time ago, it is now difficult to separate the original texts from the later ones. The student of Hindu religion should ignore any texts that might appear to establish the superiority of one sect over another, one color or race over another, or one deity over another. The differences may establish an identity, but they cannot justify superiority of any kind.

Q2. Lord Shiva is said to be the destroyer of creation. That being the case, why should we worship Lord Shiva?

A. Lord Shiva is not actually a destroyer, but the redeemer of the souls. The words *destroyer* and *destruction* have been erroneously associated with Him.

In Hindu view the creation sustains itself by a delicate balance between the opposing forces of good and evil. At the end of a cycle of creation, when this balance is disturbed and the sustenance of life becomes impossible, Lord Shiva dissolves the universe for the creation of the next cycle so that unliberated souls will have another opportunity to liberate themselves from bondage with the physical world.

From the individual standpoint, Lord Shiva protects the individual soul from pain and suffering in the physical world. When the physical body becomes too old to function or is diseased, incapacitated, and unable to function, the soul suffers pain and misery until it is freed from that non-functional body. Out of compassion Lord Shiva dissolves the body and releases the soul so that it can assume another body in its next incarnation in accordance with the Law of Karma.

Lord Shiva is the Lord of mercy and compassion. He protects His devotees from evil forces such as lust, greed, and anger. He grants boons, bestows grace, destroys ignorance, and awakens wisdom in His devotees. For these reasons the worship of Lord Shiva is very popular among Hindus.

Q3. The story of the creation of Lord Ganesha (see chapter 17) seems incredible. It seems that even God can become angry

*enough at a child that He would behead him. How could the
Lord, who is supposed to oversee world events without even
moving from His abode, not know that his own wife had created
a child? With all His supposed powers, why could He not put
the same head back on the body of Ganesha instead of
transplanting an elephant's head?*

A. The story of the creation of Lord Ganesha is incredible
because it is based upon a mythological story. Mythology was
developed to expound the higher truths of Hindu scriptures
for those who could not otherwise comprehend those truths
intellectually. Philosophy, and not mythology, provides the
adequate basis for Hindu religious beliefs and practices.
Refer to chapter 19 for a discussion of the symbolism of Lord
Ganesha and to page 175 for a discussion of the mythology.

*Q4. Why do Hindus in India waste huge quantities of food in
temple worship and yagnas when many people cannot obtain
even a single decent meal per day?*

A. Not all Hindus waste large quantities of food in temple
worships. Those who do should be reminded of the following words of Sri Krishna in the Bhagavad Gita:

"One who offers to Me with devotion only a leaf, a
flower, a fruit, or even a little water, this I accept,
because it was offered with love by one who is pure-
hearted." (BG 9.26)

As stated in chapter 14, the practice of wasting large
quantities of food in the name of an offering to deities is
against the true spirit of Hindu religion.

*Q5. Why do people offer gold ornaments and other materially
valuable objects to God in temples?*

A. Of course, God is not concerned with anything except a
devotee's true love. Offering gold to God is akin to offering

a glass of water to the ocean. Some devotees, however, wish to offer God their most expensive possessions, and gold qualifies as such an offering. In truth, there is nothing one can really offer God, since there is nothing one really owns in this world. Everything belongs to God, including ourselves. Keeping this in mind, one may offer anything one wishes as long as the offering is made with sincerity, devotion, and without expectation of any reward.

Q6. Hindus worship images and icons of stone, clay, and metal. Isn't this practice of idolatry contrary to the teachings of the Upanishads and the Bhagavad Gita?

A. Hindu worship of images and icons is not idolatry, since Hindus do not consider the images and icons as God, but *symbols* of God. Just as Christians worship the crucifix as a symbol of Christ, and Muslims adore Kaaba (Black Stone) in Mecca as the most sacred symbol of God, Hindus use images and icons as symbols of God. "Worship with the aid of images in India was not idolatry, as [was the case] in Arabia," says Al Baruni, the great Muslim scholar.

Swami Vivekananda further explains, "Idolatry in India does not mean anything horrible. It is not the mother of harlots. On the other hand, it is the attempt of undeveloped minds to grasp high spiritual truths."[21]

Q7. Why do Hindu gods have consorts?

A. Hindu gods and their consorts illustrate the importance of family life in Hindu religion. One of the three debts (see chapter 32) a Hindu must pay is to one's ancestors. This can be accomplished by raising one's family in accordance with the moral and ethical principles of the scriptures. In Hindu religion, marriage is a sacrament. The religious duty of a Hindu is to raise his or her children as responsible citizens for the sustenance of creation. A strong, well-knit family with a commitment to raising children as responsible citizens is the hallmark of Hindu culture.

Q8. What is the significance of Hindu rituals performed in homes and temples?

A.   Religious rites and rituals, if performed with under-standing and devotion, achieve the same function for the mind as soap and shampoo accomplish for the body. Rites and rituals destroy the egoism of the mind and generate God-consciousness. They turn the mind inward for worship and meditation, and purify the mind by eliminating its negative qualities. For instance, offering food to gods leads to self-sacrifice, an important virtue. Similarly, the practice of charity and fasting lead to the spirit of generosity and self-control, respectively.

Likewise, the five daily rites (*pancha maha yagnas*--see chapter 32) that a householder is enjoined to offer to the gods, sages, ancestors, and living beings, are intended to cultivate the virtues of devotion to God, to learning, to family and society, as well as kindness to animals. Hindu sages tell us that rites and rituals performed with faith, understanding, and love, help the mind to become strong, contemplative, and concentrated.

Rites and rituals performed without understanding and devotion soon become mechanical routines that do not con-tribute to a cleansing of the mind. When rituals become the ends in themselves, they do not lead to any virtues or purification of the spirit. Instead, they become impediments to the growth of the soul.

Q9. What is the significance of Hindu puja?

A. Hindu *puja* is a worship performed with faith and devotion to cultivate peace and joy in the minds of devotees. Puja is a loving entertainment to God by His devotees. According to Hindu scriptures, God manifests Himself in a subtle form in the image or idol consecrated for the *puja* by devotees. Refer to chapter 18 for a discussion of various steps involved in the performance of the *puja*.

Q10. Why shouldn't ordinary spoken languages be used in worship instead of Sanskrit?

A. The Sanskrit mantras used in religious rites and ceremonies have a special effect on the minds of those who hear them. This can be experienced by attending a religious ceremony where the Sanskrit mantras are properly recited by the priests who are specially trained to do so. The Sanskrit language has a musical, mystical, and meditative sound that is unmatched by any other language. The ancient sages revealed their truths in Sanskrit, so to use a different language would diminish the full meanings of the mantras.

The use of translations of the Sanskrit mantras into presently common languages during ceremonies are unable to produce the solemn and sacred atmosphere required for performing such holy acts. Before beginning a religious ceremony, a description of the rites and the translations of the Sanskrit mantras should be presented, followed by the performance of the rituals and the recitation of the Sanskrit hymns in the traditional manner. This will allow devotees to comprehend the full significance of rites and ceremonies while still receiving their utmost benefits.

Q11. Who are the gods a Hindu must please in order to achieve good karma?

A. There is only one Supreme Being, God (note capital G) of all religions. The Hindu gods and goddesses (note small g), also called deities, are various manifestations of the Supreme Being. These gods and goddesses are neither independent of the Supreme Being nor are they superior or inferior to each other. Just as the same man may be called a father, husband, friend, a manager, or a community worker, depending upon his particular duties at the time, the Supreme Being is called by different names, such as Brahma, Vishnu, or Shiva, when he is conceived of as creating, preserving, or dissolving the universe, respectively. Hindu religion cannot be equated with polytheism, but rather with

monotheistic polytheism, indicating that all gods and goddesses are different forms of the Supreme Being.

Good karma is not achieved by pleasing gods. Good
karma is only achieved by performing righteous work in
accordance with the moral and ethical principles of the
scriptures, and without anticipation of reward.

*Q12. Bhagavan Krishna used to steal butter when He was a
child. He also lied occasionally. Why did He not set a good
example for other children to follow?*

A. Prior to Bhagavan Krishna, the Divine was viewed as the
abstract Brahman, Who could not be seen, touched, or loved.
Brahman appeared in the body of Sri Krishna to live and act
as a common human being in order to illustrate that Brahman
can be seen, touched, befriended, and loved in a concrete
human form. This is why Krishna acted as a common human
being, laughing and crying, enjoying and suffering, loving
and hating, and promising and deceiving.

Q13. What is the significance of Vedic deities?

A. As early as the Rig Veda, a Hindu was conscious of the
fact that the One Reality can be described by various names.
The Vedic deities, which were associated with natural phenomena during the early Vedic period, represented various
names of the One Reality. This idea is expressed in what
became the famous mantra of Hindus, "They call Him Indra,
Mitra, Varuna, Agni, and even the fleet-winged celestial bird
Garuda. The One Reality, the wise speak of in many ways"
(Rig Veda I.64).

The prominent Vedic deities are Agni (god of fire), Indra
(god of Heaven), Varuna (god of the sea and waters), Vaayu
(the god of wind), and Yama (the god of death).

Part III
Hindu Epics

No Storm Lasts Forever

It will never rain 365 days consecutively. The rain may ruin your vacation or your roof! It may flood your basement. But no matter how hard it rains, one day the rain will end and water will dry up. Even snow cannot fall sixty, seventy, or eighty days in a row. Just keep in mind, all the snow piled up outside your door will melt one day. No storm, not even the one in your life, can last forever.

(anonymous)

Chapter 30
Essence of Ramayana

Ramayana, the oldest epic of Hindu dharma, narrates the story of Rama, the seventh incarnation of Lord Vishnu. The original version of Ramayana includes 24,000 Sanskrit verses and was composed by Sage Valmiki during the period 600-300 BCE. In the seventh century, Ramayana was written in the Tamil language by Kamban. Soon after, various versions of the epic appeared in other regional languages of India. In the seventeenth century a very popular version of the epic was composed in Hindi by Tulsi Das, a famous Indian poet.

The Story

The story begins in the court of King Dasharatha. He is a noble and virtuous monarch who has three queens, namely Kausalya, Kaikeyi, and Sumitra. Dasharatha is troubled because he has no sons to succeed him to the throne. He performs *Ashvamedha* (a horse sacrifice) to have a son born to him. In due course, four sons are born: *Rama* is born from Kausalya, twin brothers *Lakshmana* and *Shatrughna* from Sumitra, and *Bharata* from Kaikeyi. The four brothers are brought up in royal luxury and receive their education and training in the hands of the best known teachers and gurus of the kingdom. Although all brothers do very well in their education and training, Rama excels them all. His goodness, valor, and heroism are at their best.

When Rama is in his teens, Sage Vishvamitra approaches King Dasharatha and seeks Rama's assistance against two demons who interfered with the meditations and the austerities of the sage in the forest. The sage reveals to the king that Rama is an incarnation of God (Lord Vishnu) and has the divine power to destroy any demon who may come in his way. King Dasharatha agrees, but also sends Rama's brother (Lakshmana) along to help.

Rama and Lakshmana travel with the sage to the forest where the sage practiced his austerities. On the way Rama kills the powerful demoness Tataka. Next, Rama kills one of two demons (who had harassed the sage) and chases the other one away. Subsequently, Vishvamitra asks the two princes to accompany him to see Janaka, the king of Mithila. King Janaka had organized a *Svayamvara* (a ceremony in which the bride chooses the groom) for his daughter, Sita. Sita was born mysteriously by rising from the earth and appearing as a child to King Janaka.

At the place of the Svayamvara ceremony rests the strongest and largest bow that has ever existed. It had been dragged there by over one-hundred fifty strong men. According to the rules of the ceremony, the successful candidate must lift and string the bow, but no one had been able to achieve this feat before.

One by one, all of the kings and princes present at the ceremony--including Ravana, the demon king of the island of Lanka--attempt with all their might to lift the bow, but no one succeeds. When Rama places his hands on the bow, he not only succeeds in lifting it, but he also breaks the bow while pulling the string. Thus Rama wins Sita's hand in marriage. This humiliates Ravana, who was considered to be a king of unprecedented physical strength, but was unable to lift the bow. This was the beginning of Ravana's hatred towards Rama.

When informed of Rama's marriage, Rama's father (King Dasharatha) arrives with his other two sons. At the advice of sages Vishvamitra and Vasishtha, Sita's sister, Urmila, is married to Lakshmana and her two cousins are married to Rama's two remaining brothers, Bharata and Shatrughna. Thus in one big ceremony all four brothers are married.

Although all four brothers are equally dear to King Dasharatha, Rama has won the hearts of his parents, teachers, and the people of the kingdom. After consulting his ministers, Dasharatha decides to declare Rama the future king. Although everyone in the palace and in the kingdom rejoices at this news, Kaikeyi's (one of King Dasharatha's wives) maid-servant, Manthara, is not happy to hear this news. She

Chapter 30

pollutes Kaikeyi's ears against Rama and insists that Kaikeyi must demand that Dasharatha proclaim Bharata, Kaikeyi's own son, the future king of Ayodhya.

Thus Kaikeyi, the favorite wife of Dasharatha, announces her disapproval of Rama's coronation. She demands that Dasharatha fulfill two promises that he had sworn to her long ago, after she saved his life in a war. Kaikeyi demands that Rama be exiled to the forest for fourteen years and that her own son Bharata be proclaimed the future king. Dasharatha cannot believe his ears, but cannot rescind his promises. He is in such a state of shock that he cannot break this news to Rama.

When Rama learns of his exile, he tells his father, "Do not grieve. As your son, it is my duty to help you keep your promise. I will go to the forest to satisfy Kaikeyi's wish and all will be well." Rama's calmness, serenity, and inner joy could not be pierced by the outward circumstances of life.

Lakshmana (Rama's brother) becomes very angry with his step-mother Kaikeyi, and suggests to Rama that he ignore her and take the kingdom by force. How could Rama, the personification of dharma, succumb to such a recourse? He advises Lakshmana to give up thoughts of violence and adhere to dharma. Lakshmana, however, is not satisfied until Rama consents to also take him to the forest. Rama then tells Sita that he has been exiled and that he would have to leave her behind in the palace. How could a devoted wife like Sita allow her husband to live in the miseries of the forest while she herself stays behind to enjoy the royal luxuries of the palace? She breaks down in tears, and Rama, struck by her grief, consents to take her along. Soon Rama, Sita, and Lakshmana set out to spend fourteen years of exile in the forest.

King Dasharatha could not bear his son's separation and thus dies of grief soon after Rama leaves for the forest. It is the fruit of his own actions (karma) that King Dasharatha could not escape. In his previous life he had been fond of hunting. One day while wandering in a forest, he heard the sound of a pitcher (being filled with water) and mistook it for the sound of an elephant. He shot an arrow in the direction of the sound, which killed a boy, who was bringing water to

Chapter 30

his blind and thirsty parents. When the old parents heard about the death of their only son, they cursed Dasharatha, "The grief that you have caused us in our old age will be your grief in your old age. You will die of grief caused by the separation from your son."

Bharata, who is away from home and unaware of what had transpired and how his mother had caused Rama's exile, is immediately called upon to assume the throne following Dasharatha's death. Bharata is not happy to become the king, and instead grieves at the exile of his brother (whom he loves most) and at the death of his father. He refuses to become the king and blames his mother for the tragedy that has swept the royal family as well as the kingdom. He leaves for the forest in an attempt to persuade Rama to return and assume the throne. Rama advises Bharata, "It is my duty to honor the word of my father and I will not return to Ayodhya until the term of my exile is complete."

Bharata replies, "In that case I will rule the kingdom in your name only until you return. The kingdom rightly belongs to you and I will only act as a caretaker king." Bharata returns home with a pair of Rama's sandals, placing them on the throne to symbolize Rama's presence in the palace.

Rama, Sita, and Lakshmana continue to live in the forest, traveling from place to place. They often become the target of demons, since Rama frequently battles them to protect the sages and holy men of the forest. Finally, Lakshmana builds a hermitage in the forest to protect themselves, especially Sita, from the wrath of the demons. One day the demon king Ravana sends his sister, Surpanakha, to appear in the hermitage and beseech Rama to marry her. As a loyal husband, Rama expresses his inability to do so and advises the demoness to leave. Ignoring his advice, she makes advances toward Rama. Lakshmana then orders the demoness to leave immediately, but she continues her advances toward Lakshmana as well. This angers Lakshmana and he immediately cuts off her nose and ears.

Insulted, Surpanakha approaches her brothers Khara and Ravana (the demon king of Lanka) for revenge. Khara arrives and fights, but is killed in battle with Rama. With his sister insulted and brother killed, King Ravana cannot live in peace. In a carefully contrived plan, he sends the demon Marica, in the guise of a golden deer, to roam around Rama's hermitage. The plan is to entice Rama and Lakshmana away from the hermitage and forcibly abduct Sita.

Upon seeing the golden deer, Sita is struck by its unusual beauty and desires to have a garment made out of its charming skin. She asks Rama to go and fetch the deer for her. In order to satisfy her desire, Rama chases the animal and shoots it. While dying, the demon (in the guise of the golden deer) plays a trick to entice Lakshmana away from the hermitage so that Sita would be left unprotected. Imitating the voice of Rama, the demon cries aloud, "Lakshmana, save me!"

Upon hearing the cry for help and thinking this to be Rama, Sita asks Lakshmana to go and help his brother. Before leaving the hermitage, however, Lakshmana draws a magic line on the ground around the hermitage and informs Sita, "This line is endowed with mystic power. Any demon who crosses this line will burn to death. Stay in the hermitage and do not cross the line until we return. It will protect you from demons in our absence."

After Lakshmana leaves to search for Rama, Ravana appears in the form of an ascetic begging for food. Thinking that the recluse is genuine, Sita crosses the magic line to give food to the hungry recluse. As soon as she crosses the line, Ravana grabs her, throws her forcibly in his magic chariot, and proceeds toward Lanka, the capital city of his kingdom. Witnessing Sita's abduction, Jatayu (an old wise vulture) tries to stop Ravana, but fails. Crying helplessly, Sita drops all her ornaments, one by one, in an attempt to leave a trail for Rama to locate her. Subsequently, Ravana attempts to seek Sita's consent to marry him, but she curses him and does not even talk to him directly. On reaching Lanka, Ravana imprisons Sita in Ashoka Van (a palace garden) and gives her twelve months to change her mind, or else face death.

Upon returning to the hermitage, Rama and Lakshmana are shocked to find Sita missing. A desperate search begins immediately, but there are no clues to her whereabouts.

Chapter 30

Relying on the vulture Jatayu's account of the abduction, both Rama and Lakshmana set out toward the south.

Soon they confront a divine being, in an accursed state, who advises them to meet Sugriva (the king of monkeys) and seek his help in rescuing Sita. Sugriva had his own problems. He had been exiled by his own brother, Vali, and deprived of his kingdom.   Sugriva's brother Vali had also abducted Sugriva's wife, Tara. Rama and Lakshmana meet Sugriva and offer to help him rescue his wife and recover his kingdom from his evil brother Vali.

In the battle between the two brothers that occurs shortly thereafter, Rama kills Vali, and Sugriva regains his wife and his kingdom. In return Sugriva offers to aid Rama in rescuing Sita. He orders his commander, Hanuman, to lead an army of monkeys in a search for Sita.

With a mace in his hands, Hanuman flies over the ocean and reaches Lanka, the capital city of Ravana's kingdom. He searches for Sita all over the city and finally locates her sitting in a grove of trees in Ashoka Van. She is surrounded and guarded by demonesses. After waiting for an opportunity to find Sita alone, Hanuman introduces himself to Sita as a messenger of Rama. He shows her the ring that Rama had given him as a mark of identification. He assures Sita that Rama would soon come and rescue her. When Hanuman returns to Rama with news from Sita, preparations for war with Ravana begin immediately.

Aided by Sugriva, Hanuman, Lakshmana, and Sugriva's army of monkeys, Rama builds a bridge over the ocean and crosses over to Lanka. One of Ravana's brothers, Bibhishana, defects to Rama's side. Thus the long awaited war between Rama and Ravana (that destiny had called for) begins. The long, dreadful war somewhat slows down following the deaths of Ravana's two great warriors, Kumbhakarna (Ravana's brother) and Inderjit (Ravana's son). The war finally ends when Rama kills Ravana in the battle. Sita is freed and she returns to Rama, but her ordeal is not yet over.

Thinking that the people of his kingdom may doubt the chastity of Sita, who had been forcibly taken by Ravana, Rama suggests that Sita demonstrate her chastity. Sita is, therefore, asked to walk through burning fire to demonstrate her chastity. For the love and honor of her husband and in order to prove to the world that she is pure, Sita agrees to walk through the burning fire. Before entering the fire she prays to Agni, the god of fire. Immediately the fire god appears, pulls Sita from the fire, and delivers her to Rama. Thus the fire god himself vouches for the chastity of Sita.

By this time the term of Rama's exile is over, and along with Sita and Lakshmana, he returns to Ayodhya. On his arrival in Ayodhya, Rama is crowned the King. However, his troubles continue. After hearing that Sita had stayed in the forcible possession of Ravana for a long time, citizens of Ayodhya began doubting her chastity despite her ability to walk through fire to prove her purity. Rama is hurt by the spreading skepticism regarding his beloved wife's character, but as a loyal king he must sacrifice his personal interests and abide by the opinion of his people. He decides to abandon Sita, who is also pregnant at the time, and instructs Lakshmana to banish her to the forest. Painfully, Lakshmana accompanies Sita to the forest and abandons her in the hermitage of a very compassionate sage, Valmiki.

In due course, Sita gives birth to twin sons, Lava and Kusha, who are brought up by the sage and become two very handsome boys. They are trained in music and art by the learned sage himself. One day Valmiki is to perform a sacrifice at Rama's palace and the sage brings the twins along. During the sacrificial ceremony the twins recite the story of Rama in beautiful music as taught by the sage. The audience at the palace are delighted to hear the story in fine melody sung by the twins. When asked about the identity of the twins, Valmiki reveals that they are the twin sons of Rama whom Sita had given birth to in Valmiki's hermitage in the forest. He praises the character and the chastity of Sita and advises Rama to accept Sita back.

Rama goes to the forest to persuade Sita to return, but this was not destined to happen. Sita's divine mission is over. Upon seeing Rama, she prays to Mother Earth, "Mother, if I am pure and chaste, then accept me back."

Chapter 30

Here, the earth stretches out and Sita disappears into the
ground wherefrom she had originally risen when she appeared as a child to King Janaka. Rama takes his two sons
back with him and rules Ayodhya for a long time.

Religious and Philosophical Essence

Rama's rule of Ayodhya is called *Ramrajya*, literally meaning "the rule of Rama." The Hindu concept of Ramrajya is
centered around a society that is based upon justice, truthfulness, equality of men and women, chastity of men and women,
righteousness, morality, nobility, gentleness, goodness, humility, and valor.

The story of Ramayana illustrates the following doctrines
of the Hindu religious and philosophical traditions:

The overall functioning of the universe (i.e. cosmic operation) is controlled by divine power in accordance with a
predetermined, effective, and intelligent divine plan, known
in Sanskrit as *niyati* (meaning predetermined) or *daiva* (meaning divine). The divine plan accomplishes its goal through
the medium of human action (called karma).

In the Ramayana, the destruction of the demon king
Ravana is the goal of the divine plan. The birth of Rama and
his exile to the forest, the sighting of a golden deer by Sita
and her subsequent abduction by Ravana, and Ravana's death
in the hands of Rama, are some of the milestones of this divine
plan. The divine plan is implemented by divine power mainly
through the medium of human actions. Human actions, at
the same time, are subject to the Law of Karma, one of the
divine laws itself. For example, King Dasharatha's death by
grief (caused by the separation of his son, Rama) is the result
of his own past karma. In his earlier life he had killed the
only child of the old and blind parents.

Dasharatha's wife Kaikeyi, who had saved Dasharatha's life
in a prior battle (good karma), becomes a queen, thus reaping
the fruit of her good deed.

Sita wants an innocent and beautiful animal (golden deer)
to be killed in order to satisfy her temptation for a beautiful
garment. Her bad action (i.e. sending Rama to kill the golden

deer) results in her own abduction by Ravana. Hanuman's worship of God (in the form of Lord Shiva) and his desire to serve Him creates an opportunity for him (Hanuman) to come in contact with Rama (God in a human form). These and many other episodes of the Ramayana illustrate the workings of the Law of Karma, the fundamental doctrine of Hindu religious thought.

Ramayana illustrates the conflict between good and evil forces and the ultimate conquest of good over evil. In the Hindu view, Rama is the symbol of good and Ravana the symbol of evil. But is Rama all goodness? Is this not the same Rama who betrays his wife, Sita, who had abandoned the royal luxuries and comforts just for the sake of her husband? Does not Sita willingly walk through the burning fire to demonstrate her chastity for the love and honor of her husband? Is Ravana then all evil? Had he not done any good deeds? Had he not worked hard to create a rich and prosperous kingdom? Did he not protect his citizens? If Ravana is really all evil, why does his soul merge with Rama following his death?

To answer these apparent contradictions, we need to understand the concept of good and evil in Hindu thought. According to Upanishadic philosophy, there is nothing absolutely good or absolutely bad. The entire universe is the manifestation of Brahman, who transcends both good and evil. Therefore, the concepts of good and evil are valid only relative to the phenomenal world, which itself depends upon a delicate balance of opposing forces, such as love and hate, knowledge and ignorance, good and evil, and life and death. Whatever preserves and maintains the balance between these opposing forces is called good and whatever disturbs such a balance is termed evil.

The agency that disturbs the balance is viewed as evil only until the imbalance is corrected and the balance restored. Ravana is viewed as evil because he had disturbed the cosmic balance by his evil actions. When Ravana is killed, the balance is restored and Ravana is not evil any longer. Because of Ravana's other good deeds Ravana's soul merges with Rama after his death.

Chapter 30

The cosmic order that sustains creation by maintaining harmony (balance) between the opposing forces is called *rita*, in the Vedic language. *Rita* also ensures that the individual, social, and cosmic laws function harmoniously to support the overall cosmic order, the goal of the divine plan. Because of the relative nature of the concept of good and evil, what is good at one level may be evil at other levels, or vice versa. For example, Kaikeyi's action to have Rama exiled may be viewed as evil at the individual level, but her action is viewed as good at the social and cosmic levels, since without her action Rama could not have been exiled, and in turn, Ravana could not have been killed. The goal of the divine plan was to kill Ravana, who had disturbed the cosmic balance through his evil actions.

In the Ramayana, Rama's action to banish Sita to the forest may be viewed as evil at the individual level, but it is good at the social level, since it is the duty of Rama (as a king) to honor public opinion. Although unjustified, the public opinion in Ayodhya was against Sita, as her chastity was in question. In banishing Sita to the forest, Rama sacrifices his personal interests for the interests of his people. This is an important lesson that the present day politicians and public officials can learn from the Ramayana. In Hindu view, social duties and obligations (social dharma) take precedence over individual duties and obligations (individual dharma). A social, community, or political worker must subordinate his or her own personal interests for the larger interests of the community that he or she is called upon to serve.

Mystical Essence

From the mystical and spiritual standpoint, Ramayana illustrates how an individual soul (atman) takes a physical body, and under the influence of maya (cosmic ignorance), mistakenly identifies itself with the body and mind. This mistaken identity causes the atman to feel limited, assume individuality, and to suffer pain and enjoy pleasure in the phenomenal world. Unable to find permanent peace and happiness in the physical existence, the atman struggles through many births

in order to attain spiritual perfection, or release from the cycle
of birth and death. Here is how this fundamental doctrine
of Hindu religion is illustrated in the story of Ramayana:

"Rama" denotes the atman, the omnipresent and the
omniscient divine spirit, the core of all beings. "Dasharatha"
consists of two parts: *Dasha* (ten) and *ratha* (carriage).
Dasharatha, meaning "a carriage made of ten parts," symbolizes the human body that is made of five sense organs and
five elements (Panchamahabhutas, see chapter 37). Thus
Rama's birth as a son to King Dasharatha, symbolizes the
atman assuming a physical body to manifest in the phenomenal world.

The atman functions in the body only when it is united
with the mind. Sita symbolizes the mind and Rama's marriage
to Sita signifies that the atman unites with the mind to live in
the world as an individual. Sita was not born of human
parents, but had risen mysteriously from the ground and
appeared as a child to King Janaka. In the same manner the
mind appears mysteriously when atman takes a human body.

The city of *Ayodhya* signifies a place of no conflict (*Yuddha*
means conflict). The forest denotes Samsara, the physical
world of life's trials and tribulations. When atman takes a
body, it forgets its divinity (i.e. the leaving of Ayodhya) under
the influence of maya (cosmic ignorance), and is involved in
the cycle of birth and death. This is symbolized by Rama's
leaving Ayodhya and his exile in the forest.

Lakshmana symbolizes dharma and the austerities that
protect an individual from the troubles of Samsara.
Lakshmana accompanies Rama to protect him in the forest.
This indicates that dharma and austerities protect individuals
in the physical world.

The golden deer symbolizes the lust for sense objects.
When Sita sees the golden deer in the forest, she persuades
Rama to fetch the deer for her. This conveys the idea that
when the mind is deluded by lust for sense objects in the
world, atman is also deluded (as is Rama) because of its
association with the mind. When the mind is deluded by lust
for sense objects, it loses the power of discrimination (between
right and wrong or good and bad), leading itself to further

ruin. This is illustrated by the dialogue between Sita and
Lakshmana in which Sita, using abusive language, forces
Lakshmana to leave the hermitage to aid Rama, thus leaving
Sita unprotected.

Before leaving the hermitage, Lakshmana draws a mystic
line on the ground near the hermitage and advises Sita to stay
within the hermitage and not walk past the line. As stated
earlier, Lakshmana symbolizes dharma. The mystic line on
the ground symbolizes the boundary of dharma. Dharma can
protect an individual only if the individual stays within the
limits of dharma. When a deluded mind crosses the limits of
dharma, as does Sita by crossing the mystic line, the mind
leads itself to ultimate ruin (symbolized through the abduction
of Sita by Ravana).

Rama without Sita, but accompanied by Lakshmana, symbolizes an individual without mind (that is confused and
deluded), but in the company of dharma. The weeping of
Rama for Sita symbolizes the pain and frustration an individual suffers in Samsara. Such an individual eventually receives
divine help if he stays with dharma. This is why the weeping
Rama, accompanied by Lakshmana, meets Kabandha (a divine
being in an accursed state) who advises him to seek the help
of Sugriva (the monkey king) in order to rescue Sita.

Sugriva represents wisdom, Vali (Sugriva's brother) signifies lust. In the story, Vali deprived his brother (Sugriva) of
his wife and kingdom. Rama meets Sugriva and promises to
help him in his battle with Vali. Accompanied by Rama,
Sugriva battles his brother in order to recover his wife and
kingdom. While Vali is engaged in the battle with his brother,
Rama (who was hiding behind a tree) shoots an arrow at Vali
from behind and kills him.

Rama's shooting of an arrow at Vali from behind symbolizes the idea that lust (symbolized by Vali), being a powerful
enemy of the soul, must be fought tactfully. For example, a
man who lusts for cigarettes cannot give up smoking by
keeping a carton of cigarettes in front of him and promising
that he will not smoke. He must throw the cigarettes away
(or hide them) and not come near them, lest he be overcome
by lust.

Chapter 30

Sugriva (the monkey king) illustrates wisdom, and Hanuman symbolizes intellect. The monkeys (army of Sugriva) symbolize thoughts. When lust is destroyed, wisdom shines forth and one's intellect can control thoughts and direct their power to accomplish one's goal. This is symbolized when Sugriva tells Hanuman to organize an army of monkeys to assist Rama.

Ravana represents ego (*ahankara*). The island of Lanka symbolizes the physical body. The battle signifies spiritual discipline (meditation). Rama's battle with Ravana illustrates that an individual must struggle on the spiritual path in order to curb the senses and kill the ego. Rama's killing of Ravana and the recovery of Sita symbolizes the success of the individual in destroying worldly attachments generated by the ego.

When Sita is recovered, she is asked to walk through a fire to demonstrate her chastity. This symbolizes the first stage of the purification of the mind in its process of final purification through meditation. The final purification of the mind is symbolized by Rama's abandonment of Sita in the forest where she eventually gives birth to twin sons. When the mind is transcended (symbolized by banishing Sita to the forest), the Self shines forth and the individual becomes a *jivanmukta*, a person who has realized oneness with Brahman while still in the physical world. A jivanmukta can live in the physical and the spiritual world simultaneously without any conflict. This is symbolized by Rama's ruling of Ayodhya while living with his twin sons (Lava and Kusha), following Sita's mysterious disappearance into the ground.

Individual and Social Ideals

The Ramayana illustrates Hindu ideals such as the chastity of men and women, friendship, loyalty, sacrifice, kingly duties, and family relationships. The epic also illustrates the Hindu concept of *Ramrajya*, an ideal society based upon dharma, justice, truth, and peace. This is evident through an analysis of the main characters of the story:

Rama is the personification of righteousness, nobility, goodness, humility, and valor. As a son of a noble and virtuous king, he sacrifices his personal life in order to assist his father in fulfilling his promises to his wife Kaikeyi (Rama's stepmother). He leaves for exile in the forest without any grudge or hatred against his stepmother Kaikeyi, who was the cause of his exile. Rama advises his brother, Bharata, who was very angry at his mother (Kaikeyi) for sending Rama to exile, to love his mother and extend her the respect and reverence worthy of a queen.

At his own risk, Rama always fights the demons in the forest who harass the sages and the holy men. He weeps for Sita when separated from her by Ravana. As a devout brother, he weeps when Lakshmana appears dead when hit by an arrow in the battle with Inderjit, the valiant son of Ravana. As a man of dignity and honor, he fights Ravana and kills him. As an ideal king, he banishes Sita to the forest (and loses her forever) in order to satisfy the wishes of the people of his kingdom.

Sita is the ideal of love, devotion, and chastity in marriage for women. She loves her husband with single-hearted devotion during all trials and tribulations of her life. She fights Ravana's every attempt to win her over during the period of her forced possession.

Lakshmana symbolizes the ideal of sacrifice. He leaves his young wife behind in the palace and chooses to accompany Rama in exile. He sacrifices the amenities of his personal life in order to serve his older brother.

Bharata is the ideal of brotherly love. He becomes angry at his mother when he learns that she conspired to exile Rama. He follows Rama all the way to the forest in an attempt to persuade him to return home and assume kingship. When Rama refuses to return, Bharata assumes kingship (in the name of Rama) only as a care-taker and does not actually live in the palace.

Hanuman is the symbol of unprecedented physical strength, ultimate obedience, selflessness, sincere love and humility. Refer to chapter 28 for a discussion of the symbolism of Hanuman.

Chapter 30

Chapter 31
Essence of Mahabharata

Mahabharata, the second major Hindu epic, centers around the story of a great ancient war. This war occurred at Kurukshetra (northern part of India) , over thousands of years ago, between the families of two brothers, Dhritarashtra and Pandu. They were the descendants of the Bharata (or Kuru) dynasty of ancient India, and their families were known as Kauravas and Pandavas, respectively.

While Ramayana is essentially the story of one hero (Rama), Mahabharata is the story of many heroes (see Figure F-18) who capture our imagination. Mahabharata is the largest epic poem in the world and consists of over 100,000 Sanskrit verses organized in eighteen chapters. The *Bhagavad Gita*, popularly referred to as the Bible of Hinduism, is a part of the Mahabharata.

The Mahabharata war lasted for eighteen days and the armies of the Kauravas and Pandavas included eighteen divisions, eleven of the Kauravas and seven of the Pandavas. The epic was composed by Sage Vyasa, the author of many other Hindu scriptures. For centuries this epic was orally transmitted by bards, who may have added their own inter-pretations and content to the original story.

The Story

The Mahabharata is an epic of truly epic proportion. It is comprised of a multitude of stories within the overall narrative. The beginning of the epic takes the reader back to a time over five thousand years ago, when King Shantanu ruled the kingdom of Kurukshetra in India:

One day while wandering in a forest, the king notices a beautiful girl named Ganga standing on the banks of a river. Captivated by her beauty and charm, Shantanu proposes to her, "Would you like to be my charming queen?"

"Yes, if you promise me freedom to make my own decisions," answers the young lady. Without any hesitation, the king accepts the condition of the marriage and Ganga becomes his queen. Together they live happily, but this happiness does not last long.

Soon a baby is born and the mother immediately takes the child and drowns him in a river. The king is struck with grief, but abiding by his promise to give his wife freedom to make her own decisions, he cannot interfere. Another baby is born and the mother repeats her actions. She continues doing so to every child that is born to her. The king cannot tolerate the grief any longer and after the eighth baby is born, the king stretches out his arms and demands, "That is enough. Give this child to me. He is mine." Without saying a word, the mother hands the baby over to the king and walks towards the river. Upon reaching the river, she disappears into the water, never to be seen again.

King Shantanu names the child *Bhishma* and brings him up in the love and the luxury of the palace. Years later, while walking in a forest, Shantanu's eyes fall upon a fisher-woman by the name of Satyavati. Her charm and beauty captivate his heart. When the king proposes to her, Satyavati states her condition, "I will marry you, Oh King, if you promise that my sons will succeed you to your throne instead of your other son from your previous marriage."

The king soon finds himself in a dilemma. On one hand he loves Bhishma, who, as the eldest son, has the first right to the throne. On the other hand, he is infatuated by his passionate attraction for Satyavati.

Bhishma comes to his father's aid by voluntarily denouncing his right to the throne. In addition, he takes an oath of celibacy to ensure that he would have no heirs that may threaten the rights of Satyavati's children to inherit the throne. Thus Bhishma's sacrifice makes it possible for Shantanu to marry Satyavati.

Satyavati gives birth to two sons, *Chitrangada* and *Vicitraviraya*. A series of tragedies follow. King Shantanu passes away and Chitrangada dies young in a battle. Worried that her second son (Vicitraviraya) might also die young without

Figure F-18: Principal Characters of the Mahabharata War

Bold: Female

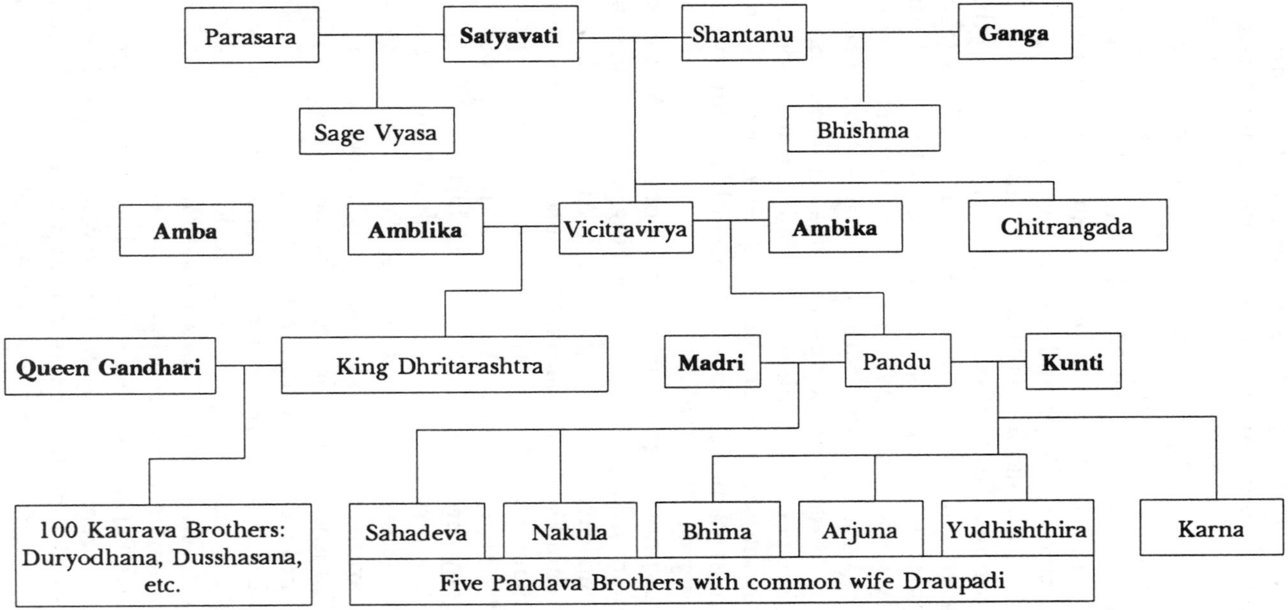

Parasara — Satyavati — Shantanu — Ganga

Sage Vyasa

Bhishma

Chitrangada

Amba

Amblika — Vicitravirya — Ambika

King Dhritarashtra — Queen Gandhari

100 Kaurava Brothers: Duryodhana, Dusshasana, etc.

Pandu — Madri — Kunti — Karna

Sahadeva Nakula Bhima Arjuna Yudhishthira

Five Pandava Brothers with common wife Draupadi

marriage and thus leave no heir to the throne, Satyavati
persuades Bhishma to quickly arrange a marriage for Vicitraviraya. Bhishma travels to Kashi and abducts the three
daughters Amba, Ambika, and Amblika of the king of Kashi
for marriage to his stepbrother. He forces the three princesses
to marry Vicitraviraya. While Ambika and Amblika agree,
Amba refuses to do so because she has been in love with
another king (Saiva) and wants to marry him.

Bhishma allows Amba to return to King Saiva, but to her
misfortune, Saiva refuses to accept Amba, saying that she has
been won by Bhishma and is not worthy of his (Saiva's) love.
Amba blames Bhishma for her misfortune and asks him to
marry her instead. When Bhishma expresses his inability to
do so (because of his oath of celibacy) Amba becomes angry
and resolves to seek revenge against him. She performs
extreme penance to please Lord Shiva, who grants her a boon.
According to the boon, her next birth would be in the body
of a man (named *Sikhandin*) who would eventually kill Bhishma
in the great Mahabharata war.

Another tragedy strikes the family of Satyavati (wife of
Shantanu). Vicitraviraya (now king) dies childless at a young
age and three widows (Satyavati, Ambika and Amblika) are
left behind with no male child to succeed the throne. Satyavati
summons Sage Vyasa (her own son from her previous husband, Sage Parasara) to use his mystic powers to create
progeny through Ambika and Amblika.

This results in the birth of a blind boy, *Dhritarashtra*, to
Ambika and an accursed boy, *Pandu*, to Amblika. Since
Dhritarashtra is blind, Pandu is crowned the new king.
Dhritarashtra is married to Gandhari, who gives birth to one
hundred sons (known as the Kauravas), including *Duryodhana*
and *Dusshasana*, prominent among the Kaurava brothers.
Pandu is married to two women, Kunti and Madri, who give
birth to five sons, *Yudhishthira, Bhima, Arjuna, Nakula,* and
Sahadeva, known as the Pandavas (see Figure F-18).

The Pandavas are not born of human parents, but are the
sons of gods. Pandu had received a curse (for insulting a
sage) which prohibited him from producing children. Pandu's
first wife (Kunti) received a magic mantra from a sage when

she was a young girl. The mantra had the power of inviting any god, who would then produce progeny through her. When she was still unmarried, she used the mantra (to test its efficacy) and invited Surya (the sun god). As a result, a son named *Karna* was born to her. Afraid of social stigma (giving birth to a child without marriage), she disposed of the child, leaving it afloat on a river. Duryodhana's charioteer rescued the child Karna and raised him (with the Kauravas).

After her marriage, Kunti discovers her husband's inability to produce children, and again uses the magic mantra to call three gods. As a result, Yama (the god of justice) sires *Yudhishthira*, Indra (the god of the heavens) sires *Arjuna*, and Vayu (the god of wind) sires *Bhima*. Kunti then gives the magic mantra to Madri, Pandu's second wife, who summons Asvins (the twin gods of medicine) who sire the twins *Nakula* and *Sahadeva*. Although Karna is the brother of the Pandavas (as he is sired by the god Surya before Kunti's marriage to Pandu), he is raised by Duryodhana's charioteer and is not counted as a Pandava. In fact, he is used by Duryodhana (Kaurava) in the war to fight against the Pandavas.

Pandu dies when his sons (the Pandavas) are still young, and Dhritarashtra, his half-brother, becomes the king. Both the Pandavas and the Kauravas are brought up together in the palace. The Pandavas surpass the Kauravas in all phases of learning and sports. This arouses jealousy among the Kauravas, a jealousy that continues throughout their lives. This jealousy becomes more critical when, at the advice of his ministers, Dhritarashtra decides to name Yudhishthira (the eldest Pandava) as the heir-apparent. This is totally unacceptable to Duryodhana, the eldest Kaurava.

In order to eliminate the Pandavas, Duryodhana arranges to send the Pandavas on a pilgrimage. Duryodhana's evil plan is to set fire to the Pandava's temporary residence they use during the pilgrimage. The Pandavas, however, escape unscathed. But to prevent the news of their escape from reaching Duryodhana, the Pandavas disguise themselves as recluses.

During the years that the Pandavas remain in disguise, *King Drupada* (the ruler of a neighboring kingdom) arranges

a Svayamvara (a ceremony in which a bride chooses a groom)
for his daughter, *Draupadi*. The successful candidate must
shoot five arrows through a revolving disc that is placed at the
top of the palace. Hundreds of contestants including Duryodhana try, but all fail. Arjuna is the only successful candidate
and he thus wins Draupadi's hand in marriage.

Upon returning home, the Pandavas jokingly announce to
their mother Kunti that they have obtained some alms for the
day. Thinking that the alms for the day must be food (which
they collected every day by begging as recluses), Kunti
commands them to share it equally. The Pandavas cannot
disobey their mother's word and thus Draupadi becomes the
common wife of all five Pandava brothers. It is at Draupadi's
marriage that the Pandavas first meet their cousin Krishna,
son of Kunti's brother Vasudeva, and consolidate their relation with him.

The news of the Pandavas' escape from the fire and their
success in winning Draupadi reaches Duryodhana and further
fuels his anger. The animosity and jealousy continue to grow
without bounds. In order to diffuse the situation, King
Dhritarashtra decides to give half the kingdom to the Pandavas, allowing them to establish a new capital, Indraprastha.

The Pandavas work hard and establish a prosperous
kingdom for themselves, with their popularity growing considerably. This further kindles Duryodhana's anger toward
his cousins. But when Yudhishthira performs a Rajasuya
sacrifice (a Vedic ceremony for royal inauguration) to lay claim
to universal sovereignty, Duryodhana decides to take action,
since a passive response would otherwise construe an acknow-
ledgment of Yudhishthira's claim to universal sovereignty.

After consulting his uncle Sakuni, Duryodhana contrives
a plan to challenge Yudhishthira to a game of dice. Their
plan would allow Duryodhana to make deceitful moves in the
game, as advised by Sakuni, and thus cheat Yudhishthira of
his riches and kingdom. Yudhishthira is fond of dice, but is
a poor player. However, as a man of honor and dignity, he
cannot reject the challenge.

And so it happens, Yudhishthira is invited to a game of
dice. He loses every move he plays. He loses his gold, jewelry,

treasure, kingdom, his brothers, himself, and finally he offers as stake his wife Draupadi, and loses her too. Duryodhana orders his brother Dusshasana to drag Draupadi into the court. When Draupadi protests, Karna commands Dusshasana (Duryodhana's brother) to disrobe her. While Draupadi is being disrobed, she cries, with tears in her eyes, and prays to Krishna for protection. As they continue pulling on her garment, a miracle occurs and Draupadi's garment multiplies endlessly. Unable to disrobe her, they give up the effort.

Draupadi then questions the court, "How could Yudhishthira use me as a stake when he had lost himself first and become a slave of Duryodhana and Sakuni (Duryodhana's advisor)?" Dhritarashtra cannot answer the question, and thinking that she may be right, addresses to Draupadi, "My daughter, ask for whatever you wish and I will grant it."

"Free my husbands and that is all," replies Draupadi. Thus the five Pandavas are freed and they begin their journey home. Soon after, Yudhishthira is invited again by Sakuni and Duryodhana to play another game of dice. The condition this time is that the loser would give up the kingdom and accept exile. Yudhishthira knows the deceitful moves Sakuni and Duryodhana played in the first game, but he still accepts another challenge. (Perhaps his obsession for the dice game clouds his wisdom, or perhaps the call of fate is too strong to resist.)

Yudhishthira thus plays again and loses again, resulting in the Pandavas and Draupadi being exiled for thirteen years. According to the terms of the exile, they must spend the last year in disguise if they wish the return of their kingdom.

After the stipulated period of thirteen years, the Pandavas return and demand half of their kingdom in accordance with the terms of the exile. Duryodhana refuses to return any territory to the Pandavas. In an attempt to settle the issue peacefully the Pandavas ask for only five villages, one for each of the five brothers, but Duryodhana refuses to return any part of the territory to the Pandavas. Krishna himself launches several peace initiatives, but they are all rejected by Duryodhana. When a war becomes inevitable, Arjuna seeks

Krishna's personal aid as an advisor. Duryodhana, on the other hand, asks for Krishna's army. Thus Krishna relinquishes control of his army to Duryodhana, but offers his personal services to the Pandavas, driving Arjuna's chariot in the battlefield. Eager to fight, both sides finalize their plans for the war. The army of the Kauravas is commanded by Bhishma and the army of the Pandavas by Dhrishtadyumna, Draupadi's brother. On the day of the war Krishna drives Arjuna's chariot between the two armies so that Arjuna can see whom he has to fight.

Upon seeing his own friends, teachers, and relatives standing on the other side of the battlefield, Arjuna is overtaken by grief at the thought of killing them all. He lays down his arms and refuses to fight. Through a spiritual dialogue (that later came to be known as the *Bhagavad Gita*, often called the Bible of Hindu religion), Krishna prepares Arjuna for the war (see chapter 9 for a discussion of the philosophy of the Bhagavad Gita).

The war is a fierce one and lasts for eighteen days. Although Krishna himself does not fight (as he has sworn not to), he provides valuable guidance to the Pandavas in the battlefield. Without Krishna's guidance and Bhishma's vow not to personally kill any of the Pandava brothers, the Pandavas could have easily been defeated by the Kauravas.

Bhishma was considered the greatest warrior of all and had received a boon from his father (after he took the oath of celibacy) that made it impossible for him to be killed against his wishes. However, after ten days of bloody war Bhishma does not see any hope for a victory by the Kauravas and he decides to give up his arms. Aided by Sikhandin, Arjuna eventually kills Bhishma (with Bhishma's permission).

Sikhandin, who was Amba in a previous incarnation, becomes instrumental in killing Bhishma. This is because, as stated earlier, Amba had received a boon from Shiva to avenge Bhishma in her next life as a man (that is, as Sikhandin).

Karna, another great warrior of the Kauravas, is eventually killed by Arjuna. Duryodhana, the leader of the Kauravas, is killed by Bhima.

Chapter 31

Thus, the bloody war of Mahabharata ends with a victory for the Pandavas. Yudhishthira is crowned the king of Hastinapura and the Pandavas rule the kingdom for thirty-six years before relinquishing the kingdom to prince Parikshit, the grandson of Arjuna.

Religious Essence

The Mahabharata is sometimes called the *Pancham Veda* (fifth Veda) since it contains the essence of the four main Vedas. With parables and anecdotes, this epic enables the average mind to comprehend the profound wisdom of the Vedas and the Upanishads. The Mahabharata is a treatise on moral and ethical values of the Hindu religious tradition. The predominant view among Hindu scholars is, "What is in the Mahabharata can be found elsewhere, but what is not in the Mahabharata cannot be found anywhere."

The teachings of the Mahabharata are often summarized in words that are similar to the Christian concept of the Golden Rule: "Thou shalt not do to others what is disagreeable to thyself." The following are some of the major elements of the religious theme of the Mahabharata:

- An important section of Mahabharata is *Shanti-Parva 329.13*, which contains the teachings of Bhishma relating to the duties of householders, kings, and monks, as well as the rules of conduct to be observed in times of crisis. The ethical laws emphasized by Bhishma are truthfulness, justice, kindness, compassion, patience, and amiability. Bhishma does not provide any categorical definitions of good and evil, or righteousness and unrighteousness, since such definitions can change with time and place. What is emphasized is that harmlessness to all creatures is good and virtuous, and injury to them is evil. Although upholding the Law of Karma, Bhishma stresses the virtue of self-effort.

- This epic illustrates the Hindu belief that whenever there is a disturbance in the cosmic order, the divine power removes the disturbance to preserve the balance between

Chapter 31

the opposite forces. For example, Duryodhana's lust for power and his evil action to order the Pandavas burnt in a fire creates a disturbance in the cosmic order. The disturbance is removed in accordance with a predetermined divine plan. Another example is the game of dice played between Yudhishthira and Duryodhana. If Yudhishthira's loss is not viewed as a destined, divine act, then it seems strange that Yudhishthira, the wisest of men, would have agreed to play a second game of dice, when he already knew that Sakuni and Duryodhana cheated in the first game and deceitfully won all his property.

- The Mahabharata illustrates the Hindu belief in the power of *tapas* (austerities and penance). During the Pandavas' exile in the forest, Arjuna performs tapas to secure a divine bow, called Gandiva, from Lord Shiva. This weapon later contributes to the Pandavas' victory in the war.

- The Mahabharata illustrates the Hindu belief that the phenomenal world emerges from Brahman, sustains itself, and merges back into Brahman. The wars and conflicts exist at the level of the phenomenal world and not at the level of the Ultimate Reality. This is symbolized by the "Vision of the Dead" that embodies this epic story: after the war, Dhritarashtra and the queens lament the loss of their children and their dead relatives. Sage Vyasa promises them that he would, by virtue of his supernatural powers, let them see the dead. So one night, while sitting on the banks of the Ganges river, Vyasa calls the dead from both sides, who appear rising from the waters of the Ganges. Dhritarashtra sees his sons together with Bhishma, Drona, Karna and others. All are happy and peaceful. There is no hatred or animosity. The Kauravas and the Pandavas are united happily. With the approach of dawn, all the dead merge back into the waters of the Ganges. The vision is so real that the war itself becomes a dream.

Chapter 31

- The story of Yudhishthira's "Journey to Heaven" in the epic illustrates that unselfishness and concern for others are supreme virtues in Hindu religion . Following their victory in the war, the Pandavas rule the kingdom for thirty-six years before deciding to retire. After retirement, the Pandavas are accompanied by their common wife Draupadi and Yudhishthira's royal dog on a pilgrimage to heaven. One by one, all die on their tough and tedious journey, except for Yudhishthira and his dog, who are left alone to complete the journey.

The Mahabharata provides the following answers to why the Pandavas (except Yudhishthira), including Draupadi, die without reaching heaven: Draupadi dies because she loved Arjuna more than her other husbands (thus reflecting selfishness); ego is the cause of Arjuna's death, as he was proud of his valor; attachment to the pleasures of the world is the cause of Bhima's failure to reach heaven, as he loved to eat and drink and was devoted to his sense of taste; Nakula dies because he was proud of his beauty; and Sahadeva fails to reach heaven because he was proud of his intelligence.

Thus only Yudhishthira, who had spent his entire life in the service of others, succeeds in reaching heaven. At the door to heaven, Yudhishthira is received by Indra, the god of heaven, who welcomes him. Yudhishthira, however, refuses to enter heaven without his wife and brothers. Indra promises him that he would meet them there. When Yudhishthira is ready to enter, Indira refuses to permit Yudhishthira's dog to enter, saying, "Heaven is not for dogs."

"This dog is my friend and I will not enter heaven if my friend is not allowed to enter," says Yudhishthira. At that moment, Dharma, the god of justice, appears and tells Yudhishthira, "You have passed the test. This dog is none other than my incarnation and I was testing you. Your unselfishness and caring for others have earned you a place in heaven."

• One of the central teachings of the Mahabharata is that one must not renounce one's duties and obligations, but perform them in the spirit of detachment, or without expectation of reward and without the fear of punishment. This ancient Hindu doctrine is eloquently expressed in many verses of the Bhagavad Gita.

• The Mahabharata illustrates the conflict between individual and social dharma. For example, Dhritarashtra's conflict is between his duties as father of the Kauravas and as a just king. Arjuna's conflict between his individual and social roles results in his indecision to fight in the war (refer to chapters 1 and 2 of the Bhagavad Gita for a detailed explanation). The Mahabharata illustrates that dharma, when correctly followed, preserves and protects the individual, social, and cosmic orders, but when violated, brings about destruction.

Allegorical Essence

From the allegorical standpoint, the Mahabharata illustrates the belief that Brahman resides in a physical body as atman. Under the influence of maya (cosmic ignorance), atman becomes involved in the workings of the phenomenal world (also called Samsara). By the power of maya we see the infinite, undivided, and changeless Reality as finite, divided, and changing in the phenomenal world, the world of maya. Maya also creates the opposing forces of good and evil to ensure the continuity of the world of maya. This is explained below:

King Shantanu, in this epic story, symbolizes both Brahman and the atman. Ganga denotes knowledge; Shantanu's marriage with Ganga conveys that Brahman unites with its own knowledge to project the universe, as knowledge is necessary for creation. The first five children born to Ganga denote five elements (earth, water, fire, ether, and air----see chapter 37); the sixth child symbolizes the mind, and the seventh denotes the intellect. The eighth child, Bhishma, symbolizes the ego. Shantanu did not save the first seven children who were thrown in the river by their mother Ganga, but he protected the eighth child Bhishma. This illustrates the idea that Brahman is not affected by His creation until the ego is born. The birth of the ego imprisons the Lord as atman in a physical body. The appearance of the ego also drives away knowledge. This is symbolized by the disappearance of Ganga immediately after she hands over the child to Shantanu.

When Bhishma reaches adulthood, he performs extreme actions, such as taking an oath of lifelong celibacy and relinquishing his right to the kingdom. This enables King Shantanu to marry Satyavati, the fisher-woman, who symbolizes maya. The idea conveyed here is that the ego manipulates atman to become involved in the phenomenal world (denoted by Shantanu's marriage to Satyavati, made possible by Bhishma's sacrifice). The deaths of Satyavati's two children (Chitrangada and Vicitraviraya) at their young ages, the birth of the accursed Pandu, and the birth of the blind Dhritarashtra all symbolize the workings of human destiny (the Law of Karma) in the world of maya.

Satyavati symbolizes maya and all her actions in the epic story illustrate the inexplicable power and influence of maya on the lives of the individuals in the phenomenal world. King Shantanu lusts after Satyavati when he first meets her. Prior to King Shantanu's marriage to Satyavati, Bhishma had given up everything in life (by taking the oath of celibacy and renouncing his right to the throne). Yet after Satyavati becomes his step-mother, Bhishma becomes a willing participant in her plan to ensure the continuity of the family she had started. He abducts three princesses, Amba, Ambika, and Amblika, for marriage to Vicitraviraya, Satyavati's second son. Satyavati even persuades Sage Vyasa to perform rituals that would enable the two childless widows, Ambika and Amblika, to have children. This shows that the incomprehensible power of maya induces even Sage Vyasa to perform actions for Satyavati (maya).

The Pandavas and Kauravas symbolize the good and evil forces in human life. The war between the Pandavas and the Kauravas denotes the struggle of the human soul (atman) to

transcend the world of maya and attain unity with Brahman.
The grace of God (symbolized by Lord Krishna in the epic
story) aids an individual to overcome evil and attain perfection.
In this regard, the opposite roles played by Krishna and
Satyavati are interesting to note. Since Satyavati symbolizes
maya and Krishna symbolizes Brahman, Satyavati does everything that she possibly can to ensure the continuity of the
family she had started. The family of Satyavati symbolizes the
world of maya, the phenomenal world of birth and death
(Samsara). Satyavati's creation of the opposite forces (the
Pandavas and the Kauravas) symbolizes the Hindu belief that
this duality in nature is created by maya.

Krishna's role in the above story is exactly opposite of that
of Satyavati. Krishna continues teaching people to mentally
detach themselves from the world of maya and perform all
actions without expectation of reward and without fear of
punishment. He teaches that actions are inescapable in the
world of maya, but attachment to the fruits of one's actions
binds the individual to the phenomenal world.

In the story of the Mahabharata, the evil forces (the
Kauravas) outnumber the good forces (the Pandavas) by
twenty to one (one hundred Kauravas fought the five Pandavas). The evil forces are also assisted by outstanding
warriors, such as Drona, Bhishma, and Karna. Their army
consists of eleven divisions against the Pandavas' seven divisions. But in the end the Pandavas are victorious. This
illustrates the power of God's grace, symbolized by Krishna's
guidance. Krishna continuously guides the Pandavas in the
battlefield until they achieve victory.

Chapter 31

Questions and Answers
Part III

Q1. Why did Bhagavan Krishna use various tricks and deceptive practices in the Mahabharata War to help the Pandavas win the war?

A. Krishna's use of tricks and deceptive practices in the Mahabharata war illustrates that one should not be afraid to fight greater evil by lesser wrong. If one party forcibly seizes the property of the second party and uses wicked means to restrain the second party from claiming its rightful property, the second party may use means that under normal circumstances would be considered unlawful, unjust, or *adharmic* (unrighteous), to repossess its rightful property. According to the *Artha-Shastra*, "In order to protect the institution [society], such measures as are treated of in secret science [as defined in the *Artha-Shastra*] shall be applied against the wicked."[19]

In accordance with the terms of the exile the Kauravas were required to return half the kingdom to the Pandavas following the Pandava's completion of the period of exile. The Kauravas refused to honor the agreement. Lord Krishna undertook several missions in an effort to settle the issue peacefully. The Kauravas not only refused to negotiate, they even threatened Krishna's personal safety. Prior to this, the Kauravas had even attempted to eliminate the Pandavas by sending them on a pilgrimage and having their temporary residence set on fire. The Pandavas, however, escaped unscathed. The Kauravas had also tried earlier to humiliate Draupadi by disrobing her in public, but Krishna came to her rescue.

As the war progressed, the Kauravas, who retained a definite edge in the battle because of their larger army and superior armament, appeared ready to defeat the Pandavas. Victory of the Kauravas over the Pandavas would have meant the victory of evil over righteousness. Thus Krishna chose to use all possible means to assist the Pandavas in destroying evil and upholding righteousness. Refer to page 225 for a discussion of the ethics of Krishna.

Q2. In Ramayana, Bhagavan Rama is projected as a perfect man and a good husband. Why did he abandon Sita just because people in his kingdom doubted her chastity? Is she not the same Sita who had abandoned royal luxuries and comforts just for the sake of her husband?

A. In abandoning Sita, Rama acted as a king and not as a husband. As an ideal king Rama subordinated his personal interests to the wishes of his people. The duties of a king are specified in Kautilya's *Artha-Shastra*: "In the happiness of his subjects lies his happiness; in their welfare his welfare; whatever pleases himself he shall not consider as good, but whatever pleases his subjects he shall consider as good."[19]
    The purpose of the secondary scriptures such as Ramayana and Mahabharata is to regulate the personal and social life of the changing society in accordance with the eternal teachings of the primary scriptures. These secondary scriptures are an *interpretation* of the primary scriptures, an interpretation which naturally depends upon the context and evolving status of society. In light of this, the Ramayana does not suggest that people of this day and age should act in the same manner as the people in Rama's kingdom acted during that time period. The reader should recognize that in Hindu view, *examples* of morality and ethics can change, but the *principles* are eternal. This is merely another way of stating that the truth is immortal and changeless, but the world of maya constantly changes.

Q3. Why is merely a reading of the Ramayana (i.e. in the traditional ceremony of Ramayana Pat) supposed to do so much good, especially reading it in a language that most readers don't even understand? How does the reading of the Ramayana at a stretch, from cover to cover and twice a year, make one a better person?

A. Whether the reading of the Ramayana will benefit one or not depends upon the *bhavana* (feeling) one puts into such reading. Take the example of two men who bathe in the River Ganges, a sacred river in India. One thinks, "What is so great about this Ganges that everyone talks about? Take two parts of hydrogen and one part of oxygen, combine them and you can make the Ganges."

The other thinks, "The holy Ganges flows from the lotus feet of Lord Vishnu. She has dwelt in the matted hair of Lord Shiva. Thousands of sages, saints, and holy men have performed sacred acts on her banks. Such is the Holy Ganges, my Mother Ganges." Filled with this *bhavana* the second man takes his bath. Both men will derive the benefit of physical cleansing from their baths. But because of his *bhavana,* the second man, in addition to physical cleansing, will also derive the benefit of inward purity; his mind will be purified by taking a bath in the River Ganges. The first man will not have the benefit of such mental purification.

Sage Valmiki was an exalted sage of his time, and a prophet in his own right. He has instilled every word of the Ramayana with mystic power. If a person reads the Ramayana with love, devotion, and with the right *bhavana,* he or she will gain the benefit of inward purity. A reading of the Ramayana is said to provide the same effect on the mind as deep meditation.

Q4. *What are the Hindu doctrines of adhikara and Ishta-devata?*

A. The Hindu doctrine of *adhikara* (spiritual competence) requires that the religious discipline prescribed for an individual should be in accordance with his spiritual competence. A laborer requires a different kind of religion than a scholar. It is useless to teach abstract metaphysics to an individual whose heart craves for concrete gods. Religious instruction should be carefully graded to suit the spiritual level of an individual.

The doctrine of *Ishta-devata* (chosen deity) requires that out of the numerous deities--various forms of the Supreme Lord as recorded in the scriptures--a worshipper should be taught to choose the one that satisfies his or her spiritual longing and to make it the object of his or her love and adoration. The chosen deity may be any one of the gods and goddesses of the Hindu pantheon, or any other form of the Supreme Lord as conceived by the heart of the worshipper.

Q5. If ahimsa means non-violence and non-injury, why is the Hindu epic Mahabharata full of violence?

A. Ahimsa does not mean pacifism, inaction, or cowardice. According to the definition of ahimsa, and when the concept of ahimsa is integrated with the other tenets of Hindu religion, injury to life for the protection of life is permitted. Virtuous and dutiful violence that is necessary for self-defense, to defend one's country and protect her honor, to protect higher life from lower life, to fight back an intruder who threatens life and property of an innocent, or to protect dharma, are all really a kind of non-violence, when viewed in the proper perspective.

The war of the Mahabharata is a war between righteousness and evil. In the end, righteousness is victorious. Resisting evil is an essential tenet of ahimsa. Inaction and cowardice are not permitted on the path of ahimsa. If violence becomes necessary to prevent violence, one must stand up against evil with ill-will toward none. This is illustrated in the Mahabharata when Bhishma, the scholarly warrior, tells his companion Karna, "Fight, but without hatred."

It must be recognized that ahimsa is a means and not the end. The true end (goal) is dharma. "I do believe that where there is only a choice between cowardice and violence, I would advise violence...I would rather have India resort to arms in order to defend her honor, than that she should in a cowardly manner become or remain a helpless witness to her own dishonor," declares Mahatma Gandhi, the apostle of non-violence.

Part IV
Other Topics

Get up and set your shoulder to the wheel—how long is this life for? As you have come into this world, leave some mark behind. Otherwise where is the difference between you and trees and stones?—they too come into existence, decay and die.

(Swami Vivekananda)

Chapter 32
Four Goals, Three Debts, and Four Stages of Hindu Life

The ultimate goal of human life is to attain spiritual perfection *(moksha)*, or freedom from transmigration of the *atman.* The social existence of an individual is a means for attaining this supreme goal. Since an individual cannot attain moksha without fulfilling his (her) individual and social duties, responsibilities and obligations, Hindu social philosophy includes the following essential social principles and practices:

- Hindu social philosophy teaches an ancient tradition of respect, freedom, equality of all men and women in the society, and dignity of the individual in relation to the society. The ultimate goal of the individual, however, is to transcend these individualistic traits and seek oneness of all existence, or unity within the diversity.

- In the interests of social welfare, Hindu social philosophy places more emphasis on the duties and obligations of a person toward the whole of society rather than on his (her) own individual rights. A person is expected to rise above his individuality and perfect himself by concentrating on his duties and obligations toward others.

- The relationship between an individual and society is established through the concept of *dharma*, one of the *Four Aims* of Hindu religious life. Dharma provides guidance for the individual, social conduct in the society for securing material and spiritual welfare, and for the growth and harmony of both individual and society. Dharma also reconciles the conflict between individual good and social good. In Hindu religion, Dharma is the cornerstone of human conduct.

The Four Goals of Human Life (*caturvarga*)

Based upon the principle of progressive evolution of the atman, Hindu thinkers have recognized *four goals* of human life: *dharma* (moral law), *artha* (wealth), *kama* (pleasure), and *moksha* (spiritual perfection, the ultimate goal). Dharma is considered the first goal, followed by artha and kama. Moksha, the final goal, is dependent upon the fulfillment of the other three goals. According to Hindu view, one must adhere to dharma (righteous living) in order to satisfy one's natural desires and material needs, with moksha as the ultimate goal. The doctrine of the four goals forms the basis of the individual and social life of a Hindu.

Dharma

The concept of dharma may have been derived from the Vedic concept of *rita*, which signifies the laws that govern the natural and moral order. No single English word can translate the word *dharma*, for it is a concept that has many connotations. The Sanskrit root of dharma is *dhr*, which means bearing, supporting, and upholding that which forms a foundation. Thus dharma means all meritorious actions of the body, mind, and speech that support the functioning of the universe. Dharma, generally translated as righteousness or duty, actually denotes much more than these translations convey. Dharma also denotes traditional duties (individual, social, and religious), good moral and ethical practices, and adherence to righteousness and the laws of the land. Dharma provides moral and ethical guidance for accomplishing material and spiritual goals and for the growth of the individual and society. Dharma holds mankind together individually, socially, politically, culturally, and spiritually, and helps a person fulfill his individual needs and his obligations to society. Finally, dharma determines the social conduct of an individual, maintaining social stability.

Besides the general prescriptions of dharma outlined above, every individual has his or her own dharma (*svadharma*), which is determined by one's position in life, with applicable moral and ethical standards. For example, a soldier's duty is different from that of a doctor. The former's dharma may require him to take a life, but the latter's dharma is to give life. Similarly, a master's dharma is different from that of a servant; a teacher's dharma is different from that of his pupil, and so on. The enemies of dharma are lust (*kama*), attachment (*moha*), egoism (*ahankara*), anger (*krodha*), jealousy (*matsarya*), pride (*mada*), and greed (*lobha*). Adherence to dharma aids an individual in conquering these enemies, live an individually and socially beneficial life on earth, and eventually attain moksha, the final goal of life.

Artha

Artha (wealth) is not an end in itself, but a basic necessity for living in this world. An individual must live physically before he can live spiritually. For this purpose a certain level of economic prosperity is necessary. Poverty is the enemy of spirituality and the fundamental cause of many ills in the world. Poverty can drive a human to commit sin, thus depriving him of spiritual progress. One must, therefore, earn enough wealth in order to raise a family, maintain a household, and ensure a reasonably comfortable life for dependents. Wealth must not be earned for hoarding, but for sharing with those who are poor, handicapped or less fortunate.

Wealth cannot lead to permanent happiness, and excessive wealth is a hurdle in the path of spiritual perfection. This was expressed by Jesus Christ, "It is easier for a camel to pass through the eye of a needle than a rich man to enter the kingdom of God." Dharma and artha, therefore, must be coordinated in order to earn a decent living while recognizing that artha is not an ultimate end of Hindu religious life.

Kama

Kama denotes the wants and appetites of an individual's body and mind in the form of one's desires, passions, emotions, and drives. Hindu thought recognizes the need for satisfying genuine human desires. Life would be dull without recreation and entertainment, such as art, music, dance, sports, conjugal love, filial affection, savory food and drink, fine clothes, jewelry, ornaments, and pleasant company. Hindu thought does not attempt to suppress these desires, but seeks to satisfy them in a controlled fashion. Excessive indulgence in desires and passions can ruin an individual's spiritual progress. Excessive desires can lead to greed, anger, jealousy, attachment, and temptation, the enemies of spiritual progress.

When desires are regulated, the energy associated with these desires can be directed into proper channels for the spiritual growth of an individual. For example, an uncontrolled sexual desire is lust that can destroy one's body and mind. However, when regulated through the process of a socially recognized marriage, the sexual energy of an individual can be dissipated in the proper channels, such as raising a family and sharing one's love with others. This results in an individual who is less egocentric and thus able to grow spiritually. Raising a family, however, is only one stage in a person's life. There is also a stage when one must renounce all desires and continue one's journey toward the final goal.

Through controlled satisfaction of genuine desires and passions, an individual becomes free from kama. This freedom from sensual desires and passions is necessary for attaining moksha, and is made possible by the proper coordination of dharma, artha, and kama.

Moksha

Although there are various views among Hindu thinkers regarding the content of moksha, all systems agree that moksha is the liberation of the soul from the bondage of flesh and the limitations of the finite body. Moksha is the ultimate goal of the Hindu religious life. Moksha is called *Mukti* by the yogis, *Nirvana* by the Buddhists, and the *Kingdom of Heaven* by the Christians. The individual soul (atman), in its liberated state, possesses divine qualities such as purity, omnipresence, and omnipotence, and is beyond limitations. Within the individual, however, the atman is involved in the workings of samsara (the cycle of birth and death in the phenomenal world), thereby subjecting itself to bondage by the Law of Karma. Moksha is attained when the individual becomes liberated from the cycle of birth and death.

Three Debts

The Hindu view of the ideal worldly life is shaped by the ethical concept of three debts that an individual must pay during one's life. The three debts are akin to three mortgages on one's life. These debts are not literal, in the sense of a liability that one is born with and spends his life trying to remunerate. Instead, the concept of three debts reflects another attempt on the part of the Hindu mind to create awareness of one's duties and responsibilities.

The first debt is to God, which one can repay by dedicating one's life to the service of God. To a Hindu, service of God means service to all mankind, regardless of caste, color or creed. Reverence for all forms of life, including plants and animals, and protection of the environment are an important part of this first debt. Service of God also includes the practice of non-violence and truthfulness, obeying scriptural injunctions, practice of self-control and purity of thought, and a pleasant and respectful attitude toward others, especially all elders. In Hindu culture, respect and reverence for the elderly is recognized as partial repayment of this debt to God. Taittiriya Upanishad 1.11 declares that parents and teachers must be treated as gods. As such, this first debt also includes service to and reverence for one's parents and teachers.

A second debt is to the sages and saints who have revealed the truths in the Vedas and other scriptures. This debt can be paid by preserving and enriching the cultural heritage that is handed down through each generation. To preserve and enrich the cultural heritage, an individual should learn and practice the philosophical and theological themes of Hindu dharma. To accomplish this goal, one should donate generously to temples and community service organizations, participate and organize pilgrimages, and support, coordinate or host religious festivals and celebrations of birthdays of saints, sages and holy men and women. An individual should help to organize religious conferences, seminars, symposiums, discussions, and debates at temples, community centers, libraries, and educational institutions. These activities help to expound the teachings of the scriptures and to illustrate how the spiritual wisdom of Hindu sages and saints can be utilized to solve problems facing the world today.

The third debt an individual is expected to pay during one's life is to one's ancestors. The repayment of this debt includes raising one's family in accordance with the moral and ethical principles of Hindu dharma. Since proper education is essential for success in raising a family, adequate education of one's children in religion, and arts and sciences is a major part of this debt.

Four Stages of Life

In order to fulfill all individual duties and obligations, Hindu thinkers have designed a plan called the four stages (ashramas) of life. These ashramas constitute a plan of action for an individual intending to lead him to spiritual perfection hereafter by living a well-disciplined life on earth. in exceptional cases, some of these stages may be skipped. The actual success depends upon the individual and his commitment to the final goal. An *ashrama* literally means a "place to stop (or rest)." In this sense, the four ashramas are the four stops (or resting places) in the journey of life.

At each stage, an individual prepares for further journey until the journey ends in moksha for the soul. Thus the four stages of life may be called the "four-step ladder to liberation." These four stages of life are *Brahmacharya Ashrama* (period of studentship), *Grhastha Ashrama* (householder stage), *Vanaprastha Ashrama* (ascetic or hermit stage), and *Sannyasa Ashrama* (life of renunciation):

Brahmacharya Ashrama

The three main goals of this ashrama are to acquire knowledge, build character, and learn to shoulder responsibilities that will fall upon the individual during adult life. This stage begins when a child enters school at an early age and continues until he or she has finished all schooling and is prepared to assume the responsibilities of the future.

The student is expected to acquire two types of knowledge. First, he or she must acquire knowledge in the arts and sciences, and learn necessary skills for earning a decent living in the world. Second, the individual must acquire religious and spiritual knowledge, the moral and ethical principles of dharma. He or she must learn to discipline the body and mind, practice self-restraint, non-violence, and truthfulness. An individual's competence in successfully assuming the duties and responsibilities of the householder stage of life depends upon the intensity and the depth of knowledge acquired during this stage of life.

Grhastha Ashrama

The beginning point for this stage is one's marriage, which is regarded as a sacrament, and not a contract, in the Hindu view of life. This ashrama forms the foundation for the support of the other two ashramas that follow. The importance of the Grhastha ashrama is often reflected in the analogy that "just like all rivers flow into the sea, all ashramas flow into Grhastha." In the Grhastha ashrama an individual pays the Three Debts. A householder earns wealth and enjoys good and noble things in life in accordance with the formula dharma-artha-kama, discussed as a part of the Four Goals.

In addition to the individual and social duties enjoined by the Four Goals and Three Debts, a householder is required to perform five dharmas (*pancha maha yagnas*) in his daily life. The first is the daily recitation of the Vedas and other scriptures (*Brahma Yagna*). This practice is intended to refresh one's mind with the sacred knowledge that was acquired during the period of studentship. This practice is also intended to preserve and enrich such knowledge.

The second dharma is the daily remembrance of one's forefathers (*Pitri Yagna*). This practice is intended to remind the individual of his duty to preserve, enrich, and continue his cultural heritage. The third dharma is to remember God through daily prayers and meditations (*Deva Yagna*).

Chapter 32

The fourth dharma is to provide food for those who are in need (*Bhuta Yagna*). This practice is intended to inculcate the spirit of sharing, a supreme virtue for all stages of life. *Bhuta Yagna* also includes care of animals and plants. In Hindu view, all life--human, animal and plant--is interdependent. A human being cannot exist in isolation without the help of other human beings, animals, and plants. The daily practice of the *Bhuta Yagna* is, therefore, important for the preservation of our environment.

The fifth dharma is to serve guests with love, respect, and reverence (*Nara Yagna*). This fifth dharma is the basis for the traditional hospitality of the Hindu households.

Vanaprastha Ashrama

After the responsibilities of Grhastha ashrama are complete, which implies that one's children have reached adulthood and have assumed the responsibilities of the household, one enters the Vanaprastha ashrama, otherwise known as the ascetic or hermit stage of life. In modern society this stage would begin at the time of retirement. In this stage one gradually withdraws from active life and begins devoting more time to the study of scriptures, contemplation and meditation. The individual, however, makes himself or herself available in order to provide guidance and share experiences with the younger generation, when requested to do so.

Sannyasa Ashrama

A Sannyasin is one who has renounced the world. This ashrama is the final stage of life in which an individual mentally renounces all worldly ties, spends all of his or her time in meditation and contemplation and ponders over the mysteries of life. In this stage of life an individual must forgo the concepts of 'I', 'My', or 'Mine', and evolve his or her consciousness to seek oneness of all existence. In ancient times one would part company with one's family and become a mendicant. In modern societies this stage can be regarded as complete mental renunciation of the world and total absorption in meditation and contemplation.

Chapter 32

Chapter 33
Hindu Samskaras

Hindu samskaras are the rites or practices enshrined and ordained in Hindu scriptures to guide an individual toward a proper sense of duty and obligation during the various stages of life. Hindu samskaras have been formulated by ancient sages based upon their own intuitive knowledge, experiences, and beliefs relating to the nature of human life.

Samskaras create a religious atmosphere conducive to the maintenance of virtuous tendencies. They purify the mind and intellect by inculcating truthfulness in the mind and purity and generosity in the heart. They create an urge for morality and righteousness. Since anger destroys nobler thoughts, greed leads to evil actions, pride hinders normal growth, and arrogance leads to irrational behavior, samskaras are designed to destroy anger, greed, pride, and arrogance. Samskaras act as signboards on the path of life and direct travelers on their journeys, thus eliminating confusion at the crossroads of life.

In Hindu dharma the birth of a child is considered a religious activity. Samskaras begin prior to birth and end with the cremation of the body following death. Although the number of samskaras prescribed in various scriptures vary from eleven to forty, the following sixteen samskaras are considered the most significant:

- *Garbhadhana* (conception): This samskara is performed by parents and consists of fervent prayers for a child in order to fulfill the parental obligation to continue the human race, one of the three debts (see chapter 32). The scriptural hymns recited by the husband and wife together during this sacrament consist of prayers for mutual love, kindness, compassion, cooperation, and enjoyment in married life.

- *Punsavana* (fetus protection): This samskara is performed during the third or fourth month of pregnancy and prior to consciousness of the fetus. The priest recites Vedic hymns to invoke divine qualities in the child. The purpose of this samskara is to create a spiritual atmosphere at home for the physical growth of the child.

- *Simantonnayana* (satisfying the cravings of the pregnant mother): This samskara is similar to a baby shower, and is performed during the seventh month of pregnancy when prayers are offered to God for the healthy physical and mental growth of the child. According to Hindu sages, the development of the mental state of a child in the mother's womb depends upon the psychological state of the mother during her pregnancy. The purpose of this samskara is, therefore, to give a sense of joy, dignity, and self-confidence to the expectant mother. As a part of this samskara, the expectant mother is advised to dwell on thoughts of nobility, goodness, and divinity, and eat *sattvic* foods (see chapter 15). Through Vedic mantras, the priest invokes the qualities of many deities (gods and goddesses) in the child.

- *Jatakarma* (child birth): Although this samskara is performed at birth, preparations for its performance occur prior to birth. This ritual welcomes the child into the family. Mantras are recited for a healthy and long life. This samskara is performed to create a pleasant atmosphere for both the new born child and the mother.

- *Namakarana* (naming the child): Name selection is performed according to scriptural procedures. The name is selected such that its meaning can inspire the child to follow the path of righteousness. The names given to newborn babies are generally suggestive of the divine qualities of the Vedic deities. A common practice among Hindus is to name their children after the names of sages, saints, holy persons, deities, and the names of the incarnations of God, such as Rama and Krishna. It is believed that by repeatedly calling such names one is reminded of the Lord.

- *Nishkramana* (taking the child outdoors for the first time): This samskara is performed in the fourth month after birth, when the child is moved outside the house and exposed to the outdoors for the first time. At this time the child is believed to be capable of bearing the effects of nature. In this samskara, parents continue to offer prayers for the good health and long life of the child. The Vedic deities are invoked to protect the child from evil forces.

- *Annaprasana* (giving the child solid food): In the sixth, seventh, or eighth month after birth, when teeth begin appearing, the child is fed solid food. Following this samskara the child can eat solid food, not having to rely on mother's milk alone. There are detailed instructions in Hindu scriptures (*Grihyasutras*) relating to the type, quality, and quantity of solid food that the child should be fed.

- *Mundan* (hair cutting): This is performed during the first or third year of age when the child's hair is removed by shaving. According to Hindu sages, this ensures the healthy growth of new hair on the clean head of the child. This popular ceremony, often an occasion for family unions, is usually celebrated with extraordinary festivity.

- *Karnavedha* (ear piercing): This samskara is performed in the third or fifth year of age. According to Hindu sages, ear piercing prevents hydrocele and hernia type diseases. For girls, ear or nose piercing is also performed to enable them to wear ornaments later in life.

- *Upanayana* (sacred thread ceremony): This introduces the male child to a teacher (guru) in order to receive education, thus marking the entry of the child into the *Brahmacharya Ashrama* (period of studentship), the first of the four stages of life (see chapter 32). This samskara is performed from the fifth to the eighth year of age, when the child is invested with a sacred thread (consisting of three strands) to be worn around the neck and waist. The three strands symbolize the three debts (see page 283) that the child repays during his adult life.

  At the time of marriage and as a part of the wedding ceremony, the bridegroom is invested with three more strands of the sacred thread, which symbolize the following three more debts: fulfilling the wedding vows (see Saptapadi on page 297), performing individual and social duties associated with the *Grhastha Ashram* (see page 285), and performing religious rites and ceremonies (*samskaras*) enjoined by scriptures. Thus the six-stranded thread around the neck of a Hindu is a reminder of the six debts that he must repay during adulthood.

- **Vedarambha** (study of Vedas): This samskara is performed at the time of *Upanayana* or within one year thereafter. The guru teaches the *Gayatri Mantra* (the most sacred Vedic mantra) to the child. In this mantra the child prays to God for illuminating his mind and intellect in order to acquire knowledge. The guru also introduces the Vedas to the pupil so that he can study the scriptures while he is still receiving his general education.

- **Samavartana** (returning home after completing education): This samskara is performed at about the age of twenty-five when the student has completed his studies. In ancient times, this samskara marked the end of the *Brahmacharya* stage, when the student was expected to return home from his guru's ashrama.

- **Vivaha** (marriage): In Hindu dharma, marriage is a sacrament and is performed after completing one's education and when two persons of the opposite sex are found compatible for marriage. The marriage enables a person to enter the *Grhastha ashrama* (householder stage), the second stage of the four stages of life. See chapter 32 for the duties and obligations of the householder stage.

- **Vanaprastha** (preparation for renunciation): This samskara is performed at the age of fifty to celebrate the departure from the second stage of life (householder stage) and the entrance into the third stage (*Vanaprastha*). In this third stage, the person renounces worldly attachments and spends increasingly more time in spiritual activities. See chapter 32 for duties and obligations in the *Vanaprastha* stage of life.

- **Sannyasa** (renunciation): This samskara is performed at the age of seventy-five to celebrate the departure from the

Vanaprastha ashrama and the entrance into the *Sannyasa ashrama*, the fourth and last stage of life. In this final stage the person completely renounces worldly attachments and performs spiritual activities. See chapter 32 for a discussion of the duties and obligations of this stage of life.

- *Antyeshti* (cremation): This is the final Hindu samskara that is performed after the death of the person by his or her descendants. In this samskara, the material elements of the physical body return to nature, and the soul (atman) is liberated from the present birth. In India, the ashes are scattered in the holy river Ganges, or other rivers symbolizing return of the material elements of the body to nature.

Relevance of Samskaras in Modern Times

In the Bhagavad Gita, Krishna advises Arjuna to control his mind by means of practice and training. Hindu samskaras create an atmosphere conducive to the training of the mind for inculcating virtuous tendencies. Just as soap and shampoo remove dust and dirt from one's body, samskaras eliminate uncontrolled sensual desires of the mind, such as anger, greed, and pride. They direct the mind toward the path of righteousness, truthfulness, compassion, kindness, and generosity. The performance of the samskaras creates a divine environment that is spiritually uplifting for all the participants, and provides an opportunity for the family members, friends, and relatives to get together and rejuvenate their relationships.

The impact of the samskaras on the training of the mind can be appreciated only when the true meanings of the mantras associated with the samskaras are understood. The persons performing the samskaras must be able to translate the Sanskrit mantras in the language understood by the congregation. When the participants involve themselves in the performance of the samskaras, with a clear understanding of the substance of each and every step of the process, the samskaras are said to have the greatest influence on the mind.

O ne of the three debts of a Hindu is his debt to the sages and saints. Preserving and enriching the samskaras is a part of this outstanding debt that a Hindu is obliged to repay.

Chapter 33

Chapter 34
Hindu Marriage

In Hinduism, marriage is viewed as a sacrament and not a contract. Hindu marriage is a life-long commitment of one wife and one husband, and is the strongest social bond that takes place between a man and a woman in the presence of their parents, relatives, friends, and society.

Grhastha ashrama (the householder stage), the second of the four stages of Hindu religious life (see chapter 32), begins when a man and woman marry and start a household. For a Hindu, marriage is the only way to continue the family and thereby repay his debt (see Three Debts in chapter 32) to his ancestors. The sacredness of marriage in Hinduism is reflected in the fact that most of the manifestations of the Ultimate Reality take the form of wedded, not single, gods and goddesses.

In Hindu view, marriage is not a concession to human weakness, but a means for spiritual growth. Man and woman are soul mates who, through the institution of marriage, can direct the energy associated with their individual instincts and passions into the progress of their souls. Family life is a training ground for a man and woman to practice divine love through human love, patience, consideration of others, forgiveness, respect, kindness, and self-control. These spiritual qualities, when developed, contribute to a happy marriage and accelerate spiritual progress.

The recognition of the spiritual ideal of Hindu marriage requires that the couple recognize marriage as a permanent lifetime relationship, and therefore an indissoluble one. In Hinduism, marriage is not an experiment to investigate whether or not one likes the other, but an irrevocable commitment for a lifetime relationship. In order to satisfy such a commitment, a couple must be ready, willing, and able to subordinate their individual interests and inclinations to the larger ideal of reflecting God's unconditional love through lifelong companionship. Hindu philosophy recognizes that there are natural differences in taste and temper, and ideals and interests of the individuals. The Hindu ideal of the institution of marriage is to reconcile these differences to promote a harmonious life.

Four Factors of a Permanent Marriage

One common notion is that "all marriages are happy; it is the living together afterwards that causes problems." From a Hindu viewpoint, four factors form the foundation for a permanent marriage. First, there must be similarity of spiritual goals and ideals and a willingness to attain them together through study, effort, and self-discipline. Physical attraction alone is not a true basis for a lifetime relationship.

A marriage is said to be like a triangle where God is at the apex and the husband and wife are at the other two corners that form the base of the triangle. As long as the couple is at the base, there is great separation between them. However, when they begin moving toward God, the distance between them decreases. The distance between them decreases to zero when they reach God and unite in Him forever in joy.

The second factor is one that an elderly Hindu would impart if asked for advice: "A wife must be wise like an elephant, pure like a dove, affectionate and home-loving like a pigeon, and loyal as a dog. A husband must be brave like a lion, wise like an owl, strong like an elephant, and faithful like a dog."

The third factor is the similarity of intellectual, social, cultural, and environmental interests. Such common interests enable a husband and wife to establish considerably more friendship and better communication between themselves. The fourth factor for a happy and permanent marriage is physical attractiveness and compatibility.

Selecting a Marriage Partner

In Hinduism, marriage is viewed as the beginning of a responsible and purposeful life. This makes the selection of marriage partners for a Hindu marriage very crucial. In order to minimize the chance of error in selecting a suitable life companion, family-arranged marriages have been a common practice in Hindu culture. An arranged-marriage is one where preliminary selection of a marriage partner, for their son or daughter, is made by parents or elders in the family. Ideally, the parents or elders use their experience in assessing the intellectual, social, psychological, and moral compatibility of the potential spouses. If the preliminary assessment indicates that the potential spouses are compatible, they are introduced to each other for their individual consent. At this stage the potential spouses may spend some time together (e.g. go out together for an afternoon or evening of recreation) in order to come to their own decision.

The Social Practice of Dating

According to the New Catholic Encyclopedia, there are six advantages and fifteen social, moral, and psychological dangers associated with the American practice of dating. The advantages of dating are the following: "It provides (1) friendly association with a member of the opposite sex, (2) permits a wide range of social contacts and experiences, (3) develops experience in adjusting to others, (4) tends to enrich the personality by providing self-identity and self-contrast with the opposite sex, (5) gives a broader freedom of choice of a marriage partner, (6) frequently reduces personal sexual tension."

The disadvantages of dating are the following: "(1) often distracts from study and self-development, (2) destroys the influence of older people of more mature and calm judgment, (3) narrows contacts by too early an involvement in steady dating, (4) offers opportunity for mutual exploitation, (5) provides opportunity for prematurely falling in love, (6) leads frequently to marriage before social or economic maturity has been attained, (7) increases the incidence of premarital pregnancy and forced marriage, and (8) leads to rebound marriages after sudden discontinuance."

Chapter 34

The psychological dangers of dating include: "(1) premature and excessive emotional pressure on the adolescent to test his dating-rating and popularity, (2) attempts to give signs of love and affection before adequate self-image and self-love are achieved, (3) false security from the too-quickly achieved permanence of the steady date, (4) falsely based jealousy and insecurity if a date fails, (5) emotional turmoil of premature love affairs and disengagements from them, (6) possible confusion of sex-role identification in the more or less equalitarian boy-girl friendship, and (7) unresolved guilts from sexual advances not judged accurately on moral principles."

Thus, in general, the practice of dating as prevalent in American society does not seem to contribute toward stable permanent marriages. Dating in America begins at an early age (often in junior high school) and begins essentially as a thrill-seeking or prestige-seeking adventure with little or no educational value.

Dating and Hindu Marriage

If the implied goal of dating is permanent marriage and if practiced only when young men and women have attained full psychological and emotional maturity, then dating can be an acceptable alternate to the arranged-marriage concept in Hinduism. In order to enhance the advantages and minimize the disadvantages associated with dating as identified above, parents as well as religious and cultural organizations must assist the youth in understanding the moral, social, and psychological consequences of dating. Parental guidance and influence, through open communication, must be available to young people to assist them in forming mature judgments necessary for perfect biological, psychological, moral, and spiritual union.

Hindu Marriage Ceremony

In Hindu religion, the marriage ceremony is entirely of a religious nature, but is preceded by supplementary rites which are of customary, traditional, or social nature. These supplementary rites may vary from place to place or region to region.

The ceremony is performed by a priest at the bride's place (or a temple), before a nuptial fire, and lasts several hours. The day and time of the wedding is set by the priest. The most important rite for the validation of a Hindu marriage is the ceremony called *Saptapadi*.

Although there are some variations among Hindus in the rites and rituals associated with marriages, the following customs and scriptural rites are central to all Hindu marriages:

Baraat--The bridegroom arrives for the wedding along with his family and friends. They are received by the bride's family and friends.

Commencement of the Marriage--The priest commences the marriage under a canopy that is specially decorated for the ceremony. The priest invokes blessings of God for the couple to be married. The bride offers yogurt and honey to the groom as a token of purity and sweetness. The bride greets the groom by placing a garland around his neck and the groom reciprocates. Both are congratulated by guests. The priest invokes the memory and blessings of forefathers of the bride and the groom for this auspicious occasion.

Kanya Dana (giving away of the daughter)--The bride symbolizes her change of status from an unmarried woman to a wife by spreading turmeric powder on her hands. *Kanya Dana* is performed by the father (or uncle or guardian) of the bride in the presence of a large gathering that is invited to witness the wedding. The father pours out a libation of sacred water symbolizing the giving away of the daughter to the bridegroom. The groom recites Vedic hymns to Kama, the god of love, for pure love and blessings. As a condition in offering his daughter for marriage, the father of the bride requests a promise from the groom for assisting the bride in realizing the three ends: *dharma, artha,* and *kama* (see chapter 32). The groom makes the promise by repeating three times that he will not fail the girl in realizing dharma, artha, and kama.

Vivaha (wedding)--The bride and the bridegroom face each other, and the priest ties their garments (the bride's sari and the groom's shirt) in a knot, symbolizing the sacred union.

Chapter 34

The bride and the groom garland each other and exchange rings. Next, a nuptial fire, symbolizing the divine witness and the sanctifier of the sacrament, is installed and worshipped. Both the bride and the groom grasp their hands together and pray to God for His blessings. *Samagree*, consisting of crushed sandalwood, herbs, sugar, rice, ghee (clarified butter), and twigs is offered into the sacred fire to seek God's blessings for the couple.

Panigrahana (holding the hand)--The bridegroom stands facing west and the bride sits in front of him facing east. He seizes her hand and recites Vedic hymns for happiness, long life, and a lifelong relationship.

Laya Homa--Here the bride offers the sacrifice of food (poured into her hands by her brother, or someone acting in her brother's behalf) to the gods for their blessings.

Agni Parinaya--The bridegroom holds the bride by the hand and both walk three times around the nuptial fire. Both offer oblations and recite appropriate Vedic hymns to gods for prosperity, good fortune, and conjugal fidelity. They touch each others heart and pray for the union of their hearts and minds.

Asmarohana (mounting the stone)--At the end of each round of the nuptial fire, both the bride and the groom step up on a stone and offer a prayer for their mutual love to be firm and steadfast like the stone.

Saptapadi (seven steps, the wedding vows)--This is the most important rite of the entire wedding ceremony. Here the bride and the bridegroom take seven steps together around the nuptial fire (Agni) and make the following seven wedding vows to each other:

> With God as guide, let us take,
> the first step to nourish each other,
> the second step to grow together in strength,
> the third step to preserve our wealth,
> the fourth step to share our joys and sorrows,

the fifth step to care for our children,
the sixth step to be together forever,
the seventh step to remain lifelong friends,
perfect halves to make a perfect whole.

The *Saptapadi* ceremony concludes with a prayer that the union is indissoluble. At the end of this ceremony the bridegroom and bride become husband and wife.

Suhag--The groom places *sindhoor* (red powder) on the bride's hair indicating that she is now a married woman.

Ashirvad (blessings)--The groom's parents bless the couple and offer cloth or flower to the bride (now their daughter-in-law), symbolizing her joining of the groom's family. All those assembled shower flowers on the couple and bless them, completing the marriage.

A Rig Vedic Hymn for Wedding

Among many hymns from the Vedas and other scriptures, the following Rig Vedic hymn is used in the wedding ceremonies (Rig Veda Book X, Hymn LXXXV):

(*Husband*) I take thy hand for good fortune so that with me, thy husband, thou may attain old age; the solar deities give thee to me to live family life. (*To both the husband and wife*) May thou not be separated; may thou reach thy full years, sporting with children and grandchildren and rejoicing in thy house. (*To the Bride*) Flourish thou with thy husband, be good to all men and women, to the animals, be of amiable mind and of great splendor; be the mother of heroes, be devoted to Gods. Bounteous Indra! Endow this bride with excellent children and fortune; give her ten sons and make her husband the eleventh [i.e., the husband should be attended with love and care as if he were the youngest child]. So may the Universal Gods, so may the waters join our hearts! May Gods together bind us close!

Chapter 34

Chapter 35
Some Popular Mantras

A mantra is a sacred syllable, word or verse which has been revealed to a sage in deep meditation. A mantra, when recited with devotion, concentration, and understanding, revitalizes the body and mind with mystic power, and harmonizes thought and action. There are thousands of mantras in Hindu scriptures that are recited during prayers, meditations, and religious functions in homes and in temples.

A mantra, when repeated constantly during meditation, first loudly and then through silent and mental chanting, changes the consciousness. A mantra produces a change in one's consciousness depending upon the mystic power associated with the mantra. Although one can chant any mantra with faith and devotion during meditation and derive significant benefit from it, a mantra must be sought from a spiritual master (guru) in order to derive full benefit. The success of a particular mantra in affecting one's consciousness depends upon the inherent tendencies (samskaras) of an individual. The guru possesses the required intuition and wisdom to determine which mantra would be effective for a particular individual. The following are a few of the most popular mantras used by Hindus in prayers and meditations.

Gayatri Mantra
The Gayatri Mantra is the most sacred Rigvedic mantra. *Gayatri* means "the savior of the singer." The mystic power of this mantra is considered so significant that it is called "the mother of the Vedas." There is nothing higher than the Gayatri in the Vedas. Gayatri Mantra is also called *Savitri Mantra*, as it is addressed to *Savitri* (i.e., the Sun as the creator).

Facing east (symbolically the sun), a devotee repeats this mantra a number of times (usually a fixed number). This mantra is imparted to a young child at *Yagnopaveet* (*Upanayana*, the sacred thread ceremony) for initiation into the religious and spiritual order of the Vedas:

> *Om bhoor bhuvah svah; tat savitur varaynyam; bhargo*
> *dayvasya dheemahi; dhiyo yo nah prachoda-yat; Om.*
> (Rig Veda 3.62.10 and Yujur Veda 36.3)

Om (God), *bhooh* or *bhoor* (earth, the giver of life), *bhuvah* (atmosphere, the dispeller of miseries), *svah* (wealth, the bestower of happiness), *tat* (that), *savitur* (creator), *varaynyam* (most worthy, acceptable, and desirable), *bhargah* or *bhargo* (personification of knowledge), *dayvasya* (of divine), *dheemahi* (meditate), *dhiyah* or *dhiyo* (minds, intellects), *yah* or *yo* (one who), *nah* (our), *prachoda-yat* (inspire, lead).

> God is the giver of life, the dispeller of miseries, and the bestower of happiness. Let us meditate upon that Creator, the most worthy and acceptable Almighty God. May He inspire and lead our minds and intellects.

Guru Mantra

In this mantra the devotee worships God as Supreme Guru (teacher, spiritual preceptor) of the universe.

> *Gurur Brahma gurur Vishnuh, gurur devo Maheshvarah;*
> *gurussakshat param Brahma, tasmai shri gurave namah.*
> (Guru Gita)

Gurur (Guru, the spiritual preceptor), *Brahma* (the creator within the Hindu Trinity), *Vishnu* (the preserver in the Hindu Trinity), *devo* (God), *Maheshvarah* (Lord Shiva, the destroyer within the Hindu Trinity), *gurur+sakshat* = *gurussakshat* (Guru alone), *param Brahma* (supreme Brahman, the Absolute), *tasmai* (to Him), *shri gurave* (respectable Guru), *namah* (be my salutation).

> The Guru is Brahma (the creator within the Hindu Trinity); the Guru is Vishnu (the preserver in the Hindu Trinity); the Guru is the great God Shiva (the

final dissolver of the universe within the Hindu Trinity); the Guru alone is the Supreme Brahman, the Absolute. To Him, the great Guru, I offer my salutations.

Prayer and Meditation Mantra

This mantra is popularly used in prayer and meditation:

Akhanda-mandala-karam, vyaptam yena chara-charam;
tat padam darshitam yena, tasmai shri gurave namah.
(Guru Gita)

Akhanda (the entire), *mandala-karam* (cosmos), *vyaptam* (is pervaded), *yena* (by whom), *chara-charam* (the animate and the inanimate), *tat* (that), *padam* (state or goal), *darshitam* (is indicated), *tasmai* (to that), *shri gurave* (respectable Guru), *namah* (salutations or prostrations).

Salutations to the Supreme Guru by whose grace the ultimate state of being, which pervades the entire cosmos and everything animate and inanimate, is realized.

God's Grace

In the following verse of the Bhagavad Gita, Lord Krishna promises His grace to those who surrender to Him:

Sarva-dharman paritya-jaya, maam ekam sharanam vraja.
Aham tvaa sarva-paape-bhyo, moksha-yisyaami maa suchah. (BG 18.66)

Sarva dharman (all religious concepts), *prityajaya* (having abandoned), *maam* (to Me), *ekam* (alone), *sharanam* (refuge), *vraja* (take), *aham* (I), *tvaa* (thee), *sarvapaapebhyo*, (from all sins), *moksha-yisyaami* (will liberate), *maa* (not), *suchah* (grieve).

Abandoning all religious concepts, take refuge in Me alone. I will liberate thee from all sin; grieve not.

Chapter 35

Prayer to God as Divine Mother

This is the most popular mantra for praying to God in the form of Divine Mother:

> *Sarva mangala mangalye, shive sarva artha sadhike.*
> *Sharanye trayambake gauri, narayani namostute.*
> (Durgasaptasati or Chandi 11.10)

Sarva (all), *mangala* (auspicious), *mangalye* (all auspicious things), *shive* (good and noble), *sarva* (all), *artha* (wealth), *sadhike* (the shelterer, the fulfiller), *sharanye* (salutations), *trayambake* (multi-formed), *gauri* (bright one), *narayani* (Divine Mother), *namostute* (salutations to Thee).

> Salutations to Thee, O Divine Mother. Thou art
> the auspicious of all auspicious, essence of all good
> and noble, fulfiller of desires, multi-formed, bright
> one, the shelterer of all.

Complete Surrender to God

This mantra is usually recited at the conclusion of a prayer, meditation, or religious function. Here the devotee surrenders his or her individuality to the Lord for His grace:

> *Twameva mata cha pita twameva, twameva bandhuscha*
> *sakha twameva.   Twameva vidya dravinam twameva,*
> *twameva sarvam mama deva-deva.*

Twameva (you alone), *mata* (mother), *cha* (and) *pita* (father), *bandhu+cha = bandhuscha* (brother and), *sakha* (friend), *vidya* (knowledge), *dravinam* (wealth), *sarvam* (everything), *mama deva-deva* (my God of all gods).

> O h Lord! You alone are my mother, father, brother,
> friend, the knowledge, and wealth. You are every-
> thing to me and the God of all gods.

Universal Prayer

The following is the most popular mantra, for the well-being of the entire world. It is usually recited at the conclusion of a prayer, meditation, or other religious rite:

Chapter 35

Om sarve bhavantu sukhinah, sarve santu nira-maya-ah;
sarve bhadrani pashyantu, ma-kaschit dukha-bhak bhavet.
Om shantih, shantih, shantih.

Om (God), *sarve* (all of mankind), *bhavantu* (may be),
sukhinah (happy), *santu* (may be, become), *niramayaah* (free
from disease), *bhadrani* (prosperity, auspiciousness), *pashyantu*
(may see, experience, enjoy) *ma* (not), *kaschit* (any one),
dukha-bhak (experiencer of misery), *bhavet* (may be, become),
shantih (peace).

Oh lord, may all of mankind be happy; may all of
mankind be healthy; may all of mankind experience
prosperity; may none (in the world) suffer. Peace,
peace, peace!

Peace Invocation
The following Upanishadic mantra affirms that this universe is a manifestation of Brahman:

Om poornam-adah poornam-idam, poor-nath poornam-
udachyate; Poor-nasya poornam-adaya, poornam-eva-va-
sishyate. (Isavasya Upanishad)

Om (God), *poornam* (whole, full), *adah* (that), *idam* (this),
poornath (the whole, the full), *udachyate* (comes out, manifests),
poornasya (from the whole), *adaya* (appears, is taken out),
evavasishyate (still remains).

That is full, this is full; the full comes out of the full.
Taking the full from the full, the full still remains.

The true meaning of the above mantra is not reflected in
the literal translation provided above. The word "that" refers
to the Absolute Brahman, the unmanifested state of the
Absolute. The word "this" refers to the universe, the manifested state of Brahman. The meaning of the above mantra
is that Brahman is infinite, undivided, and changeless before
and after creation. Brahman does not change and there are
no modifications involved in the process of creation of the

universe. Refer to chapter 37 for further discussion of this subject.

Morning Prayer
The following prayer is recited in the morning while looking at one's hands:

Karaagre vasate Lakshmiih, kara madhye Saraswati.
Karamuule tu govindah, prabhaate kara darshanam.

On the tip of your fingers is Goddess Lakshmi and in the middle of your palm is Goddess Saraswati. On the base of your palm is Lord Govinda [Vishnu]. Realizing this, look at your hands every morning.

Prayer for Education, Enlightenment, and Success
The following prayer is recited by the disciple and his guru together for removing obstacles so that the guru can successfully impart higher knowledge to the disciple. This prayer is also recited by a devotee, at the commencement of any venture, for removing obstacles for the success of that venture.

Om sahanaav-avatu, sahanaav bhunaktu. Saha veeryam karavaa-vahai. Tejaswinaa-vadheetam-astu, ma vidvishavahai. Om shantih, shantih, shantih.
(Taittiriya Upanishad II.1)

Om (God), *sahanaav* (us both together), *avatu* (may protect), *bhunaktu* (may cause us to enjoy), *saha* (together), *veeryam* (with great energy), *karavaavahai* (let us do), *tejaswinaa* (brilliant), *vadheetam* (study), *astu* (may become), *ma* (not), *vidvishavahai* (may hate each other).

Om...May He protect us both (guru and disciple). May He cause us to enjoy (the Supreme). May we both work with great energy. May our study become brilliant. May we not hate each other.
Om...peace, peace, peace.

Chapter 35

Universal Prayer for Enlightenment and Immortality

The following mantra is most popular among Hindus. The mystic power of this mantra has been recognized by Hindu sages from time immemorial. In this mantra the devotee prays to the Lord for freedom from ignorance and attainment of immortality (union with God):

Asato ma sad-gamaya; tamaso ma jyotir-gamaya; mrtyor-ma amrutam gamaya. Om...shantih, shantih, shantih.
(Brihadaranyaka Upanishad 1.3.28)

Asato (unreal), *ma* (from), *sad* (real), *gamaya* (lead me), *tamaso* (darkness), *ma* (from), *jyotir* (light), *gamaya* (lead me), *mrtyor* (death), *ma* (from), *amrutam* (immortality), *gamaya* (lead me), *shantih* (peace).

Lead me from unreal to real; lead me from darkness to light; lead me from death to immortality. O m...peace, peace, peace.

In the above hymn *unreal* means death, *real* means immortality, *darkness* means death, and *light* means immortality. Thus the meaning of the entire hymn in short is *make me immortal*, i.e. lead me to the Truth, the Absolute Reality, so that I may free my atman from the cycle of birth and death and eternally unite with the Supreme Lord.

Popular Short Mantras

The following are some of the short mantras popular among Hindus:

Aham Brahmasmi - I am *Brahman* (the *atman* or spirit).
(Brihadaranyaka Upanishad)

This mantra affirms that an individual is essentially the spirit (*atman*) living in a physical body. The spirit is immortal, whereas the physical body is subject to death and decay. In the absence of the spirit, a body is dead, and in the absence of a body, the spirit cannot manifest itself in the phenomenal world.

Chapter 35

Tat Tvam Asi----That thou art.
(Chandogya Upanishad)

In this mantra "That" refers to *Brahman*, the Absolute. The meaning of this mantra is that Brahman alone exists and is the essence of everything in the universe. Brahman alone is real and everything else is only an appearance of Brahman.

Prajnanam Brahma---Brahman is pure consciousness.
(Aitareya Upanishad of the Rig Veda)

Ayam Atma Brahma---This self is Brahman.
(Atharva Veda)

The above four mantras are famous Upanishadic declarations from the four Vedas, expressing the highest Vedantic truths. These four sentences are called *Mahavakyas* or "great utterances."

Om Tat Sat---O m! That is Being.
(Bhagavad Gita 17.23-26)

In this mantra, "That" refers to Brahman, manifested as creation and "Being" refers to Brahman in the unmanifested state. Thus the mantra means, "What we perceive as creation is in reality Brahman." This mantra usually appears at the end of scriptures. The significance of this mantra is explained in Slokas 23 through 26 of Chapter 17 of the Bhagavad Gita. Each chapter of the Bhagavad Gita ends with this mantra.

Om Namo Narayanaya---O m! Honor be to God in man. (Narayana Upanishad Sloka 5)

This mantra glorifies the atman in a human being and is used as a traditional form of greeting among saints and holy persons.

So-ham Ham-sah---I am He, He is I.

In this mantra "I" refers to the *atman* and "He" refers to *Brahman*. Thus the mantra affirms that the *atman* and

Brahman are one and the same; an individual is the atman wrapped up in a physical body.

Sarvam khalvidam Brahma - Everything [animate and inanimate] is indeed Brahman.
(Chandogya Upanishad 3.14.1)

Popular Mantras of Various Traditions (*Sampradayas*)

The following are some of the mantras which are popular among the followers of various religious traditions (*sampradayas*) within Hindu religion:

The most sacred "mantra of the sixteen names," the "Great Mantra" of the devotees of Bhagavan Krishna:
Hare Krishna Hare Krishna Krishna Krishna Hare Hare
Hare Raama Hare Raama Raama Raama Hare Hare.

The most auspicious mantra of Vaishnavism:
Om Namo Naaraayanaaya - Adoration to Lord Vishnu.

The most auspicious mantras of Shaivism:
Namah Shivaaya ca Shivataraaya ca - Obeisance to Lord Shiva, who is supremely auspicious.
Om Namah Shivaaya - Adoration to Lord Shiva.

The most sacred mantra of Shaaktism (worship of the Supreme Lord as Divine Mother):
Om Hrim Chandikaayai Namah - Homage (adoration) to the Divine Mother, Goddess Chandika (Durga).

The most sacred mantra of Ganapathyam (worship of Lord Ganesha):
Om Sri Ganayshaaya Namah - Homage (adoration) to Lord Ganesha.

The most sacred mantra of Kaumaaram (worship of Lord Karttikeya or Subramanya):
Om Kaarttikeya Namah - Adoration to Lord Karttikeya.

Chapter 35

Chapter 36
Major Hindu Festivals

Festivals are an important means of spiritual regeneration in Hindu religion. In addition to national festivals, there are many state festivals celebrated by Hindus in India. In one way or another, Hindu festivals are associated with Hindu deities. Through these festivals, Hindus affirm their faith in their religion, culture, and spiritual heritage that has existed for thousands of years.

The fixed dates for the celebration of festivals are determined by the Hindu lunar calendar, called *Panchanga* ("the five limbs"). The lunar calendar (*Panchanga*) is based upon the daily rising and setting of the moon, and on its waxing and waning characteristics.

The lunar month is divided into two fifteen-day parts. Beginning with the new moon, the subsequent fifteen days culminating in the full moon (*Purnima*) are called waxing or bright fortnight (*Shukla Paksha*). The next fifteen days following the full moon culminate in the new moon (*Amavyasa*) and are called waning or dark fortnight (*Krishna Paksha*). Each day of the month is associated with either the bright fortnight or the dark fortnight.

The lunar year consists of twelve months of thirty days each. The calendar adds an extra month once every five years to correct for the difference between the solar and the lunar year. The names of the months of the lunar year are: *Chaitra* (March-April), *Vaisakha* (April-May), *Jyeshtha* (May-June), *Ashadha* (June-July), *Sravana* (July-August), *Bhadrapada* (August-September), *Asvina* (September-October), *Karttika* (October-November), *Agrahayana* (November-December), *Pausha* (December-January), *Magha* (January-February), and *Phalguna* (February-March).

In the Hindu calendar, the days of the week are believed to be governed by deities. Sunday is ruled by the Sun (*Ravi*) and is called *Ravivar* (*var* means day); Monday is called *Somavar* and is ruled by the moon (*Soma*); Tuesday or *Mangalvar*, is ruled by Mars (*Mangal*); Wednesday is ruled by Mercury (*Budh*), hence *Budhvar*; Thursday is ruled by Jupiter (*Brhaspati*) and is called *Brhaspativar*; Friday or *Shukravar* is ruled by Venus (*Shukra*), and Saturday is ruled by Saturn (*Sani*) and is called *Sanivar*.

Although there are many other festivals celebrated by Hindus, this chapter includes a brief discussion of only the major festivals and religious fairs (*melas*).

Vasant Panchami

This festival falls on the fifth day of the bright fortnight of Magha (January-February) and is dedicated to the worship of Saraswati, the goddess of knowledge and learning (see chapter 25). The celebration includes dances and the singing of bhajans (devotional songs of love) in honor of the goddess. Because Saraswati reigns over education, Vasant Panchami is especially observed by teachers and students. Special celebrations are held in schools by children, who worship and offer flowers to the goddess.

Mahashivaratri

Mahashivaratri (the great night of Shiva) falls on the fourteenth day of the dark fortnight of Phalguna (February-March), and is dedicated to the worship of Lord Shiva. This festival is purely religious in nature and universally observed by all Hindus. On this day devotees sing bhajans in honor of Shiva, recite Sanskrit shlokas (verses) from scriptures, offer prayers in the morning and evening, and some observe fasting throughout the day. People visit nearby temples of Shiva and offer prayers in large crowds. The prayers and worship continue late into the night when the devotees offer coconut, Bilva leaves, fruits, and specially prepared sacred food to Shiva and his divine consort Parvati. Offering Bilva leaves to Shiva on Shivaratri is considered very auspicious by his devotees.

The origin of Shivaratri is attributed to several stories in Hindu mythology. One very popular story traces the origin of this festival to the churning of the Ocean of Milk by *devas* (gods) and *asuras* (demons). It is said that when both gods and demons were churning the Ocean of Milk to obtain *amrita* (water of immortal life), they came across many unusual substances, including the deadly poison *Kalakuta*. As soon as they touched the poison, it exploded into poisonous fumes that threatened to envelope the entire universe by darkness. When the destruction of the universe seemed inevitable, the gods ran for assistance from Brahma and Vishnu, but neither was able to help. At last they ran to Lord Shiva, who raised his trident and condensed the fumes. To save creation, Shiva swallowed the poison without spilling a single drop. The poison left a dark blue mark on Shiva's throat. The gods praised and worshipped Shiva for saving the universe.

The philosophical essence of the above story is as follows: gods and demons symbolize all kinds of individuals (both good and bad) in the world. The Ocean of Milk represents the ideal world that is full of peace and happiness for all human beings. Churning the Ocean of Milk signifies the human activity in the world. The amrita symbolizes happiness and the poison represents human greed and selfishness. Shiva symbolizes the atman (self), the spiritual essence of an individual. Worship of Shiva denotes meditation and contemplation by an individual on his or her own self.

The above story is symbolic of the fact that individuals perform actions in the world in order to achieve happiness. In this process a person is usually overpowered by greed and selfishness, ruining his or her efforts for obtaining peace and happiness. Thus the only way to achieve peace and happiness is by worshipping Shiva at night, that is, by meditating on one's own self during the night when the individual is free from the distractions of the physical world. When the individual attains self-knowledge, he or she can live in the world without being affected by craving, anger, greed, attachment, pride, jealousy, and egoism, the seven enemies of the soul. Therefore, Shivaratri symbolizes the worship of the atman within.

Another story in Hindu mythology also emphasizes the auspiciousness of Shivaratri: On the day of Shivaratri, a hunter, who had killed many birds in a forest, was chased by a hungry lion. The hunter climbed a Bilva tree to save himself from the lion's attack. The lion waited throughout the entire night at the bottom of the tree for its prey. In order to stay awake to avoid falling from the tree, the hunter kept plucking the leaves of the Bilva tree and dropping them below. The leaves fell on a Shiva Linga that happened to be located at the bottom of the tree. Shiva was pleased by the offering of the Bilva leaves by the hunter, although inadvertently, and saved the hunter in spite of all the sin the hunter had committed by killing the birds. This story emphasizes the auspiciousness of worshipping Shiva with Bilva leaves on Shivaratri.

Holi

Holi is a very popular and colorful festival celebrated with more vigor in North and Central India than in the South. In the South, a similar festival occurs simultaneously, known as the *Kama Festival*, celebrated in honor of Kama, the god of love. Although there seems to be no direct link between the two occasions, both are age-old traditions of celebrating the arrival of spring.

Holi is celebrated at full moon in the month of March, corresponding to the month of Phalguna in the Hindu lunar calendar. Although there exist several stories relating to the origin of this festival, the following are the two most popular, as told in Hindu folklore:

King Hiranyakashipu was a devotee of Shiva and had received boons of power and wealth. He became obsessed with his power and claimed sovereignty over the gods. He demanded that his subjects stop the worship of the other gods and instead worship him. He tortured those subjects who did not agree. His own son, Prahalada, was a staunch devotee of Lord Vishnu even when he was a little boy. He challenged his father's claim of sovereignty over the gods and the world. He prayed to Lord Vishnu, "I want no kingdom, heaven, or freedom from birth. All I want is an end to the miseries of the people caused by my father."

Hiranyakashipu, realizing his own son to be a potential threat to his authority, decided to do away with him. When all his efforts to kill Prahalada failed, the king sought the help of his sister, Holika or Holi, who had received a boon that she could not be killed by fire. Holika placed the litle boy in her lap and lit a fire around her in an attempt to burn Prahalada in fire. However, Lord Vishnu rose from the fire, revoked Holika's boon, burnt her to ashes, and saved the life of His devotee Prahalada.

To celebrate this victory of virtue over sin, fires are lit on the eve of Holi. People collect wood and pile it around a central pole. Sometimes a pot is filled with seeds and buried under the pole. The pole symbolizes Prahalada and the wood symbolizes Holika. The pole survives the fire, whereas the wood is burned to ashes. People also throw coconuts in the fire to help burn Holi. Some people forecast the success or the failure of future crops by interpreting the direction of the flames or the condition of the seeds in the pot buried under the pole. The ashes from the fire are sometimes collected as protection against diseases and evil spirits.

Another legend of the Holi festival is that the female demon Pootana, under orders from King Kamsa, attempted to kill the infant Krishna on this day by feeding him poisoned milk. In the process, however, Krishna killed Pootana. To celebrate this event, people enact divine plays that Krishna enjoyed with the cowherd boys and girls. Sometimes women beat (lovingly, of course) the men with sticks and the men must accept this light punishment. People of all ages, castes, and classes sing, shout, and throw colored water at each other, all of which is intended to symbolize the tricks and pranks played by Krishna on the gopis (cowherd girls).

Whatever may be the origin of the festival of Holi, its celebration symbolizes the happiness of the arrival of the spring season. A long and cold winter can be an emotional setback. Holi provides hope for a new year with new aspirations. This may explain the erotic and occasionally curious moods and attitudes of the people while playing Holi. This is symbolized by people wearing peacock feathers on their heads, and their clothes and faces stained with different colors.

Chapter 36

Ugadi

Ugadi, the Telugu New Year's Day, falls on the day of the new moon in the month of March-April. Both Maharastrians and Kannada people also consider Ugadi as the start of their new year. On this occasion people wear new clothes, greet one another, prepare feasts, light fireworks, and celebrate the event with great rejoice. This day is also the beginning of the new fiscal year for public institutions. The officers of the government prepare revenue accounts for the ending year and farmers renew their leases, if any, for their lands.

At approximately the same time as Ugadi, Telugus also celebrate another festival, called Panchganga. This festival is considered very auspicious for the start of new ventures, including jobs. On this occasion, a savory food item, known as chutney, is made from neem flowers, fresh green mangoes, jaggery, and tamarind. This delicacy is considered highly nutritious and, as a part of the celebration, is distributed to as many people as possible.

Ramanavami

Ramanavami, the birthday of Lord Rama, the sixth incarnation of Lord Vishnu (see chapter 26), falls on the ninth lunar day of the bright fortnight of Chaitra (March-April). This festival, celebrated with great sanctity and fasting, is one of the five important fasts (Maha-vratas) observed by Hindus since ancient times. On this day temples are specially decorated, and religious discourses narrate the life story of Rama (see chapter 30). Chariot processions (Ratha Yatras) carrying the idols of Rama, his wife Sita, brother Lakshmana, and devotee Hanuman are held in major cities and towns. An extraordinary religious function consisting of sacred discourses, the singing of bhajans, and dramas depicting the life story of Rama, is held at Ayodhya, India, the birthplace of Lord Rama.

In Andhra Pradesh, India, Ramanavami is celebrated for nine days. One of the significant events of the celebration is the re-enactment of the wedding ceremony of Rama and Sita, known as Srirama Kalyanamahotsavam.

Chapter 36

Rakhsha Bandhan

The festival of Rakhsha Bandhan, also known as Rakhi, is widely celebrated by Hindus in order to strengthen the bond between a brother and sister. *Rakhsha* means security and *Bandhan* means relation or bond. Rakhsha Bandhan, therefore, means a "bond of security" that is renewed between a brother and sister.

On the day of Rakhsha Bandhan each girl ties a thread (known as Rakhi) on the wrist of her brother. In return the brother gives a gift (usually cash) to the sister to indicate the acceptance of the Rakhi. By accepting this thread the brother pledges to support and protect his sister in times of distress. This tradition of tying the thread by a girl continues even after she is married. If the brother and sister cannot meet each other on the day of Rakhsha Bandhan, the Rakhis and the gifts are exchanged via mail.

If a girl does not have a brother, she can offer to tie a Rakhi (or send by mail) on the wrist of any man, and if accepted by the man, he becomes her adopted brother for the rest of his life. If a girl adopts someone as her brother on Rakhsha Bandhan, she must tie or send a Rakhi to her adopted brother every year thereafter.

The origin of the festival of Rakhsha Bandhan can be traced to the Mahabharata: In order to punish Shishupala for his repeated criminal offenses and sinful deeds, Lord Krishna threw a celestial weapon at Shishupala. In the process of throwing the weapon, Krishna injured his own finger, which bled profusely. At that moment Draupadi tore a piece of her sari to wrap it around Krishna's finger, stopping the bleeding. For Draupadi's favor Krishna promised her his help in the hour of need. Later, Krishna kept his word when he came to Draupadi's rescue, while she was being dishonored by the Kauravas following the game of dice between the Pandavas and the Kauravas (see chapter 31).

A piece of Draupadi's sari was the first Rakhi that gave rise to the festival of Rakhsha Bandhan. Later this festival gained further popularity in India in the old days of foreign domination when the womenfolk needed protection. By performing a simple rite of thread-binding, a woman had the opportunity to claim any man as her brother, who was then obliged to protect her honor even at the cost of his life. This thread-binding ceremony is so sacred that even the ancient Muslim ruler of India, Humayun, could not resist his responsibility to protect the Hindu princess Karmavati (from the tyranny of the Muslim rule), who had just sent a Rakhi to him.

Janmashtami

Janmashtami marks the celebration of Lord Krishna's birthday. Krishna, the eighth incarnation of Lord Vishnu, the eighth child of his parents, was born at midnight in a prison on the eighth day of the dark fortnight of Bhadrapada (August-September). Krishna's father Vasudeva and his mother Devaki (sister of King Kamsa) had been imprisoned by Kamsa, the demon king of Mathura.

Kamsa was a cruel, oppressive, and arrogant king who had unleashed terror in his kingdom by his cruel acts. After astrologers announced that he would be killed by a son born to his sister Devaki, Kamsa killed each of her first seven children soon after they were born. He also imprisoned Devaki and her husband in order to ensure that every child born was killed and that none would escape.

At the time Krishna was born, the prison guards fell asleep and Vasudeva, Krishna's father, managed to escape with the baby out of the prison. Vasudeva took Krishna to Gokula where he was exchanged for the baby daughter of Yashoda and Nanda. Vasudeva returned to the prison with the baby girl. When Kamsa was informed that a girl, and not a boy, was born to Devaki, he decided to kill even this girl. When Kamsa took the girl in his hands and tried to strike her against the ground, the girl slipped away from his hands and flew into the sky announcing, "Kamsa, the savior of the earth is already born and he will soon kill you." Meanwhile, in Gokula the cowherd family of Yashoda and Nanda brought up Krishna, who eventually killed King Kamsa.

Krishna's birthday, the most popular festival among Hindus, is celebrated with great festivity. The entire day and evening is filled with religious activities that include dancing, offering prayers, and singing bhajans in homes and nearby temples. Some devotees also fast on Janmashtami. Throughout India, especially at Mathura and Vrindavan, where Krishna was born and spent his early childhood, colorful plays are staged to depict the popular episodes of Krishna's childhood. The festivities continue until the clock strikes midnight, at which time Krishna's birth is celebrated by momentarily turning off all lights. Following this event, sweets and fruits are distributed, concluding the celebration of Janmashtami.

Ganesha Chaturthi

Ganesha Chaturthi celebrates the birth of Lord Ganesha (see chapter 19). Ganesha, the elephant-headed god, is the son of Lord Shiva and Goddess Parvati. The following story in Hindu mythology explains the birth of Ganesha: Once Parvati was alone in her house. She wanted to take a bath but there was no one in the house to watch for visitors. Parvati created young Ganesha from the dust of her own body and placed him at the entrance of the house, with instructions not to allow anyone inside until she finished her bath.

During this time Shiva returned, but was prevented by Ganesha from entering the house. Shiva was enraged for being denied entrance to his own house and he cut off Ganesha's head in anger. When Parvati learned of this tragedy, she appealed to Shiva for mercy. Shiva ordered his servants to go out and bring the head of the first creature they saw. The servants' eyes laid upon an elephant. They cut the elephant's head and brought it before Shiva. Shiva used the elephant-head to bring Ganesha back to life, thus giving birth to the elephant-headed god. Shiva also pronounced Ganesha the god of wisdom and prosperity. (Refer to Chapter 19 for a true understanding of the symbolism of Lord Ganesha.)

The Ganesha Chaturthi festival lasts for one week. During this festival the devotees offer prayers, perform dances, and worship Ganesha in homes and temples. On the last day, clay models of Ganesha are carried through a procession for immersion into water at a sea, river or lake. Ganesha Chaturthi is a very popular festival in Maharashtra, India, where huge clay models of Ganesha are carried on floats in a procession that is marked by singing, playing of drums, blowing of conches (huge seashells), and the striking of cymbals. The procession ends at a seashore, river, or a lake, where Ganesha is immersed into the water.

A large body of water (sea, river, or lake) symbolizes the impersonal aspect of Brahman, the sole essence of the universe. An icon of a deity (god or goddess) represents the personal aspect of Brahman. Thus immersing clay models of Ganesha in water indicates that in the ultimate analysis the personal and impersonal aspects of Brahman are one and the same, a truth that can be realized only through one's own spiritual experience.

Durga Puja

Durga Puja, also known as Navaratra (nine nights), is a festival observed in honor of Goddess Durga. This festival continues for nine nights and is celebrated during the first nine days of the bright fortnight of the month of Asvina (September-October). The tenth day of this festival coincides with another festival known as *Dussehra*, or *Vijaydashmi.*

In Hindu mythology the Goddess Durga (see chapter 23) is one of the principal forms of the divine spouse of Shiva. Durga Puja is a festival that celebrates her victory over the buffalo demon Mahisasura. According to the mythological story, Mahisasura was so powerful that none of the gods were able to destroy him. The gods, therefore, approached Goddess Durga for help. Each god gave her his best weapons. Equipped with the most powerful weapons, Durga destroyed the powerful demon that the gods had been unable to overcome.

The main ritual of this festival consists of placing images of the Goddess in homes and temples through the entire nine nights of the ceremony. During the entire ceremony the Goddess is worshipped with offerings of flowers, fruit, food, and bhajans sung in praise of the deity.

Chapter 36

In India the celebration of Navaratra varies significantly from one region of the country to another. In Tamil Nadu, for example, Goddess Durga is worshipped daily, but on the ninth day the Goddess is worshipped in the form of Saraswati, the Goddess of knowledge and learning. In some regions of India, kanyas (young girls) are worshipped as embodiments of the Goddess and the worship is called *Kanya Puja* (the worship of young girls). For this worship nine girls are worshipped on the fifth day of the celebration, known as *Lalita Panchami*.

In Bengal huge images (icons) of the Goddess are beautifully decorated and worshipped during all nine days. The colorful dances and the devotional singing reach their climax on the night between the eighth and ninth days. On the final day, large colorful processions, marked by singing and dancing, carry the images of the Goddess to the sea, river, or lake for immersion into the water. As explained above under the discussion of Ganesha Chaturthi, immersion of the icons of the Goddess in water indicates that the personal and impersonal aspects of Brahman are one and the same.

Onam

Onam, the most important festival of Kerala, is observed in August-September for ten days. The festival celebrates the symbolic return of the legendary demon-king, Mahabali, who is said to have been very popular among his subjects. Mahabali was a two-sided character: he brought tremendous prosperity to his kingdom and was therefore loved and respected by his people. On the other hand, the king had deprived the gods of all their possessions and due to his egotistic attitude, had declared supremacy over the earth and the heavens.

In his fifth incarnation, known as the Dwarf incarnation, Lord Vishnu assumed the form of a dwarf Brahmin boy in order to punish Mahabali for his devilish deeds. One day Mahabali performed a horse sacrifice, and because of his generosity, declared that he would grant anything that anyone asked for. The Dwarf approached the court of the king and asked for enough space in which the Dwarf could take three

Chapter 36

steps. The king granted the request, and the Dwarf suddenly assumed a gigantic form. His first step covered the earth, the second the heavens, and the third step landed on the head of the king, sending him flying to the underground. Thus the earth and the heavens, which had been claimed by Mahabali, were recovered for the gods by Lord Vishnu.

The above mythological story has deep philosophical significance. Mahabali, the demon-king, symbolizes a human being who normally has both the bright and the dark side to his character. The three steps of the Dwarf represent the three states of human consciousness (awake, dream, and deep sleep). When the ego is destroyed (symbolized by the Dwarf's third step landing on the head of Mahabali), an individual gains divine consciousness, which leads to eternal joy.

Onam is celebrated in the spring season in Kerala, when the sky is blue, the fields are green, the rivers are full with calm and clear water, and the gardens are abundant with fruits and flowers. In this backdrop of natural joy, young children gather flowers during each morning of the festival and arrange them in circles. Also during each day of the festival, a new, larger concentric circle is added. The flower decorations are eventually replaced by a deity made of clay or mud, known as the Lord of the Onam festival. The deity has a square bottom, four faces, and a pointed top. The flower designs, which are expanded each day of the festival, symbolize the slow and steady blossoming of the flower of life in an individual. The square bottom of the deity symbolizes an individual, the four faces represent the four stages of life (see chapter 32), and the pointed top indicates pure divinity (union with God). Thus the entire celebration of Onam symbolizes the slow ascent of an individual from individual consciousness to the divine consciousness, the storehouse of eternal joy.

On the social side, Onam provides an opportunity for family reunions, exchanging presents between friends and relatives, filling one's wardrobes with beautiful clothes, reviving social contacts through dinner parties and gifts, and eating delicacies prepared specially for the festival. Overall, the festival inculcates a sense of oneness among people.

Chapter 36

Dussehra

Dussehra is a ten-day festival beginning on the first day of the month of Asvina (September-October). This festival symbolizes the victory of good over evil and is celebrated in various, extraordinarily festive forms. In Bengal, for example, Dussehra is celebrated concurrently with Navaratra (Durga Puja) to honor Goddess Durga for her victory over the demons. The final celebration (on the tenth day of Dussehra) is the culmination of Navaratra.

In most of North India, Dussehra celebrates Rama's victory over the demon-king Ravana, as described in the Hindu epic Ramayana. During the ten days of the festivities every city and village in North India enacts the story of Rama's life as told in the Ramayana. The festival ends on the tenth day of the month of Asvina, when huge effigies of Ravana are carried to an open space and burnt to symbolize the defeat of Ravana. The effigies are usually stuffed with fire crackers that explode to the cheers of huge crowds.

Diwali

Diwali is derived from the Sanskrit word *Deepawali,* meaning "a row of lights." This festival falls on the new moon night of Kartika (October-November) and is celebrated over a period of five days. The first day is considered very auspicious for the purchase of new clothes, utensils, housewares, and other such items.

Diwali is associated with several mythological stories. According to one story, Lord Krishna is believed to have destroyed the demon Narakasura on the first day of Diwali. In some parts of India, effigies of Narakasura are burned on Diwali to celebrate the victory of Lord Krishna over the demon. In North India, the second day of Diwali is dedicated to the worship of the sacred hill Govardhana, near the town of Mathura, the birthplace of Krishna, a site of deep religious significance to the devotees of Lord Vishnu and Krishna, the eighth incarnation of Lord Vishnu. Hindus also believe that on the day of Diwali, Rama returned to Ayodhya after defeating Ravana, and the people of Ayodhya celebrated the return of Rama by lighting thousands of clay lamps.

Diwali is celebrated by Hindus with extraordinary festivity. Houses are cleaned and painted to sanctify them. Utensils are cleaned, and cushions and upholstery of furniture are changed. People wear new clothes and take pledges to begin a new life. Shops and offices are decorated with colored electric lights. Businessmen close their old account books and begin new ones. At dusk, homes and shops are illuminated with colored lights, followed by fireworks. People exchange gifts and visit friends and relatives.

Pongal

Pongal, also known as Makar Sankranti, is a state festival closely associated with the agricultural life of the people in the states of Tamil Nadu and Karnataka. This festival is celebrated over three days in the middle of January to mark the joy of the new harvest season. On the first day, known as *Bogi*, people throw away some of their old belongings (or burn some of their old pots and clothes in a village bonfire), symbolizing the dispelling of evil spirits from their homes. Next, houses are cleaned, painted, and decorated. Women draw beautiful patterns (*kolams*), with colored and moistened rice flour, on pots, pans, the fronts of door-steps, and at places where special food is prepared for the festival. The next day is the first of the month, *Thai*. The celebrations begin with the cooking of newly harvested rice, which is allowed to boil and overflow, symbolizing the hope of abundance of harvest or wealth.

The third day is *Mattuppongal,* or "the thanking of the farmer's best friends," the cows and the bulls. The cows and bulls are sprinkled with turmeric powder to ward off evil spirits. Their foreheads are lovingly decorated with red powder, their horns are polished, and garlands of beads, flowers, and jewelry are placed around their necks or hung from their horns. The specially decorated animals are paraded through villages to the cheers of huge crowds. The festival concludes with people playing games, such as *Manja*

Virattu, a chase for turmeric, and *Jalli Kattu,* a game similar to a rodeo where men chase a bull and the winner takes whatever is hung from the neck and horns of the bull.

Rath Yatra

Rath means chariot and *Yatra* means procession. Rath Yatra is a procession of chariots held in June or July every year in Puri, Orissa. The city of Puri, one of the holiest places in India, is the location of the famous temple honoring Lord Jagannath. Rath Yatra is held in honor of Jagannath, the Lord of the universe. *Jagat* means universe and *nath* means savior. Jagannath (*Jagat* + *nath*) is another name for Lord Vishnu, the Lord of the universe.

The main event of this festival is the procession of three huge wooden raths (chariots), each about forty-five feet high with wheels approximately seven feet in diameter. The first chariot carries the image of Lord Jagannath, accompanied by over fifty priests who perform the necessary rites. The other chariots carry the statues of Balbhadra, brother of Jagannath, and Subhadra, sister of Lord Jagannath. Devotees from all over India come to Puri to pull the chariots in the procession. The procession begins from the temple of Lord Jagannath at Puri, continues through the city, and culminates in a garden (known as "God's garden"), where the images are maintained for one week before being returned to the temple.

The image of Lord Jagannath, used for the Rath Yatra, is carved out of wood and depicts only the face of the Lord. This figure has no arms, legs, or other parts of the body. According to one legend, when Krishna (incarnation of Lord Vishnu) entered into *Mahasamadhi* (a conscious exit from the physical body) his body was placed on a pyre for cremation. The cremation fire only consumed the legs and arms of Krishna's physical body. The unconsummated portion of the body was immersed into the waters of the ocean. This unconsummated and immersed portion of Krishna's physical body transformed into a log of wood that floated in the ocean toward the beach at Puri. This wooden log was the original image of Lord Jagannath worshipped in the Jagannath temple at Puri.

Amarnath Yatra

The famous Amarnath cave, high in the Himalaya mountains, about seventy miles from Pahalgam (in Kashmir, India), is the destination of thousands of pilgrims on the full moon day (Purnima) in the month of Sravana (July-August). The cave is located about 13,000 feet above sea level and is considered very sacred by the devotees of Lord Shiva. The cave is about 150 feet wide at the entrance, 90 feet high, and can accommodate about six hundred standing people. There are two holes in the northern wall of the cave from which water trickles down to form an ice lingam (pillar), the symbol of Lord Amarnath (Shiva). Although the formation of the lingam is naturally symmetrical, it appears as if it is hand-carved. The size of the lingam naturally changes with the waxing and the waning of the moon. The lingam reaches about eight feet in height in July, diminishes to four feet in August, and drops to about one foot in September.

The Amarnath cave is the sacred place where Lord Shiva taught His wife Parvati the secrets of the universe. Here in this cave, Lord Shiva bestows His vision to those who are pure at heart. Swami Vivekananda had the vision of Lord Shiva in this cave and was blessed with the boon of death-at-will (*iccha-mrityu*).

Pushkar Mela

Pushkar Mela (*mela* means fair) is an annual festival celebrated at Pushkar, in Rajasthan, about a week before the full moon in the beginning of November. Pushkar, a holy town on one side of a lake in Rajasthan, is the location of the famous temple in India dedicated to the worship of Lord Brahma, the first member of the Hindu Trinity.

Thousands of people throughout Rajasthan and other parts of India, including holy men, travel to Pushkar to bathe in the lake on the day of the festival. Bathing in the lake during the festival is believed to be very auspicious.

Kumbha Mela

Kumbha Mela (*kumbha* means pot) is a sacred Hindu pilgrimage that takes place at the following four locations of India: (1) Prayag (near the city of Allahabad, in the state of Uttar Pradesh), at the confluence of the three rivers Ganges, Yamuna, and Saraswati, (2) Haridwar (in the state of Uttar Pradesh), where the river Ganges enters the plains from the Himalayas, (3) Ujjain (in the state of Madhya Pradesh), on the banks of the Ksipra river, and (4) Nasik (in Maharashtra), on the banks of the Godavari river. The pilgrimage occurs four times every twelve years, once at each of the four locations. Each twelve-year cycle includes the Maha (great) Kumbha Mela at Prayag, attended by millions of people, making it the largest pilgrimage gathering in the world.

The observance of Kumbha Mela is based upon the following mythological story: thousands of years ago, perhaps in the Vedic period, gods and demons made a temporary agreement to work together in obtaining *amrita* (the nectar of immortality) from the Milky Ocean, and to share this equally. However, when the Kumbha (pot) containing the amrita appeared, the demons ran away with the pot and were chased by the gods. For twelve days and twelve nights (equivalent to twelve human years) the gods and the demons fought in the sky for the possession of this pot of amrita. It is said that during the battle, drops of amrita fell onto four places: Prayag, Haridwar, Ujjain, and Nasik. Thus Kumbha Mela is observed at these four locations where the nectar fell.

Kumbha Mela is attended by millions of people on a single day and is the most sacred religious event for Hindus. A ritual bath at a predetermined time and place is the major event of this festival. Other activities include devotional singing, mass feeding of holy men and the poor, and religious assemblies where doctrines are debated and standardized. The auspiciousness of Kumbha Mela is in part attributed to the gathering of thousands of holy men at one place on earth.

Chapter 36

Chapter 37

Hindu Religion and Science-- a Complementary Outlook

Religion without science is blind, science without religion is lame.
                                                        Albert Einstein

A religion or philosophy is a myth if it cannot face the scrutiny of science. Religious, philosophical, and scientific concepts should be in reasonable agreement if such concepts are to shape the minds of young people. Young men and women cannot possibly have much faith in their religion or philosophy if teachings at school contradict teachings at home.

In recent times we have seen several major religions, including Christianity, faced with a dilemma. The theory of creation taught by Christianity is not compatible with the concept of evolution proposed by science. The Vedic view is that "religion must be founded on reason and experience. It should not be contrary to natural law and should be part of a way of objectively understanding the inner or higher truth of the human being and the universe. Likewise science must address the ultimate issues of life and death and not merely concern itself with the transient matters. It must not merely turn its eye upon the outer world but also look into the inner world of consciousness." [28f]

The obvious question is, how does Hindu religion square with science? Since science does not yet recognize the concept of the individual soul (atman) of Hindu philosophy, the discussion in this chapter applies only to the evolution of the observable matter in the universe.

The most popular system of Hindu philosophy, known as Vedanta, is essentially a synthesis of the six systems (or schools) of Hindu philosophy (see chapter 6). There are basically two schools of thought in Vedanta: *Advaita* (non-dualism) and

Dvaita (dualism). *Advaita* holds that this universe is an appearance of Brahman. The individual soul (atman) and Brahman appear to be different as a result of maya, but in Reality they are identical.

Dvaita holds that Brahman and prakriti (matter) are two distinct realities, implying that atman is different from Brahman. When compared with science, however, the *Advaita* school of Hindu philosophy is in better agreement with scientific laws and theories governing the existence of the universe. In order to explain the parallels, we must first define some of the major Sanskrit terms as follows:

Definitions

Vivarta - "apparitional causation." This is a transformation by appearance only. In this kind of transformation a cause produces an effect without itself undergoing any change. A classical example of this kind of causation is mistaking a rope for a snake. Nothing really happens to the rope, but in twilight it may appear as a snake.

Parinama - "transformational causation." In this kind of transformation, energy is changed from one form to another without any change in its total amount.

Maya - usually translated as *avidya* or cosmic ignorance; actually means apparitional causation, that is, the mistaken perception of one object for another. In this sense, maya and Vivarta are synonyms and can be used interchangeably. Maya is caused by the three inherent qualities of prakriti (see chapter 4), known as *sattva, rajas, and tamas*. These three subtle qualities of prakriti are also known as the triple powers of maya.

Panchamahabhutas - "the five great elements." According to Hindu sages, the Panchamahabhutas are the ingredients of all matter (gross and subtle) in the universe, including our own physical bodies. There are five Panchamahabhutas:

Panchamaha-bhutas	Conventionally Translated As	Proposed Interpretation
Akasha	Ether	Gravitational energy
Vayu	Air	Kinetic energy
Tejas	Fire	Radiation (or light)
Ap	Water	Electricity
Prithvi	Earth	Magnetism

The reader should note that the earlier translations of the Sanskrit terms *akasha, vayu, tejas, ap,* and *prithvi* as ether, air, fire, water, and earth, respectively, were cited in the nineteenth century, when the classical physics of that time could not correctly explain the creation of the universe. With the advent of Einstein's Relativity Theory, a better understanding of the universe has emerged. It is, therefore, proposed that the Panchamahabhutas be interpreted as the five energies listed above for the purpose of investigating the parallels between Advaita Vedanta and modern science.

Hindu sages have associated the Panchamahabhutas with the five sense organs of human perception. *Akasha* is associated with the ear since the saccule is sensitive to our orientation in a gravitational field. *Vayu* is associated with the skin, because temperature, a measure of kinetic energy, is sensed by the skin. *Tejas* is associated with the eyes because light is visible to the eyes. *Ap* is associated with the tongue because an electric shock leaves a sour taste (protons taste sour). *Prithvi* is associated with the nose since the molecular configurations that produce smell are the result of the magnetic pairing of molecules. In Sanskrit literature, the presiding deities for *ap*

Chapter 37

and *prithvi* are twins. In science, electricity and magnetism are indeed twins, since the two are directly intertwined.

Evolution of the Universe

According to the *Taittiriya Upanishad*, the universe arises from Brahman:

"From Brahman arises akasha [gravitational energy]. From akasha arises vayu [kinetic energy]. From vayu arises tejas [radiation]. From tejas arises ap [electricity] and from ap arises prithvi [magnetism]." (Taittiriya Upanishad 2.1)

The arising of gravitational energy from Brahman is the first cause of the universe and we will discuss it later in this chapter.   The other transformations stated in the above Upanishad statement are discussed below:

Science tells us that the materials of this universe, including the materials of our bodies, are made of 92 naturally occurring chemical elements. All these chemical elements were created from primordial hydrogen gas in the bellies of stars, during billions of years of stellar evolution. Each of these elements consists of a different number of hydrogen atoms and the mass of each of these elements equals the mass of the hydrogen atoms constituting the element.

Billions of years ago there was no sun, no earth, and no planets. The great space of this universe was filled with hydrogen gas, with each atom consisting of one proton encircled by an electron. For billions of years the hydrogen atoms floated in the vastness of space, colliding and drifting on. After an almost endless period of colliding and drifting, the spatial density of atoms increased as they began falling together, in the gravitational field, to form the sun and other stars. In the process of forming stars, including the sun, some of the gravitational energy transformed into the kinetic energy of atoms. Thus from *akasha* arose *vayu*.

While hydrogen was fusing to form stars, the collisions became more frequent and furious. In the collision process some of the kinetic energy was converted into heat energy.

Some of this heat radiated into space and the remaining heat began warming the star. Thus from *vayu* arose *tejas*. When the star became hot, the collisions became wild, emitting electrons from some atoms. Thus from *tejas* arose *ap* (electricity, or the movement of electrons). From *ap* arose *prithvi*, since magnetism is associated with electricity. This explains how, through the process of transformational causation (parinama), the four forms of energy (vayu, tejas, ap, and prithvi) arose from the initial energy within the primordial hydrogen (i.e. from akasha, gravitational energy).

The process of stellar evolution continued. The protons, in the absence of the shielding electrons, repelled each other and flew wildly apart in search of electrons. In the intense heat of the star (ten to twenty million degrees centigrade), the protons fused together to form alpha particles. As the star became hotter, at extremely high temperatures (in the range of two hundred million degrees centigrade), the alpha particles combined together to form the nuclei of carbon and oxygen. At still higher temperatures the carbon and oxygen combined to form the nuclei of the heavier elements, such as iron. When the centers of the stars formed iron, those centers became heavy and collapsed by gravity, producing explosions brighter than a billion suns. These explosions blew up the entire outer layers of the stars, scattering the materials (star dust) all over the galaxy. These are the materials that formed the earth some five billion years ago.

What sustains our lives on earth? Our lives are sustained by the chemical energy that we obtain from the food we eat and the oxygen we breathe. However, the energy actually comes from sunlight. The oxygen comes from the environment and food is grown in the soil. In the presence of sunlight, plants use carbon dioxide, water, and a few other materials to release oxygen. We breathe this oxygen and release carbon dioxide that plants use. With sunlight, plants grow and provide food for the animals. Thus the energy that living beings use comes from the sun.

Where does the sun get its energy from? The sun forms energy from the hydrogen falling under gravity in the core of the sun. Hydrogen combines together to form helium,

emitting radiation in the form of heat and light. Therefore
we see that not only has the primordial hydrogen produced
the universe through stellar evolution, but the current hydrogen in the sun also supports life on earth. Thus the
Panchamahabhutas, through *transformational causation* (parinama), are the ingredients of this universe, and also support
life on earth. The question now is: how did akasha (gravitational energy) arise from Brahman? In other words, what is
the first cause of the universe?

The First Cause

According to *Advaita Vedanta*, akasha (gravitational energy
of the primordial hydrogen) does not arise from Brahman by
transformational causation, as do all subsequent formations in
the universe. According to the Isavasya Upanishad, everything visible or invisible arises from Brahman:

"That is fullness, this is fullness; the fullness comes out
of the fullness. Taking the fullness from the fullness,
the fullness itself remains."

Everything arises from Brahman, but according to the
above verse, *Brahman remains unaffected by such arisings.* Therefore, akasha cannot arise from Brahman through the process
of transformational causation, since this process is by definition a conversion process that would alter the original substance or energy. Thus, the first cause must be *apparitional
causation* (vivarta). We see this universe by mistake (maya or
avidya), says Advaita Vedanta. Under the influence of maya,
the infinite, undivided, and changeless Brahman appears to
us as the universe, just as in twilight a rope appears as a snake.
Because of error in our perception caused by maya, the
infinite, undivided, and changeless appears as finite (small
electrical particles of primordial hydrogen), divided (into
atoms or protons and electrons), and changing (motion of
electrical particles in matter).

According to Advaita Vedanta, the three powers of maya
(*sattva*, *rajas*, and *tamas*) are the causes of error in our
perception. In the above analogy, when one mistakes a rope

for a snake in darkness, the three powers of maya can be explained as follows: by the revealing power of sattva we see the rope; by the veiling power of tamas we fail to see the rope correctly, and by the projecting power of rajas we see the rope as something else (a snake). Likewise the changeless Brahman has not changed (just as the rope did not change), but appears as the universe to our senses because of our faulty perception. Thus the goal of Hindu religious life is to correct our perception using the techniques of Jnana Yoga, Karma Yoga, Raja Yoga, or Bhakti Yoga. We will discuss the scientific bases for these spiritual disciplines later in this chapter.

Without space, electrical and gravitational fields of electrical particles (electrons and protons) of primordial hydrogen could not be perceived. Without time, the changes in energies of these particles could not be perceived. Since we perceive matter in space as finite (small electrical particles) and divided (into atoms), what is beyond space must be infinite and undivided. As changes are perceived in time, what is beyond time must be changeless. Since Reality is said to transcend the divided and the changing, then Reality must be beyond space and time. This definition of Reality can thus be derived from science.

We said earlier that the primordial universe consisted of hydrogen gas dispersed in space. Hydrogen gas consists of protons and electrons. The question we must now answer is, how has this finite, divided, and changing world arisen from the infinite, undivided, and changeless Reality? The process could not be through transformational causation (parinama), because hydrogen gas is energy (gravitational and electrical) and energy cannot initially arise from the *transformation* of energy. Thus by implication (if not directly) science points to apparitional causation as the first cause of the universe.

In apparitional causation, when a rope is seen as a snake, some characteristics of the rope must appear in the snake. The length and the diameter of the rope must be seen as the length and diameter of the snake. If the rope is short and fat the snake is seen as short and fat. If the rope is long and thin the snake is seen as long and thin. A rope cannot be seen as a desk or a chair. Thus if Reality is seen by

Chapter 37

apparitional causation as hydrogen gas dispersed in space, then what is infinite, undivided, and changeless must be seen in the minute particles (protons and electrons) of hydrogen gas, just as some characteristics of the rope are seen in the snake as stated above.   This condition is satisfied in the following manner: the infinite is seen in the electrical charges of the protons and electrons, since like charges repel each other toward infinite expansion. The undivided is seen in the gravitational energy of the protons (and of all matter). The tendency of protons (and of all matter) to fall together due to gravity is the undivided seen in the divided. The property of inertia, which accounts for the tendency of particles (and of all matter) to resist changes in their state of rest or motion, unless acted upon by some external force, is the changeless seen in the changing.   Thus, the infinite, undivided, and changeless Brahman is seen as finite, divided, and changing, under the influence of maya (apparitional causation).

Yoga Philosophy and Science

As living organisms, we are genetically programmed to fulfill biological necessities to ensure our survival (as species) and to pass the genetic code to future generations. We fulfill these biological necessities by transformational causation. We ensure our survival by breathing and eating, and our ego performs this function by discriminating between us (as eaters) and the environment (as food).   But fulfilling biological necessities does not fulfill our yearnings that drive our bodies, such as love, freedom, and peace.

In human beings, love is the undivided seen in the divided (we are divided as individuals), freedom is the infinite seen in the finite (we are finite beings), and peace is the changeless seen in our changes (both mental and physical).   By our yearnings for love, freedom, and peace, we are intuitively seeking the undivided, infinite, and changeless (the God of all religions). The problem is that we are seeking these goals by fulfilling biological necessities (transformational causation), as dictated by our genetic programming.

Chapter 37

Transformational causation cannot lead us to Reality because we did not come into existence by transformational causation. We can reach our goal only by reversing the way we came. We entered existence through indiscrimination (as in the mistake of perceiving a rope for a snake). We can exit only through discrimination (by observing the rope as a rope and not a snake). Thus, we must deprogram our genes to reach our goal.

Hindu religion recommends four methods for deprogramming our genes. These four methods have given rise to the four spiritual disciplines of Jnana Yoga, Karma Yoga, Bhakti Yoga, and Raja Yoga. Jnana Yoga teaches to discriminate the real from the transient. Here the discrimination is not between the organism and the environment, as genetic programming dictates, but between the perceiver (the ego) and the perceived. In this case everything external to the organism, including its body, becomes perceived. This helps the ego to eliminate the notion that it (the ego) is the doer of actions, thereby imparting right knowledge of the Reality to the individual. The right knowledge of Reality enables an individual to have a glimpse of Reality.

Karma Yoga teaches that one should perform all actions without the expectation of reward. The actions dictated by genetic programming always look for reward (fulfillment of biological necessities). Thus Karma Yoga is another deprogramming method in which actions performed do not perform a genetic job. On the contrary, such actions contribute to discrimination, which is the road to Reality.

In Bhakti Yoga one performs all actions as an offering to God. An individual establishes a personal relationship with God in such a way that genetic programming is directed away from our current goal of life, the fulfillment of biological necessities.

Raja Yoga teaches one the control of mind and senses such that genetic programming is directed away from biological necessities (as the goal of life) and toward discrimination. Since the mind sees the rope as a snake, it is the mind that must discriminate between the two by focusing its attention on the rope.

Chapter 37

Hindu Dharma and Heisenberg's Uncertainty Principle

We have seen above that Hindu religion and science walk hand-in-hand in their descriptions of Reality. Now we will see that they also walk together in recognizing the natural limitations of human knowledge.

According to Hindu religion, the impersonal aspect of Brahman (the Ultimate Reality) is immeasurable and beyond human knowledge. Thus there is a natural limitation to what a human being can know. This doubt is expressed in the last four lines of the hymn of creation in the *Rig Veda*:

"None knoweth whence the creation has arisen, and whether He has or has not produced it. He who surveys it in the highest heavens, he only knows, or perhaps he knows not." (Rig Veda 10.129)

According to Advaita Vedanta, we see Brahman as the universe because of maya (cosmic illusion), just as we see a rope as a snake in twilight. However, when we see a rope as a snake, it is impossible for us to identify the snake properly. We cannot know whether the snake is a viper pit or a cobra. Similar uncertainty arises in modern physics and is expressed by Heisenberg's Uncertainty Principle, which states that we cannot measure accurately both position and momentum of a moving particle at the same time. If we precisely determine the momentum of a moving particle, there is no way to measure its position, and vice versa. Thus the Uncertainty Principle reveals that nature itself presents a barrier which we cannot cross in our attempt to understand nature.

Hindu religious thought is complementary with modern science, declares Prof. Klaus K. Klostermaier; "A fair number of leading physicists and biologists have found parallels between modern science and Hindu ideas."[25d] Science emphasizes reason and experiment, but religion is commonly based upon faith and dogma. Our challenge today is to harmonize religion and science to create a spiritualized science, that can objectively explore the ultimate spiritual truth and provide a direct experiential access to the inner reality.[28f]

Chapter 37

Chapter 38
Contribution of Hindus
to World Culture

From the invention of the decimal system in mathematics to the noble philosophy of ahimsa, Hindus have contributed their share in all fields of knowledge and learning. Hindu society had advanced itself at a very early time. Over five thousand years ago, when Europeans were only nomadic forest dwellers, ancient Hindus had established a civilization known as the Harappan culture in the Indus Valley, the northwestern region of India.

Archaeologists have discovered over 285,000 square miles of ancient city life, of which Harappa and Mohenjo-Daro are considered the most significant sites. The archaeological excavations have revealed that as early as 3000 BCE, cities were constructed with major streets, which were further divided into small lanes. The houses were constructed on the sides of streets, using standard baked bricks of 9.5 x 5.5 x 2.75 inches. Large public buildings with public baths were designed on brick platforms. The houses included bathrooms with drains connected to a large central drainage system via sewer lines. The sewer lines were constructed with regular inspection holes and were covered with bricks.

When much of the world was still in the primitive state, people of the Harappan culture were conducting trade workshops in weaving, bead-making, pottery, dying of fabrics, and metallurgy. The archaeological discoveries include jewelry made of copper and bronze, beautiful sculptures of clay and bronze, pottery, and beads made of various metals, including gold, silver, and copper. This shows that the people of the Harappan culture were familiar with industrial processes, such as the grinding and boring of stones, and the melting, molding, and shaping of metal.

The people of the Indus Valley also produced seals, used for documenting business transactions. The seals were made of stone (in the form of square tablets) and were engraved with figures of animals, such as goats, buffalo, elephants, and tigers. The discovery of these seals in distant lands suggests that the Harappan navigators must have sailed as far as Mesopotamia for trade.

Some of the knowledge that ancient Hindus had acquired in the fields of arts and sciences passed on to Egypt and subsequently to Greece and Europe. A summary of some of the achievements of the ancient Hindus is outlined below:

Education

The world's first university was established at Takshashila (northwest region of India) in approximately 700 BCE. The campus accommodated 10,500 students and offered over sixty different courses in various fields, such as science, mathematics, medicine, politics, warfare, astrology, astronomy, music, religion, and philosophy. The minimum age for admission was sixteen years and students from as far as Babylonia, Greece, Syria, Arabia, and China came to study at this university.

Another large university was established at Nalanda around 500 AD. Approximately one mile long and a half-mile wide, this campus housed a large library, called *Dharam Gunj* (Treasure of Knowledge), that was spread over three buildings, known as Ratna Sagar, Ratnadevi, and Ratnayanjak. Among other facilities, the university included 300 lecture halls, several laboratories, and an astronomical research observatory, called *Ambudharavlehi*. The university used handwritten manuscripts for teaching and attracted students and staff from many countries, including China, Korea, and Japan. According to the Chinese traveler Hieun Tsang, the campus housed 10,000 students, 2,000 professors, and a large administrative staff.

Mathematics

Ancient Hindus provided the concept of zero to the world. In early Sanskrit texts and in Pangala's *Chandra Sutra* (200 AD), "zero" is called *shunya*. Later, Bhaskaracharya (400-500 AD) showed that any number divided by zero becomes infinity, and infinity divided by any number remains infinity. The first inscription of zero dated 585-586 AD was found on the Sankheda Copper Plate in Gujarat, India. Zero is also described by Brahmagupta in his famous seventh century work, called *Brahma Bhuta Siddhanta*. Later, Hindu "Shunya" became "Sifir" in Arabic language in 770 AD, "Ziffre" in Latin texts, and finally "Zero" in English language in 800 AD. "We owe a lot to the Indians, who taught us how to count, without which no worthwhile scientific discovery could have been made," says Albert Einstein.

The Brahmi Inscription shows that a system of symbols to represent numbers, that eventually led to the modern numerals, was developed in India as early as 300 BCE. The decimal system was developed in India as early as 100 BCE and the number-names were coined to denote numbers, such as *eta* (1), *dvi* (2), *tri* (3), *nava* (9), *dasha* (10), *vimshathi* (20), *trimshat* (30), *navati* (90), *shata* (100), *sahasra* (1,000) and *ayuta* (10,000). India gave to the world the place-value system of numeration. In the words of Laplace, French Mathematician, "We shall appreciate the grandeur of this achievement when we remember that it escaped the genius of Archimedes and Appolonius."

The largest number known to the ancient Greeks was *Myriad* (i.e., 10^4) and to the Romans *Mille* (10^3). However, ancient Hindus had developed the prefixes for raising ten to powers as high as fifty-three. The small and large numbers used in ancient computations were: *kala* (1/16), *kushtha* (1/12), *shapha* (1/8), *pada* (1/4), *koti* (10^7), *titilamba* (10^{27}), *sarvabala* (10^{45}), and *tallakshna* (10^{53}).

The significance of the invention of the base-10 numerical system is easily overlooked, since we take the present-day system of mathematics for granted. But this idea was revolutionary in its time. Prior to the advent of the decimal system, the Roman numeral system was commonly used. Of course, no formal mathematical operation, not even multiplication or division, can be carried out with Roman numerals. On the other hand, the base-10 system allows problems to be worked out simply by hand or in the mind. The decimal system paved the way for the future of mathematics and science.

Square and Cube Roots

The present method of extracting the square and cube root by division was invented by the ancient Indian mathematician, Aryabhatta in 476 AD.

Value of *Pi*

Pi is the ratio of the circumference of a circle to its diameter. An ancient Sanskrit text says, "Add four to one hundred, multiply by eight and then add sixty two thousand; the result is approximately the circumference of a circle of diameter of twenty thousand." In 497 AD, Aryabhatta calculated the value of *pi* as 3.146, as a ratio of 62832/20000. The modern value of pi is 3.1415926. In 825 AD, Mohammad Ibna, an Arab mathematician, stated, "This value 62832/2000 has been assigned to *pi* by Hindus."

Pythagorean Theorem

Pythagoras is credited with the invention of the Pythagorean Theorem in 500 BCE. According to this theorem the square of the hypotenuse of a right-angled triangle equals the sum of the squares of the two sides. However, this theorem was developed by the Hindu mathematician Baudhayana one hundred years earlier in 600 BCE. In his book *Baudhayana Sulba Sutra* (600 BCE), Baudhayana states, "The area produced by the diagonal [i.e. the area of the square formed by the diagonal] of a right-angled triangle is equal to the sum of the areas produced by it on two sides [i.e. the sum of the areas of the squares formed by its two sides]."

Area of a Triangle

In 476 AD, Aryabhatta said, "The area of a triangle is the product of 1/2 of any side and the perpendicular [from opposite vertex] to it." In modern language, this means that the area of a triangle = (1/2) x Base x Altitude.

Chapter 38

Theorems in Sulva Sutra

There are many important theorems stated in the ancient Sanskrit text *Baudhayana Sulva Sutra* (600 BCE), such as (1) diagonal of a rectangle bisects the rectangle, (2) diagonals of a rectangle bisect each other, and (3) diagonals of a rhombus bisect each other at right angles.

Trigonometry

One of the significant contributons of India to the world of mathematics is the invention of trignometry. The Sanskrit concepts of *Jya* and *Koti Jaya* became the *sine* and *cosine* in European language.

Quadratic Equation

The present "Completing the Square Method" of solving the quadratic equation ($ax^2+bx+c=0$) was given by Sridharacharya in 991 AD, as follows: "Multiply the two sides [of the above quadratic equation] by four times the coefficient of the square of the unknown ($4a$); and add the square of the coefficient of the unknown (b^2) to both sides [and solve for the unknown]."

Permutations and Combinations

The following equation was given in the text form by Mahaviracharya of Karnataka, India, in 815-878 AD:

$nC_r = \{n(n-1)(n-2)...(n-r+1)\}/(1,2,3...r) = n!/r!(n-r)!$

Indeterminate Equation

Indian mathematician Bhaskara (1114 AD) invented the *Chakravala* (Cyclic) method to solve indeterminate equations (*Varga Prakrti*). His solution to $61x^2+1=y^2$ is $x=226,153,980$ (9 digits) and $y=1,766,319,049$ (10 digits). It was over 600 years later that Euler, an eminent mathematicain of Switzerland, solved the same equation in 1732 AD.

Law of Gravity

In *Surya Siddhanta*, dated 400-500 AD, the ancient Hindu astronomer Bhaskaracharya states, "Objects fall on the earth due to a force of attraction by the earth. Therefore, the earth, planets, constellations, moon, and sun are held in orbit due to this force." Approximately 1200 years later (1687 AD), Sir Isaac Newton rediscovered this phenomenon and called it the Law of Gravity.

Botany *(Vrkshayurveda)*

In 300 BCE, Theoprastus (Greek philos.) classified plants as trees, herbs, and shrubs. Over six thousand years earlier, Rig Veda had already classified plants as *Vruksha, Osadhi,* and *Veerudha.* In 100 BCE, Sage Parashara classified the flowering plants into three familes of *Samiganiya, Kurchaganiya, and Swastikaganiya.* Approximately 1800 years later, Swedish botanist Linnaeus rediscovered this classification in 1700 AD and called it Leguminosae, Compositae, and Cruciferae. Reflecting upon this, Indologist Sir William Jones says, "Had only Linnaeus known Sanskrit, he would have vastly improved his own system of nomenclature."

Sage Parashara identified various parts of a plant cell as *Kalavestana* (outer wall), *Sukshma Patrak* (inner wall), *Ranjakayukta Rasashrya* (colored sap), and Anvasva (invisible stuff). Over 1700 years later and with the aid of the microscope, Robert Hooks rediscovered in 1665 AD that plants contain cells which are like a honyeycomb in structure.

Mahabharata Shantiparva XII,177,16 states that roots absorb water and the sap ascends in the plants by the force generated by air. Over a thousand years later, this phenomenon was rediscovered by Dickson and Jolly in 1894 and came to be known as the theory of Suction Force.

Yajurveda classifies parts of a plant as *Pushpa, Parna, Valsa, Kanda, and Moola.* In modern language, the same classification is now known as Flower, Leaf, Twig, Stem, and Roots. Brihat Samhita, a 500 AD Sanskrit text of Varahamihira, classifies plant disease into four categories: *Pandu Patrata, Pravala Avriddhi, Shakhashosha, and Rasasruti.* The modern names for these parts of the disease process are: chlorosis of leaves, falling of buds, drying of branches, and exudation of sap.

Astronomy

In his treatise *Aryabhateeyam*, dated 500 AD, the Hindu genius Aryabhatta states, "Just as a person traveling in a boat feels that the trees on the bank are moving, people on the earth feel that the sun is moving." He also explains that the earth is round, rotates on its axis, orbits the sun, and is suspended in space. The lunar and solar eclipses are further explained by Aryabhatta as the interplay of the shadows of the sun, moon, and earth.

Calculation of Time

According to modern calculations, the time taken by the earth to orbit the sun is 365.2596 days. In *Surya Siddhanta*, dated 400-500 AD, Bhaskaracharya calculated this time as 365.258756484 days.

Metallurgy

Ancient Indians had considerable expertise in mining, processing and application of various metals. Archaeological excavations show that gold jwelery was used as early as 3000 BCE at Mohenjo-Daro. The iron pillar of Delhi dates back to 400 AD and has been existing for the last 1600 years without rust or decay. The pillar is 24.3 ft. high, 12.05 inches diameter at the top and 16.4 inches at the bottom, and weighs approximately 6 tons. Lord Buddha's copper statue found in Sultangaz, Bihar, India (exhibited at Birmingham Museum, U.K.) is approximately 7.5 ft. high, weighs one ton, and is dated back to 500 AD.

Transportation

The Rig Veda, the oldest document of the human race, includes references to the following modes of transportation:

Jalayaan--a vehicle designed to operate in air and in water. (*Rig Veda* 6.58.3)
Kaara--a vehicle that operates on ground and in water. (*Rig Veda* 9.14.1)

Tritala--a vehicle consisting of three stories.
(*Rig Veda* 3.14.1)
Trichakra Ratha--a three-wheeled vehicle designed to oper-
ate in air. (*Rig Veda* 4.36.1)
Vaayu Ratha--a gas or wind-powered chariot.
(*Rig Veda* 5.41.6)
Vidyut Ratha--a vehicle that operates on power.
(*Rig Veda* 3.14.1)

Medicine

Ayur Veda, or "the science of life," is the traditional system
of Indian medicine that originated from the fourth book of
Vedic literature, the *Atharva Veda*. This system of medicine,
developed in 1000-500 BCE, uses natural herbs to cure
diseases, and is still used in India and many other countries
of the world.

The Greek physician Hippocrates (460-377 BCE) is honored as the father of medicine. However, well before Hippocrates, Maharshi Charaka had already written the *Charaka
Samhita* ("Handbook of a Physician") in 500 BCE. In this
handbook Maharshi Charaka includes the following:

• the anatomy of the human body with methods of diagnosis
  and treatment of diseases.

• a listing of plant substances, mineral substances, and substances of animal origin for the preparation of medicines
  used in the treatment of diseases.

• a classification of Ayur Veda into eight categories: *Agada
  Tantra* (treatment for venoms), *Bhutividya Tantra* (treatment
  for mental diseases), *Kaumarbhrutya Chikitsa* (pediatrics),
  Shailya Chikitsa (general surgery), *Shaalakya Chikitsa* (treatment for the head and eyes), *Rasaayana Tantra* (pharmacol-
  ogy), and *Vaajeekarana Tantra* (treatment of infectious
  diseases).

↞ Surgery

The earliest known work relating to human surgery is *Shushruta Samhita*, written in approximately 600 BCE by the Hindu surgeon Shushruta, who performed plastic surgery as early as 600 BCE. Shushruta Samhita mentions over 120 surgical instruments in use at that time. It describes over three hundred surgical procedures and classifies human surgery into eight categories. In addition to Shushruta Samhita, there are many ancient Sanskrit texts that describe various surgical procedures. For example, *Agni Karma Vidhi* is a method in which heat and light rays are used for treatment, eliminating in some cases the need for surgery. *Jaluka Prayog* describes methods for purifying blood. Chanakya's *Arthashastra* describes post-mortems, and *Bhoja Prabandha* describes brain surgery, successfully performed in 927 AD by two surgeons on King Bhoja to remove a growth from his brain.

Yoga

The science of yoga originated from the Vedas. Today many variations of Hatha Yoga, in the form of a system of exercises, are used in many countries for the preservation and growth of the human body. Other forms of yoga are also used for attaining mental control and well-being.

Religion and Philosophy

Hindu religion has given the world the wisdom of the Vedas, the Upanishads, and the Bhagavad Gita. Free from any kind of dogma, Hindu scriptures teach universal harmony, self-dignity, and reverence for all forms of life. "All mankind is one family," is the slogan of Hindu sages. In the following words, Henry David Thoreau pays tribute to the wisdom of the Vedas:

"Whenever I have read any part of the Vedas, I have felt that some unearthly and unknown light illuminated me. In the great teaching of the Vedas, there is no touch of the sectarianism. It is of all ages, climes, and

nationalities and is the royal road for the attainment
of the Great Knowledge. When I am at it, I feel that
I am under the spangled heavens of a summer night."

Language and Literature

Sanskrit (meaning, "cultured"), the classical language of
Hindu religion, is the oldest and the most systematic
language in the world. The vastness, versatility, and power
of expression of Sanskrit can be appreciated by the fact that
this language has 65 words to describe various forms of
earth, 67 words for water, and over 250 words to describe
various types of rainfall. Some scholars (see references
below) maintain that Sanskrit is the most convenient
language for computer software programming.

In the following words, Juan Mascaro pays high tribute
to the glory of the Sanskrit literature, "Sanskrit literature is
a great literature. We have the great songs of the Vedas,
the splendor of the Upanishads, the glory of the Bhagavad
Gita, the vastness (10,000 verses) of the Mahabharata, the
tenderness and the heroism found in the Ramayana, the
wisdom of the fables and stories of India, the scientific
philosophy of Sankhya, the psychological philosophy of
yoga, the poetical philosophy of Vedanta, the Laws of
Manu, lyrical poetry and dramas of Kalidasa. Sanskrit
literature, on the whole, is a romantic literature interwoven
with idealism and practical wisdom, and with a passionate
longing for spiritual vision."[9]

Panini's Sanskrit grammar, produced in about 300 BCE,
is the shortest and fullest grammar in the world.
According to Sir Monier-Williams (Eng. Sanskrit scholar,
1819-1899), "The Panini's grammar reflects the wondrous
capacity of the human brain, which till today no other
country has been able to produce except India."

References:
Briggs, Rick. *Knowledge Representation in Sanskrit and Artificial
Intelligence.* AI Magazine 6, pp. 22-38, 1985
Kak, Subhash. *The Paninian Approach to Natural Language
Processing.* International Journal of Approximate Reasoning, Vol.
1, pp. 117-130, 1987

Chapter 38

In his book *The Wonder that Was India,* A. L. Basham notes: "Though its fame is much restricted by its specialized nature, there is no doubt that Panini's grammar is one of the greatest intellectual achievements of any ancient civilization, and the most detailed and scientific grammar composed before the 19th century in any part of the world."

Music and Dance

The sacred syllable O M, believed to be the sound of creation when correctly intoned, is said to include all sounds of music and associated rhythms. The Vedic hymns are metrical and were recited in music over five thousand years ago. The *Sama Veda* is the source of Indian classical music, which is heavily rooted in spiritualism. Indian music is not only a melody, but an experience in the unity of the body, mind, and spirit.

Indian dance involves the body as well as the mind. Hindus consider dance as a form of worship and meditation. The following are the major schools of classical Indian dance:

Bharatanatyam--a traditional Indian dance (after the name of Sage Bharata, the author of the *Natyashastra,* the manual of dramatic art) that originated in temples and is largely used to enact religious themes. This dance involves an elaborate system of postures, hand gestures, and foot movements (13 postures of the head, 9 of the neck, 36 of the eye, and 37 of the hand).

Kathakal--a spectacular lyric dance of southern India involving intensive footwork. This dance is performed with acrobatic energy and highly stylized pantomime.

Manipuri--a dance associated with Manipur in northeastern India and characterized by a gentle lyrical style.

Kathak--an intricate dance of northern India that includes passages of narrative pantomime.

Chapter 38

Odissi--a romantic dance of love and passion.

Other Achievements

In an ancient Sanskrit text known as *Saudamini Kalla*, Maharshi Matanga describes the art of photography and various ways of analyzing sound waves.

In the ancient Sanskrit text *Meghotpatti Prakaranam*, Maharshi Angirasa describes over sixty kinds of lightning, over thirty forms of thunder, many types of hail storms, and many types of thunderbolts and clouds.

In an ancient Sanskrit text, *Shakti Tantram*, Maharshi Agasatya describes various forms of natural energy and illustrates how these natural sources of energy can be used for the welfare of mankind.

The game of chess was developed in India and was originally called *Astapada* (sixty-four squares). Later this game came to be known as *Chaturanga* (four corps). In 600 AD, this game was learned by Persians who named it Shatranj (derived from the original word *Chaturanga*).

The Noble Laureates

Rabindranath Tagore
Noble Prize for Literature, 1913

Venkata Raman
Noble Prize for Physics, 1930

Har Gobind Khorana
Noble Prize for Physiology or Medicine, 1968
(shared with Robert W. Holley and Marshal W. Nirenberg)

Subrahmanyan Chandrasekhar
Noble Prize for Physics, 1983
(Shared with William A. Fowler)

Amartya Sen
Noble Prize for Economics, 1998

Chapter 39
Vedic History in the
Proper Perspective

The Rig Veda, the world's oldest scripture of mankind, refers to a stellar configuration that corresponds to a date from 6000 to 7000 BCE.[12] Based upon the literary evidence included in the Rig Veda and other ancient Hindu scriptures, Indian scholars have always maintained that early hymns of the Rig Veda were developed four to five millennia, if not earlier, prior to the beginning of Judaism and Christianity. They have further noted that the Vedic culture flourished in the northwestern region of India in prehistoric times and that the Indus Valley civilization was a continuation of the same culture. The Western scholarship has overwhelmingly denied antiquity to the ancient Indian history. In spite of the mounting evidence otherwise, the Western educational institutions are still telling their students that the Vedic religion was founded in India by the Aryan invaders in 1500 BCE. This is being taught under the pretext of what is known as the Aryan invasion theory.

The Aryan Invasion Theory

The so-called Aryan invasion theory was put forth by 18th and 19th-century Western scholars at the time when the British were still ruling India. Most of these scholars were Christian missionaries whose scientific reasoning was influenced by religious and political overtones. They could not mentally conceive that an entirely different civilization far more ancient than those of the Greeks and Romans could have existed in India. The principal architect of the Aryan invasion model was Max Muller (1823-1900), a British philologist and a Sanskrit scholar.

According to the Aryan invasion theory, the Vedic culture was established by light-skinned nomadic, Indo-European tribes from Central Asia (known as Aryans), who invaded India around 1500-1000 BCE. The Aryan invasion destroyed an earlier, more advanced urban civilization (known as the Indus Valley settlement) that had been established by the dark-skinned Dravidians, the natives of India.

Basis of the Aryan Invasion Theory

The following are some of the reasons that were used by Western scholars to support the Aryan invasion model:

- The Western scholars (who were mostly Christians) believed in Biblical chronology, according to which the world was created in about 4000 BCE. Thus they rejected *outright* any literary evidence in the Rig Veda and other ancient Hindu scriptures that pointed to dates and events earlier than 4000 BCE.[12]

- Linguistic data shows that the Vedas and the Upanishads were developed over a long period of time, that can be divided into five distinct time intervals. Max Muller, as a Christian himself, believed that the world was created around 4000 BCE, as endorsed by Biblical chronology. He thus *arbitrarily* assumed each time interval for development of the Vedas to be at 200 years. Any time period assumed to be greater than 200 years would have pushed the date of the composition of the Vedas earlier than 4000 BCE, thus conflicting with Max Muller's religious belief about the creation of the world. Knowing that Buddha lived around 500 BCE and that the Vedas were composed prior to Buddha, Max Muller calculated the date of the arrival of Aryans in India as 500 BCE + 200 years (per time interval) x 5 (time intervals) = 1500 BCE.

- The Vedas often speak of the war between "the forces of light" and "the forces of darkness." Although these expressions are only poetic metaphors (to illustrate a war between virtue and evil) in the Vedas, they were nevertheless interpreted by Western scholars to indicate a war between light-skinned Aryans and dark-skinned Dravidians. Thus it was concluded that India was invaded by Aryans, who destroyed the supposed pre-Aryan Indus Valley culture.

- The literary evidence of the Vedas and the Puranas was handled in two different ways. If the evidence showed that the Vedic culture existed prior to 1500 or 2000 BCE, such evidence was declared mythical. If the evidence could be somehow interpreted (or perhaps misinterpreted) to fit the idea of an Aryan invasion, every effort was made to do so. The following are two examples:

- The astronomical sightings of the equinoxes and solstices included in the Vedic texts were completely ignored, since the calculations based on such data showed that Vedic culture existed earlier than 7000 BCE, and thus conflicts with the Christian view that the world was created in 4000 BCE.

- Although the correct translation of the Sanskrit term *samudra* is ocean, it was initially translated as "a body of water." Hence the references to ships in the Rig Veda and to the ancient river Saraswati (and other ancient rivers) were considered false and mythical by Westerners. If *samudra* had been translated correctly as ocean, the references to ships and the vast trade over water would have been considered real and not mythical, and would have also indicated that the Aryans were civilized people and not nomads. The idea of nomadic Aryans had been assumed by Western scholars to fit their idea of the Aryan invasion.

Implications of the Aryan Invasion Theory

The following are the major historical, political, and social implications of the Aryan invasion theory:

- The theory declares the Vedic culture to be primitive, as it was established apparently by Aryan nomads who overthrew a more advanced, earlier civilization. The Puranas, Mahabharata, and Ramayana are labeled as mythical, and approxi-

mately seven thousand years of Vedic culture are left
without any historical basis.

• It may have driven South Indians to think that the inhabitants of the North (so-called Aryans) had destroyed their
ancient civilization and dominated them. This perhaps
divided Indians, making it easier for Western interests to
rule India.

• The theory implies that Vedic culture established itself
subsequent to Middle-Eastern culture, thus raising the
possibility that the Vedic civilization may have been derived
from Middle-Eastern cultures, which are historically linked
with the Bible and Christianity. This also implies that
scientific discoveries made by ancient Hindus were based
upon Greek civilization rather than being derived independently and well before the Greeks.

Current Evidence and the Fresh Insights

In their book *In Search of the Cradle of Civilization,* authors
George Feuerstein, Subhash Kak, and David Frawley have
generated seventeen scholarly arguments challenging the
validity of the Aryan invasion model. The authors conclude
that when their arguments are combined with other additional
evidence not specifically cited in their book, "we obtain a
picture of ancient India that diverges considerably from the
inherited Aryan invasion model."[28]

The modern archaeological evidence suggests that the
Indo-Aryans were present in India as an ethnic sub-group of
the Vedic people 6500 BCE or earlier, and that the Harappan
culture was a continuation of the Vedic culture.[10] Current
archaeological data have revealed that the Indus Valley culture
was not destroyed by any outside invasion, but by natural
causes. J. G. Schaffer thus summarizes the current archaeological evidence: "Current archaeological data do not support
the existence of an Indo-Aryan or European invasion into
South Asia at any time in the pre- or proto-historic periods.
Instead, it is possible to document archaeologically a series of
cultural changes reflecting indigenous cultural development

from pre-historic to historic periods...The Indo-Aryan invasion(s) as an academic concept of the 18th and 19th century Europe reflected the cultural milieu of that period. Linguistic data were used to validate the concept that in turn was used to interpret archaeological and anthropological data."[11]

In ancient Hindu literature, the term "Arya" is an adjective and does not refer to any particular race. The word "Arya" is derived from the Sanskrit root *Ar* and means "to attain" or "to know." Arya means "one who is wise as a result of education or experience." The Vedic people called themselves Aryas not because they belonged to a unique race, but because they were enlightened and cultured rishis of mixed races. There never was a supposed "non-Aryan" race of "Dravidians" existing in India anywhere at any time. If the word "Dravidian" has any historical or racial connotations, it is with reference to the local name of a certain tribe of the Aryans who colonized South India in ancient times.

Conclusion

There is agreement among many modern scholars of both East and West that the Aryan invasion theory is a scholarly fiction and that the Rig Vedic people, so-called Aryans, were the original inhabitants of India. The early hymns of Rig Veda were composed by them in India in 6500 BCE or earlier. The modern archaeological and literary evidence suggests that the Vedic religion evolved in India from prehistoric times and that the Indus Valley civilization was a continuation of the Vedic culture.

In the words of Feuerstein, Kak, and Frawley, "The early Indic civilization, as we know it from towns like Mohenjo-Daro and Harappa, but even from the much earlier settlement of Mehragarh, was multiracial and multiethnic, similar to compositions of groups living in India today. Skeletons found at those sites have been identified as belonging to the Proto-Australoid, Mediterranean, Alpine, and Mongoloid races...The Mediterranean race, such as most of the people in India today belong to, including the so-called Aryans and Dravidians, appear to have been the majority group."[28g]

Chapter 40
Hindu Religion--a Religion
Of World Brotherhood

Hindu religion, a religion of universal harmony and peace, views mankind as one large family, and is concerned with the perennial philosophy that defines the universe, the individual, and God. The primary Hindu scriptures, the Vedas, are the earliest expression of the universal principles that deal with global spirituality and moral values. Following are some of the major features of Hindu religious thought that contribute to its universal outlook and vision:

Sacredness of the Individual

In Hindu view, an individual is in essence one with the Divine. Each individual, regardless of religion, geographic region, color, or creed is in reality *atman* (individual spirit or soul) clothed in a physical body. The atman, the spiritual center within the human body, is the source of unlimited knowledge, power, love, and purity. According to the predominant Hindu view, the same atman resides in all beings, from the lowest worm to the perfect human being. The difference is not in the atman, but in the level of its manifestation, which itself depends upon the kind of physical body the atman is associated with. In a human body the atman has the highest manifestation. In Hindu view, therefore, each human being is potentially divine, eternally perfect, and pure. Truth and goodness are buried deep in the nature of each individual. However, due to ignorance (*maya* or *avid*ya) an individual feels limited, weak, and imperfect, and commits sin. Just as darkness quickly disappears upon the appearance of light, an individual's delusion quickly vanishes when he (or she) gains Self-knowledge.

In Hindu view, an individual is not born a sinner, but becomes a victim of ignorance under the influence of maya. In the World Parliament of Religions held in Chicago in 1893, Swami Vivekananda declared the divinity of the entire human race: "You are the children of God, the sharer of immortal bliss, holy and perfect beings. You divinities on earth, sinners? It is a sin to call a man so, it is a standing libel on human nature."

Universal Tolerance and Harmony

One of Hindu religion's greatest gifts to mankind is the attitude of religious tolerance and universal harmony. Through their spiritual experiences, the *rishis* (ancient sages and seers) discovered that there are many ways of conceiving the Ultimate Reality and numerous ways of approaching It. Thus they declared in the Rig Veda, over eight thousand years ago (Rig Veda 1.164.46):

"Ekam sat vipraha bahudha vadanti."
"Truth is one, the wise call it by various names."

The Ultimate Reality or Truth was called *Brahman* by the sages of the Upanishads. "The manifestation of Brahman in each and every human being is the atman," the sages declared. "Brahman and atman are one. All is One and One is in all." This doctrine of the oneness of mankind is further elucidated by Sri Krishna in the Bhagavad Gita:

"In whatever way humans love Me, in the same way they find My love. Various are the ways for humans, but in the end they all come to Me." (BG 4.11)

The Hindu concept of the unity of all existence has two aspects. First, all beings are different manifestations of one Supreme Being, or God. "Different people may have different skins and different colors, but beneath these different skins runs the blood of one color," is a popular maxim.

Secondly, the unity of an individual and God is also the unity of one individual and another. All human beings are thus members of one large family of God, where He is the father, mother, friend, and savior of all. Therefore, it is wrong, and harmful, Hindus say, to insist that one's own path toward God is the only way. This vision of religious tolerance is rooted in the kind of doubt reflected in the last verse of the Hymn of Creation in the *Rig Veda*:

> "None knoweth whence creation has arisen, and whether He has or has not produced it. He who surveys it in the highest heavens, he only knows, or *perhaps he knows not*." (Rig Veda 10.129)

This hesitancy (reflected in the words *perhaps he knows not* of the above verse) to claim superiority and exclusiveness of thoughts, beliefs, and practices, has minimized dogmatism in Hindu religion. For this reason, the belief in religious tolerance, universal brotherhood, and the love of mankind has been the living ideal of Hindus throughout the ages. There are many historical examples of this ideology, including India's providing shelter to Zoroastrians when Persia was conquered by the Arabs. At that time a large number of Zoroastrians were forced to accept Islam, but many devout followers left Persia and traveled to India where they were given refuge by Hindus. Since that time their descendants, the Parsees, have kept their faith alive in India.

Diversity of the Human Mind

Hindu religion does not accept dictatorship in religious and spiritual matters. In other words, Hindu religion recognizes the diversity of the human mind. Hinduism declares that a human being is governed by three powers of nature, called the three *gunas* (namely *sattva*, *rajas*, and *tamas*). According to the Bhagavad Gita, "sattva, rajas, and tamas [light, fire, and darkness respectively] are the three constituents of nature. There is nothing in heaven or on earth which is free from these three powers of nature." (BG 14.5 and 18.40)

Chapter 40

Sattva represents the qualities of goodness, balance, and harmony. *Rajas* denotes restless passion, and *tamas* indicates dullness, inertia, and laziness. These three attributes determine the nature and character of an individual, depending upon the proportion in which each attribute is present. Each individual, therefore, lives life according to his (or her) own inherent nature, determined by the gunas.

In Hindu view, there is no one God or Goddess for all humanity, but there is one Truth, or Reality that expresses itself in many ways and forms. Hindu religion thus offers different spiritual paths to individuals of different aptitudes, depending upon whether one is a scholar or an illiterate, a philosopher or a poet, a simple man of faith, a mystic, or an ordinary man of action. This religious freedom is a unique feature of Hindu religious tradition, as it permits one's work preference combined with one's mode of worship to determine one's overall spiritual path. In the words of Sir Monier-Williams (Eng. Sanskrit scholar, 1819-1899):

"And, in real truth, Hindu religion has something to offer which is suited to all minds. Its very strength lies in its infinite diversity of human character and human tendencies. It has its highly spiritual and abstract side suited to the metaphysical philosophy, its practical and concrete side suited to the man of poetic feeling and imagination, its quiescent and contemplative side suited to the man of peace and lover of seclusion."

Purity of Reason

Hindu religious tradition does not prescribe central authority, hierarchy, dogma, or a rigid or narrow moral code for living. Instead, Hindu tradition relies upon pure reason and true knowledge as an essential prerequisite for recognizing the oneness of all mankind. God has given human beings the faculty of reason so that men and women can distinguish true emotion from false emotionalism, faith from fanaticism, and imagination from fancy. When reason is clouded by selfishness, greed, or prejudices of race or religion, human beings fail to see themselves as the children of one God. The importance of pure reason is heavily emphasized in Hindu scriptures. In the *Gayatri Mantra*, the highest and the most sacred Vedic mantra, a Hindu does not pray for wealth and riches for himself, his family or his community. Instead he prays for purity of reason for all beings of the world:

> "God is the giver of life, the dispeller of miseries, and the bestower of happiness. Let us meditate upon that Creator, the most worthy and acceptable Almighty God. May He inspire and lead our minds and intellects."
> (Rig Veda 3.62.10 and Yajur Veda 36.3)

Capacity to Absorb Ideas

Hindu religion is not a religion of a single book or a particular founder. Hindu tradition is therefore always ready to inquire, investigate, and assimilate new experiences and insights. Hindus have a great capacity for absorbing ideas and adapting to new conditions. When Buddha challenged Hindu religion in the sixth century BCE, Hindus incorporated some of Buddha's teachings and accepted him as an incarnation of God. Thereafter Buddhism virtually disappeared from India. Likewise when Christianity arrived in India, Hindu religion absorbed much of the Christian message by popularizing Bhakti Yoga, which eventually unified various Hindu sects around the belief in God and faith in the Vedas. New laws were passed to abolish social injustices. A new attitude towards social issues was developed, and a distinction drawn between religious life and social practices.

Non-violence

The Hindu doctrine of non-violence (*ahimsa*) toward all forms of life is an essential prerequisite for universal coexistence. A universal vision of mankind was conceived by Hindu sages when they declared: *Vasudhaiva kutumbakam*, or "All of mankind is one family." (Hitopadesh, a popular scripture)

Bhagavan Krishna further declares in the Bhagavad Gita:

"He who sees Me [God] in all beings and all beings in Me, from him I vanish not, nor does he vanish from Me." (BG 6.30)

For this very reason every religion or every race that arrived in India has found a permanent home there. Mahatma Gandhi was the greatest exponent of *ahimsa*. Prior to him, the doctrine of *ahimsa* had been applied only in religious and spiritual spheres of human activity. He was the first leader who extended this doctrine to the actions of social, political, and community leaders. He used non-violence as a successful tool in leading India to independence from British rule.

Gandhi's concept of *ahimsa* was based upon his belief that Truth and *ahimsa* are two sides of the same coin. He believed that there can be no Truth without non-violence and therefore, non-violence is implied in Truth. It was this vision of Truth that Gandhi held all his life. He wrote in *Young India* in 1925: "*Ahimsa* is my God; Truth is my God. When I look for *ahimsa*, Truth says, 'Find it out through me'; when I look for Truth, *ahimsa* says, 'Find it out through me!'"[13]

To a world torn by violence and hatred, Gandhi brought the ancient Hindu doctrine of *ahimsa*. To a world divided by prejudices and racial arrogance, Gandhi came to show the path of love and understanding through the doctrine of *ahimsa*. By successfully leading India's freedom struggle against British rule through non-violence, Mahatma Gandhi demonstrated that people irrevocably bonded to the path of non-violence are stronger than an empire built on huge armies and armaments.

Universal Prayers

Another notable feature of Hindu religion is the universality of its prayers. Hindus do not pray for themselves alone. Their prayers are designed for all of mankind. This is evident from the words of the following typical prayer that millions of Hindus sing everyday at the conclusion of their worship or religious ceremony:

"May all of mankind be happy; may all of mankind be healthy; may all of mankind experience prosperity; may none [in the world] suffer."

If there must be a religion that recognizes mankind as one family of God, where the members can live in love, dignity, peace, and harmony, Hindu religion has the religious depth to accommodate such a world brotherhood of souls. This universal view of Hindu religion is expressed in the following words of Dr. Sarvepalli Radhakrishnan:

"The basic principles of Hindu faith have sufficient breadth and resilience to serve as the background of a universal religion of humanity that is yet to arise, a religion which refuses to build on any dogmatic creed but has room for all the truths that old times have won, as well as those which will rise from the 'unspent deep things of God,' a religion that welcomes into its fold all who are pure in heart and sincere in worship, and thus fosters a life of the Spirit which will be too vast and rich to be reduced to any one form...It will survive the attacks of the modern social movements, for it aims at human unity through the Spirit."[14]

Conclusion
What mankind needs today is a global civilization that can integrate all the diverse aspects of human creativity. To create such a global culture, the world religions will have to rise above narrow-mindedness and dogma and seek unity within the inherent diversity of various traditions. Unity should not be turned into an ideological stereotype that destroys the diversity, nor should diversity become divisive and thereby destroy unity. The Hindu religious tradition has sufficient spiritual depth to nourish such a global civilization. Its openness to new ideas, its experimental and experiential character, its refusal to dogmatize what is beyond human understanding, and its genuine spiritual insights are the ingredients for such a global civilization.

Chapter 40

Questions and Answers
Part IV

Q1. What is the purpose of Hindu religious life?

A. The purpose of Hindu religious life is three-fold. First, to teach how one can employ righteous means to successfully accomplish the four goals of human life: *dharma, artha, kama,* and *moksha* (see chapter 32). Second, to assist an individual to acquire sufficient mental and spiritual strength in order to face the trials and tribulations of worldly life. This can be accomplished by yoga, prayers, meditations, as well as through rites and rituals. The third purpose is to guide an individual on a spiritual path culminating in union with God, the ultimate goal of Hindu religious life.

Q2. What is the essence of Hindu culture?

A. As any other culture, Hindu culture has both extrinsic as well as intrinsic values. The extrinsic aspect includes temples, music and dance, traditional customs, foods, arts and crafts, and rites and ceremonies. The real essence of Hindu culture, however, is in its intrinsic values which include, but are not limited to, the following:

Belief in divinity: Everything animate or inanimate is considered divine. Hindus say "*Sarvam Brahmamayam,*" meaning "everything is full of Brahman," or "Brahman is the essence of all that exists."

The Upanishads say, "He is the sun dwelling in the heavens, the air dwelling in the sky, the fire existing on the altar...He is in man, in gods, in the sacrifice [work performed as one's duty], in the sky; [He is] born in water, born on earth, born in the sacrifice, born on the mountains...."[20] This forms the basis of a Hindu's respect for all aspects of nature--plants, animals, the earth, sky, air, water, fire, and so on. According to Hindu culture there is nothing unholy in nature. The doctrine of ahimsa is the direct consequence of this broad view of divinity.

Unity in diversity: Hindu culture recognizes that differences in opinion between any two individuals are natural and inevitable. No two persons, animals, or plants--no two of anything in nature--are identical. Underlying the apparent diversity is the perfect unity of existence, as life is interdependent. Unity in diversity is, therefore, the quintessence of this culture. Hindu culture includes a broad spectrum of faiths and a wide range of philosophical diversity.

Family concept: Elders are an integral part of the family. Informality and family togetherness are important characteristics of Hindu culture. Whether at a marriage party, a temple occasion, or a cultural program, all age groups can be seen socializing together, where adults are talking, teenagers discussing, children arguing, and infants running around. Such a scene may appear disorderly, but it helps in keeping family members close to each other, and may help in reducing the generation gap.

Duties and responsibilities: Individuals are taught to be dutiful and caring. Wealth is necessary to make a decent living, but amassing wealth is considered undesirable. Integrity, contentment, non-violence, and obedience to the laws of the land are essential characteristics.

Personal character: A high premium is placed on individual character and chastity in marriage. One-wife-one-husband is the banner of Hindu culture. Premarital or extramarital sex is sinful in this culture.

Freedom of thought: Hindu culture believes in full freedom of thought and expression. Nobody is punished for criticizing or speaking against established traditions or beliefs. Hindus have hailed the critics of their religion such as Buddha, Mahavira, and Guru Nanak as reformers instead of dubbing them as heretics. "I am overjoyed that my own disciple has defeated me," remarked Ramanuja's teacher after being defeated in a philosophical discussion by his own disciple, Ramanuja. Hence, one can see that Hindu religion does not punish or label one as an infidel for presenting a point of view that may be contrary to established beliefs or practices.

Reverence for the elderly: Mother, father, and teacher have been given the highest place of honor in Hindu culture. Respect--not blind obedience or conformity--for parents, teachers, and elders in and outside one's family is a hallmark of this culture.

Q3. Do the words "Hindu religion" and "Vedanta" mean the same? The authors of Hindu religious writings appear to use these words synonymously.

A. Vedanta literally means "the end of the Veda." It refers to the name prescribed to the teachings of the Upanishads, the end or concluding portions of the Vedas, and various other religious writings, such as the Brahma Sutra and the Bhagavad Gita, that interpret the teachings of the Upanishads. Vedanta (or Uttara Mimamsa--see page 70) is also one of the six systems of the orthodox school of Hindu philosophy. A Vedantist is one who follows one of the three major subsystems of the Vedanta philosophy (see Figure F-4).

Hindu religion is a broader term than Vedanta and includes Vedantic as well as non-Vedantic systems of religious thought, all deriving their authority from the Vedas. Included in Hindu religion are many schools of religious thought, including the six popular systems of philosophy, and their subsystems (see chapter 6). Thus a Hindu is one who follows any school of Hindu philosophy, including Vedanta. Therefore, we can say that every Vedantist is a Hindu, but every Hindu is not a Vedantist.

Q4. What are the Hindu concepts of virtue (punya) and sin (papa)?

A. In Hindu view, whatever retards an individual's spiritual progress or harms others is sin or evil. Performing one's duties and actions in accordance with moral and ethical

principles and doing good to others is considered virtue. The
Mahabharata prescribes the following rules:

"...abstention from injury, truthfulness of speech, justice,
compassion, self-restraint. Procreation [of offspring with
one's own spouse], amiability, modesty, patience--the
practice of these is the best of all religions...." (Shantiparva 21.11-12)

"Abstention from injury by act, thought, and word, in
respect of all creatures, compassion, and gift [charity],
constitute behavior that is worthy of praise. That act or
exertion by which others are not benefited, or that act in
consequence of which one has to feel shame, should never
be done." (Shantiparva 124.65-6)

Q5. Does Hindu religion teach asceticism?

A. Hindu religion teaches self-control as opposed to asceticism. When self-control exceeds certain levels, asceticism
predominates. Some critics argue that Hindu religion emphasizes asceticism and that followers are required to suppress human desires altogether. This is a false notion, as
evident by the fact that Hindu religion preaches four goals
of life: dharma (righteousness), artha (wealth), kama (genuine
desires), and moksha (liberation). The only condition in
achieving these goals is that one must learn dharma first and
use this in earning a living and in satisfying legitimate desires.
Lust, greed, anger, and jealousy must be controlled at all
costs. These are the four enemies of the soul, and the major
causes of human misery in the world (see also chapter 32).

Q6. What is the significance of a temple? How are temples constructed? How are the icons made and installed in temples?

A. Although God exists everywhere, His presence can be felt
more easily in temples and places of worship. Just as a library
offers a suitable environment for study and research, a temple
offers a convenient place to think of God and meditate on

Him. The architecture and the design of a typical Hindu temple symbolizes God as a Cosmic Person, with various parts of the temple representing major parts of the Cosmic Body of God, as follows:

Temple Structure	Description	Symbolizes
Garbha Griha or Sanctum Sanctorum	Innermost chamber, housing the icon of the major deity	Head of Cosmic Person (God)
Antarala	Adjoining passage	Neck
Shukanasi	Adjoining passage	Nose
Prakaras	Surrounding high walls	Hands
Gopura	Tower at the main entrance	Feet
Navaranga or Mantapa	Multipurpose hall for temple activities	-
Balipitha	Pedestal for offering	-
Dhvajastambha or flag post	Pedestal for offering	-

The bigger temples may have smaller shrines for other deities. The construction and the consecration processes of a temple are very elaborate and are performed in accordance with *Silpa Shastra*, the Hindu architectural book. Two of the major rituals associated with the construction and consecration of a Hindu temple are *Pratishta* (installation of icons) and *Kumbhaabhishekam* (temple dedication). Pratishta is a sacred ceremony by which icons are endowed with divine power. The cosmic pillar is an important part of a Hindu temple, as it is supposed to be the communication channel between the humans and the gods.

The construction of an icons is a very elaborate process in itself. Icons are formed out of special wood and stones. The trees used in the creation of icons are cut on auspicious days as determined by astrologers. The artisan who makes the icons is known as *Silpi*. Prior to the construction of an icon, the *Silpi* performs sacred rites and rituals to purify himself. He meditates, mentally visualizes the icon, and prays for divine guidance in making the icons. After completion, the icon is purified with water and by other sacred articles in an elaborate and colorful ceremony. Finally, a special *Nyasa* ritual is performed with great devotion to infuse *prana*, or *the breath of life*, into the icon by a special mantra. This completes the process of the creation of an icon for a temple.

Q7. What is the role of a temple in the Hindu community?

A. Mahatma Gandhi was once asked, "why do you go to the temple?" "I do not go to a temple, my soul does," replied the Mahatma. Just like a library provides the facilities, environment and the inspiration to study or do research, a temple provides the right environment and facilities for pursuing religious and spiritual life. Religious sacraments purify the mind in the same manner soap and shampoo clean the physical body. These sacraments can be more effectively performed in temples where the facilities exist for such group activities. All religions consider group prayers more powerful than individual prayers. The temples have resources to invite scholars and speakers to enlighten the devotees on various issues associated with religious life. Swami Vivekananda says that individual salvation is not possible without social salvation. Therefore, temples are best equipped to organize social and community activities and involve and train the youth in such activities. In short, the temple is to the Hindu community what the heart is to the human body.

Q8. What is the significance of pilgrimages in Hindu religion?

A. Pilgrimages (see Appendix A-3) are an important feature of Hindu religious life. In Hindu view, the routines of daily life may lead to mental boredom, thereby weakening the mind of its moral and ethical qualities. Pilgrimages reinvigorate the mind just as recharging reactivates a weak battery.

Hindu sages tell us that God exists everywhere, but His presence is more tangible at places of pilgrimages as a result of the intense spiritual environment created by the holy people and devotees who visit such places. The sanctity of pilgrimage sites free the mind from egotism, envy, pride, and malice.

For an effective pilgrimage, Hindu scriptures recommend fasting, self-control, inward purity (freedom from envy, pride, and malice), physical cleansing, charity at the place of pilgrimage, and worship of gods with love and devotion, before and during the pilgrimage.

For those who are unable to embark on a pilgrimage, Hindu scriptures provide a method by which they can receive the benefit of a pilgrimage through another pilgrim, known as the substitute pilgrim. The substitute pilgrim creates an icon of *kusha grass* (herbage) to represent the original person who is unable to undertake the pilgrimage. The icon is bathed at the place of pilgrimage via a religious ritual, treating the idol as the original person who was unable to make the pilgrimage.

Q9. What is the status accorded to a woman in Hindu Society? Does she have equal rights?

A. From the religious aspect, a woman has the same religious and spiritual freedom as a man. Like a man, she is the soul in bondage and the goal of her life is the same as that of man, spiritual perfection or moksha. Hindu religion has elevated women to the level of divinity--only Hindus worship God in the form of Divine Mother (see chapter 5).

This concept of the spiritual equality of souls naturally influenced the status of women on an individual and social level. "Where women are honored, there the gods are pleased; but where they are not honored no sacred rite yields rewards," declares Manu Smriti (III.56), a religious text on social conduct

However, the status of women in Hindu society has also been affected by factors other than the ideals set forth in the Vedas and Upanishads, such as cultural mores and the exploitation of the biological and psychological differences between men and women. Therefore, on an individual and social level, complete and total equality between men and women is a goal that Hindu society (and other societies) is still striving for. As Swami Vivekananda said, we must realize that man and woman are two wings of the same bird; that in order to truly soar to great heights, a man and woman must work in unison in order to achieve greater harmony in life.

Q10. The caste system and untouchability are in violation of the teachings of the Upanishads, Brahma Sutra, and the Bhagavad Gita, the major scriptures of Hindu religion. Why then did these practices originate in Hindu religion ?

A. Untouchability and the caste system, two elements of ancient Hindu social philosophy, found their way into Hindu society because Hindus failed to incorporate the teachings of their scriptures into their social philosophy. There is no religious sanction to these practices in the primary Hindu scriptures. Refer to chapter 4 for a discussion of the Varna System of the Vedas and chapter 17 for a discussion of how the Varna System degenerated into the hereditary caste system of the post-Vedic period. As previously stated in this work, the caste system and untouchability violate the spirit of Hindu religious tradition.

Q11. What role have reform movements played in the evolution of Hindu religion ?

A. Hindu religion has been shaped, sustained, and strengthened by several reform movements over thousands of years. Its resilience can be directly traced to these reform movements. The first reform activity was initiated by the sages of the Upanishads themselves, when the original, elegant religion of the Rig Veda deteriorated under a system of bewildering sacrifices, as a result of the incorporation of the Brahmanas into the Vedas.   Ceremonial sacrifices became commonplace, prompting the sages of the Upanishads to reject excessive sacrifices and advocate meditation upon and knowledge of Brahman as the Supreme Path for self-realization.

Sri Krishna initiated the second reform movement by harmonizing various spiritual disciplines (Jnana, Karma, and Bhakti) and eliminating the disputes stemming from claims of superiority of one path over another. His greatest contribution, the doctrine of selfless work, requires that one perform a duty for its own sake, as well as to contribute to the social well-being.

The third reform moment, implemented by Buddha and Mahavira, emphasized the importance of moral and ethical principles in life. Both sages spoke against excessive ritualism and the caste system, which had gained a strong hold in Hindu society.   In the course of time, when Buddhism weakened as a result of strife in its organization, Adi Shankaracharya appeared on the scene and launched the fourth reform movement to re-establish Hindu religion in India.

Then came a series of invasions in which Hindu society in India succumbed to foreign powers. First the Muslims and then the British assumed control of India, not merely physically, but also in the realm of thought. The Muslims attempted to undermine Vedic culture and thought as much as possible. However, during this most critical period in India's history, scores of great religious and spiritual leaders (see chapter 1 and Table T-1) appeared on the scene to protect the Hindu religious tradition from the onslaughts of the invaders. If not for the great and noble souls who initiated the Bhakti movement during this critical period, Hindu religion might have disappeared from its own place of birth, India. This was the fifth reform movement of Hindu religion.

During the period of colonialism in India, the British created a different sort of problem by the import of religious and cultural ideas from the West. The British virtually succeeded in degrading the religious thought of traditional India. Thus, initially, British-educated Indians were apparently ashamed of their own religious and philosophical traditions, since their measure of intelligence was a reflection of European values, including the mastery of the English language.

During this period the sixth reform movement was launched by organizations such as the Brahmo Samaj and the Arya Samaj, as well as many individual reformers (see Table T-1). Since the re-establishment of India as a free and independent nation, the revival of Hindu philosophy and the consciousness of the eminence of its philosophical past have been the most prominent developments. In recent times the Hindu mind has continued to be influenced by Western thought, but Western mind has also been influenced by Hindus more than ever before, through the writings of contemporary poets, sages and philosophers such as Paramahamsa Sri Ramakrishna, Swami Vivekananda, Sri Aurobindo Ghose, Sri Ramana Maharshi, Sarvepalli Radhakrishnan, and Mahatma Gandhi.

Q12. Why do Hindus believe that their religion is universal? Don't all religions have some universal aspects anyway?

A. It is true that all religions have *some* universal aspects. In Hindu religion , however, *all* aspects are universal and for this reason Hindu religion is called *Sanatana Dharma*, meaning "universal [or eternal] religion." There is no touch of sectarianism in the teachings of the Vedas, the Upanishads, the Brahma Sutra, or the Bhagavad Gita, the major Hindu scriptures. All doctrines of Hindu religion have universal application and character. The doctrines of the harmony of religions and universal brotherhood (*Vasudhaiva kutumbakam*) are applicable to all peoples of all times and climes. The doctrine of the divinity of *atman* (soul) says that every person, regardless of color, creed, religious affiliation, gender or geographic location, is potentially divine and the goal of life is to express this divinity in whatever one does in this world. Hindu prayers are also universal in content and character. Hindus say "*Surve bavanto sukhinah*'" which means "let all the people of the world live in peace." The most sacred prayer of Hindus is the *Gayatri Mantra*, which concludes in the following words, "May the Lord sharpen the human intellect."

The law of Dharma is the law of growth and harmony for every human being, and ahimsa is the universal law of kindness and compassion towards all God's creatures. The law of karma is the universal law of justice. Thus, we can see that right from its inception, the foundation of Hindu religion is cast in the bedrock of universalism. Refer to chapter 40 for additional discussion on this subject.

Q13. How does one practice Hindu religion in this world of cut-throat competition, when every morning one wakes up and worries about one's job, material needs of the present, and financial security for the future?

A. In order to survive in this world of "cut-throat" competition, one requires a healthy body, a strong mind, and faith in one's own self. These are the elements of success for an individual in a modern society. Hindu religion provides these ingredients to anyone who is interested in using them in daily life.

Daily meditation helps an individual to reduce (even eliminate) the physical and mental stresses caused by excessive competition. Yoga maintains one's body and mind in a healthy condition. Faith in the Universal Self (of Whom the individual self is a reflection) provides the necessary confidence and mental power to handle any situation in life.

Apprehension, anxiety, and daily worries kill more people than the tasks we are to accomplish. Anxieties stem from helplessness, which is in itself the direct consequence of an individual's lack of faith in the Divine. Essentially, Hindu scriptures say that "we should do the best, and let God do the rest." We have barred God from our lives by our egotistic thoughts. "God will get in, if man lets Him in," is an old adage. A religious mind is never full of worry. Such a mind knows that all an individual can be asked of is his (or her) best effort. Beyond this the Divine will play His role.

Hindu religious rites have been designed by God-realized sages to provide peace of mind, freedom from worries, and to revive faith in the workings of the Divine. Faith in the Divine is very necessary in today's environment for an individual to maintain the proper physical and mental balance. The performance of such rites as well as the daily puja of a family deity will go a long way in boosting an individual's ability to survive the stresses and strains of the present life.

Q14. Describe a distinct "Hindu personality" who could be viewed as a role model for youth?

A. Swami Vivekananda, a saint, scholar, author, reformer, intellectual, and a guardian of the poor, is one role model for the future of mankind. With his deep insight into the current problems of the human race, a sincere desire to uplift the living conditions of the poor and less fortunate, reverence and regard for women and an advocate of their rights, and with compassion for mankind, Swamiji was a spokesman of the human race.

In his historical speech at the World Parliament of Religions in Chicago in 1893, Swamiji presented the idea of a universal religion, unhampered by sectarian insularities, tolerating every attitude of the human mind, and respecting every path that leads to the realization of the unity of existence. Swamiji said that if our religious leaders recognize and accept that all different paths and practices are good for those who follow them with faith, without dismissing others or trying to convert them by exploiting their condition, humanity can make great progress toward the glorious world of our vision. The goal of any religion should be the unfolding of human consciousness to its ultimate limits of divinity. "Offer such a religion," he said, "and all the nations will follow you."

Swami Vivekananda taught that while man can know God in various forms, his greatest attainment is the realization of his identity with the Supreme Reality. He declared that all yogas can be harmoniously combined and freedom attained "by work, or worship, or psychic control, or philosophy, by one, or more, or all of these." Swamiji also declared the following:

- a person's highest achievement and greatest happiness lies in manifesting his own divinity.
- a person's clearest vision lies in his perception of divinity everywhere.
- a person's truest worship is the selfless service of his fellow man, for his fellow man is, in reality, God himself.

Q15. The doctrine of nishkama karma (desireless action) states that one can attain moksha (salvation from the cycle of birth and death) by performing righteous actions but without desire for their fruits. How can one perform righteous actions without desire for their fruits when moksha itself is the fruit of such actions?

A. Moksha, a state of eternal peace and freedom, is realized when the mind transcends all worldly desires and enters a state of total desirelessness. Moksha is not possible as long as any worldly desire is still left, including the desire for moksha itself. All desires must end before one can attain desirelessness, that is, salvation from the cycle of birth and death in the phenomenal world. A person performing *nishkama karma* should not cling to the desire for moksha, since such a desire will prevent him from attaining spiritual perfection. Moksha may be said to be the fruit of desireless action, but with a desire for such a fruit, there will be no salvation or spiritual freedom.

Q16. Hindu religion advocates the philosophy of desireless action (nishkama karma) for attaining spiritual perfection. In as much as desires are natural to human beings, isn't it inhuman to advocate the philosophy of desireless action?

A. *Nishkama karma* (desireless action) does not mean that one should suppress all desires. Genuine desires must be satisfied, as life would be dull without recreation and entertainment, such as art, music, dance, sports, conjugal love, filial affection, savory food and drink, fine clothes, jewelry, ornaments, and pleasant company. Lord Krishna does not ask Arjuna (in the Bhagavad Gita) to kill all desires. On the contrary, Krishna tells him that he (Krishna) himself is the desire, when this desire is not directed against righteousness:

> "I am the power of those who are strong, when this power is free from passion and selfish desires. I am desire when this is pure, and when this desire is not against righteousness." (BG 7.11)

Desireless actions do not imply motive-less or disinterested actions. Desireless actions are those that are not motivated by ego, but by reason and wisdom, and for the good of all. *Nishkama karma* means performing all one's duties in accordance with dharma, without desire for reward. The reward, when received, should be used for the welfare of all beings, including the doer himself. The Bhagavad Gita does not advocate the negative form of desirelessness:

> "Set thy heart upon thy work, but never on its reward; but never cease to do thy work." (BG 2.50)

Q17. Hindus in the U.S. have an excellent opportunity to select the best of the two cultures. What are the values of Western culture that should be incorporated in Hindu culture in order to obtain the best of the two worlds?

A. There are five Western cultural values that should be incorporated into our daily lives:

• *Volunteerism*: Historically, Hindus have been preoccupied with the idea of individual salvation, thus ignoring the needs of their society. The Ramakrishna Mission, founded by Swami Vivekananda, was the forerunner of the movement to redirect our attention from individual salvation to social salvation. Much more needs to be accomplished in this regard. We must join forces with the West to identify and resolve social and community concerns, such as homelessness, environment, and education.

- *Respect for law in politics*: Just as the doctrine of ahimsa was introduced to the social and political arena by Mahatma Gandhi, the concept of dharma must be incorporated into politics. Currently, political leaders among Hindus apparently do not retain the same respect for the law as in the West.

- *Punctuality:* Although the informality of Hindu culture is praiseworthy, respect for others, particularly the elderly, is also given a high priority. In this regard, one's respect for time is a mark of one's attitude and respect for others, as well as a measure of self-discipline. Therefore, our sense of punctuality, though gradually improving, must continue to be adopted by all.

- *Sharing:* Sharing of resources, not only amongst ourselves but also with the underprivileged, is the hallmark of a community-conscious society. Thus we need to launch and become more involved in community service projects, and increase contributions to non-profit community service organizations.

- *Unity:* The diversity of Hindu culture is commendable, as it provides an individual with freedom of thought and expression. In order to strengthen the society, however, unity of all members of a society is essential. We must recognize common underlying principles and work toward unity in order to solve community problems that need our attention.

Q18. The doctor has just told me that I have about six months to live. I am not ready to die and I am in panic. What should I do? I admit that I have never thought of God. Is it too late to think of God?

A. Doctors only know the physical aspect of life, but their is the spiritual dimension which is beyond the realm of science. You should immediately turn to God and put your faith in

Him.   Invoke His mercy by continuous faith and unceasing prayer. Do not be despondent, develop a will to live and do everything to stay healthy. There are numerous documented cases where the patients lived way beyond their physicians' predictions.

It is never too late to turn to God. Sri Krishna says in the Bhagavad Gita, "If one remembers Me at the time of death, one will surely come to Me." Thus it is obvious that if a person turns to God as late as the time of death, he (she) is still cared for by the Divine. In another verse Sri Krishna again says, "Leave all thoughts of right and wrong and come to Me for salvation. I will save you from all sins. Grieve not." The last words of this verse "*grieve not*" are God's promise to help anyone who turns to Him for help.

In his book *Man's Eternal Quest*, Paramahansa Yogananda says, "The man who clings to the Divine is bound to be healed, because God knows that the devotee is praying, and He cannot but respond. But when you give up, the Father says, 'All right. I see that you can do without Me. I shall wait for you.'"

Q19. Why does God want us to pray? Doesn't He know what we need?

A. God knows what we need, but He has given us free will to either turn to Him for help, if we want, or take care of our own affairs by ourselves. A prayer denotes our conscious decision to turn to God for help rather than going on our own.

According to Paramahansa Yogananda, "The first rule in prayer is to approach God only with legitimate desires. The second is to pray for their fulfillment, not as a beggar, but as a child of God: 'I am Thy child. Thou art my mother and father. Thou and I art one.' When you pray deeply and continuously, you will feel a great joy welling up in your heart. Don't be satisfied until that joy manifests; for when you feel that all-satisfying joy in your heart, you will know that God has tuned in your prayer broadcast. Then pray to Him: 'Lord, this is my need. I am willing to work for it; please guide me and help me to have the right thoughts and to do the right things to bring about success. I will use my reason, and work with determination, but guide Thou my reason, will, and activity to the right thing that I should do.'" (*Man's Eternal Quest*, by Paramahansa Yogananda - see Suggested Readings)

Q20. My father was a devout Hindu. He used to sing bhajans regularly and perform many charitable acts as his devotion to God. We always performed prayers and to me he was a model Hindu. He was a very loving person endowed with saintly qualities. He was unfortunately involved in a fatal car crash. I am still trying to figure out why he was not protected by God from the horrible accident that took him away from us.

A. Good actions of one lifetime do not necessarily guarantee that one's overall past karma will be positive, just as a large amount deposited in a bank on a single day does not necessarily guarantee that the overall balance in the bank on that day will be positive. The overall bank balance on a particular day will depend upon the sum total of all the previous deposits and withdrawals made as of that day. Hindus believe that God is too merciful to punish anyone. Whatever we receive is the result of our own overall past and present karma, which is the sum total of the karma of all previous lives and this life. Since an ordinary person may only know what is happening in this life and does not know the content of his (her) past karma, the only choice we have is to perform righteous actions and have faith in the cosmic laws, in spite of our difficult times. When the mind is agitated by the tragedy that you have suffered, this explanation may not be enough for you. This, however, is the truth of the matter, as far as our scriptures are concerned.

Q21. Also, even through all his good acts, he was always struggling to keep his head above water financially. The Tirukural says, "Virtue leads to heaven's wealth and earthly riches here", so I ask, what went wrong?

A. Tirukural (a popular Hindu scripture) does not refer to the "virtue of one lifetime." What is implied is the sum total of all virtues of this and the past lives. Again, since we do not know the virtues of the past lives, we have no choice except to increase our virtue in this life to counter any bad karma we may have committed in our past lives.

Q22. Since the origin of the world as we know it is not clear according to Hindu religion (i.e., early Hindu scriptures portray the world as already existing at the beginning), where did the universe come from? If the world is a cycle of illusion (maya), as many Hindu texts seem to indicate, then why try to understand it scientifically at all? Why not focus all our efforts on escape from the cycle of illusion?

A. The origin of the universe is clear in Hindu religion . The universe arises from pure consciousness or *Paramatman* via its creative will (*Ishvara*) and creative power *(Ishvara-Shakti)*. We must strive to understand this world, which is not only knowable, but one with pure consciousness. The illusion is that the world exists apart from consciousness and that our true Self is limited to a bodily expression. This illusion persists as long as one perceives the world with the mind and the senses alone.

O nce the mind and the senses are transcended through a spiritual experience, the illusion disappears and the individual consciousness becomes one with the cosmic consciousness (i.e., one attains *samadhi*, or union with God). In this experience, the objective universe disappears and the sense of individual separateness and differentiation is lost. This spiritual transformation occurs when one follows the path of knowledge (*Jnana Yoga*), selfless service to mankind (*Karma Yoga*), love of mankind (*Bhakti Yoga*), or contemplation and meditation (*Raja Yoga*). None of these paths is exclusive or superior to others. The suitability of a particular path depends upon the emotional, intellectual, and spiritual dimensions of one's personality. Refer to chapter 8 for more details.

Part V
References

Strength is the one thing needful. Strength is the medicine for the world's disease. Strength is the medicine which the poor must have when tyrannized over by the rich. Strength is the medicine which the ignorant must have when oppressed by the learned. And it is the medicine the sinner must have when tyrannized over by the other sinners.

(Swami Vivekananda)

History of Hinduism

(see Note 1)

Date	Activity
10000 BCE	Last Ice Age ends. The world population is estimated at 4 million and that of the Indian subcontinent 100,000 (see Note 2).
8000-5000 BCE	The Mehrgarh site, located at the foot of the Bolan Pass in the region of Baluchistan, is comprised of multiethnic and multiracial settlements. Residents domesticate cattle, sheep and goats. The archaeological evidence suggests that Mehrgarh was a center of technical innovations and a marketplace for imports and exports. People were involved in overseas trade of the precious stones and sea shells.
6500 BCE or earlier	Aryans are present in India as one of the multiethnic groups of the ancient Indian people (see Note 3).
6500 BCE	According to David Frawley, a Western researcher, Rig Vedic hymns refer to an astronomical configuration that corresponds to 6500 BCE, placing the composition of the early Rig Vedic hymns at this date.

Date	Activity
6000 BCE	Archaeological data suggests the presence of Shiva worship in the Indus Valley civilization at this time.
6000-2000 BCE	Vedic period (see Note 4).
5500 BCE	Mehrgarh villagers make female statues of several Goddesses, suggesting the existence of early Shakti worship (worship of God as Divine Mother in India.
5000-1500 BCE	The Indic civilization (popularly but misleadingly called Indus Valley civilization) flourished with its peak around 3700 BCE. This prehistoric civilization spread from western to central India. Cities with multiethnic and multiracial populations were established from present-day Pakistan to Gujarat, Punjab and Uttar Pradesh.
ca. 4750 BCE	Traditional date for Bhagavan Rama's period (see Note 5).
ca. 3112 BCE	Traditional date for Krishna's period, end of the Mahabharata war, and beginning of the *Kali Yuga* (see Note 6).
ca. 2000 BCE	Early version of the Mahabharata is written, but enlarged later during ca. 700 BCE-300 AD.
2000-1000 BCE	Brahmanas and Aranyakas are composed.
1500-1250 BCE	Major Upanishads are composed.

Table T-1

Date	Activity
ca. 1500-500 BCE	Sutra period; the philosophical sutras (basic texts for *Sankhya, Nyaya,* and *Vaiseshika* systems of philosophy) are developed.
ca. 700 BCE	The Bhagavad Gita, originally narrated during the Mahabharata War, is written down (see Note 7).
600-300 BCE	Ramayana is written as a poem by Valmiki, but is enlarged further sometime later.
599-527 BCE	Mahavira teaches Jainism.
550-480 BCE	Gautama Buddha preaches Buddhism.
500-200 BCE	The *Brahma Sutra* is developed by Sage Badarayana.
ca. 500 BCE	Panini develops Sanskrit grammar (see Note 8).
ca. 300 BCE	Kautiliya's *Arthashastra* (according to some scholars: 100 AD), Gautama's *Nyaya Sutra,* and Kanada's *Vaiseshika Sutra* are written.
ca. 273-237 BCE	Buddhism flourishes in India under the reign of Ashoka.
200 BCE-100 AD	*Manusmriti* is compiled.
ca. 200 BCE	Sage Patanjali writes *Yoga Sutra.*
100 BCE-800 AD	Tirukkural, a popular Hindu scripture, is composed.
57 BCE	*Samvat* calendar of Hindu religion starts at zero.

Table T-1

Date	Activity
320-520 AD	Hindu culture flourishes under the Gupta empire (see Note 9).
300-1500	Puranas and Tantras were developed.
400-500	Kalidasa, a famous poet, develops Sanskrit literature.
400-500	Aryabhata, a famous mathematician, astronomer and founder of the decimal system makes many discoveries. For example, he suggests that the earth is round, rotates on its axis, and revolves around the sun.
600	Varahamihira, a famous astronomer, makes discoveries (see Note 10).
788-820	Adi Shankaracharya, a medieval sage known for his spiritual and intellectual genius, teaches Advaita (non-dualism) Vedanta philosophy. His dynamic teachings demolish the influence of Buddhism in India and contribute to the rapid revival of Hinduism.
900	Great temples are constructed, bronze castings are produced, and beautiful bronze statues of gods and goddesses are built under the Chola dynasty that rules much of South India.
ca. 1100	Buddhism is virtually extinct in India. Abhinavgupta, known for his intellectual and spiritual genius, develops the philosophy of Kashmiri Shaivism. Various Hindu Tantras are composed.

Table T-1

Date	Activity
1055-1137	Ramanujacharya expounds *Visishtadvaita Vedanta*.
1199-1278	Madhvacharya teaches Dvaita (dualism) Vedanta.
1380-1460	Kabir, a famous mystic poet, popularizes the bhakti (devotion) movement of Hinduism.
1469-1538	Guru Nanak, a famous Saint, establishes Sikhism.
1483-1563	Surdas, a renowned poet, contributes to the revival of devotionalism.
1486-1533	Chaitanya, the most revered Vaishnava saint and believed to be an incarnation (avatara) of the Divine, revives the bhakti movement of Hinduism.
1498-1546	Mira Bai, a famous female poet saint, strengthens the bhakti tradition.
1503-1623	Tulsi Das, one of the popular mystic poets, composes the Hindi version of Ramayana and influences Hindu devotionalism.
1774-1833	Ram Mohan Roy, a social and religious reformer, establishes Brahmo Samaj (see Note 11).
1824-1883	Swami Dayananda establishes Arya Samaj (see Note 12).

Date	Activity
1836-1886	Paramahamsa Sri Ramakrishna, the most revered sage who is now worshipped as an avatara, expounds the Vedanta philosophy (see Note 13).
1863-1902	Swami Vivekananda, the foremost disciple of Sri Ramakrishna, teaches the Vedanta philosophy in and outside India (see Note 14).
1869-1948	M. K. Gandhi, an apostle of peace and non-violence, preaches the Hindu doctrine of ahimsa (non-violence).
1872-1950	Sri Aurobindo Ghose, a philosopher, poet, and a yogi, teaches *Integral Yoga* for the evolution of human consciousness and transformation of the physical world.
1879-1950	Sri Ramana Maharshi, a famous sage of modern times, expounds teachings of the Upanishads and Advaita Vedanta. Through the writings of Maharshi's Western disciples, especially Paul Brunton, Advaita Vedanta becomes popular in the West. Paul Brunton's book *A Search in Secret India* makes Maharshi's teachings widely known outside India.
1888-1975	Through his numerous scholarly and authoritative writings, Sarvepalli Radha-krishnan, a philosopher, statesman, and the second President of India, interprets the classical Hindu religious thought (Vedanta) in the light of the modern world.

Table T-1

Date	Activity
	He views Hindu religion as a "way of life," the most successful of all the ways, and thus superior to all others. Two of his popular works are: *The Hindu View of Life* (1926) and his notable introduction and commentary on the *Bhagavad Gita*.
1893	The World Parliament of Religions is held in Chicago, where Swami Vivekananda introduces the Vedanta philosophy to the Western world.
1893-1952	Paramahansa Yogananda establishes the Self-Realization Fellowship International Headquarters in Los Angeles, California, for the worldwide dissemination of the ancient science of Kriya Yoga and meditation (see also Glossary).
1896-1977	Bhaktivedanta Swami Prabhupada establishes the International Society of Krishna Consciousness (ISKCON).
1916-1993	Swami Chinmayananda establishes the Chinmaya Mission for the dissemination of the teachings of Sanatana Dharma.
1990	A school of Vedic Studies, the only one of its kind, is opened at the Rabindra Bharati University, India.
1995	A biggest Hindu temple in the Western world, built by Swaminarayan *Sampradaya* (religious tradition), opens in the Neasden district of London.

Table T-1

Notes on Table T-1:

1. Traditional Indian chronology after Buddha is the commonly accepted chronology of the ancient Indian history. However, the traditional Indian chronology prior to 600 BCE differs significantly from the Western chronology, which is based upon the Aryan invasion theory (see Chapter 39). Based upon the current archaeological and astronomical findings, a growing number of both Eastern and Western scholars have rejected the Aryan invasion theory and challenged the Western chronology of the ancient Indian history. Most of the dates in this timeline prior to 600 BCE are based upon the findings of S. B. Roy, an Indian researcher. Roy provides a fairly convincing basis for his chronology, such as carbon-14 dating, cross-referencing the early Indian historical events with other well established historical traditions, and using astronomical observations recorded in the Rig Veda. See S. B. Roy, "Chronological Framework of Indian Protohistory," published in the Journal of the Bihar Research Society (1972): 44-78; and "Chronological Framework of Indian Protohistory - the Lower Limit," published in the Journal of Oriental Institute (Baroda), nos. 3-4 (1983): 254-274. For a detailed timeline, refer to the timeline published in Sivaya Subramuniyaswami's book "Dancing With Shiva," published by Himalayan Academy, US.

2. Paleolithic sites using stone tools have been unearthed in Tamilnadu and Punjab (India) that are dated 470,000 years ago or even earlier. The so-called Soan culture is reported to have flourished in India between 400,000 and 200,000 BCE. See H. D. Sankalia, "Paleolithic, Neolithic and Copper Ages" in The History and the Culture of the Indian People (general ed., R. C. Majumdar), vol. 1 , pp. 125-142.

3. See Subhash C. Kak, "The Indus Tradition and the Indo Aryans" in *The Mankind Quarterly,* Vol. XXXII, Number 3, Spring, 1992.

4. Most of the modern scholars agree that 2000 BCE is the conclusion of the Vedic period. The main support for this argument is that the current archaeological data shows that the ancient Saraswati River, the principal river of the Rig

Table T-1

Veda, dried up around 2000 BCE. There is a wide variation among scholars on the beginning of the Vedic period. David Frawley thinks that the early hymns of the Rig Veda were composed around 6500 BCE, S. C. Kak arrives at 6000 BCE, P. V. Kane assumes 4000 BCE or earlier, and B. G. Tilak arrives at 4500 BCE.

5. There is a wide difference of opinion among scholars regarding the date of Rama's period. S. B. Roy's estimate is 1950 BCE, K. K. Klostermaier suggests ca. 2350-1950 BCE, and other scholars give different dates. The traditional date, however, is ca. 4750 BCE.

6. Regarding the Mahabharata war and Krishna's period, there is also wide speculation among scholars. Roy's estimate for Krishna's period is 1400 BCE, C. Sengupta sets Krishna's birthdate on July 21, 2501 BCE, and the date of Mahabharata war on 2449 BCE. The Mahabharata text itself refers to winter solstice as having been observed at Dhanishtha, which corresponds to 1400 BCE. This does not necessarily mean that the actual war occurred at this date, since we know that the Mahabharata text was written long after the original war actually took place. The traditional date for Krishna's period is 3112 BCE.

7. S. C. Kak's estimate for the composition of the Bhagavad Gita is ca. 700 BCE, P. V. Kane suggests ca. 500-200 BCE, and yet others date it ca. 100 BCE-100 AD.

8. According to S. B. Roy, Panini developed the Sanskrit grammar in 1300 BCE.

9. The Gupta empire is also called the Golden age of Hindu culture. During this period large temples were built, sculptures and paintings were produced, and great discoveries were made in the fields of science, mathematics, and astronomy. Kalidasa, the great poet and playwright, composed the classics of Sanskrit literature. This was the period of the famous mathematicians and astronomers, such as Aryabhata and Varahamihira.

10. Varahamihira is the author of many astronomical works, including Brhatsamhita (Great Compendium) that

Table T-1

explains the astronomical influence of heavenly bodies on human behavior.

11. Ram Mohan Roy, a social and religious reformer (sometimes called the "father of modern India"), founded Brahmo Samaj to rectify social abuses, such as the early marriage of girls, denial of widow remarriage, and denial of equal rights to women. He advocated the Western system of education in India and pressed for religious reform based on what he considered the Upanishadic doctrine of monotheism or Unitarianism.

12. Swami Dayananda, a social and religious reformer, launched a forceful effort to abolish the caste system, image worship, and excessive ritualism. He united all Hindus through the belief in one God and a common faith in the Vedas. He revitalized a new pride in the Hindu community. According to Swami Dayananda, the Vedas taught monotheism and morality and were the ultimate source of religious authority.

13. Sri Ramakrishna is one of the most revered sages of India. Through his own spiritual experiences, he illustrated the fundamental Hindu doctrine that all true religions lead to the same goal. He unified many Hindu religious sects through his teachings. His main teaching was that religion is not a matter of doctrine or belief, but of realization.

14. Swami Vivekananda first arrived in America in 1893, and soon afterwards attended the World Parliament of Religions in Chicago. Following his remarkable performance at the Parliament of Religions, Vivekananda stayed in America for an extended period to teach the Vedanta philosophy to Americans. He established the Vedanta Society of New York before returning to India in 1896. In India he established the Ramakrishna Mission, to spread the teachings of Sri Ramakrishna through the monks of the Mission. Many centers were established throughout India, and later centers were also established in London and San Francisco on Vivekananda's second U.S. visit. Since then, many new Vedanta centers have been established throughout the world. (See also Glossary and answer to Q14 on page 370.

Table T-1

Table T-2
Hindus Around The World
(1996 Estimate)

Country	Hindus	Country	Hindus
Bangladesh	1,795,000	Pakistan	600,000
Bhutan	415,000	South Africa	594,000
Canada	500,000	Sri Lanka	2,540,000
Fiji	270,000	Suriname	115000
Guyana	214,000	Thailand	54,000
Guade-loupe	16,000	Trinidad	280,000
India	761,687,000	U.K.	350,000
Indonesia	3,770,000	U.S.A.	825,000
Martinique	20,000	*Other Countr.*	345,000
Mauritius	540,000		
Nepal	18,145,000	*Total World*	793,075,000

Summary:
The total population of Hindus in the world (1996 est.) is 793,075,000, which is 13.7% of the world population. Of this 761,687,000 (96%) live in India; 31,043,000 (3.9%) live in countries listed above, and the remaining 345,000 (.04%) live in other parts of the world.

Sources:
- 1997 Book of the Year Encyclopedia Britianica.
- The World Factbook, 1996 (http://www.odci.gov).
- Illustrated Book of the World Rankings, 1997.
- The Universal Almanac, 1996.

Table T-3
Concept of God in Hinduism and Christianity

Concept	Hinduism	Christianity	Remarks
Ultimate Reality (impersonal aspect, unmanifested cosmic Absolute)	Brahman	none	see Note 1
Ultimate Reality (personal aspect)	Ishta-deva or Ishta-devata	none	see Note 2
Ultimate Reality (as creator and controller of the universe)	various names, such as Ishvara, Divine Mother, Paramatma, and Purusha	God	see Note 3
Three-fold Nature of the Ultimate Reality	Sat, Tat, O M	Father, Son, and Holy Ghost	see Note 4
Individual aspect of the Ultimate Reality	atman	soul, spirit, self	see Note 5
Sacred Trinity	Brahma, Vishnu, and Shiva	none	---
Nature of creation	cyclic and evolutionary	non-cyclic and non-evolutionary	see Note 6

Concept	Hinduism	Christianity	Remarks
Cause of suffering in the world	maya (cosmic ignorance)	Original Sin	see Note 7
Spiritual discipline	Karma Yoga, Bhakti Yoga, Jnana Yoga, Raja Yoga	Karma Yoga, Bhakti Yoga	see Note 8

Notes on Table T-3:

1. There is no equivalent word for "Brahman" in Christianity since this concept is not present in Christian theology.

2. The Hindu concept that God can be worshipped by any name and in any form does not exist in Christianity. As such there is no equivalent word for "Ishta-deva" or "Ishta-devata" in Christian theology.

3. In Hindu religion, God is the creator, controller (sustainer) and the dissolver of the universe. Since creation appears in cycles, dissolution of the universe is necessary for its recreation. In Christianity, God is only the creator and the controller and not the dissolver of the universe, since Christianity believes that God created the universe only once.

4. The meanings of the words Sat, Tat, and OM of the Hindu scriptures are somewhat similar to the meanings of the Biblical words Father, Son, and Holy Ghost (Spirit). In Hindu scriptures, *Sat* refers to the cosmic Absolute, the unmanifested aspect of the Ultimate Reality, and in Christianity, the same meaning is generally assigned to the word "Father." The word *Tat* is the manifested aspect of the Ultimate Reality. The word "Son" is the Christ consciousness (Brahma or Kutastha Chaitanya of the Hindu scriptures) existing within creation,

Table T-3

which is the manifestation of the cosmic Absolute. The "OM" vibration or sound is what Christians call the "Holy Ghost."

5. In Christianity the individual soul (spirit) is created by God. In Hindu religion the individual soul (atman) is a spiritual reality which, being eternal, is not created by God, but is part of God. See chapter 4 for further discussion of atman.

6. In Hindu religion, creation exists in cycles. In each cycle the individual soul evolves from lower forms of life to higher ones until it obtains a human body. In a human body the individual soul becomes conscious of itself and is capable of attaining moksha (liberation)---freedom from the cycle of birth and death in the phenomenal world. See chapter 2 for further discussion of creation.

7. According to the Christian theology, Original Sin is transmitted from one generation to the next and inherited by each person as a consequence of the original sinful choice made by Adam, the first man of the human race, who sinned in the Garden of Eden. The concept of Original Sin leads to the conclusion that God punishes each and every person of each and every generation for the mistake committed by one person. Such a view is not accepted in Hindu religion. According to Hindu view, an individual is potentially divine, but he or she commits sin due to *maya* (cosmic ignorance), which is a metaphysical principle and not a moral one. See chapter 4 for discussion of maya and sin in Hindu religion, and chapter 13 for information relating to the Law of Karma.

8. Although Christianity does not label its spiritual disciplines as Karma Yoga and Bhakti Yoga, the Christian emphasis on love of mankind with one's duties dedicated to the service of God, is essentially a path of Bhakti Yoga and Karma Yoga.

Table T-3

Table T-4

Energy Centers (Chakras)

Name	Symbol	Location	Color	Sense	Spiritual Qualities
Muladhara chakra	square/ cross	base of spine	yellow	smell	peace, security and freedom
Swadhis- thana chakra	crescent moon	pelvis	silver	taste	creativity
Manipura chakra	triangle	navel	red/ yellow	sight	power of understanding, clarity, and expansiveness
Anahata chakra	circle	heart	sky blue	touch	love, compassion, kindness
Vishuddha chakra	oval	throat	purple	hear- ing	purity, power of speech and expression
Ajna chakra	third eye	between eyebrow	orange	mind	wisdom and intuition
Sahasrara chakra	thousand- petaled lotus	crown of head	white	---	cosmic consciousness (God com- munion)

Note:

The colors associated with the chakras, as listed above, are not visible to the naked eye. Only a spiritually adept can perceive these colors in deep meditation. A chakra can be awakened by using a mantra in accordance with the instructions of a guru. When a particular chakra is awakened, an individual develops spiritual power along with the qualities associated with that chakra.

Table T-5

Comparative Principles in Hinduism, Christianity and Judaism

Hinduism	Christianity	Judaism
Hindu religion is the world's oldest surviving religion. It has no human founder, and is beginningless, as it predates recorded history. The major scriptures are the Vedas, Bhagavad Gita, the epics, Agamas and others. Hindu religion has three main denominations: Shaivism, Shaktism, and Vaishnavism. The following are the major beliefs of Hindu religion:	Christianity was founded by Jesus of Nazareth about 2000 years ago in what is now Israel. The major scriptures are the Bible, Old and New Testament. Christianity has three main denominations: Roman Catholic, Eastern Orthodox and Protestant. Among Protestants there are numerous denominations. The following are the major beliefs of Christianity:	Judaism, the religion of the Jews, began about 3700 years ago in what is now Israel. The founders are Abraham, the first in the lineage, and Moses, who brought the Commandments and established religious laws and traditions. The major scripture is the Torah (the first five books of the Old Testament) and Talmud. The three main denominations of Judaism are: Orthodox, Conservative, and Reform. The following are the major beliefs of Judaism:

Hinduism	Christianity	Judaism
1. There is but one Supreme Being, Who is absolute existence, knowledge, and bliss. He is both immanent and transcendent, and both Creator and Unmanifest Reality. There is no duality of God and the world, but only unity.	1. There is but one God, Who reveals Himself as Father, Son and Holy Ghost. God is the Creator, Sustainer and Redeemer of the world, but is distinct from His creation. There is duality of God and the world.	1. There is but one God, Yahweh, Who is incorporeal, and transcendent, beyond the limitation of form. God is the Creator of the world, which He rules and guides. He is distinct from His creation. There is duality of God and the world.
2. There is no absolute beginning or end of the universe. The universe has existed eternally and undergoes cycles of creation, preservation, and dissolution.	2. The world was created once by God, but was corrupted by sin. Under a divine scheme, the world moves towards God for final perfection.	2. The universe is not eternal, but was created by God and will be destroyed by Him.
3. Each soul is potentially divine. Sin is of the mind and not of the soul. Man commits sin because of the ignorance of his own true nature. Self-knowledge destroys ignorance, just as fire burns fuel to ashes.	3. As a result of the Original Sin (Adam's Sin) the human race was spiritually corrupted and thereby alienated from God. Thus man is born a sinner.	3. None is born a sinner. Man has two natural impulses: good and evil. He can either follow God's law, or rebel and be influenced by Satan.

Table T-5

Hinduism	Christianity	Judaism
4. The ultimate goal of Hindu religion is the personal and direct experience of God, which frees the soul from the cycle of birth and death.	4. The goal of Christianity is eternal life with God in heaven by accepting Christ as savior and living life according to his teachings.	4. The goal of Judaism lies in obedience to the Torah, which can alleviate the plight of the individual and of society.
5. Each soul evolves toward union with God by his own effort. No savior can achieve this for him. No soul will be eternally deprived of union with God. The soul suffers in the world only until it frees itself from the cycle of birth and death (samsara).	5. Salvation is only through the savior, Jesus Christ, God's only begotten son. Those who obey God's commands will have eternal life. Those who persist in rebellion will be lost eternally.	5. Man's spiritualization is only possible through adherence to the Torah, God's only immutable law. God punishes those who rebel against His law.
6. The soul incarnates, evolving through many births, until all its karmas have been resolved and liberation attained.	6. It is ordained by God that human beings die once and after that face judgment.	6. It is ordained by God that human beings die once and after that face judgment.
7. The soul is not created by God, but is a part of God. It suffers in the world due to maya, the cosmic ignorance.	7. The soul is created by an act of God. It suffers in the world because of the Original Sin.	7. God is Creator of the Soul. As the spirit of God in man, the soul is immortal.

Table T-5

Hinduism	Christianity	Judaism
8. A spiritually awakened master (guru) is essential to realize the Transcendent Absolute, as are personal discipline, good conduct, purification, self-inquiry, yoga and meditation. `	8. God has given revelation of Himself in Jesus and the sacred scriptures. Prophets, apostles, evangelists, and pastors are empowered by God to guide individuals.	8. No one can intervene in the relationship of man and God, nor can God be represented in any form, nor can any being be worshipped other than the one God, Yahweh.
9. Hindu religion believes that there is no one religion that teaches an exclusive way to salvation. All genuine spiritual paths are valid and all great religions are equally true. The different religions are like the branches of a tree--the tree of religion.	9. Christianity believes that it is the only true religion, and the only path to salvation. It also believes that the Bible is the only word of God.	9. Judaism believes that God has established a unique spiritual covenant with the Hebrew people. Jews thus consider themselves a chosen people apart from all other peoples of the earth.
10. The Law of Karma, the law of cause and effect, is the divine law of justice by which an individual creates his own destiny through thoughts, words, and deeds.	10. Through God's grace and favor, lost sinners are rescued from the guilt and eternal consequences of their evil thoughts, words and deeds.	10. Proof of God's love and promise to man comes from obedience to the Torah, which pleases God, Yahweh.

Table T-5

Hinduism	Christianity	Judaism
11. Hell and heaven are neither physical places, nor are they eternal. They exist only in the astral world as periods of temporary stay for the unliberated soul, following its departure from the physical world and prior to its next incarnation into the physical world.	11. On Judgment Day the physical body of every soul that ever lived will be brought to life. The pure souls will be consigned by God to heaven to enjoy everlasting life, and sinners to hell, a physical place where the soul suffers eternally.	11. Obeying God's law brings rewards in the future life when the Messiah will come to overthrow evil and reward the righteous in God's kingdom on earth, the Day of the Lord. Thereafter the soul will enjoy God's presence and love.
12. Upon death the soul enters the astral world and remains there until it reincarnates in accordance with the Law of Karma. In Hindu religion God neither judges nor punishes the soul, and as such there is no Judgment Day for the soul. The soul is born again and again on earth to reap the fruits of its own past actions until all its karmas have been resolved.	12. Upon death the soul enters Heaven or Hell, depending upon its quality of life on earth. On Judgment Day the dead are brought back to life and the redeemed are rewarded eternal life with God in Heaven. The sinners are consigned to Hell by God, where they suffer eternally.	12. Upon death the soul migrates to Heaven or to Hell, depending upon its quality of life on earth. One day the Messiah will appear on earth and there will be a Day of Judgment, and the dead shall arise to everlasting life.

Table T-5

Hinduism	Christianity	Judaism
13. Hindu religion believes that there is neither any intrinsic evil in Nature nor any evil force in the world to oppose God. Man commits evil due to Cosmic Ignorance (maya) and remains separated from God, suffering in the world until he attains salvation.	13. There is indeed genuine evil in the world. The evil is embodied in Satan (Devil), who opposes God's will and is the personification of evil, deception and darkness.	13. There is indeed genuine evil in the world. The evil is embodied in Satan (Devil), who caused God's creation to go astray.
14. Proof of God's existence lies in direct communion with Him, through the grace of a guru, who guides an individual on a spiritual path.	14. Jesus is God incarnate, and therefore the only sure path to salvation. Other religions may offer spiritual insights, but only Jesus is the Way, the Truth, and the Life.	14. Moses was God's foremost prophet, who delivered the Commandments, man's highest law, revealed to him by God on Mount Sinai.
15. Worship of God is in the form of a deity (a particular manifestation of God) and is both ritualistic and meditative, centering around the temple and home shrine.	15. Worship of God is congregational with simple rituals centering around the place of worship in the church.	15. Worship of God is through devotion, rituals, and prayers centering around the synagogue and home.

Table T-5

How to Meditate

This appendix provides basic instructions on a simple meditation technique for the beginner. This technique is based upon the common underlying principles of various types of meditations. If practiced regularly, this technique will enable one to efficiently learn more advanced techniques later, through initiation by a spiritual master.

As stated in chapter 8, meditation is a scientific means for experiencing perfect physical and mental relaxation by uniting the joy of the individual self (atman) with the vast joy of the Cosmic Self (Brahman). Meditation is a special form of concentration in which the mind is essentially liberated from restlessness and is focussed on the Self within.

Benefits of Meditation

- Relaxes the body by removing tension from nerves and muscles. Studies have shown that one hour of deep meditation is equivalent to several hours of deep sleep, as far as relaxation of the body is concerned.

- Decreases mental restlessness, thereby relaxing the mind. A relaxed mind is stronger and more efficient. A strong mind, in turn, adds solid moral and ethical direction to one's life.

- Purifies the mind of mental pollutants such as anger, short temper, craving, lust, and envy. A pure mind is a source of peace and tranquillity, as well as wisdom and joy.

- Meditation sharpens one's memory and intelligence. In her book *Meditation for Children*, Dr. Deborah Rozman states, "It is a well-known scientific fact that the average person is using only about ten to fifteen percent of his brain cells at this time in history."[22] The remaining 85 to 90% of brain cells are inactive and thus practically useless. The energy one taps from within by meditation is believed to gradually stimulate inactive brain cells by activating the brain's neurons, thereby bringing more awareness to an individual's consciousness.

• Meditation brings one in touch with one's self (atman), which is the source of unlimited power within. Because of maya, an individual's attention is normally directed outside of himself. Meditation focuses one's attention inward and guides one in discovering one's own true nature, full of purity and divinity. The purpose of life is to seek union with God, and meditation provides both the map and the vehicle for such a journey to the kingdom of God. Hindu sages bear testimony to this fact.

Steps for Meditation

1. Set aside a separate room, where possible, or a corner of a room for the sole purpose of meditation. Do not use that space for any purpose other than meditation. If you associate holiness with any images or pictures, locate them in the meditation room. Burn incense and place flowers in that room, if you like. Consider the meditation room as a shrine so that the moment you enter this room, your mind will be filled with spiritual vibrations.

2. Early morning and late evening, before going to bed, are the best hours to set for meditation. During these times the mind is relatively calm and thus receptive to meditation. Once meditation times are established, be regular and do not change them.

3. Choose a convenient meditation posture (see Q3 below) facing the east or the north (where possible; see Q1 and 2 below). Hold the spine erect, abdomen in, chest out, shoulders back, and the chin parallel to the floor. Keep the spine vertical, with waist, back, and neck in a straight line. Keep the head upright.

4. Inhale slowly and deeply through the nostrils to a fixed count (six to ten); hold your breath to the same count, and

Practice this ten times. Then inhale through the nostrils, tensing the whole body and clenching the fists. Relax all the body parts at once and, as you do so, exhale completely through the mouth in a double exhalation, "huh huh." Repeat this exercise six times. Now inhale and exhale normally.

5. Close the eyes and mentally offer the following prayer to the Lord, with the deepest devotion of your heart:

> *"Asato ma sad-gamaya; tamaso ma-jyotir gamaya; mrtyor-ma amrutam gamaya. OM--Shantih, Shantih, Shantih."*

> "Lead me from unreal to real; lead me from darkness to light; lead me from death to immortality. OM--Peace, Peace, Peace."

6. Chant the following mantra loudly, semi-verbally (silently) or mentally twenty times with the deepest devotion of your heart:

> "Om bhoor bhuvah svah; tat savitur varaynyam; bhargo day-vasya dheemahi; *dhiyo yo nah prachoda-yat; Om."*

> "God is the giver of life, the dispeller of miseries, and the bestower of happiness. Let us meditate upon that Creator, the most worthy and acceptable Almighty God. May He inspire and lead our minds and intellects."

7. Choose a Divine name or a short mantra that helps you to feel the Divine presence in your heart. The mantra can be in any language, but should be short and once selected, should not be changed. If you have not been given a mantra by a guru, you may select any one of the following popular mantras or any other mantra listed in chapter 35:

Rama Rama Rama	*Krishna Krishna Krishna*
Om Om Om	*Om Namah Shivaya*
Om Tat Sat	*Tat Tvam Asi*
Om Sri Ram Jai Ram Jai Jai Ram	*Aham Brahmasmi*
So-ham	*Ayam Atma Brahma*
Om Namah Narayanaya	*Ayam Atma Brahma*

Appendix A-1

8. With the eyelids half-closed (or completely closed, if this is more comfortable to you), look upward, focusing your gaze and attention at the spot between the eyebrows. Do not cross the eyes or strain them. It is important to fix the whole of your attention at the point between the eyebrows, *Ajna Chakra* or the *third eye* (see Table T-4). Watch your mind as a disinterested observer would. If the mind wanders, chant the chosen mantra a few times and bring the consciousness back to the point between the eyebrows. Again observe the mind, keeping your attention focussed at the point between the eyebrows. If the mind wanders again, chant the mantra again a few times and keep watching your mind. Go back to the repetition of the mantra whenever the mind wanders. Repeat this process until you feel the divine response as a calm, deep peace and inner joy. Do not chant the mantra mechanically; pour your entire devotion from your heart into the chanting of your mantra.

9. When the meditation session is completed, do not arise quickly and leave in a hurry. Doing so is akin to filling a glass with milk to the brim and then running with it; the milk is bound to spill over. To terminate meditation, open your eyes and slowly move your head around to look at objects in the vicinity. Arise slowly and stretch your muscles. Spend some time reading the scriptures, dwelling on divine thoughts, or listening to devotional music. Let the peace and calm of meditation permeate your body and mind before you leave the place of meditation.

10. A beginner should practice meditation for at least 30 minutes per session. The longer one meditates, enjoying the peace and calm, the faster one can progress spiritually. The calmness derived from meditation helps to bring harmony and happiness into one's daily activities. The following is a suggested meditation schedule for for the beginner:

Physical relaxation (step 4 above)	5 to 10 minutes
Prayer and chants (steps 5)	5 to 10 minutes
Meditation (step 8)	15 to 30 minutes
Post-meditation period (step 9)	5 to 10 minutes
Total	30 to 60 minutes

Questions and Answers

Q1. *Why is it necessary to meditate in a particular place and direction. Is not God present everywhere?*

A. By sitting in one particular place or direction one does not gain any extra spirituality. However, some guidelines are helpful to the beginner in meditation. To illustrate, a seedling planted along a roadside should be protected from animals by a fence until the seedling grows into a tree. The fence does not help in the growth of the plant, but protects the plant when it is young. If the fence is not removed when the plant grows, the same fence can impede the growth of the tree. Similarly, all guidelines directed for the practice of meditation protect the beginner from environmental distractions and should be considered as a fence around the little plant of spirituality. The fence must be removed when the plant grows, lest the barbed wire fence of rituals and regulations impede further growth of the tree of spirituality. Until a swimmer learns to swim skillfully, he or she should not take the risk of swimming into deep water. We may select a room or a corner in the beginning to meditate, but we should not remain there all our lives. When the plant of meditation becomes a tree, one will be able to meditate anywhere and any time.

Q2. *Many teachers suggest that, where possible, one should meditate facing the east or the north. What is the significance of meditating in these two directions?*

Appendix A-1

A. The daily rotation of the earth is from the west to the east. A meditator facing the east faces the direction of the earth's motion. This is similar to riding a train and facing the direction of the train's motion; some people become sick riding backwards in a train, that is facing the direction opposite to the train's motion. Yogis have found out that during meditation the nervous system becomes very sensitive and in some cases the earth's motion may cause mental distractions. When it is not possible to face the east, one should face the north. The earth's magnetic field is such that the polar magnetic current flows from the south to the north. Yogis have found that meditating in the direction of the magnetic current eliminates the subtle effect of the earth's magnetic current on the nervous system.

Yogis also tell us that if the head is placed toward the south during sleep, the magnetic current passes from the head to the feet and helps to improve the quality of sleep. Similarly, placing the head toward the east during sleep helps one to enjoy a better sleep, since the sleeper is oriented in the direction of the earth's motion. Many cases of insomnia are reported to have been cured by simply rearranging the bed. Thus for meditation, where possible, one should face the east or the north, and for sleeping one should place the head toward the south or toward the east.

Q3. *What is the purpose of an asana (posture) in regards to meditation? Of the many different asanas that are taught, which one is the best for meditation?*

A. The purpose of an *asana* is to hold the spine vertical, ensure overall stability of the body, and prevent the body from bending during meditation. The *asana* must be comfortable and not cause any discomfort that would harm the meditator. Thus the best *asana* is one that is comfortable and holds the body in the correct position for meditation. The following four *asana*s are common and any of these can be used:

Asana	Description
Padm-asana (lotus posture)	Sit on the floor on a cushion. Place the right foot on the left thigh, left foot on right thigh, soles of the feet upwards, with the feet held on the thighs. Lay the palms on your lap, the right one over the left, and with the palms facing up. This asana holds the knees firm on the floor, presses the waist forward, and locks the spine in the vertical position. This asana is best for longer and deeper meditations, but may cause discomfort to those whose legs are not supple.
Svasti-kasana (posture of peace and success)	Sit on the floor on a cushion. Put the right toe inside the left knee-pit. Holding the left toe with the left hand, and with the help of the right hand under the right leg, draw the left toes into the right knee-pit. Lay palms on your lap, the right one over the left, with the palms facing up. This asana maintains the spine perfectly vertical.
Sukh-asana (cross-legged)	Sit on the floor on a cushion, with the upper and outer parts of your feet resting on the floor. Lay the palms on your lap, the right one over the left, with the palms facing up.
Sitting on a chair	Sit on a straight armless chair with the feet resting flat on the floor. Hold the spine erect, abdomen in, chest out, shoulders back and chin parallel to the floor. Turn the palms upward and rest them on the legs at the juncture of the thighs and the abdominal region, in order to prevent the body from bending forward. The meditation chair should be of comfortable height, neither too high nor too low, and neither too soft nor too hard. Keep the spine vertical, with waist, back, and neck in a straight line. Keep the head upright.

Appendix A-1

One can use any of the above asanas for meditation depending upon whether one is accustomed to sitting on the floor (although sitting on the floor is generally recommended). Perfection cannot be attained by an *asana* alone. The mind must be brought under control for success in meditation and for proper living as well.

Q4. *What is the significance of breathing with respect to meditation?*

A. According to the science of breathing, the pattern of breathing is indicative of the nature of one's consciousness. A mental disturbance or restlessness is signaled by shallow and irregular breathing. Regular and deep breathing is a sign of mental poise and tranquillity. Regular deep breathing should, therefore, be practiced prior to meditation (see meditation step 4 above).

Q5. *What are the key factors for success in meditation?*

A. The following are the key factors for success in meditation:

- Bathing has a cleansing effect on the body as well as the mind, and is thus a beneficial practice before meditation. Sages tell us that spreading a woolen blanket or a silk sheet (or both with silk on top) to cover meditation seat has a beneficial effect on meditation. If sitting on a chair, spread the cloth over the back of the chair and under your feet.

- To avoid being sleepy, do not meditate just after eating. Wait at least an hour. Eat more vegetables and fruits and avoid consuming meat products, as much as possible.

- Meditation is a divine appointment to commune with God. Keep your appointment at all costs. God does not appreciate people missing their appointments!

- Do not give up meditation if the mind is restless and you think that you are wasting time. If your mind is too restless to meditate, read a scripture or listen to devotional music, but *never* leave your meditation seat. Know that the single factor that ensures success in meditation is one's persistence. If you persist, the mind will eventually learn to meditate. The mind is difficult to control, but it can be controlled by regular practice, Sri Krishna declares in the Bhagavad Gita (BG 6.35).

• Without true love and devotion for God, one can never succeed in meditation. One must look forward to one's meditation with love and devotion, thinking, "This is the only time in my life that I will have an opportunity to converse with my own Creator. He is the One Who sent me here on this earth, and He is the One Who will receive me back, and determine my new assignment. I better make friends with Him now, lest it be too late." With this kind of *bhavana*, one will certainly succeed in meditation.

Q6. *What is the difference between meditation and prayer?*

A. A prayer is a devotee's request or plea to the deity (God), in word or thought, with adoration, confession, supplication or thanksgiving. In prayer, the devotee talks and the deity listens, but the separation between devotee and deity is maintained. Meditation, on the other hand, is the act or process of engaging in divine contemplation or of focussing one's thought on the deity. In meditation, the deity talks in the language of silence and the devotee listens in silence. In the highest form of meditation (i.e., *samadhi*), the separation between the devotee and the deity disappears and the devotee realizes the deity as his (her) own Self. Refer to Question 19 on page 374 for a discussion of the rules for success in prayer.

Arati
Om Jaya Jagadeesha Hare

Om jaya jaga-deesha hare
Swaamee jaya jaga-deesha hare
Bhakta jano ke sankata, daasa jano ke sankata
Kshana ma*y doora kare
Om jaya jaga-deesha hare

Salutations to Thee, the Lord of the universe
Salutations to Thee, the Protector of all
O instant remover of the troubles of the devotees
Salutations to Thee, the Lord of the universe

Jo dhyaa-ve phala paave
Duhkha vinashe mana kaa
Swaamee dhukha vinashe mana kaa
Sukha sampatti ghara aave
Sarva sampatti ghara aave
Kashta mite tana kaa
OM jaya jaga-deesha hare

He who surrenders to Thee obtains the fruit
The afflictions of his mind disappear
Peace and prosperity dawns on him
All the body's troubles disappear
Salutations to Thee, the Lord of the universe

Maata pitaa tuma mere sharana gahoo* ma*y kisakee
Swaamee sharana gahoo* ma*y kisakee
Tuma bina aura na doojaa, prabhu bina aura na doojaa
Aasa karoo* ma*y jisakee
Om jaya jaga-deesha hare

Thou art my mother and my father
Who else can I surrender to, who else can I surrender to
There is none I can rely upon
Other than Thee, other than Thee
Salutations to Thee, the Lord of the universe

Tuma poorana para-maatmaa tuma antar-yaamee
Swaamee tuma antar-yaamee
Paara-brahma para-meshwara
Paara-brahma para-meshwara
Tuma sabake swaamee
Om jaya jaga-deesha hare

Thou art the absolute and omnipresent Lord of all
Thou art the omnipotent and omniscient Lord of all
Thou art the Supreme Lord of the universe
Thou art the Supreme Lord of all
Salutations to Thee, the Lord of the universe

Tuma karunaa ke saagara, tuma paalana-karta
Swaamee tuma paalana-karta
Mai sayvaka tuma swaamee
Mai sayvaka tuma swaamee
Kripaa karo bhar-taa
Om jaya jaga-deesha hare

Thou art the ocean of compassion
Thou art the ultimate Protector of all
I am Thy servant, Thou art my Master
Have mercy on me, O merciful Lord
Salutations to Thee, the Lord of the universe

Tuma ho ayka agochara, saba ke praana-pati
Swaamee saba-ke praana-pati
Kisa vidhi miloo* da-yaama-ya
Kisa vidhi miloo* da-yaama-ya
Tuma-ko ma*y ku-mati
Om jaya jaga-deesha hare

Appendix A-2

Thou art the only One invisible, the beloved of every heart
How can I reach Thee, O Supreme Lord?
I am weak and ignorant, O merciful Lord
Salutations to Thee, the Lord of the universe

Deena bandhu dhukha-hareaa, tuma rakshaka mere
Swaamee tuma rakshaka mere
Karuna-hath uthaao, apanay sharana lagaavo
Dwaara padaoo* ma*y tere
Om jaya jaga-deesha hare

O support of the weak, the Remover of sorrows
Bestower of peace and the Lord of the universe
Bless me with Thy compassionate hands
I am at Thy doorstep, O Supreme Lord
Salutations to Thee, the Lord of the universe

Vish-aya vikaara mitaavo, paapa haro devaa
Swaamee paapa haro deva
Shradhaa bhakti ba-dhaa-vo
Shradhaa prayma ba-dhaa-vo, santana kee sevaa
Om jaya jaga-deesha hare

Relieve me of passion and suffering, O merciful Lord
Protect me from sin, O Supreme Lord
Bless me with ever increasing faith
Bless me with divine love and spirit of service for the holy
Salutations to Thee, the Lord of the universe

Pronunciation Guide

Use the pronunciation scheme provided in the glossary with
the following supplementary guide:
  a to be pronounced like *u* in *cut* (never as *a* in *cat*)
  aa to be pronounced like *a* in *father*
  ee to be pronounced like *ee* in sheep

The star mark * next to a vowel or a consonant indicates the
nasalized pronunciation of that letter.

Appendix A-2

Table A-3
Sacred Pilgrimages (*Tirthas*)

Pilgrimages (*tirthas*) are an integral part of Hindu religious life. The Puranas and the Mahabharata describe many of these sacred places in India, which are visited by millions of Hindu pilgrims every year. Pilgrimages are essential for mental peace, spiritual growth, penance for past sins, and cultivation of piety.

Three Main Tirthas

The significance of the three main sites of tirthas (Prayaga, Gaya, and Kashi) is reflected in the ancient maxim: "One should shave one's head (symbolizing surrender to God) in Prayaga, offer *pindas* (small balls of rice offered as oblations to the departed ones) in Gaya, and die (to attain moksha) in Kashi."

Prayaga: At the confluence of the holy rivers Ganga (Ganges) and Yamuna at Allahabad in Uttar Pradesh, Prayaga (renamed Allahabad by Muslims in 1584) is considered the king of tirthas. In ancient times, Lord Brahma is said to have performed a great Yajna here. An annual event, Magh Mela, lasting from 15 days to a month, is held here with great religious fervor during January-February. Every 12th year Magh Mela is known as Kumbha Mela when millions of pilgrims come here to bathe in the holy rivers and perform religious rites and ceremonies. A huge temporary township is set on the river bank to celebrate the Kumbha festival. The Ardha Kumbha festival is held every sixth year. An ancient banyan tree (near Allahabad Fort), called Akshya Batt (immortal banyan tree), is considered very auspicious. Kumbha Mela is also held at three other locations in India (see chapter 36).

Gaya: About 58 miles south of Patna in Bihar, Gaya is a tirtha of supreme sanctity. The grace of God is said to be so localized here that offering oblations to the departed souls provides them immediate peace and raises them to heavenly abode. Millions of devout Hindus come here from all walks of life and offer *pindas* for their departed ones. The pilgrims bathe in the holy Phalgu river and visit the Vishnupad temple, said to have been built over the footprints of Lord Vishnu. About ten miles south of Gaya is Bodh Gaya, where Buddha attained enlightenment under a Peepal tree over 2500 years ago. The present Bo tree is believed to be the direct descendent of the original tree under which Buddha attained nirvana.

Kashi: Located on the western banks of the holy river Ganga in Uttar Pradesh, Kashi (also called Varanasi or Banaras) is the most famous of all holy cities in India. Kashi literally means "full of divinity," or "spiritually resplendent." Devout Hindus have been visiting this holy city from times immemorial for religious merit and atonement of their past sins. Every devout Hindu aspires to visit Kashi at least once in the lifetime. The holiest place in Kashi is the Vishwanath Temple, the golden spiraled temple where Lord Shiva resides as the Lord of the city. In the Matsya Purana (a Hindu scripture) Lord Shiva says, "Varanasi is always my most secret place, the cause of liberation for all the creatures."

The most fascinating part of Kashi is the crescent-shaped river front, approximately three miles long. It has bathing ghats (banks with steps) where pilgrims bathe in the holy waters of Ganga early in the morning, and perform religious rites and ceremonies with great sanctity. In the evening, lighted lamps are set afloat on tiny leaf boats in Ganga with the loud chanting of prayers and holy hymns. The lighted lamps in the water provide colorful scenes of enchanting beauty. Nine miles north-east of Kashi is a town called Sarnath, where Lord Buddha gave his first sermon after attaining enlightenment.

Four Tirthas of Special Sanctity (*Chardham*)

Badrinath: At the confluence of Rishi Ganga and
Alaknanda rivers in the Himalayas, about 185 miles north
of Rishikesh, lies Badrinath.   Lord Vishnu is said to have
done penance here in prehistoric times.   The image of
Badrinath (another name for Lord Vishnu) was installed by
Adi Shankaracharya in the present temple. This holy place
takes its name after "badri," meaning "wild berries," which
once grew here in plenty.   The two mountain peaks Nar
and Narain stand like two guards on either side of
Badrinath.   The towering Neelkanth mountain stands at a
distance.   The ancient scriptures declare that no pilgrimage
is complete without a visit to Badrinath.   Just opposite the
shrine on the banks of Alaknanda lies a hot sulfur spring,
called Tapt Kund.   Yamunotri and Gangotri, the popular
centers of pilgrimage, are also located in this region.

About three miles from Badrinath is a village called Mana.
Tradition says that the Vedas were compiled and divided into
four books in the Vyas Gufa (cave) of this village.   Many
Puranas were also written in this gufa. In addition to the
numerous places of religious and spiritual interest around
Badrinath, the area abounds in picturesque places of splendid
beauty.

Dwarka: Located on the west coast (in Gujarat)
overlooking the Arabian sea, Dwarka is a sacred pilgrimage
center due to its association with Sri Krishna, who was the
king of Dwarka in his time.   The famous temple in Dwarka is
Jagat Mandir, which is said to have been built by the
grandson of Sri Krishna.   There are numerous holy places,
temples and shrines in and around Dwarka that devout
Hindus visit regularly, especially on Janmashtami, the birthday
of Sri Krishna.

Rameshwaram: Literally, "abode of Rama," Rameshwaram is known as "Kashi of the South," and is located on an
island about 100 miles from Madurai. Here Bhagavan Rama
erected a lingam, the symbol of Lord Shiva, before killing the
demon-king Ravana.   Rameshwaram is said to be the
culmination point in the quest for moksha for all devout
Hindus.   The holy island is filled with many temples that

enshrine the images and icons of Rama, Sita, Lakshman, and Hanuman.

Puri: About 40 miles from Bhubaneswar, Puri is a popular pilgrimage center that offers a number of colorful fairs and festivals throughout the year.   The famous temple of Puri is the Jagannath Temple (Jagannath means "the Lord of the Universe"). Puri is said to be the abode of the Lord of the Universe.   The Rath Yatra (see page 322) is a spectacular event that is held every year with great religious fervor. There are many sacred temples and shrines located in the three cities of Puri, Konark and Bhubaneswar, which form a triangle, popularly known as the Golden Triangle.

Seven Sacred Tirthas

Ayodhya: Located in Uttar Pradesh, Ayodhya is a popular pilgrimage center as it is the birthplace of Bhagavan Rama.   Among the places of religious interest in Ayodhya are the Kanak Bhawan, Bharat Kund and Hanuman Garhi, and the birthplace of Rama, known as Janambhoomi.

Haridwar: Literally, "abode of the gods," Haridwar is located on the banks of the holy river Ganga and is a pilgrimage center of great antiquity.   The most sacred spot here is Har-ki-Pauri, a bathing ghat (bank), where devotee Hindus congregate to bathe in the holy waters of Ganga. Haridwar is also one of the four places (see chapter 36) where Kumbha Mela is held every 12 years.   About 13 miles from Haridwar is Rishikesh, said to be the gateway to the kingdom of gods.   Rishikesh is a famous center of renunciation, yoga, meditation, penance, and salvation.   There are many popular ashrams (spiritual centers) in Rishikesh.

Kanchipuram: Also called "Varanasi of the South," Kanchipuram is a city of temples and a very important pilgrim center.   It includes as many as 124 beautiful temples and   shrines.   This   is   also   the   seat   of   Jagadguru Shankaracharya, a famous saint of India.   Thousands of devout Hindus visit this city to seek his blessings and guidance.

Mathura: About 30 miles from Agra in Uttar Pradesh is Mathura, the birthplace of Sri Krishna.   Many bathing ghats (banks) on the river Yamuna, which flows through this town, are intimately connected with the legends of Sri Krishna. There are many places of religious interest around Mathura, such as Govardhan Hill and Vrindavan. Pilgrims can be found on the streets of Mathura year-round, especially at the time of Holi and Janmashtami (see chapter 36) festivals.

Ujjain: Located on the banks of the holy river Shipra, Ujjain is a popular pilgrim center in Madhya Pradesh. It is the site of the famous Kumbha Mela (see chapter 36). Ujjain has many temples, of which Mahakala Temple dedicated to Lord Shiva is an ancient temple. One of the twelve famous *jyotirlingas* is installed in this temple. Gopal Mandir is another famous temple renowned for its image of Sri Krishna in silver. About two miles from the city is the ancient Sandipani Ashram, where Sri Krishna, along with his elder brother Balaram and his friend Sudama, is said to have received education from Rishi Sandipani.

The two remaining tirthas of this category are Dwarka and Kashi, which are discussed above.

Other Sacred Pilgrimages

Amarnath, the abode of Shiva, is located in Kashmir (see chapter 36). The massive ice lingam in the holy cave waxes and wanes with changing seasons. The holy cave is located at an altitude of 9500 ft. above sea level.

Kedarnath shrine in the Himalayas, the abode of Lord Shiva, is located 11800 ft. above sea level. The holy shrine is said to have been built by the Pandavas on their way to paradise (see chapter 31), following the battle of Mahabharata. The region around Kedarnath is considered highly sacred and contains many holy places of religious interest. Various gods, goddesses, munis, sages and saints are said to have their abode in this region.

Tirupati temple in Andhra Pradesh is the world famous shrine of Lord Venkateswara Balaji. Tirupati is the richest shrine in India and perhaps in the world! Thousands of pilgrims visit this shrine daily throughout the year.

Khir Bhawani, the abode of the Divine Mother in Kashmir, is located about 16 miles from Srinagar. A marble shrine with a gold-plated dome houses the image of the Divine Mother. The shrine stands in the midst of a spring.

The color of the water in the spring changes from time to time.

Kanya-Kumari is the southern tip of India where three seas (the Bay of Bengal, the Indian Ocean, and the Arabian Sea) meet. According to tradition, Parvati performed great penance here to seek the hand of Lord Shiva in marriage; hence the name Kanya-Kumari or the "virgin girl." There is a temple dedicated to Kanya-Kumari and offshore there are two huge rocks where Swami Vivekananda meditated before coming to the United States. On one of the rocks stands a magnificent statue of Vivekananda, known as Vivekananda Rock Memorial.

Meenakshi temple, a sculptural wonder with twelve Gopurams (tower at the main entrance) and four gateways, is itself a city within a city. There is a hall of one thousand pillars, with lavish sculptures of gods and goddesses--an archeological and engineering marvel. There are two main shrines, one dedicated to Goddess Meenakshi and the other to Shiva Sundareshwara, her Lord.

Vaishno Devi: This is the most popular and sacred shrine dedicated to the Divine Mother, known as Vaishno Devi. About 40 miles from Jammu, the holy shrine is located at an altitude of 5300 ft.

Kurukshetra: About 100 miles from Delhi, Kurukshetra is one of the most sacred places for Hindus. Here Sri Krishna imparted the eternal teachings of the Bhagavad Gita to Arjuna. According to tradition, Vedic rishis composed hymns and sage Vyasa wrote the Mahabharata here at Kurukshetra. Devotees congregate here to bathe in the Sarovar pond on the occasion of the festivals.

Other famous pilgrimage sites include Bhubaneshwar and Konark in Orissa; Chidambaram, Tanjavur, Trichi, and Mahabalipuram in Tamil Nadu; Pawapuri in Bihar; and Pushkar in Rajasthan. Pawapuri is the site where Vardhman Mahavir (see chapter 11), the great Jain Tirthanker, delivered his last sermon and attained nirvana in 527 BCE. Pushkar is the site of the magnificent Brahma temple (see Pushkar Mela on page 323), the only one of its kind in India.

Popular Spiritual Centers (Ashrams for the Elderly)

There are many ashrams (spiritual centers) all over India that have been established to cater to the spiritual needs of people, especially the elderly. In principle, an ashram is a residential place that caters to the needs of the Vanaprastha Ashram of religious life (see chapter 32). These ashrams function like small retirement communities and provide spiritual guidance for the residents. The following are some of the most popular ashrams that have stood by their excellent reputation for decades. For more information, please contact the head of the ashram directly:

- Sri Ramanasramam, Sri Ramanasramam P.O. Tiruvannamalai - 606 603, India.

- Anandashram, P.O. Anandashram, Kanhangad, Kerala, India 671531. (established by Swami Ramdas)

- Shivananda Ashram of Rishikesh, The Divine Life Society, P.O. Shivanandanagar, Pin Code 249 192, District Tehri-Garhwal, U.P., India.

- Satya Sai Baba Ashram, Puttaparthy, Andhra Pradesh, India.

- Sri Aurobindo Ashram, Pondichery, Tamil Nadu, India.

Hindu Temples Around the World

Refer to the following websites to obtain information about Hindu temples around the world:

For temples in U.S.A.:
http://www.hindunet.org/temple_info/

For temples in Canada:
http://www.hindunet.org/temple_info/canada_list.html

For temples in U.K.:
http://www.hindunet.org/temple_info/uk_list.html

For temples in India:
http://www.hindunet.org/temple_info/india_list.html

For temples Worldwide:
http://www.hindunet.org/temple_info/

Appendix A-3

Works Cited

1. Radhakrishnan, S. *The Hindu View of Life* (p. 12).

2. Moore, Charles A.C. (editor). *The Indian Mind*. Hawaii: East West Press, University of Honolulu, 1967 (p. 181).

3. *Rig Veda 1.164.46* (mandala 1, hymn 164, and mantra 46).

4. Nikhilananda, Swami. *The Gospel of Sri Ramakrishna* . New York: Ramakrishna-Vivekananda Center, 1977.

5. *Thus Spake Vivekananda*. India: Ramakrishna Math.

6. Prabhavananda, Swami and Christopher Isherwood. *Shankara's Crest Jewel of Discrimination* (Viveka-Chudamani). California: Vedanta Press, Hollywood.

7. Yogananda, Paramahansa. *Autobiography of a Yogi*. California: Self-Realization Fellowship.

8. Jyotirmayananda, Swami. *Advice to Students*. Florida: Yoga Research Foundation, South Miami.

9. Mascaro, Juan (trans.). *The Bhagavad Gita*. The Penguin Classics.

10. Kak, Subhash C. "The Indus Traditions and the Indo-Aryans," published in *The Mankind Quarterly*, Volume XXXII, Number 3, Spring , 1992.

11. Shaffer, J.G. *The Indo-Aryan invasions: cultural myth and archeological reality*, published in J.R. Lukacs (ed.), *The People of South Asia*. New York: Plenum Press, 1984.

12. Frawley, David. *Gods, Sages and Kings*. Salt Lake City: Passage Press.

13. *Young India*, dated September 17, 1925. A weekly journal edited by Mahatma Gandhi; ceased publication in February 1932.

14. Radhakrishnan, Sarvepalli. *Hinduism and the West: Modern India and the West* (p. 359).

15. *Complete Works of Swami Vivekananda*, Volume 4 (pp. 356-360).

16. Radhakrishnan, Sarvepalli. *Eastern Religions and Western Thought*. London: Oxford University Press, 1940 (p. 323).

17.   Ibid., p. 57.   18.   ibid., pp. 54-55.

19.   *Kautilya's Artha-Shastra,* Book 14, chapter 1 and Book 15, chapter 19.

20.   *Katha Upanishad* II.2.2.

21.   *Chicago Address*, Swami Vivekananda.

22.   Rozman, Deborah. *Meditation for Children.* Millbrae, California: Celestial Arts.

23.   Monier-Williams. *Sanskrit -English Dictionary.* London: Oxford University Press.

24.   *Bhagavad Gita,* Chapter 2, Slokas 18-20 and *Chandogya Upanishad* 8.12.1.

25.   Klostermaier, K. Klaus. *A Survey of Hinduism.* Albany, New York: State University of New York Press, 1994, (p. 31).

25a. Ibid., p. 438.   25b. Ibid., p.19.   25c. Ibid., p.415.

25d. Ibid., p. 476.   25e. Ibid., chapter 9.

26.   *Manusmriti,* Chapter I, Verses 65-74.

27.   *Sukla Yajurveda, Satapatha Brahmana* XI.3

28.   Feuerstein, George, Subhash Kak and David Frawley. *In Search of the Cradle of Civilization.* Wheaton, IL.: Quest Books, 1995 (p. 281).

28a. Ibid., p. 105.   28b. Ibid., p. 282.   28c. Ibid., p. 276.

28d. Ibid., p. 40.   28e. Ibid., pp. 91-107.   28f. Ibid., p. 279.

28g. Ibid., p.102.   28h. Ibid., p. 161.

29.   Radhakrishnan, Sarvepalli. *The Bhagavad Gita.* Bombay, India: Blackie &Son, 1982 (p. 75).

30.   Dayananda, Swami. *The Teachings of the Bhagavad Gita.* New Delhi, India: Vision Books, 1990 (p. 53).

31.   Satchidananda, Swami. *The Yoga Sutras of Patanjali.* Yogaville, Virginia: Integral Yoga Publications, 1990 (pp. 231-232).

32.   Muktananda, Swami. *Play of Consciousness.* South Fallsburgh, New York: Syda Foundation, 1978 (p. 27).

33.   Harris, Marvin. *Cows, Pigs, and Witches: The Riddles of Culture.* New York: Random House, 1974

Suggested Readings

Basham, A. L. *The Wonder That India Was*. New York: Grove Press, 1959.
A scholarly presentation of the development of Indian culture from prehistoric times to 1000 AD.

Bishop, Donald H. *Indian Thought*. New York: John Wiley and Sons.
A collection of essays by leading Hindu scholars, providing a thorough introduction to Hindu religious traditions.

Capra, Fritjot. *The Tao of Physics*. New York: Bantam Books, 1984.
A pioneering work that reconciles Eastern philosophy and Western science through a humanistic vision of the universe.

Chidbhavananda, Swami. *The Bhagavad Gita*. India: Sri Ramakrishna Tapovanam, 1977.
The original Sanskrit verses are included with transliteration, a word-for-word English translation, followed by a commentary--an excellent text for the students of the Bhagavad Gita.

Complete Works of Swami Vivekananda. Vols. 1-8. Calcutta: Advaita Ashram.
A most comprehensive and authoritative source of information on all aspects of Hinduism--essential reading for all students of Hinduism.

Encyclopedia of Eastern Philosophy and Religion. Boston: Shambhala, 1989.
An informative source of basic terminology and doctrinal systems of Buddhism, Hinduism, and Taoism.

Frawley, David. *Gods, Sages and Kings*. Salt Lake City: Passage Press, 1991.

This well-written, completely absorbing book brings to light the Vedic/Indo-European heritage that is the basis of contemporary European and American as well as Far Eastern civilizations.

Moore, Charles A.C. (ed.). *The Indian Mind.* **Hawaii: East-West Press University of Honolulu, 1967.**

An excellent collection of essays written by experts in their respective fields, explaining the fundamentals of Hindu religion, philosophy, and social practices.

Klostermaier, Klaus K. *A Survey of Hinduism.* **Albany, New York: State University of New York, 1995.**

A comprehensive survey of Hindu tradition, including its history, sacred writings, and major systems of religious thought. Klaus K. Klostermaier is a Professor of Religion at the University of Manitoba.

Nathan, R.S. *Symbolism in Hinduism.* **Bombay: Central Chinmaya Mission Trust, 1983.**

An authoritative discussion of the symbolism of Hindu Gods, sacred articles used in worship, and the significance of auspicious days.

Pandey, Ray Balli. *Hindu Samskaras.* **Delhi: Motilal Banarsidass.**

An excellent explanation of the purpose of Hindu Samskaras with a detailed discussion (about 100 pages) of the importance of the Hindu marriage ceremony (vivaha) and related issues. The book includes a step-by-step procedure of the various Samaskaras.

Pandharipande, R.V. *The Eternal Self and the Cycle of Samsara.* **Needham Heights, MA: Ginn Press, 1990.**

A scholarly and systematic overview of Indian, Chinese, and Japanese mythologies with a comparative discussion of their underlying philosophies.

Dayton, Brandt (ed.). *Practical Vedanta, Selected Works of Swami Rama Tirtha.* **Pennsylvania: Himalayan International Institute, 1978.**

A remarkable collection of the lectures delivered by Swami Rama Tirtha during his American tour of 1902-4. With profound and humorous tales, these lectures expound the ancient philosophy of Vedanta with simple reason.

Radhakrishnan, Sarvepalli (edited and translated). *The Principal Upanishads.* **London: George Allen and Unwin, 1953.**
Complete Sanskrit texts of eighteen Upanishads, with excellent translations, explanatory notes, and an historical/philosophical introduction by a well-known scholar.

Radhakrishnan, S. and Moore, Charles A. (editors). *A Source book in Indian Philosophy.* **Princeton: University Press.**
A splendid coverage of Indian philosophy provided in selections from well-known sources such as the Upanishads, Bhagavad Gita, Laws of Manu, six schools of Vedanta philosophy, Sri Aurobindo, and some less commonly known works such as Kautilya's Artha Shastra.

Radhakrishnan, S. *Eastern Religions and Western Thought.* **London: Oxford University Press.**
With earnest conviction and conspicuous ability, this book shows that the insights of the Eastern religions, especially Hinduism and Buddhism, are necessary for the enrichment of human spirit. This work has significantly influenced the Western mind and marked a turning point in Western civilization.

Robins, J. *Diet of a New America.* **U.S.A.: Still Point Publishing, 1987.**
An account of the inhumane conditions under which animals are raised for food; an excellent survey of the food choices for health and pleasure.

References for Spiritual Knowledge:

Nikhilananda, Swami. *The Gospel of Sri Ramakrishna.* **New York: Ramakrishna-Vivekananda Center, 1977.**
Religious and spiritual conversations of Sri Ramakrishna with his disciples, devotees, and visitors. Like a powerful cleanser, this book purifies the reader's heart and mind in order to accelerate his (or her) spiritual growth; a masterpiece that fills one's heart with love for God.

Talks With Sri Ramana Maharshi. **Tiruvannamalai, India: Sri Ramanasramam, 1984.**
A reading of this book automatically drives a sincere devotee inward to the source, and is thus a complete *sadhana* in itself.

Although Ramana Maharshi taught for the most part through silence, he did instruct through speech also, and these talks contain the essence of his teaching--Self-inquiry. The book also contains a listing of other books in English pertaining to the life and teachings of Bhagavan Sri Ramana Maharshi.

Ramdas, Swami. *God-Experience*. Vols. 1-2. India: Anandashram, P.O. Kanhangad, Dist. Kasaragod, Kerala 671531, South India.

These volumes include the teachings of Swami Ramdas (affectionately called 'Papa') based upon the fullness and richness of his own direct experience of God. Each page is filled with the divine wisdom ever flowing from the lips of the Master. Even a casual reading of these volumes awakens one to awareness of God; a valuable guide to all spiritual aspirants.

Yogananda, Paramahansa. *Autobiography of a Yogi*. California: Self-Realization Fellowship, 1988.

As an authoritative introduction to the science of Yoga, this book is a spiritual classic, revealing the scientific foundation underlying the great religious paths of both the East and the West. Translated into seventeen languages, this book is used as a text for reference in colleges and universities throughout the world; a must for every spiritual aspirant.

Yogananda, Paramahansa. *Man's Eternal Quest*. California: Self-Realization Fellowship, 1988.

The wisdom in this book is not merely that of a learned scholar. It is the empirical testimony of a spiritual genius whose life was filled with inner joy and outer accomplishment, born of his own direct experience of God.

Self-Realization Fellowship Lessons.

The SRF Lessons teach the universal spiritual principles of self-realization and are grouped into "six steps," each of which contains approximately twenty-five lessons. Those who complete Steps I and II and have a sincere desire to embrace the spiritual lineage of the SRF Gurus (Babaji, Lahiri Mahasaya, Sri Yukteswar, and Paramahansa Yogananda), become eligible to receive initiation in Kriya Yoga, a sacred spiritual sadhana. Lessons are available from Self-Realization Fellowship, 3880 San Rafael Avenue, Los Angeles CA 90065; Tel. (213) 225-247.

Glossary

Pronunciation Guide

	Pronounced like			Pronounced like	
a	u	in but	m	m	in map
ã	a	in father	ṁ or ṃ	semi-nasal sound	
ai	ai	in aisle	n	n	in not
au	ou	in house	ṅ or ñ	n	in sing
b	b	in bear	ṇ	n	in none
bh	bh	in abhor	o	o	in go
c	ch	in check	p	p	in put
ch	chh	in church-hill	ph	ph	in uphill
d	d	in dice	r	r	in red
ḍ	d	in drum	ri	ri	in rich
dh	dh	in adhere	ṝ	ri	in marine
ḍh	dh	in mad-house	s	s	in since
e	e	in prey	ś	su	in sure
g	g	in gun	ṣ	sh	in shut
gh	gh	in log-hut	sh	sh	in shut
h	h	in him	t	t	in dot
ḥ	h	h (aspirated sound)	ṭ	t	in time
i	i	in fill	th	th	in nut-hook
î	i	in police	ṭh	th	in boat-house
j	j	in jump	u	u	in full
jh	dgeh	in hedge-hog	û	u	in rude
k	k	in kind	v	v	in ivy
kh	kh	in ink-horn	y	y	in yes
l	l	in lull			

Notes on Pronunciation:

The above pronunciation guide is based upon the Sanskrit-English transliteration commonly used in scholarly literature. The pronunciation system used in the glossary of this book, however, is a simplified version of the above pronunciation guide and is based upon the following considerations:

- Consonants with undershots such as ṣ, ṭ, ṭh, ḍ, ḍh, and ṇ are not used, since they do not differ greatly in pronunciation from their unmarked counterparts.

- v is pronounced with the upper teeth lightly pressed against the lower lip, not as forcefully as when pronouncing the English v. Therefore, the sound created is between English v and w.

- h occurs only at the end of syllables and is pronounced with a light h-sound. ṁ or ṃ serves to nasalize the preceding vowel.

With the exceptions noted above, the simplified system of pronunciation used here differs from that of the scholarly transcription as follows:

Scholarly Transcription	Simplified System
c (cakra)	ch (chakra)
ṃ (Dipaṃkara)	m (Dipamkara)
ṃ (Saṃskrit)	n (Sanskrit)
ṛ (Ṛgveda)	ri (Rigveda)
ś (Śiva)	sh (Shiva)
ṛ, ṣ, ṇ (Kṛṣṇa)	ri, sh, n (Krishna)
ṭ, ḍ, ṇ, ḥ	t, d, n, h

abhishêka: symbolic bathing of a deity during worship.

āchārya: a spiritual teacher who has mastered the scriptures and realized the truths they teach.

adharma: opposite of dharma; absence of righteousness.

adhikāra: spiritual competence; the principle that religious teaching should be graded according to the spiritual competence of the student.

advaita: philosophy of monism or non-dualism.

Āgamas: Hindu sectarian scriptures, mainly pertaining to Shaivism, Vaishnavism, and Shaktism.

āgāmi karma: future karma arising through one's present actions.

Agni: the Vedic deity of fire.

ahankāra: literally, "I do"; ego; egoism; I-consciousness.

ahimsā: non-violence; non-injury; abstinence from injuring any living creature by thought, word, or deed.

ākāsha: the void; ether; space.

akrodha: freedom from anger.

Ālvārs: twelve medieval Vaishnava poet-saints of South India.

Ambā: another name for Shakti, the Divine Mother.

amrita: the nectar of immortality; the water of immortal life.

anādi: without beginning; beginningless.

ānanda: bliss; absolute joy.

ananta: infinite; endless.

āp: water.

apara vidyā: lower knowledge; the relative knowledge gained through senses and intellect that helps in daily life.

apaurusheya: having no human origin; the Vedas are called apaurusheya, since they are of the divine origin (i.e., spoken by God).

Āranyakas: literally, "belonging to the forests"; Vedic writings proceeding the Brāhmanas and preceding the Upanishads.

ārati: Hindu worship of God with flowers, incense, and lighted candles that are waved in front of an image or icon of a deity or a holy figure.

Arjuna: one of the five Pandava brothers; a friend and disciple of Sri Krishna.

artha: wealth, material possessions; one of the four goals of human life.

Ārya Samāj: a nineteenth-century Hindu social and religious reform movement, founded by Swami Dayananda in India.

āsana: any of the various bodily postures in Hatha Yoga; a body posture in meditation.

asat: literally, "nonbeing, nonexistence"; that which is inaccessible to speech or thought.

āshrama: a center for religious study and meditation; one of the four stages of Hindu religious life.

Ashtānga Yoga: literally, "eight-limbed yoga"; the term refers to Rāja Yoga, which contains eight limbs or steps.

asteya: literally, "non-stealing"; one of the five virtues of the first stage (yama) of Rāja Yoga.

āstika: literally, "orthodox, true to Veda"; name for the six popular systems of Hindu philosophy.

asuras: demons, devils, evil spirits; enemies of gods and goddesses.

Atharva Veda: the fourth Veda, concerning the affairs of daily life.

ātman: individual self, soul, or spirit; the spiritual essence of the individual. In Hinduism, the individual self is a spiritual reality which, being eternal, is not created by God. Ātman is pure consciousness.

AUM: see O M

avatāra: an incarnation of God on earth. An avatāra is born as an act of divine will and not as a result of karma.

avidyā: the original ignorance, nescience; the cause of the cosmic illusion that leads to the false perception that the ātman (individual self) is identical with the body and mind.

Āyurveda: an ancient system of medicine that originated from the Atharvaveda.

Badarāyana: author of the *Brahma Sūtra*. See also Vyāsa.

Bhagavad Gītā: literally, "The Song of the Lord"; the spiritual dialogue (700 verses) between Sri Krishna and Arjuna on the battlefield of Kurukshetra, in the war of Mahābhārata; the Gospel of Hinduism.

Bhagāvan: Lord; an incarnation of the Lord in human form; personal God of the devotee.

bhajana: a song expressing love and devotion for God.

bhakta: a devotee who worships God through love and self-surrender.

bhakti: supreme love of God; self-surrender to the guru and the chosen deity (*Ishta Devā*).

Bhakti Yoga: the spiritual path of love and self-surrender; one of the four yogic paths to union with God as taught in the Bhagavad Gītā.

Bhārata: a king and sage of the ancient Bhārata clan whose descendents, the Pāndavas and Kauravas, fought the Mahābhārata war. India was once called *Bhāratavarsha* (i.e., the land of Bhārata) after the name of king Bhārata.

bhāvanā: idea; feeling; attitude; meditation.

Bhīma: one of the five Pāndava brothers, famous for his physical strength.

Bhīshmā: granduncle of the Pāndavas and Kauravas; one of the warriors in the war of Mahābhārata.

bindu: literally, "particle, dot, spot"; a symbol representing the universe in its unmanifest form.

Brahmā: Hindu god of creation; the first god of the Hindu Trinity of Brahmā, Vishnu, and Shiva.

brahmachārya: vow of celibacy; a complete discipline of body, mind and senses.

brahmachārya āshrama: student stage of life.

Brahman: the cosmic Absolute, the ultimate principle underlying the universe; Supreme Being; Universal Spirit; Ultimate Reality; Self.

Brāhmanas: a portion of the Vedas consisting of discussion and elaboration of the Vedic mantras dealing with rituals; members of the priestly class, one of the four castes of the ancient Hindu social order.

Brahma Sûtra: a collection of the aphorisms and verses on the teachings of the Upanishads, also known as the Vedānta Sûtra.

Brāhmin or **Brāhmana**: a member of the priestly class, one of the four castes of the ancient Hindu social order. Technically speaking *Brāhmin* is not a correct Sanskrit term, but is commonly used in preference to Brāhmana, since the latter term also refers to a portion of the Vedas, and thus may lead to confusion.

buddhi: intelligence; the faculty that enables the mind to perceive objects in the phenomenal world.

chakras: literally, "wheels"; the seven psychic centers of life and consciousness in the human spine and brain. When these psychic centers are awakened by yoga and meditation, the devotee attains samādhi (union with God).

Chandī: another name for the Divine Mother or Goddess Durgā; a sacred text in which the Divine Mother is described as the Ultimate Reality.

Chandikā: another name for the Divine Mother of the universe.

darshanas: a school of philosophy or a view of life inspired by the Upanishads; philosophical or religious doctrines.

Dasharatha: Rāma's father; ancient king of Ayodhyā.

Devākī: Sri Krishna's mother.

dharma: religion; righteousness; the path that one should follow in accordance with one's nature and responsibilities; one of the four goals of a human being.

dharma lakshanas: characteristics of dharma.

Dharma Shāstras: Hindu religious writings concerning rules of conduct, morality, and social law.

dhārna: concentration.

Dhritarāshtra: the blind king and father of the Kauravas.

dhupa: incense.

dhyāna: meditation; contemplation; absorption.

Draupadī: common wife of the Pāndavas.

Drona: the famous warrior-teacher of the Kauravas and Pandavas.

duhkha: suffering; misery.

Durgā: literally, "the unfathomable one"; popular name for the Divine Mother; the consort of Shiva.

Duryodhana: eldest son of Dhritarashtra, the leader of the Kauravas in the war with the Pāndavas.

Dussehrā: a popular Hindu festival, ako called Durgā Pūjā.

dvaita: duality; one of the three schools of Vedānta philosophy based on dualistic theism.

gadā: mace.

Ganesha or **Ganapatî:** the god with an elephant head, worshipped as the god of success and remover of obstacles.

Gangā: the river Ganges, the most sacred river of India.

garuda: a mythical bird, the vehicle of Lord Vishnu.

Gāyatrî Mantra: the most sacred Vedic mantra, in the form of a prayer to the sun, for the enlightenment of the intellect.

ghāt: steps; a flight of steps leading to a river; a bathing place on a river bank.

Gokula: the pastoral district on the river Yamunā where Krishna passed his boyhood with his foster parents, Yashoda and Nānda.

gopî: a cowherd girl; a devotee of Krishna.

grhastha āshrama: the householder stage of life.

gunas: the three constituents of the primal matter Prakriti: sattva, rajas, and tamas.

guru: religious teacher; spiritual guide; a spiritual master who has realized union with God.

Hanumān: the monkey hero of the Rāmāyana who helped Rāma to recover Sitā from Rāvana.

Hari: another name for Lord Vishnu.

hatha yoga: yoga based upon bodily postures and control of the physical processes in the human body.

himsā: violence; opposite of ahimsā (non-violence).

Hiranyagarbha: universal consciousness: totality of the minds.

idi: a major channel of subtle energy in the human body.

Indra: the Vedic god of the heavens; god of rain.

Indus or Sindhu: the Indus river, one of the seven sacred rivers of India.

Ishta-devā or **Ishta-devatā**: a personal god; a chosen deity to whom a devotee offers worship and devotion.

Ishvara: God; the Supreme Being as the Creator of the universe. "Ishvara is the supreme interpretation of the Absolute [Brahman] by the human mind," says Swāmī Vivekānanda.

Ishvara-prāni-dhāna: surrender of one's self to God.

japa: the repetition of a sacred word, syllable, name, or mantra.

jīvā: the individual embodied self.

jīvanmukta: one who has attained spiritual freedom (moksha) while still living in a body.

jnana: supreme knowledge of the Ultimate Reality.

Jnāna Kānda: the portion of the Vedas dealing with knowledge.

Jnāna Yoga: the path of supreme knowledge and intellectual analysis that leads to union with God.

Jyotirlinga: literally, "pillar of light." A Jyotirlinga is a symbol for Lord Shiva. Twelve Jyotirlingas are said to have mysteriously appeared in the ancient times. They are installed at twelve sacred places (each a center of pilgrimage) in India. Numerous miracles have been reported around these Jyotirlingas, as they are said to manifest special potency.

Kāla: literally, "time"; a name for Yama, the god of death.

Kālī: Shakti (cosmic energy), another name for the Divine Mother of the universe.

kaliyuga: literally, "dark age"; one of the four ages of the world, whose time is reckoned in divine years.

kalpa: the length of one complete cycle of creation and dissolution, equivalent to 12,000,000 human years.

Kāma: the god of love.

kama: love, pleasure, sensual desire; one of the four goals of human life.

Kapila: an ancient sage; the founder of the Sankhya school of Hindu philosophy.

karana sharîra: causal body.

karma: action (physical, or mental); deeds; results of the past actions.

Karma Kānda: the portion of the Vedas dealing with rituals, sacrifices and ceremonies.

Karma Yoga: the path that leads to union with God through selfless action (i.e. by performing one's duties).

Kārttikeya: the warrior god; commander of the divine army, the son of Shiva and Parvatī, also called Skanda, Kumāra, or Subramanya.

Katha Upanishad: an Upanishad belonging to the Yajur Veda.

Kauravas: the one hundred sons of the blind king Dhritarāshtra. They are the cousins and opponents of the Pāndavas in the Mahābhārata war.

kīrtana: reciting, chanting, singing, or dancing for God.

Krishna: the eighth and most popular incarnation of Vishnu; the teacher of the Bhagavad Gītā to Arjuna on the battle field of Kurukshetra, where the Mahābhārata war was fought.

Kriya Yoga: a yogic technique whereby the life-energy is freed from the senses and directed inward to rejuvenate the brain and spinal centers, which in turn unites the individual consciousness with the cosmic consciousness (i.e. union with God). See Chapter 26 of *Autobiography of a Yogi* (see Suggested References) for details. (See also Yogananda, Paramahansa)

Kshatriya: the warrior class; one of the four castes of ancient Hindu social order.

kumbhaka: retention of breath between exhalation and inhalation.

Kumbha Mela: a sacred Hindu pilgrimage attended by millions of people, making it one of the largest pilgrimage gatherings in the world.

kundalanī: the cosmic energy (Shakti) that usually lies dormant at the base of the spinal column. When awakened through spiritual exercises, the kundalani power rises through the six centers (chakras) along the spine and reaches the seventh center at the top of the head, and the individual enters into samādhi (union with God).

Kundalanī Yoga: tantra yoga; the yogic path that leads to union with God by awakening the kundalani shakti.

Kurukshetra: the battlefield where the Mahābhārata war was fought.

kusha: sacred grass, used to cover the place of meditation and also employed in worship rites.

Lakshmana: the beloved half-brother of Rama in the story of Rāmāyana.

Lakshmî: the divine consort of Vishnu; the goddess of wealth and power.

laya: dissolution.

Laya Yoga: a yogic discipline that seeks to merge the individual spirit in the Ultimate Reality.

lîla (or leelā): the divine sport or play of God; Hindus describe creation as the lila of God.

linga or lingam: a pillar of stone used as a symbol of Lord Shiva.

lobha: greed.

mada: pride.

Madhva or Madhvāchārya: the thirteenth-century religious reformer, philosopher, and scholar who developed the Dvaita school of Vedānta philosophy.

Mahābhārata: one of the two great epics of Hindus.

Mahādeva: Great God; another name for Lord Shiva.

mahākaruna: unlimited compassion.

mahāmaitrî: deep friendship.

Mahāmāyā: the great illusion; Shakti (cosmic energy); another name for the Divine Mother of the universe.

maharshi: great rishi (seer or sage).

mahāvākyas: the sublime pronouncements; great utterances; the four Upanishadic declarations (see Chapter 35) expressing the highest Vedāntic truths.

Maheshvara: another name for Lord Shiva, the Great God.

mālā: garland; a rosarv of 108 beads.

manana: meditation; reflection.

manas: the mind; the thinking faculty.

mandala: literally, "circle"; a circular diagram of a complex design; the voluminous collection of verses that makes up the Rig Veda.

mantra: a divine name, sacred syllable, word, or verse used for worship and prayer.

Mantra Yoga: the yogic path that aims to achieve union with God by means of repetition of a mantra.

Manu: an ancient Hindu sage who developed the code of conduct (social and moral) for Hinduism.

Manu Smriti or **Manu Samhita**: a Hindu scripture containing ethical laws.

māyā: literally, "deception, illusion, infatuation, appearance"; ignorance or cosmic illusion. According to Advaita philosophy, māyā draws a veil over Brahman and also veils our vision and causes humans to perceive the infinite, undivided, and changeless reality (Brahman) as finite, divided, and changing. According to Sānkhya philosophy, māyā, the inseparable power of Brahman, is the cosmic energy, the material cause of the universe. Māyā and Brahman together are called Ishvara, the personal God, who creates, preserves, and dissolves the universe.

Mimamsā: one of the six schools of Hindu philosophy emphasizing the ritualistic aspect of the Vedas.

moha: egoism; attachment; bond; deluded love; deception.

moksha: final liberation or release from samsara (the cycle of birth and death); one of the four goals of human life.

mukti: see moksha.

mūlādhāra: one of the yogic centers of the body located at the bottom of the spine.

muni: a holy man who practices solitude and contemplation.

nadī: literally, "tube, vessel, vein"; the nadis are the subtle energy channels through which life energy passes to all parts of the body.

namaskāra: prostrating before God or Guru.

Nandi: the sacred bull, the vehicle of Shiva. Nandi, one of the great worshippers of Shiva, is said to have taken the form of a bull, because the human body was not strong enough to bear the devotional ecstasy he experienced.

Nārāyana: another name for Lord Vishnu.

nāstika: literally, "atheistic"; term referring to the unorthodox philosophical schools, which do not believe in the authority of the Vedas.

Natarāja: the dancing pose of Shiva, symbolizing cosmic evolution.

Nāyanārs: medieval mystical Shiva poet-saints (traditional number 63) of South India.

Neela Kantha: literally, "blue throat"; another name for Lord Shiva, whose throat turned blue when he swallowed poison (see Mahāshivaratrî in Chapter 36) to save the universe.

Nibandhas: Hindu religious writings that include social law and rituals.

nididhyasana: literally, "contemplate, consider"; the last of the three stages of the Vedantic realization; uninterrupted contemplation.

nirdaya: devoid of compassion; opposite of *daya* (compassion).

Nirguna Brahman: Brahman without attributes; a term used in Vedānta to describe the Absolute, in its quality-less aspect.

nirvāna: literally, "extinction"; a state of liberation or illumination that frees an individual from birth and death. This term denotes the highest transcendent consciousness, which is also denoted by various other terms: *Brahman-nzrvāna* (Bhagavad Gîtā), *turîya* (Upanishads), *nirbzja samādhi* (Yoga philosophy), *nirvikalpa-samādhi* (Vedānta), and *moksha* (other religious literature).

nirvikalpa samādhi: the highest state of consciousness in which the soul loses sense of being different from the Universal Self. It is a temporary state from which there is a return to the ego-consciousness.

nishkāma karma: an action performed without expectation of any reward; selfless action.

nishvasitam: the breath of Îshvara (God). The Vedas, spoken *by* God, are called *nishvasitam*.

niyama: ethical observances; the second step of Patanjali's Yoga.

Nyāya: one of the six popular schools of Hindu philosophy that is based upon analytical and logical inquiry for attaining true knowledge of the atman.

OM or AUM: the most sacred symbol and the source of mystic power in Hinduism. O M (also called *Pranava*) symbolizes both the personal and the impersonal aspects pf the Supreme Reality.

OM Tat Sat: literally, "0 M! That is Being"; the sense of the words is that what we perceive as the creation, the world of appearances, is in reality Brahman.

pancha kosha: five sheaths (coverings).

panchamahabhutas: literally, " five great elements"; the five elements *ether, air, fire, water,* and *earth* are the ingredients of all observable matter in the universe.

pancha mahā yagnas: five great daily sacrifices (duties) of a devout Hindu.

Pancharātra: name of a Vaishnava sect following the doctrine of the sacred texts called Pancharātra, believed to have originated in Kashmir during first and third century BCE.

Panchatantra: a collection of popular tales and fables comprising five *(pancha)* books *(tantra).*

Pāndavas: the five Pandava brothers: Yudhishthira, Arjuna, Bhima, Nakula, and Sahadevā.

Pāndu: brother of the blind king Dhritarāshtra; father of the Pandavas.

Paramahamsa or **Paramahansa:** literally, "the highest swan"; a title that indicates the highest stage in spiritual development, that is union with God.

Paramātma: the highest Self; the Supreme Self.

Parameshvara: the highest Lord of all Being, beyond any possibility of description.

Para vidyā: higher knowledge; spiritual knowledge.

Pārvatī: the daughter of Parvata, the personification of Himalaya; wife of Lord Shiva.

Patanjali: the ancient sage and founder of the yogic discipline based upon the Sankhya philosophy.

pinda: small ball of rice that is offered to ancestors as oblation.

pingalā: literally, "yellow"; one of the major mystic channels *(nadis)* of the human body.

prakriti: the unconscious primal matter, the material cause of the universe; ultimate cosmic energy.

pralaya: complete dissolution, when the cosmos merges into the Unmanifest Supreme Reality.

prānamaya Kosha: vital sheath.

Pranava: another term for O M.

prānāyāma: control of prana, the fourth step of Rāja Yoga; prānāyāma consists of breathing exercises (which may be combined with the practice of a mantra) that include inhalation *(purak)*, retention of breath *(kumbhaka)*, and exhalation *(rechak)*.

prārabdha karma: the part of one's past karma which is to bear fruit in this life.

pratyāhāra: one of the steps in Rāja Yoga; withdrawal.

pnithvî: earth, personified in the Vedas as the *mother* of all beings.

pūjā: a religious ceremony; ceremonial worship of God in the form of a deity.

Puranas: Hindu mythology; religious writings (based upon stories and legends about gods, ancient kings, sages, and saints) that are used to illustrate the religious and spiritual doctrines of Hinduism.

purusha: pure consciousness; the term used in Sānkhya philosophy to denote the Ultimate Reality; the principle of consciousness as opposed to prakriti, or matter.

Rādha or **Rādhikā:** the childhood playmate and favorite disciple of Krishna. In Hinduism the relationship between Rādha and Krishna is viewed as the divine relationship between an individual soul and God.

Rādhāknshnan, Sarvepālli: a philosopher, statesman, and the second president of India (1888-1975).

rāga: a musical note or melody; a particular musical mode or order of sound.

rajas: one of the primal qualities; rajas is the subtle element of prakriti that causes activity, restlessness, and greed.

Rāja Yoga: the royal yoga, a yogic path that aims at union with God through control of the body, mind, and intellect.

rākshasas: demons; devils; evil spirits; see also asuras.

Rāma: the seventh incarnation of Vishnu, the hero of Rāmāyana.

Rāmakrishna: a nineteenth century sage of India, now worshipped as an avatāra; the guru of Swāmî Vivêkânanda, founder of the Rāmakrishna Mission.

Rāmānuja or **Rāmānujāchārya**: a saint and philosopher (1055-1137), founder of the Visishtādvaita (qualified non-dualism) school of Vedānta philosophy.

Rāmāyana: the life story of Rāma, the oldest Hindu epic in Sanskrit literature describing the story of Lord Vishnu's incarnation as Rāma.

Rāvana: the demon-king of Lankā, who abducted Sitā, wife of Rāma, and was defeated and eventually killed by Rāma in a war that is described in the Rāmāyana.

Rig Veda: the oldest of the four Vedas, the primary scriptures of Hinduism.

rishi: a seer or a sage. Although there are many rishis noted in Hindu scriptures, the following seven are said to have had the Vedas revealed to them: Gautama (not Buddha), Bharadvaja, Vishvamitra, Jamadagni, Vasishtha, Kashyapa, and Atri.

rita: literally, "truth, divine order"; cosmic law; the moral and the natural order in the universe.

Rudra: the Vedic god now called Shiva.

sādhana: a spiritual path or discipline that leads to moksha (i.e., union with God).

Saguna Brahman: Brahman with attributes; Īshvara; the personal god whom one may worship and adore.

sahasrāra chakra: the yogic center located in the brain.

samadhi: a state of higher consciousness (beyond the waking, dream, and deep sleep states) in which all mental activity ceases; the final stage in yogic discipline in which one attains union with God.

Sāma Veda: one of the four Vedas.

Samhitās: the collection of the mantras in the first portion of the Vedas.

sampradaya: a Hindu theological tradition.

Samsāra: the world of phenomenal experiences; the phenomenal world in which an individual soul passes from one life to another, in perpetual cycles of birth and death.

samskāras: sacraments; natural impressions and the tendencies of an individual; residual impressions created by karma.

Sanātana Dharma: eternal or universal righteousness; original name of Hinduism.

sanchita karma: accumulated karma of former births that has yet to bear fruit.

Sānkhya: one of the six schools of Hindu philosophy based on dualistic realism.

sannyāsa: renunciation; the fourth and the final stage of Hindu religious life.

sannyāsin or **sannyāsi:**   one who has renounced the world and lives totally without possessions.

Saraswatī: the Goddess of knowledge and learning; the divine consort of Brahmā; an ancient river of India that dried up around 1900 BCE.

sat-chit-ānanda: "being-consciousness-bliss"; conceptual description of the Absolute, Who is actually beyond description.

satsanga: company with the holy people or devotees of God.

sattva: one of the three primal qualities; the subtle element of prakriti, characterized by harmony, peace, and wisdom.

satya: truthfulness; thinking, speaking and acting on the basis of truthfulness.

Satyanārayana Pujā: a special worship performed to seek divine help for satisfying material desires or attaining success in a given venture.

savikalpa samādhi: a state of consciousness in which the distinction between the knower, knowledge and known is not yet lost.

Self: see Brahman.

Shaivism or **Shivaism:**   one of the three major traditions of worship in Hinduism. The followers of Shaivism worship the Supreme Being as Lord Shiva.

Shakti: force, power, energy; the consort of Shiva, worshipped as the Divine Mother; the personification of the primal energy of the Lord with which He creates, preserves, and dissolves the universe.

Shaktism or **Tantrism:**   one of the three major traditions of worship in Hinduism.

Shankara or **Shankarācharya**:   the medieval saint and scholar, known as the spiritual genius of India. Shankara was the greatest exponent of the Advaita Vedānta.

sharira: body; perishable form.

shaucha: purity of the body and mind; one of the five virtues of the second step of Rāja Yoga.

Shesha Nāg: the great serpent upon whose coils Lord Vishnu rests; shesha (snake) symbolizes time.

Shiva: the third member of the Hindu Trinity of Brahmā, Vishnu, and Shiva; the dissolver and regenerator of the universe.

Shivarātri: literally, "night of Shiva"; a special annual festival dedicated to the worship of Shiva.

shravana: hearing of truth from a Guru.

shûnya: zero; void; nothingness; indeterminate. In Buddhism shûnya represents "void" of the Ultimate Reality when it is stripped of Its empirically conceived attributes.

siddhis: supernatural powers; realization; attainment.

sindhoor: vermillion.

Sindhu: the Indus river.

Sîtā: the wife of Rāma; the heroine of the Rāmāyana. Hindus worship Sîtā as an incarnation of goddess Lakshmi.

sloka or **shloka**: a stanza in Sanskrit.

Smriti: literally, "that which is remembered"; Hindu religious writings that interpret and/or elaborate upon the teachings of the Vedas.

srishtî: creation; the term is used in reference to the development of the universe from its seed state.

Sruti: literally, "that which is heard"; the primary scriptures of Hinduism, the Vedas and Bhagavad Gîtā..

sthûla sharîra: gross or physical body.

sûkshma sharîra: the subtle body.

Sûrya: the Sun god.

sûrya namaskāra: adoration to the Sun; a set of twelve simple exercises for the physical body per Hatha Yoga.

sushumnā: the most important occult energy channel or passage that connects the lower end of the spine with the brain. According to the Tantric literature, when Kundalinî is awakened the spiritual power rises through Sushumnā.

sushupati: the state of deep sleep, in which neither the mind nor ego exist.

Sûtra: thread, a thread of words or phrases; abbreviated words or phrases that cannot be normally understood without a commentary.

svadharma: one's own dharma regulated by thoughts and actions; one's profession.

swāmî: a spiritual title of respect and reverence.

tamas: one of the three primal qualities; the element of prakriti that is characterized by dullness, ignorance, inertia, and laziness.

Tantras: Hindu religious writings that describe spiritual disciplines related to Shakti (i.e. Divine Mother), the creative power or cosmic energy.

Tantra Yoga: synonymous with Kundalinî Yoga.

tattwa or **tattva**: element; truth; essence of a thing.

tejas: light; effulgence.

tilak: a mark made of ashes, sandal paste, or vermillion and placed on the head or between the eyes on the forehead.

tirtha: pilgrimage site.

tirthayātra: pilgrimage

Tryambaka: literally, "three eyes"; another name for Lord Shiva.

tulsî: the Basil plant. Tulsi leaves are popularly used in the worship of Lord Vishnu.

turîya: the fourth state beyond waking, dreaming and sleeping; the superconscious state of illumination.

Umā: another name for Pārvatî, the wife of Shiva.

Upanishads: literally, "sitting near"; the final or concluding portion of each Veda.

Vaiseshika: one of the six popular schools of Hindu philosophy.

Vaishnava: one who follows Vaishnavism. Vaishnavas worship the Supreme Being in the form of Lord Vishnu and His incarnations.

Vaishnavism: one of the three major theological traditions of Hindu religion.

Vaisya: name given to the agricultural and business communities; one of the four castes of ancient Hindu society.

Vālmikī: an ancient sage, the author of the epic *Rāmāyana.*

varna: literally, "color, class"; a social class system of the ancient Hindu society.

Varuna: the Vedic deity of water.

Vasishtha: one of the prominent Vedic rishis; see also rishis.

Vāsudevā: another name for Sri Krishna.

Vāsudhaiva Kutumbakam: "all of mankind is one family," one of the most important doctrines of the Hindu religious tradition.

vāyu: air.

Vedāngas: literally, "the limbs of the Vedas"; the six auxiliary branches of instruction supplementing the Vedas.

Vedānta : literally, "the end of the Vedas"; the name given to the teachings of the Upanishads and other religious writings that interpret or elaborate upon the teachings of the Upanishads. The *Upanishads, Brahma Sūtra,* and *Bhagavad* Gītā are the three main pillars of Vedānta.

Vedānta Sūtra: see Brahma Sūtra.

Vedas: the primary scriptures of Hinduism.

vilva: a sacred tree, also called the bel tree. Vilva (or bel) leaves are used for the worship of Lord Shiva.

Vishnu: the second member of the Hindu Trinity of Brahmā, Vishnu, and Shiva; the preserver of the universe.

Vishvāmitra: literally, "friend of the world or universe"; one of the eminent Vedic sages. (see also rishi)

Visishtādvaita: the system of philosophy based upon qualified monism as taught by Rāmānuja.

Viveka Chūdāmanī: literally, "the Crest Jewel of Discrimination"; an important work on Advaita Vedānta by Adi Shankara.

Vivekānanda: Swami Vivekānanda (1863-1902), the beloved disciple of Paramahamsa Rāmakrishna. Vivekānanda electrified the American audience by his historic speech on Hinduism in the World Parliament of Religions held in Chicago in September of

1893; the founder of the Rāmakrishna Mission (see also Note 7 of Table T-l).

Vrindāvan: a sacred forest of India by the river Yamunā near Mathurā, the birthplace of Sri Krishna.

Vyasa: author of the *Mahābhārata,* founder of the Vedānta school of philosophy, the compiler of the *Pûranas,* and the author of the *Brahma Sûtra.* Some scholars believe that the author of the *Brahma Sûtra* is Badarāyana, others point to Vyāsa, and still others believe that these two are the same person.

yajna: worship; sacrifice; Vedic ceremony, sacrament; religious duty.

Yajur Veda: one of the four Vedas.

Yama: the Vedic god of death.

yama: ethical restraints; the first step of Rāja Yoga.

Yashodā: Krishna's foster mother who brought him up in the cowherd village of Gokula.

yoga: literally, "union"; a spiritual path that leads to union with God.

Yogānanda, Paramahansa (1895-1952): author of *Autobiography of a Yogi,* one of the most popular books in the world on Indian spirituality. Paramahansa Yogananda came to the United States in 1920 as India's delegate to an International Congress of Religious Liberals. As a most revered religious and spiritual teacher, Yogananda lived in the U.S. for thirty-two years. He taught the science of Kriya Yoga, meditation, and the art of spiritual living through lectures, books, and special lessons that he prepared for the dissemination of his teachings. In 1925 he established the Self-Realization Fellowship (SRF) International organization in Los Angeles, California, from where SRF Lessons are made available to students worldwide. The goal of Paramahansa Yogananda's teachings is the direct personal experience of God through balanced development of the body, mind, and soul. For information on SRF teachings, write to: Self-Realization Fellowship, 3880 San Rafael Avenue, Los Angeles, CA 90065, Tel: (213) 225-2471.

Yudhishthira: the eldest of the five Pandava brothers who fought the Mahābhārata war against their cousins, the Kauravas. The Mahābhārata describes Yudhishthira as a symbol of dispassionate judgment and incorruptible righteousness.

Subject Index